Blame

Blame

ITS NATURE AND NORMS

Edited by D. Justin Coates
and
Neal A. Tognazzini

OXFORD
UNIVERSITY PRESS

OXFORD
UNIVERSITY PRESS

Oxford University Press is a department of the University of Oxford.
It furthers the University's objective of excellence in research, scholarship,
and education by publishing worldwide.

Oxford   New York
Auckland   Cape Town   Dar es Salaam   Hong Kong   Karachi
Kuala Lumpur   Madrid   Melbourne   Mexico City   Nairobi
New Delhi   Shanghai   Taipei   Toronto

With offices in
Argentina   Austria   Brazil   Chile   Czech Republic   France Greece
Guatemala   Hungary   Italy   Japan   Poland   Portugal   Singapore
South Korea   Switzerland   Thailand   Turkey   Ukraine   Vietnam

Oxford is a registered trade mark of Oxford University Press in
the UK and certain other countries.

Published in the United States of America by
Oxford University Press
198 Madison Avenue, New York, NY 10016

Library of Congress Cataloging-in-Publication Data
Blame : its nature and norms / edited by D. Justin Coates & Neal A. Tognazzini.
p.   cm.
Includes bibliographical references (p.   ).
ISBN 978-0-19-986084-5 (pbk. : alk. paper)—ISBN 978-0-19-986082-1 (hardcover : alk. paper)
1. Blame. 2. Faultfinding. 3. Criticism, Personal. I. Coates, D. Justin. II. Tognazzini, Neal A.
BJ1535.F3B53   2013
128'.4—dc23   2012014063

1 3 5 7 9 8 6 4 2

Printed in the United States of America
on acid-free paper

For Stephanie and Anna,
wholly praiseworthy partners

{ CONTENTS }

{ ACKNOWLEDGMENTS }

First, our sincere thanks to the contributors, both for writing such great essays and also for being such a pleasure to work with.

Second, we are grateful to several teachers and friends from whom we have learned much about blame and moral responsibility over the years, especially John Martin Fischer, Coleen Macnamara, Angie Smith, and Gary Watson. John in particular has been an exemplary teacher, mentor, and good friend to both of us, and he helped us get this project under way.

Third, thanks to the editors and reviewers at Oxford University Press for their patience and insight, especially Peter Ohlin and Lucy Randall.

And finally, thanks to The College of William & Mary, the University of California, Riverside, the American Council of Learned Societies, and Portland State University for the hospitality and financial assistance that made possible the editing of this book and the research for our introductory chapter.

DJC
Riverside, CA

NAT
Williamsburg, VA
April 2012

{ CONTRIBUTORS }

Macalester Bell is an assistant professor of philosophy at Columbia University.

Christopher Bennett is a senior lecturer in philosophy at the University of Sheffield.

D. Justin Coates is the Law and Philosophy Fellow at the University of Chicago Law School.

Christopher Evan Franklin is an assistant professor of philosophy at Marymount University.

Erin I. Kelly is an associate professor of philosophy at Tufts University.

Coleen Macnamara is an assistant professor of philosophy at the University of California, Riverside.

Victoria McGeer is a research scholar at the University Center for Human Values at Princeton University and a fellow in the school of philosophy at the Australian National University.

Michael McKenna is a professor and Keith Lehrer Chair of Philosophy at the University of Arizona.

Derk Pereboom is a professor of philosophy at Cornell University.

T. M. Scanlon is the Alford Professor of Natural Religion, Moral Philosophy, and Civil Polity at Harvard University.

George Sher is the Herbert S. Autrey Professor of Philosophy at Rice University.

David Shoemaker is an associate professor in the Department of Philosophy and the Murphy Institute at Tulane University.

Angela M. Smith is an associate professor of philosophy at Washington & Lee University.

Neal A. Tognazzini is an assistant professor of philosophy at The College of William & Mary.

R. Jay Wallace is a professor of philosophy at the University of California, Berkeley.

Gary Watson is Provost Professor of Philosophy and Law at the University of Southern California.

Blame

The Contours of Blame

D. Justin Coates & Neal A. Tognazzini

1. Introduction

Whether or not P. F. Strawson was right about the precise attitudes and emotional reactions that constitute interpersonal relationships, he was surely right to think that our commitment to such relationships is "thoroughgoing and deeply rooted" (p. 81).[1] These relations vary widely—we relate "as sharers of common interest; as members of the same family; as colleagues; as friends; as lovers; as chance parties to an enormous range of transactions and encounters" (p. 76)—but they "form an essential part of the moral life as we know it" (p. 91). That much of Strawson's picture, at least, should be uncontroversial. Also uncontroversial is the fact that *blame* is, for better or worse, a central part of human relationships. The essays in this volume, then, attempt to deepen our understanding of our own moral lives.

When we say that blame is central to human relationships, we don't mean that it *belongs* at the center. We are merely making the undeniable point that we are (in fact) beings who evaluate, react, and respond to each other (and ourselves) along various normative dimensions. How we should feel about the role that blame plays in our lives is itself one of the interesting philosophical questions about blame. But there are also the questions of what precisely blame is, who its appropriate subjects and objects are, when it is (and is not) called for, and what functions (if any) it serves. Each of these questions is addressed, at least to some extent, by one or more of the essays collected here, which together represent the current state of the philosophical conversation about the nature and ethics of blame. Our primary aim in this chapter is to situate those essays within the broader context of recent work on blame.[2]

For helpful comments on earlier versions of the material in this chapter, thanks to John Martin Fischer, Samantha Matherne, Ben Mitchell-Yellin, and Matt Talbert.

[1] All quotations from Strawson are from his 1962, as reprinted in Watson (2003).

[2] It's important to note, however, that work on blame is still in its infancy, so there is no generally accepted way of framing these issues. The way we frame things in this chapter does not always map

1.1. PRELIMINARY APOLOGIES

We begin, however, with two apologies (in the Socratic sense). First, you will not find much talk about free will in this volume. It is perhaps surprising that although the founding document of contemporary work on blame (Strawson 1962) is an essay on the problem of free will and determinism, the work inspired by Strawson's essay does not much concern itself with free will. But this is less surprising once we recall that while Strawson's particular suggestion for "reconciling" the libertarian and the compatibilist has been widely rejected,[3] his exhortation "to keep before our minds . . . what it is actually like to be involved in ordinary interpersonal relationships" (p. 77) has been heeded with vigor.[4] This is not to say that recent work on blame is wholly divorced from concerns about free will, but the emphasis is now much more on moral psychology and the significance of blame in moral life. The essays collected here reflect this emphasis.

As for the second apology: you will have noticed that our topic is simply *blame* rather than *praise and blame*. Why the exclusively negative focus? Several responses come to mind. For starters, we would endorse what Gary Watson has to say on this point:

> We seem to have a richer vocabulary of blame than of praise. This slant is not due solely to mean-spiritedness. At least part of the explanation is that blaming tends to be a much more serious affair; reputation, liberty, and even life can be at stake, and understandably we are more concerned with the conditions of adverse treatment than with those of favorable treatment. (Watson 1996, as reprinted in Watson 2004, p. 283)[5]

But we would also be inclined to challenge the two presuppositions behind the question. First, it's not at all clear that praise and blame are, upon reflection, a usefully opposed pair after all.[6] As we will note below, the idea of *private* blame

---

neatly onto the way the other authors frame things, and there's certainly nothing hallowed about the taxonomy we suggest. For a truncated and less detailed version of what follows, see Coates and Tognazzini (2012).

[3] And, in our view, almost as widely misunderstood.

[4] At least one of the things that Strawson was exhorting us to do was to pay more attention to the moral emotions. When Strawson was writing in 1962, he was able to say, "It is a pity that talk of the moral sentiments has fallen out of favour. The phrase would be quite a good name for [the reactive attitudes]" (p. 92). In large part due to Strawson's essay, talk of the moral sentiments is now decidedly "in favor."

[5] This is not to deny, of course, that *part* of the explanation is the human tendency toward mean-spiritedness, as Watson slyly acknowledges with the word 'solely'.

[6] Strawson says of resentment and gratitude that they are "a usefully opposed pair" (p. 77), and that may well be true. But we note that it seems much more natural to say that feeling resentment is a way of blaming than it does to say that feeling gratitude is a way of praising. Perhaps another explanation for the tendency of philosophers to focus on blame, then, is that many of them follow Strawson in thinking that blame is to be understood in terms of the moral emotions (see section 2.3 below).

seems coherent in a way that private praise does not. You might discover to your horror that your spouse continues to blame you for something you did several years ago, but it seems at best awkward to say that you might discover that your spouse has been praising you for several years without anyone's knowing about it. The fit between being praised and having one's praises *sung* seems quite tight indeed.[7] Second, it's not clear, upon reflection, that to focus on blame *is* to focus on something negative. Perhaps on some conceptions of blame, a blameless world would be a better place. But on many of the conceptions endorsed by the philosophers in this volume, blame is actually required for, or even partly constitutive of, goods that we would prefer not to do without. This is not to say that a world with blame may be an acceptable compromise; rather it may be the only sort of world humanly possible.

But here we've already stepped into controversial territory, so let's take some time to orient ourselves.

1.2. STRAWSON AND THE PRIMACY OF BLAME

We've said that "Freedom and Resentment" is the founding document of contemporary work on blame, so we begin with a brief discussion of it. It provides both the inspiration for one of the most influential contemporary accounts of blame and the conceptual framework for understanding just how important an inquiry into blame is.[8]

Strawson's essay is an attempt to carve out a middle ground between two equally implausible proposals for how to justify blame, both of which are guilty of "over-intellectualizing the facts" (p. 92). On the one hand, there is the "one-eyed" utilitarian (best exemplified, perhaps, by Smart 1961), who tries to justify blame by "[pointing] to the efficacy of the practices of [blame] in regulating behaviour in socially desirable ways" (Strawson 1962, p. 73) and in the process "loses sight (perhaps wishes to lose sight) of the human attitudes of which these practices are, in part, the expression" (p. 92). On the other hand, there are those who think blame cannot be justified without "recourse to the obscure and panicky metaphysics of libertarianism" (p. 93), arguing that blameworthy

---

[7] A point noted long ago by Richard Brandt (1958, p. 8 n. 5). In fact, Brandt's essay is strikingly prescient on a number of issues surrounding blame, including the reactive attitudes (pp. 24–27), the question of standing (p. 27), and the problem of moral luck (p. 30 n. 31).

[8] Strawson's essay may be the start of *contemporary* work on blame, but it clearly has important historical antecedents, especially in the eighteenth century in Scotland. David Hume is perhaps the clearest example: "The mind of man is so formed by nature, that, upon the appearance of certain characters, dispositions, and actions, it immediately feels the sentiment of approbation or blame; nor are there any emotions more essential to its frame and constitution. . . . [T]hese sentiments are not to be controlled or altered by any philosophical theory or speculation whatsoever" ([1748] 1977, p. 68). Strawson is not only often read as a sort of Humean naturalist, but he also alludes to this period in the history of philosophy when he laments the fact that "talk of the moral sentiments has fallen out of favor" (see note 4 above).

agents need to possess "contra-causal freedom or something of the kind" (p. 92) in order to truly *deserve* blame. If these are our options for dealing with the free will problem, then, given the practical inconceivability of skepticism, we are forced to choose between inadequacy and inanity (to borrow Strawson's words [p. 92]).

The details of Strawson's proposed alternative are controversial, but here's the basic idea. Instead of viewing blameworthiness as an independent meta-physical fact about an agent (or based on such a fact), as the libertarian does, the utilitarian is right to view it as somehow essentially tied to our blaming practices. But the libertarian is right to insist that our blaming practices are more than just instruments for the regulation of behavior. As Strawson puts it, "Our practices do not merely exploit our natures, they express them" (p. 93). And the relevant aspect of human nature is "that complicated web of attitudes and feelings which form an essential part of the moral life as we know it" (p. 91), namely the *reactive attitudes* of resentment, indignation, and guilt (among others). These attitudes are precisely what is left out of the utilitarian picture of blame, but, according to Strawson, "it is just these attitudes themselves which fill the gap" (p. 92) and not some mysterious appeal to meta-physical freedom. To be morally responsible, on this account, just is to be a member of the moral community, to be someone toward whom others feel the reactive attitudes. And these attitudes are "something we are given with the fact of human society" (p. 91), not something it is in our nature to be able to give up.

For our purposes we need not evaluate the details of Strawson's proposal.[9] We only wish to point out two ways in which its influence continues to be felt by philosophers working on blame and moral responsibility. First, although Strawson himself never identifies the reactive attitudes with blame, it is an extremely natural and plausible extension of his essay, and accordingly many contemporary philosophers favor such an account (including many in this volume). Second, perhaps the most common way of conceiving of moral responsibility these days is along broadly Strawsonian lines, emphasizing the importance and explanatory priority of our practices of blaming and holding one another responsible. These practices (together with their associated norms) are not (taken to be) constrained by any independent "moral responsibility facts" about the agent in question; rather they are what partly determine which facts about an agent even *count* as the moral responsibility facts in the first place.[10]

Taken together, these Strawson-inspired views suggest another way in which blame is central to our moral lives. If the picture painted here is right,

---

[9] See McKenna and Russell (2008) for discussion of Strawson's essay.

[10] See, e.g., Wallace (1994, ch. 4). This is not to say that our practices are not constrained by any facts about the agent whatsoever. The reactive attitudes may still be inappropriate if the agent lacks certain crucial capacities. The Strawsonian point is simply that those particular capacities count as relevant to moral responsibility only *in the context of* and *in light of* our practices.

then blame is not only the natural human response to actions that display a kind of interpersonally significant ill will or disregard, but it is also the lens through which we can even know what counts as a free action in the first place. In this sense, the free will problem is, perhaps paradoxically, just one of the many problems that can be categorized as part of *the ethics of blame* (see section 3 below). If free will is, as many contemporary theorists think, the control required for moral responsibility (whatever it turns out to be), and moral responsibility is to be understood in terms of the propriety of blame, then an implication of the Strawsonian picture is that any philosophical examination of free will must begin with an inquiry into the nature of blame. We can add freedom, then, to the host of puzzling philosophical issues—including hypocrisy, forgiveness, mercy, and apology—that revolve around and ultimately depend upon a satisfactory account of blame.[11] All the more reason to get started as soon as possible.

2. The Nature of Blame

So what is it to blame someone? What mental states or activities are involved, and how can they help us understand the broader blaming context?[12] One relatively straightforward way to tackle these questions is to imagine a robust blaming context—one that seems clearly to involve blame *somewhere*, even if we aren't yet sure where—and then take each candidate mental state or activity one by one to see whether it can perform the tasks that blame performs. In a standard sort of blaming context, candidate mental states and activities abound: beliefs, desires, emotions, dispositions, overt behaviors, and speech acts all can seem, from certain perspectives, like plausible candidates for what's essential to blame. Accordingly, accounts of the nature of blame vary widely.

To help focus the inquiry, let's start by briefly mentioning two ways in which the term 'blame' gets used that are philosophically interesting but are at best only part of the story. The first is what Elizabeth Lane Beardsley (1969) calls the "whodunit" (or "whatdunit") sense of blame (see also Hart 1968, ch. 9; Kenner 1967). If your car won't start in the morning, some simple diagnostics may reveal that the culprit is a dead battery. In a causal sense, then, your dead battery may be *to blame* for your being late to the office. This sort of blame is

---

[11] And let's not forget those theorists whose substantive moral theories depend on the notions of blame and blameworthiness (e.g., Gibbard 1990).

[12] As a first approximation, this broader context seems to involve a back-and-forth exchange: someone who is regarded as a fellow member of the moral community transgresses in some way, leading to blame, which (ideally) encourages apology and in turn forgiveness. On moral responsibility as a conversation, see Watson (1987b), McKenna (2012), and Shoemaker (2007).

no doubt philosophically interesting, but it doesn't amount to the sort of *moral* blame with which the essays in this volume are primarily concerned.[13]

At the other extreme is the idea that blaming is some sort of overt action, perhaps telling someone that his behavior is substandard, or perhaps scolding him, in an attempt to get him to change his behavior in the future.[14] These actions certainly do seem to be ways of blaming—or, perhaps better, expressing blame—but again they are at best only part of the story that moral philosophers are interested in telling.[15] At its core, blaming seems like something one can do in the privacy of one's own study (for example), and its proper objects do not seem limited to those who are in the here and now.[16]

Still, a wide spectrum lies between judgments of causal responsibility and overt expressions of blame: Where will we find the essence of blame?

2.1. COGNITIVE ACCOUNTS

Taking seriously the distinction between blame and expressed blame may naturally lead us to think that blame must be located somewhere inside the blamer's head.[17] Judgments of causal responsibility are clearly not enough, but perhaps other sorts of judgments will do the job. There is a rather wide array of judgments one could appeal to here, but we can borrow a phrase from Gary Watson and categorize them all as judgments about "the quality of the other's moral self as exemplified in action and attitude" (1987b, as reprinted in his 2004, p. 226).

Jonathan Glover (1970), Ishtiyaque Haji (1998), and Michael Zimmerman (1988), for example, all seem to view blame as though it is a type of "moral accounting" (Glover 1970, p. 64). When we blame someone, we judge "that there is a 'discredit' or 'debit' in his ledger, a 'negative mark' in his 'report card,' or a 'blemish' or 'stain' on his 'record'; that his 'record' has been 'tarnished'; that his 'moral standing' has been 'diminished'" (Zimmerman 1988, p. 38).[18]

---

[13] Recent work in experimental philosophy, however, provides some reason to think that even judgments of causal responsibility are not wholly divorced from moral concerns. See, e.g., Knobe and Fraser (2008).

[14] Writers who focus on blame's outward manifestations include Altham (1973), Beardsley (1969), Duff (1986), French (1976), and Talbert (2012).

[15] But they are a part of the story. It's not for nothing that the word 'blame' has the same etymological root as the word 'blaspheme' (both come from the Greek for *evil-speaking*).

[16] "[I]t is surely possible to blame someone—say, a persuasive salesman for your financial difficulties—without ever telling anyone. Blame is more like holding an opinion than expressing it" (Squires 1968, p. 56). See also Sher (2006, p. 74); Wallace (1994, p. 56).

[17] Again we stress that the taxonomy we construct here is not to be taken as the obviously correct way of characterizing the literature but merely as one helpful way to get a grip on things. The accounts discussed in this section, for example, are probably best described as *tending to emphasize cognitive elements*. Similar remarks apply to our categories below.

[18] It seems likely that this is the sort of view that Smart thought of as exemplifying "a rather pharisaical attitude to sinners" (1961, p. 305) and that pushed him to defend the utilitarian view, which he saw as the only alternative once the metaphysics of libertarianism was rejected as incoherent.

Gary Watson outlines an account of blame according to which it involves a negative *aretaic* judgment, a judgment that the person blamed has displayed some sort of vice or fault. To blame, in this sense, is "to see [the conduct] as 'inferior goods,' as a poor exercise of human evaluative capacities, as characteristic of someone who cares little about standards of excellence in human affairs" (1996, as reprinted in his 2004, p. 265).[19]

Nomy Arpaly (2006) and Pamela Hieronymi (2004) emphasize the sort of judgment that Strawson takes to occasion the reactive attitudes, namely a judgment that someone displayed ill will.[20] T. M. Scanlon (1988, 1998) and Angela Smith (2008a) focus on related judgments, such as the judgment that the wrongdoer's action "violated a norm of mutually respectful relations with others" (Smith 2008a, p. 36).[21]

These accounts all capture something deep and important: blaming involves *evaluating*.[22] When we blame others, we see them as having dropped below some standard that we accept (or perhaps that we think they should accept), whether of excellence, morality, or respectful relationships. The judgments involved here are tinged with normativity, and because of this they carry a certain *force*: they are the sorts of judgments that we would rather not have made about us, even if the person doing the evaluating never says anything to us. It matters a great deal to us whether those we respect consider our own conduct subpar.[23] And blame certainly seems to have this characteristic too.

Nevertheless, just as overt action accounts appeared to conflate the distinction between blaming and expressing blame, cognitive accounts may appear to conflate the equally useful distinction between blaming and judging blameworthy.[24] To elide this distinction may seem to turn blame into what Watson

---

[19] Watson makes clear that he does not think this sort of judgment exhausts the nature of blame. Aretaic judgments are primarily associated with what he calls "responsibility as attributability" (1996, as reprinted in his 2004, p. 271), and other blaming responses are relevant to the *accountability* face of moral responsibility.

[20] We say that Arpaly and Hieronymi *emphasize* this judgment, but strictly speaking they do not identify blame solely with this judgment. Arpaly thinks that the blamer must also be "'in favor' of morality at some level" (2006, p. 25), and Hieronymi suggests that a "commitment to morality" is going to be central to an adequate account and defense of the propriety of blame (2008, p. 29), but she does think that judgments of this sort can account for the characteristic force of blame (see note 23 below).

[21] We note, however, that neither Scanlon nor Smith seems to endorse purely cognitive accounts of blame any longer (if they ever did). Scanlon's most recent view is articulated in his 2008 (we discuss it below) and is further elaborated and defended in chapter 5 of this volume. Smith also develops a distinctive view in her contribution to this volume, chapter 2.

[22] Other authors who focus on the connection between blaming and judging include Beardsley (1970), Squires (1968), and Stern (1974).

[23] "It seems quite plausible to me that standing in relations of mutual regard is of considerable importance to creatures like us. Thus the content of a judgment of ill will can carry a certain amount of force—despite being descriptive. If it is true, then you no longer stand in such a relationship" (Hieronymi 2004, p. 124).

[24] Angela Smith suggests that perhaps this seeming infelicity ought to be tolerated, since it reflects "a deep ambiguity in our use of language, an ambiguity that shows up precisely when we ask whether

calls a "fault-finding appraisal." Cognitive accounts may make it seem "as though in blaming we were mainly moral clerks, recording moral faults," which is something that can be done "from a detached and austerely 'objective' standpoint" (Watson 1987b, as reprinted in his 2004, pp. 226–27). But is genuine blame something that can be so detached? When we blame someone, we're not simply *noting* the fact that she falls below some standard; rather, blame seems also to be about our own attitudes toward how the agent has negotiated (or failed to negotiate) that standard. Accordingly, we might accept a cognitive account about what it is to *judge blameworthy* while insisting that blame itself must be more robust.[25]

2.2. CONATIVE ACCOUNTS

One natural way to augment a cognitive account is by adding conative elements, such as desires, intentions, expectations, and dispositions, all of which might account for the way true blame seems to involve being *engaged* or *exercised* by the substandard action. We not only *evaluate* when we blame, but we also *respond*. There are two prominent contemporary accounts that take this route.

The first of these accounts is articulated and defended by George Sher (2006). According to Sher, what we need to add to a judgment of blameworthiness in order to get blame is a backward-looking desire "that the person in question not have performed his past bad act or not have his current bad character," which, when added to the relevant belief, anchors "a set of affective and behavioral dispositions," such as dispositions to anger and reproach, that are traditionally associated with blame (p. 112). The backward-looking desire is the crucial motivational element that, in Sher's view, ties the (potentially) detached judgment of blameworthiness to the robustly non-detached ways in which we tend to react to blameworthy action. Moreover, the very same

---

blame necessarily involves an emotional or behavioral element" (2008a, p. 38). For another defense of the conflation, but in the opposite direction, see Hertzberg (1975), who says, "Actually, wanting to provide a theory of blame involves a misconception. This notion presupposes that we can distinguish judgments of blameworthiness, and the reasons for them, from the emotional attitude of blame and the circumstances which produce it. But these are not two separate things, but two ways of viewing one side of human life. Only for someone who can feel resentment towards another for his conduct will anything count as a reason for judging him blameworthy" (p. 511).

[25] This seems a good place to mention an early writer on blame who produced a series of insightful and unduly neglected papers: Elizabeth Lane Beardsley (1957, 1960, 1969, 1970, 1979). Beardsley for the most part was concerned to bring speech act theory (as developed in Austin [1962]) to bear on issues of praise and blame (a project that has recently been taken up again by Coleen Macnamara [2011 and chapter 8 in this volume]), but she also made the intriguing claim that once the nature of blame is properly articulated, we will see that blameworthiness cannot be understood in terms of whether there is something that the blameworthy agent is *worthy* of. Beardsley's claim seems to be that an attitude will count as a *blaming* attitude only if it already involves a judgment about blameworthiness. Hence the attempt to spell out blameworthiness in terms of an agent's being worthy of certain blaming attitudes will be caught up in a vicious circularity. See Beardsley (1970, especially pp. 174–76).

backward-looking desire is implicated in our commitment to morality itself. Sher argues, then, that his account reveals a satisfying way in which blame is central to our moral lives: in the end, part of what it is even to accept moral principles at all is to have the desire that partly constitutes blame. The justification of blame and the justification of morality, therefore, go hand in hand (Sher 2006, ch. 7).

Sher's account is elegant and satisfying, but not surprisingly it has received much critical attention in the literature. Pamela Hieronymi (2008) and Angela Smith (2008a) both raise important worries for the account, and several of our authors discuss it. In her contribution to this volume, Smith (chapter 2) gives an extended critique of Sher's account, arguing that the belief-desire pair he appeals to cannot anchor the emotional and behavior responses that are characteristic of blame after all. Victoria McGeer (chapter 9) and Christopher Franklin (chapter 11) both accuse Sher's account of being too "sanitized" (McGeer's word), leaving out the emotional core, which is needed both for a psychologically realistic account of blame (McGeer) and a fully adequate vindication of blame against those who think it ought to be discarded (Franklin).[26] Even Derk Pereboom, a well-known skeptic about the existence of moral responsibility (if not about its possibility; see his 2001), argues in his contribution (chapter 10) that the sort of blame Sher has in mind can still exist in a world without moral responsibility. Pereboom paints this as a happy state of affairs, but we have reason to suspect that Sher will not think it so happy. After all, at the beginning of his book, Sher says that Pereboom "vividly, if unwittingly, illustrates just how strange—I am tempted to say 'inhuman'—a world without blame would be" (Sher 2006, p. 5).

Another conative account (broadly speaking) that has taken hold in the contemporary literature is T. M. Scanlon's (2008). Like Sher, Scanlon begins with a judgment of blameworthiness, though the precise content of the judgment that Scanlon has in mind emphasizes the importance of "the expectations, intentions, and other attitudes that constitute" our interpersonal relationships (p. 128). Scanlon sketches his proposal as follows:

> Briefly put, my proposal is this: to claim that a person is *blameworthy* for an action is to claim that the action shows something about the agent's attitudes toward others that impairs the relations that others can have with him or her. To *blame* a person is to judge him or her to be blameworthy and to take your relationship with him or her to be modified in a way that this judgment of impaired relations holds to be appropriate. (pp. 128–29)[27]

---

[26] In fairness, Sher expresses his own doubts about the alleged emotional core of blame: "That we would be better off if we were to weaken the connection between blame and rancor may be the kernel of truth in the anti-blame ideology" (2006, p. 138).

[27] We should be wary of taking Scanlon's italics too seriously here; on the next page (2008, p. 130) he indicates that in some contexts, to judge blameworthy may itself be a way of blaming.

We need not go into the details here—and in any case Scanlon elaborates on
and more fully defends his account in chapter 5—but the basic idea is simply
that to blame someone is to recognize, and make modifications that express
that one recognizes, that things cannot go on as before with that person. The
relationship has been impaired, and blame is a way of marking that fact (where
'marking' of course goes beyond merely judging *that it is a fact*).

How exactly the blamer marks the impairment will depend on any number
of particular details of the context and the relationship in question, but Scanlon gives the following examples:

> I might, for example, cease to value spending time with him in the way
> one does with a friend, and I might revise my intentions to confide in
> him and to encourage him to confide in me. Third, I might complain
> to [him] about his conduct, demand an explanation or justification, or
> indicate in some other way that I no longer see him as a friend. (2008,
> pp. 129–30)

It is an advantage of Scanlon's account (and of Sher's) that "it accounts for what
seems to be the evident variability of blame, and its clear dependence on particular relationships" (Scanlon 2008, p. 212). Sometimes blame will involve
speech acts, sometimes cold shoulders, sometimes more subtle responses, all
depending on the particular relationship that is taken to be impaired.[28]

Scanlon's account is also elegant and satisfying and has been the target of
much criticism. Perhaps the most common objection has been expressed
pithily by R. Jay Wallace (2011, p. 349), namely that it "leaves the blame out of
blame." Wallace goes on:

> Blame has a quality of opprobrium that is not captured by the consid-
> erations about the normative significance of impaired relationships that
> are at the center of Scanlon's approach. I believe that this important di-
> mension of blame can be made sense of only in terms of the reactive
> sentiments. (p. 349)[29]

Several of the authors in this volume critically discuss Scanlon's account,
though the charge that it is too mild is not the only objection raised (but
McGeer does touch on it, and Pereboom once again shows how even the moral
responsibility skeptic can countenance blame in Scanlon's sense). In her contribution, Smith worries that Scanlon's account, somewhat surprisingly, fails to
take relationships as seriously as an adequate account of blame should. Sher
(chapter 3) argues that Scanlon's account has difficulty accounting for cases in

---

[28] Another underappreciated virtue of Scanlon's account is that it can explain our blaming judgments in cases of "moral outcome luck" (see Nagel 1979, ch. 3). Scanlon himself takes this to be one of
the desiderata any adequate account of blame must satisfy (2008, p. 126).

[29] This sort of criticism has also been pressed by Mason (2011) and Wolf (2011).

which we blame strangers, people with whom it is a stretch (at best) to say that we have anything resembling a *relationship*. Christopher Bennett (chapter 4) also raises this concern and adds worries about how Scanlon can make sense of desert and proportionality, among other issues. (Bennett then goes on to construct his own broadly conative account, according to which blame consists in a symbolic withdrawal of goodwill.)

Scanlon addresses some of these issues in his own essay and elaborates his account in illuminating ways (chapter 5). He also admits (as he did in his 2008, p. 212) that his account is revisionary in certain respects. This is something we do well to keep in mind, especially if Scanlon is right that "the things we are inclined to believe about blame form an inconsistent set" (chapter 5). Perhaps the most any account of blame can inspire to be is an "interpretation."

David Shoemaker, in his contribution to this volume (chapter 6), discusses whether it is possible to extend Scanlon's interpretation of blame in a way that can account for institutional blame. And although Shoemaker argues that it cannot, this is not meant as an *objection* to Scanlon's view; rather, Shoemaker concludes that perhaps moral blame and criminal blame are just two different beasts.

2.3. THE STRAWSONIAN ACCOUNT

If cognitive and conative elements together still don't seem enough to explain the precise way we are exercised by wrongdoing when we blame, then you may want to follow R. Jay Wallace (who follows Strawson) and include the reactive emotions as well:

> To blame someone is a way of caring about the fact that they have treated others with contempt or disregard; when you experience indignation, resentment, or guilt, you are not merely left cold by the immoral attitudes that form the object of blame, but find that those attitudes engage your interest and attention. (2011, pp. 367–68)

We began this chapter by drawing attention to two of Strawson's insights—that the realities of interpersonal relationships ought to be front and center in any attempt to understand moral responsibility and that the moral sentiments are a crucial component of such relationships—and we have now worked our way back up to an account of blame that features these two insights. Given how thoroughly his essay has influenced contemporary work on blame, perhaps it is not surprising that the Strawsonian account of blame is widely accepted. On this view, to blame someone is to target her with one of the reactive emotions.[30]

---

[30] Variants of this account are endorsed by Cohen (1977), Fingarette (1957), Wertheimer (1998), and Wolf (2011), and it is often taken for granted in many other discussions. See, e.g., Darwall (2006); Talbert (2012).

Wallace (1994, 2011) has done the most to articulate and defend this view, and he puts it to work in a broader theory of moral responsibility, according to which our susceptibility to blame someone is what constitutes the stance of holding that person responsible, the appropriateness of which is in turn crucial to determining whether someone is a morally responsible agent.[31] But one need not accept the details of Wallace's broader theory in order to agree with him when he says:

> [Blame] includes an attitudinal aspect, where the attitudes in question have a distinctive content and focus. It is this attitudinal aspect of blame that is accounted for by the reactive emotions. Those emotions are essentially backward-looking, being responses to particular violations of moral obligation, and in this respect they capture exactly the attitude characteristic of blame. Thus, I think it would indeed be strange to suppose that one might blame another person without feeling an attitude of indignation or resentment toward the person, or that one might blame oneself without feeling guilt; attempts to communicate blame generally do function, at least in part, to give expression to such attitudes. (1994, p. 75)

The reactive emotions that Strawson was at pains to emphasize, it seems, can easily perform the tasks that we ask blame to perform. They can be kept private, but they can also be expressed. They are responses triggered by judgments about another person's "moral self," and they may even include propositional components, but they are not experienced from an austere and detached perspective. Moreover, they can easily explain why being blamed tends to be unwelcome and why concerns about fairness might arise when we think about the possibility of determinism. Perhaps we have finally discovered the nature of blame.

As always, however, things are not so simple. George Sher (2006, ch. 5) raises several worries for the Strawsonian account, including that it may be *too* robust. Is it really the case, Sher asks, that blame is always so emotional? On the contrary, he says:

> We may, for example, feel no hostility toward the loved one whom we blame for failing to tell a sensitive acquaintance a hard truth, the criminal whom we blame for a burglary we read about in the newspaper, or the historical figure whom we blame for the misdeeds he performed long ago. As [these] examples suggest, blaming is something that we can do regretfully or dispassionately. . . . We simply do not have the emotional resources to muster even a twinge of hostility toward each of the innumerable miscreants, scoundrels, and thugs—many of them long dead—whom we blame for what we know to be their bad behavior or bad character. (pp. 88–89)

---

[31] John Martin Fischer and Mark Ravizza (1998) have also developed an influential Strawsonian theory of moral responsibility, though they don't seek to give an explicit account of blame (in contrast to Wallace).

The Strawsonian could simply insist, of course, that there is no blaming going on in these examples, but that can easily seem like an ad hoc response in this context.[32] A more promising response will involve giving a theory of the reactive emotions according to which resentment need not involve "a twinge of hostility." But that is a large (albeit worthwhile) undertaking (cf. Hurley and Macnamara 2010).[33]

Several of our authors explore accounts that are broadly Strawsonian. Michael McKenna (chapter 7), for example, argues that the best account of blame will include an emotional component, and he situates such a view in his broader *conversational theory* of moral responsibility, according to which "the actions of a morally responsible agent are potential bearers of a species of meaning, *agent-meaning*," to which the blamer then responds, opening up a conversation of sorts. In his essay McKenna elaborates on this account (which he has articulated and defended in his 2012), and he considers its connection with the notion of desert.

Coleen Macnamara, in her contribution (chapter 8), starts by assuming the Strawsonian account for the sake of argument and explores how we ought to think about what's going on when we *express* our blame by giving voice to the reactive emotions. Many contemporary theorists, including Wallace (1994), Stephen Darwall (2006), and Margaret Urban Walker (2006), argue that the expressed reactive attitudes are best understood as *demands*, but Macnamara questions this assumption. Along the way she touches on the relationship between blame and holding responsible, as well as the sense in which the reactive attitudes may (*pace* Wallace 1994, pp. 63–64) be responses to *bad* actions as well as *wrong* actions.

And while Wallace (chapter 12) does not further defend a Strawsonian account of blame here (he has done that admirably in previous work), his essay demonstrates how well such an account fits with other aspects of morality and moral motivation.

2.4. FUNCTIONAL ACCOUNTS

If you remain skeptical about the adequacy of any overt action, cognitive, conative, or affective account of blame, then it's hard to know what other mental states or activities might do the job.[34] Then again, perhaps what dissatisfies you

---

[32] Wallace tries to make this response seem a bit more plausible by explaining that we might still be taking up the stance of holding those miscreants responsible (which one can do simply by believing that a reactive emotion would be fitting). See Wallace (1994, pp. 76–77).

[33] Another objection to the Strawsonian account is that it seems to shield blaming responses themselves from moral criticism, since reactive emotions are not typically thought of as under our control. But sometimes it does seem like one ought not to blame, so how can the Strawsonian account for this? Hieronymi (2004) raises this sort of objection, as does McKenna (chapter 7 in this volume).

[34] Perhaps a *volitional* account holds some promise. For an attempt to spell out such an account, drawing inspiration from the work of Harry Frankfurt, see Tognazzini (2012).

is that each of these accounts seems right in certain cases but wrong in other cases. Can't we construct a hybrid account of some sort?

Two of our authors, McGeer and Smith, argue that we can. Or rather, they argue that instead of asking which mental state or activity can perform the tasks that blame performs, we should simply identify blame with its tasks. That is, we should figure out what *function* blame serves and then allow the particular context to determine which mental state or activity best serves that function, and so let context determine which way of responding counts as blame.

Smith identifies blame, in all of its manifestations, with *protest*.[35] She builds on Scanlon's account but argues that it fails to capture the sense in which blame is communicative. Merely marking an impaired relationship does not count as blaming someone, Smith argues, unless it is done "as a way of *protesting* (i.e., registering and challenging) the moral claim implicit in her conduct, where such protest implicitly seeks some kind of moral acknowledgment on the part of the blameworthy agent and/or on the part of others in the moral community." And once we bring the idea of protest into the picture, we can allow blame to be the sort of variable phenomenon that we ordinarily take it to be.[36] (To be sure, both Sher and Scanlon can allow for the variability of blame, but Smith argues forcefully that an adequate account of blame needs to include explicit reference to its *aim* in order to get the right extension.)

McGeer is explicit that she understands blame in functionalist terms: "[Blame] is a state that is apt for being caused by perceived wrongdoing and apt for producing certain behavioral effects." She agrees with the Strawsonian that "the state that typically plays the causal role of blame in human beings is an affective state," though she is careful to point out that on a functionalist understanding of blame, affective states need not *always* be involved. In fact, McGeer presents a challenge to the standard methodology here, so it's worth elaborating on this point a bit.

Inquiry into the nature of blame typically proceeds by considering a candidate mental state or activity to see how well it fits with our considered judgments about the sort of work that blame is supposed to do. If it seems possible for blame to do its work without that particular mental state or activity, then we conclude that it cannot be part of the essence of blame. Each failed proposal will yield some data that we can add to a growing list of desiderata that any adequate account of blame must meet.

McGeer argues, however, that certain mental states or activities may well figure into an adequate account of blame even if they are not *always* or *necessarily* present in cases of blame. She distinguishes between "features whose

---

[35] Talbert (2012) also attempts to articulate a sense in which blame is a form of protest (though he focuses on blame's outward manifestations). Both Smith and Talbert draw on Boxill (1976) to make their case.

[36] See also Hieronymi (2001), which explains how the reactive attitude of resentment can be seen as a kind of protest.

contingent association with the phenomenon in question is of no criterial significance," on the one hand, and "features that . . . account for our interest in identifying a kind as such, even though things belonging to the kind do not invariably manifest the feature in question," on the other hand, and she argues that features of the latter sort may, despite being inessential, be included in an adequate account of blame. Respecting this point, she argues, will help us to construct an account of blame more psychologically realistic than many currently on the market.

In accordance with this distinction, McGeer maintains that "exceptional cases" (cases of emotionless blame) need not tell against an account of blame that puts the emotions front and center. She then goes on to explore the role that anger plays in human psychology, ultimately suggesting that our best bet for dealing with the emotionally unsavory side of blame is to admit that some of our practices and institutions need to be reshaped.

Other functionalist accounts of blame are possible, of course, depending on what one takes to be the aim of blame. Franklin (chapter 11), for example, argues that experiencing and expressing the reactive attitudes should be seen as a way of valuing morality. He presupposes a Strawsonian account of blame, but his claims about the aim and value of blame can stand alone and might serve as the foundation for alternative functionalist accounts. (We return to Franklin's approach below.)

3. The Ethics of Blame

However, it's not enough simply to give an analysis or interpretation of blame. Nor can we rest content with an explanation of its role or its significance in moral practice. We must ask a further question: When is it appropriate to blame?[37]

Following Scanlon (2008, p. 123), we use 'the ethics of blame' as a capacious (and apt) characterization of the diverse set of norms that govern our practices of blame. When we are sensitive to these norms, our blame will be appropriate; when we fail to blame in accord with these norms, our blame will be inappropriate. A satisfactory ethics of blame, then, will provide a systematic account of the norms that identify the *propriety* conditions on blame (i.e., the conditions that, when satisfied, render blame appropriate, all things considered). And there are at least three interdependent sets of propriety conditions governing blame. Specifically, there are conditions that (1) the transgressor,[38] (2) the would-be

---

[37] We use the word 'appropriate' at this juncture to cover a wide range of normative terms, since we may ask when blame is good, or permissible, or fair, and so on, each of which may raise distinct issues.

[38] A note on terminology: we use the unwieldy 'transgressor' in place of the more common 'wrongdoer' to leave open the possibility that sometimes blame is legitimately targeted at individuals who have merely acted badly (but not wrongly). On blame for bad actions, see Macnamara's essay (chapter 8).

blamer, and (3) the blaming interaction must satisfy in order for blame to be appropriate. We'll (somewhat hesitantly) call these the conditions of blameworthiness, the conditions of jurisdiction, and the conditions of procedure.[39]

3.1. CONDITIONS OF BLAMEWORTHINESS

The first set of propriety conditions governing blame are those conditions under which transgressors are blame*worthy* or are *deserving* of blame.[40] Admittedly it might seem odd to characterize blameworthiness as falling within the purview of the ethics of blame since blameworthiness has been more traditionally associated with metaphysical questions concerning free will and moral responsibility. But as we suggested in section 1.2, blame is, in some important sense, prior to blameworthiness.[41] So understood, the free will debate is an aspect of an overall account of the ethics of blame. An agent will presumably be *unworthy* of blame—that is, he will be *excused* or *exempted* from blame—if he lacks certain capacities, but which capacities are relevant here will depend on the *nature* of blame itself and the *norms* of our blaming practices. As Smith points out (chapter 2):

> If we interpret blame as mere negative moral evaluation, for example, then it would seem that the conditions of moral responsibility may be quite weak. . . . If, on the other hand, we interpret blame as a kind of explicit moral sanction involving harsh treatment, then it would seem that the conditions of moral responsibility may be more stringent.

Presumably the reason that the conditions on being morally responsible would be weaker if we interpreted blame primarily as a form of negative moral evaluation than they would be if we interpreted blame primarily as an explicit moral sanction is that negative moral evaluations aren't rendered *unfair* in cases in which the agent lacks certain relevant agential capacities, but plausibly, explicit moral sanction would be.

Of course, these issues naturally lead us to questions of free will, since it's plausible that some form of agential control is one of the relevant capacities.

---

[39] The conditions are distinguished roughly as follows. When the conditions of blameworthiness are satisfied, it will be appropriate for would-be blamers to blame *transgressors*. When the conditions of jurisdiction are satisfied, it will be appropriate for *would-be blamers* to blame transgressors. And when the conditions of procedure are satisfied, it will be appropriate for would-be blamers to *blame* transgressors. Obviously this is not perfect, and as Kelly's, Bell's, and Watson's contributions to the volume make clear (chapters 13, 14, and 15), these conditions are importantly related and interdependent. But for now we think they provide a useful way of carving up the conceptual landscape.

[40] For more on what it may mean for an agent to deserve blame, see McKenna's contribution to this volume (chapter 7).

[41] In addition to Strawson (1962), here we also follow, among others, Watson (1987b), Wallace (1994), and Fischer and Ravizza (1998), who all accept some version of this claim.

Since we have little to contribute to these debates here, we'll now turn to the other two sets of propriety conditions governing blame.

3.2. CONDITIONS OF JURISDICTION

The conditions of jurisdiction pick out those conditions that would-be blamers (or "blamers," for short) must satisfy if their blame is to be appropriate. Thus when blamers meet the conditions of jurisdiction,[42] it is appropriate for *them* (i.e., *those particular blamers*) to blame transgressors for their actions (or character, beliefs, emotions, etc.). After all, an instance of blame can be inappropriate if the transgression that triggers the blame is not within the blamer's *jurisdiction*. And as we understand it, a blamer's jurisdiction refers to her moral and relational standing, her authority, and her normative powers: the "place" from which she blames. Thus threats to a blamer's moral and relational standing, authority, and normative powers are plausibly seen as threats to the propriety of her blame.

To illustrate the need for this set of propriety conditions, consider the following case (well-known from ninth-grade English classes) in which we cannot explain the impropriety of blame in terms of agents not being blameworthy:

> "Wait a minute," snapped Tom, "I want to ask Mr. Gatsby one more question."
> "Go on," Gatsby said politely.
> "What kind of row are you trying to cause in my house anyhow?"
> They were out in the open at last and Gatsby was content.
> "He wasn't causing a row." Daisy looked desperately from one to the other. "You're causing a row. Please have a little self control."
> "Self control!" repeated Tom incredulously. "I suppose the latest thing is to sit back and let Mr. Nobody from Nowhere make love to your wife. Well, if that's the idea you can count me out. . . . Nowadays people begin by sneering at family life and family institutions and next they'll throw everything overboard." (Fitzgerald 1995, pp. 136–37)

In this tense scene, it's natural to interpret Tom as blaming Daisy and (especially) Gatsby for their affair. After all, it's plausible to think that his incredulity reveals a deep resentment for how he has been treated—how Daisy and Gatsby have failed to regard his standing as her husband. And taken in isolation, such blame seems to be appropriate. If *anyone* has the standing to blame another for an affair, certainly it is the aggrieved spouse.

---

[42] "Conditions of jurisdiction" is a bit misleading. However, because the more accurate "conditions related to the jurisdiction of a would-be blamer" is unwieldy, we'll stick with it.

The problem here, though, is that Tom himself is involved in a tawdry affair. So if you're like us, you probably think that Tom's blame in this scene is hypocritical, and hence in some sense objectionable. And if we're right in thinking that Tom's blame is inappropriate, then this alone shows that the blameworthiness of the transgressors is not sufficient for the propriety of blame. After all, surely Gatsby and Daisy are blameworthy for their affair. Yet something still seems inappropriate about Tom's blame. This (and a wide range of similar cases) suggests that there is a set of propriety conditions that must obtain if particular blamers are to be justified in their blame. And plausibly, if the above case is any indication, hypocrisy undermines the propriety of a blamer's blame. But while a great number of theorists agree on this point, there's often disagreement about why hypocrisy undermines Tom's standing (disagreement that reflects broader disagreements about what blame is).

To explain the impropriety of blame like Tom's, T. M. Scanlon (2008) has suggested that hypocrisy undermines a blamer's standing to blame because in cases of hypocritical blame, it is the blamer rather than the transgressor who has impaired the relationship. And since, on Scanlon's account, blame *marks* an impairment in a relationship, the hypocritical blamer fails to mark any impairment at all, since her relationship has already been impaired in the relevant way by her own transgressions. Her blame is therefore inaccurate. In the above case, Scanlon would explain the impropriety of Tom's blame simply by pointing out that it wasn't appropriate for him to adjust his intentions toward Daisy since his own affair was responsible for undermining the fabric of fidelity that underwrites marriages.

But Scanlon's account is not without its detractors. In contrast to Scanlon, Wallace (2010) argues that hypocrisy undermines a blamer's standing to blame because hypocritical blame essentially involves a denial of the equal moral standing of persons. Wallace claims that when we submit others to the burdensome sanctions associated with blame while shielding ourselves from such affects (say, by not feeling guilty enough to refrain from continued wrongdoing, by not regarding ourselves as owing others apologies, etc.), we attach "differential significance to the interests of the persons whom [we] blame and to [ourselves]" (p. 333). But to attach a differential significance in this way is to violate the standard of equal consideration for all persons—that is, the very standard that underwrites the possibility of moral community. On Wallace's view, an agent's moral standing to blame cannot outstrip her commitment to the equal standing of persons. Thus some transgressions and transgressors do not fall within the jurisdiction of the hypocrite. And this certainly seems to be the case for Tom. While he affords himself leniency, he refuses to extend the same freedom to his wife and her lover. Accordingly, his blame is objectionable.

But despite widespread agreement that hypocrisy is a threat to the propriety of blame, Macalester Bell (chapter 14) forcefully and provocatively argues that it is not. Rather than seeing hypocritical blame as something a transgressor should be protected from, she emphasizes our role as *targets* of blame. According to Bell, when it satisfies at least one of its five aims, blame helps to shield moral communities from the serious moral damage done by transgressions. So when we are targeted with blame—even hypocritical blame—we shouldn't rely on deflecting defenses that dismiss the content of the blame (e.g., "Who are *you* to criticize me?"); instead we should take seriously the content of the blame and respond to it accordingly.

But even if Bell is right to think that hypocrisy doesn't threaten the propriety of blame, there are other potential threats to a blamer's jurisdiction. For example, the nature of the relationship between transgressor and blamer is also relevant. Whereas Jennifer's parents can blame her for flunking out of school, we can't.[43] Because of their close relationship, Jennifer's failure has a significant impact on her parents' lives; she has (perhaps) wasted thousands of dollars of their money. By contrast, her failure has little or no impact on our lives.[44] Accordingly, blame doesn't seem appropriate; it's simply none of our business.[45] Of course, even strangers have some relationship grounded in their equal standing as persons in the moral community. And this explains why some of Jennifer's actions, even when we don't know her, plausibly fall within our jurisdiction. Though it may be inappropriate to blame Jennifer for her failure at school, it would certainly be appropriate to blame her if we discovered that she was responsible for a murder.

In her contribution to this volume (chapter 13), Erin Kelly discusses what can be thought of as a further propriety condition on jurisdiction. Kelly considers the nature and significance of excusing conditions—conditions under which we should excuse transgressors from blame. According to Kelly, "[E]xcuses represent a threshold of reasonable expectations formed by reference to norms about the burdens we morally expect persons, generally speaking, to bear in order to do the right thing." Thus in seeing a transgressor as excused, we are regarding her in ways that invite compassion. Accordingly, we regard her as having acted wrongly (or badly, as the case may be) but as nevertheless an inappropriate target of our blame. Of course, we regard her in these ways not simply because we recognize something deficient in the transgressor, but also because we recognize that *we* cannot have reasonably expected better from her.[46] This suggests that whether we have the jurisdiction to blame will

---

[43] We could presumably judge Jennifer blameworthy, but, as we suggested above, there is a distinction between judging blameworthy and blaming.

[44] Of course, the impact of their attitudes and actions on our lives isn't what grounds our relationships with others, but the degree to which others' attitudes and actions impact our lives often reflects the depth of the relationships.

[45] "If the harm isn't gross or the injustice egregious (no crime against humanity), if our concern, though earnest, is idle, then high-minded indignation has odors of moral self-indulgence" (Wertheimer 1998, p. 499).

[46] For a similar set of cases, see Fischer and Tognazzini (2011).

ultimately depend on what we can reasonably expect of others. It likewise suggests that the propriety of our blame will depend on whether reasons of compassion, which arise when we are sufficiently reflective about the potentially excusing conditions transgressors find themselves in, are especially weighty.

Of course, these are not the only considerations that go into determining whether the blamer has jurisdiction in a particular case. (G. A. Cohen [2006] and Angela Smith [2007], for example, have more to say about these particular issues.)[47] But rather than focus on these specific norms, we turn now from issues related specifically to would-be blamers to issues tied to the propriety of specific blaming interactions.

3.3. CONDITIONS ON PROCEDURE

The final class of propriety conditions that we'll consider are those conditions that must obtain if particular blaming interactions are to be appropriate. Although it's hard to say exactly where conditions of blameworthiness and conditions of jurisdiction end and where conditions of procedure begin, these conditions are usefully distinguished, since it's possible that even if the conditions of blameworthiness and the conditions of jurisdiction are satisfied, particular instances of blame are nevertheless inappropriate. For example, one way that particular instances of blame might be inappropriate is if the transgression that triggers the blame is relatively minor but the blame manifests itself in extremely severe and burdensome ways. While it might be appropriate to chide a friend for being fifteen minutes late, surely it's inappropriate to end the relationship over the same slight. Just as the punishment must fit the crime, so too must the blaming interaction fit the transgression.

There is also an epistemic condition that blaming interactions must satisfy. Just as we think criminal courts shouldn't convict if there is a reasonable doubt as to the defendant's guilt, it's plausible to think that we shouldn't blame others if there are good reasons to doubt that the potential target of blame is blameworthy for her actions.[48] It's plausible that the epistemic standards on criminal punishment should be higher than the epistemic standards on blame in informal interpersonal contexts, in part because there's a great deal more at stake in the case of criminal punishment. This would suggest that we had better be sure of what we're doing to a much greater degree when we threaten a transgressor with coercive detainment or execution than in cases of interpersonal blame (which threatens transgressors with comparatively light sanctions, if any). But

---

[47] For insightful discussions of a blamer's jurisdiction, as applied to a legal context, see Duff (2010); Tadros (2009).

[48] In chapter 6 of this volume, David Shoemaker argues that criminal punishment and informal blame are importantly dissimilar. However, as you'll see there, the dissimilarities that Shoemaker points to do not impugn our invocation of legal contexts on this point.

notice that although blamers must be epistemically responsible in their blame, this is not an issue of jurisdiction. A jury that convicts a defendant even though there are good reasons to doubt her guilt has done something inappropriate, but this impropriety doesn't arise from issues of jurisdiction. Rather, something about how they have deliberated and issued a verdict has gone wrong— that is, it's a procedural issue. And the same is true in cases of epistemically irresponsible blame.

In his contribution to the volume (chapter 15), Gary Watson considers two procedural issues relating to the vice of judgmentalism, which he understands as an overwillingness to criticize and blame others for their faults. Specifically, Watson considers and analyzes two forms of judgmentalism, the first of which involves a failure of interpretive generosity and the second of which involves a lack of acceptance of others' faults. His penetrating discussion connects the ethics of blame to the ethics of interpersonal relationships more generally, while weaving together issues related to jurisdiction and procedure.

Of course, there is much more to say about the ethics of blame (e.g., see chapters 12–15), and we haven't even touched on the ethics of the broader blaming context, including the norms governing apology, mercy, and forgiveness. It's undeniable that reasons for compassion, mercy, and forgiveness sometimes outweigh the reasons for blame, and a full ethics of blame will appreciate and reflect this fact.[49] Hence, given the richness of these topics, as well as their significance for meaningful relationships of the sort that we regularly enjoy, we simply note that this is an area especially ripe for future research.

4. Skepticism about Blame

We want to conclude by considering whether blame is valuable, something worth preserving. If blame turns out to have little or no value, then shouldn't we try to excise it, and its associated pain and suffering, from our moral lives?

Watson raises this challenge forcefully for Strawson's account of blame in his "Responsibility and the Limits of Evil" (1987b). Pointing to Strawson's (1962) discussion of resentment, Watson notes that for Strawson, blaming others is typically a retributive act, one that involves a withdrawal of goodwill toward transgressors and a willingness to participate in or otherwise sanction the suffering of the transgressor. But Watson notes that this seems to tell against an ideal of human relationships that regards such retributive responses as poisonous. The ideal in question is "an ideal of human fellowship

---

[49] A full ethics of blame may also need to appreciate the point made forcefully by Cheshire Calhoun (1989, p. 405) that "it may be reasonable to reproach moral failings even when individuals are not blameworthy."

or love which embodies values that are . . . important to our civilization"
(Watson 1987b, p. 257). When we laud revolutionaries like Mahatma Gandhi
or Martin Luther King Jr., we are celebrating this ideal—one that takes seriously the wrongs perpetrated against oppressed groups without acquiescing
to the desire to inflict suffering on transgressors. The success of Gandhi and
King in bringing about significant social change without succumbing to
unhealthy drives aimed at causing suffering provides us with a reason to
doubt the value of blame, at least on some interpretations of blame. Even if
there are some pro tanto reasons for blaming, it doesn't follow that blaming is
a valuable activity that should be, all things considered, endorsed and pursued. If we are to make room for blame as an activity to be engaged in, we
need an account of the value and significance of blame that either sidesteps
the issue by showing why blame doesn't involve the dispositions to inflict
suffering that Watson points to, or justifies the worrisome infliction of suffering that seems internal to many extant accounts of blame.[50]

In our view, this is a significant challenge.[51] Pereboom (chapter 10) reiterates
this challenge when he argues that several extant conceptions of blame are
consistent with thinking that retributive blaming responses to transgressions
are never justified, since such conceptions are divorced from the retributive
reactive attitudes.[52] Specifically, Pereboom argues that both Sher's and Scanlon's accounts of blame are consistent with the human ideal that Watson points
to, since neither of these accounts involves essential reference to the retributive
sentiments. After all, blame (as understood by Sher and Scanlon) is an activity
that facilitates and maintains meaningful human relationships. Here we see a
central value of blame—namely its role in underwriting interpersonal relationships. But it's important for Pereboom that blame play this role without
presupposing the legitimacy of or otherwise involving retributive responses.
In this sense, Pereboom shows us a way we can sidestep Watson's challenge.

Of course, since Watson's challenge is really only a challenge for reactive
attitude theorists (i.e., those who identify blame with the reactive attitudes of
resentment, indignation, and guilt), Pereboom's reply isn't so much an answer
to Watson's challenge as it is a concession (one that Pereboom is all too happy
to make!) that the retributive features of (some conceptions of) blame are not
only poisonous but unimportant. But what of those who take the reactive attitudes to be essential to blame? Do they have a leg to stand on?

---

[50] In her contribution (chapter 9), McGeer calls the first project that of "domesticating blame," and
she thinks that at best it produces a psychologically distorted view of blame. She prefers to engage in
the project of (merely) "civilizing blame," accepting its potentially troubling emotional core but urging
a revision in some of our blaming practices.

[51] For some other potential pitfalls of blaming that might make one worried about its value, all
things considered, see Williams (2003).

[52] For Pereboom, such responses are never justified because we are never morally responsible (and
so never blameworthy) for our actions.

In his contribution to this volume (chapter 11), Franklin argues that the re-active attitude account of blame does have the resources to answer Watson's challenge. According to Franklin, when we blame others for their transgres-sions, we are valuing moral values. And because the reactive attitudes are internal to blame on Franklin's account, they are directly implicated in the activity of committing ourselves to moral values. Franklin argues for this claim by considering what our commitment to moral values would look like if we were to abandon blame as a sensible response to transgressions. He argues that if we failed to respond emotionally in the ways characteristic of blame to mor-ally significant transgressions, then we would have good reason to doubt our commitment to moral values in the first place. Thus for Franklin, the value of blame is itself tied to its role in cementing our commitment to moral values.[53]

But this isn't to deny that in certain circumstances our emotional responses can lead to the unhealthy or poisonous acquiescence to the suffering of trans-gressors. This is certainly true (and not something, we think, that Franklin would want to deny).[54] But to take seriously Watson's challenge or Pereboom's restatement of Watson's challenge would be, on Franklin's view, to make an equally extreme mistake. Though we shouldn't celebrate the unhealthy aspects of retributive blaming responses, to fail to engage with transgressors via the reactive attitudes is ultimately to fail to take seriously the significance of the offense in question. This suggests a further value in blame, one articulated by Bell (chapter 14). According to Bell, blame is valuable because it "helps to shield and protect [the moral community] from the moral damage wrought by wrongdoing." So not only is blame a way in which we value moral values, but it also plays this role in part because it protects the moral community from the damage done to our values by transgressions.

While Franklin and Bell seem to point to genuine values associated with blame, we wonder whether they provide an adequate response to Watson's challenge. In particular we wonder why blame pruned of its essential connec-tion to the reactive attitudes cannot play the roles that Franklin and Bell point to. (Franklin himself addresses this in his objection to Sher's view.) Indeed, this is Pereboom's view. After all, suppose that an agent responds to an instance of wrongdoing by blaming the wrongdoer in those ways characterized by Scanlon. Though she is not essentially emotionally exercised, it's plausible to think that her marking of an impairment in her relationship with the wrong-doer in a way that affects her standing intentions toward the wrongdoer itself constitutes a form of valuing moral values. Moreover, such a response to wrongdoing plausibly can, in certain circumstances, serve to shield and pro-tect the moral community from the moral damage of moral transgression.

---

[53] Wallace (2011) also seems to accept something like this view.

[54] Of course, if McGeer is correct, then even these potentially unhealthy or poisonous responses to blame can be normatively and interpersonally significant.

Thus ultimately, whether the reactive attitudes are required for blame to have the sort of value Franklin and Bell point to will depend on whether the reactive attitudes are really required for the activities of valuing and protecting respectively. And if so, then plausibly Franklin and Bell are on to something important concerning the value of blame. But if not, more needs to be said. Thus this too points to important directions for future research concerning both the nature of the reactive emotions and their role in our valuation of moral values.

5. Conclusion

We hope we have made clear that blame is an extraordinarily rich topic, and we are grateful to each of the authors in this volume for helping to advance our understanding of it. Yet there is still much work to be done. By way of conclusion, we'll mention a few issues that seem especially ripe for future research.

The first is the nature of the reactive emotions. It doesn't take a very detailed understanding of resentment to see the plausibility of the Strawsonian account of blame, but we suspect that coming to a deeper understanding will help to further clarify the account and will likely shield it from some of the objections raised above.

Another issue is the nature of praise. We raised some doubts at the beginning of this chapter about whether praise is truly analogous to blame in any morally interesting sense, and similar suspicions have cropped up here and there in the contemporary literature (see, e.g., Wolf 1990; Watson 1996). Recent work by Coleen Macnamara (2011) also explores some interesting disanalogies between praise and blame. This suggests that a full understanding of praise will require an independent inquiry, which is something very few philosophers have undertaken.

Finally, given the rise of accounts of blame that emphasize relationships, it would be good to try to get a better understanding of what exactly they involve. Wallace suggests in his essay (chapter 12) that relationships will lie at the very heart of morality itself, and that certainly seems like an attractive view. But what sorts of relationships are involved, and what actions and attitudes ground those relationships?

One of the difficulties of working on a topic like blame—though perhaps any philosophical topic is like this—is that, as Robert Frost put it, "way leads on to way," and soon you feel the need to have a theory about everything in order to write about anything. At those times we do well to take Strawson's advice to remember "what it is actually like to be involved in ordinary interpersonal relationships" and resist the urge to "over-intellectualize the facts." For a philosopher, that's an exceedingly difficult task. But at least we have an example to follow.

Moral Blame and Moral Protest

Angela M. Smith

1. Introduction

One of the most interesting recent developments in the literature on moral responsibility is the increased focus on the nature of moral blame. If we understand what it *means* to be morally responsible for something as a matter of being a sensible target, in principle, of moral praise or blame for that thing, then our account of the conditions of moral responsibility will certainly depend on how we interpret these distinctive forms of moral response. If we interpret blame as mere negative moral evaluation, for example, then it would seem that the conditions of moral responsibility may be quite weak: in order to be a sensible target of negative moral evaluation, it is plausible to claim that one need only be capable of expressing a morally significant "quality of will" through one's conduct. If, on the other hand, we interpret blame as a kind of explicit moral sanction involving harsh treatment, then it would seem that the conditions of moral responsibility may be more stringent: in order to be a sensible target of ill treatment, it is plausible to claim that one should have had an opportunity to avoid that ill treatment. Thus our willingness to ascribe moral responsibility to some agent for something may depend, significantly, on what we think blame itself is.[1]

Like many recent writers on this topic, I am dissatisfied with both the "moral assessment" account of blame and the "moral sanction" account of blame. The sort of blame associated with our ascriptions of moral responsibility seems to me to go beyond the mere negative assessment of a person for her attitudes or

I am indebted to Jason Benchimol, Rahul Kumar, Janice Moskalik, Sandra Reiter, and Lad Sessions for stimulating discussions about the topic of this paper. I also received extremely useful written comments on an earlier draft of this paper from Justin Coates and Neal Tognazzini. I would like to thank the audiences at the College of William and Mary and Virginia Tech University for their many helpful comments and suggestions. My work on this paper was supported by a summer Lenfest Grant from Washington and Lee University, for which I am very grateful.

[1] For the remainder of this paper, I will be using the term 'blame' to refer to 'moral blame,' unless otherwise noted.

conduct, but it also does not seem to me to be a matter of anything akin to a punishment or penalty for wrongdoing. If we think carefully about mundane cases of moral blame arising in everyday interactions between normal competent adults, it seems clear that we are not simply evaluating one another against a moral standard, but it also seems wrong to say that we are "punishing" or "sanctioning" one another (in the way that we may punish or sanction a small child in an effort to foster her moral development).[2] But what, then, is this attitude or activity of moral blame, which goes beyond mere assessment but does not involve the deliberate infliction of punishment or penalties?[3]

Probably the most influential contemporary answer to this question has its roots in the reactive attitude theory put forward by P. F. Strawson in his famous 1962 article "Freedom and Resentment." According to this theory, blame is neither a mere assessment nor a form of sanctioning activity but rather a distinctive emotional response we have to perceived manifestations of ill will or disregard on the part of others. To blame a person, on this view, is to feel a reactive emotion of resentment or indignation toward her for violating the basic moral demand for goodwill or reasonable regard. But this theory too has come under attack recently by some who have argued that such emotional reactions are not, in fact, essential to moral blame. Both George Sher (2006) and T. M. Scanlon (2008) have argued against the Strawsonian account on these grounds and have put forward distinctive new proposals about how we should understand the nature of moral blame.

My aim in this paper is to critically evaluate these two new accounts of blame and to offer an alternative account that remedies what I see as some of the shortcomings in their approaches. Both Sher and Scanlon seek to provide an account of blame that falls between the mere assessment account and the sanction account, but they reject the appeal to the Strawsonian reactive attitudes as a way of splitting the difference. While I agree with them that the reactive attitudes are not necessary for blame, I will argue that each of these new accounts leaves out something that is absolutely essential to the kind of blame associated with ascriptions of moral responsibility, something that the Strawsonian theory comes much closer to capturing: namely, the element of moral

---

[2] Kyla Ebels-Duggan (2010) emphasizes how distorting it is to think of blame as a kind of "punishment" in ordinary interpersonal relations between competent adults. As she notes, questions of punishment arise most clearly in child-rearing and institutional contexts. In ordinary interpersonal contexts, however, punishment is usually not at issue.

[3] One might doubt whether there *is* a single phenomenon at issue here—"moral blame"—that is susceptible to philosophical analysis. Indeed, the wide variety of accounts that have been given of the nature of moral blame might suggest that there is no such phenomenon. Still, I agree with R. Jay Wallace (2011, fn. 1 p. 370) that there does seem to be a special kind of reaction (or set of reactions) that we have *only* toward individuals whom we judge to be morally responsible for exercises of immoral agency, a kind of reaction that we do not have toward unfortunate occurrences of other kinds. This at least will be my working assumption in what follows.

protest.[4] To morally blame another, in my view, is to register in some significant way one's moral protest of that agent's treatment of oneself or others. Such protest need not be outwardly expressed in any way, and it need not take the form of a Strawsonian reactive attitude. But what unites all of the behavioral and attitudinal responses we are inclined to categorize as instances of blame, I will argue, is that they share this element of moral protest. This element, in turn, is what explains how moral blame differs from the sorts of negative attitudes and responses we might have toward individuals and creatures whom we do not regard as morally responsible for their conduct.

My strategy will be as follows. In the next section, I will very briefly discuss some of the well-known objections that have been raised to the sanction view, the assessment view, and the reactive attitude view of moral blame. By examining these objections, we will be in a position to spell out some of the basic desiderata that an adequate account of moral blame must meet. In sections 3 and 4, I will discuss Sher's and Scanlon's recent accounts of blame and explain why, despite their improvements over these traditional views, neither of these accounts successfully explicates the true nature of moral blame. Finally, in section 5, I will put forward my alternative account, which I will argue does a better job of capturing the distinctive force and significance of moral blame.

2. The Nature of Blame: Sanction, Assessment, or Reactive Attitude?

Moral blame of the sort I am concerned with in this paper is characteristically a response to a *person* on the basis of some wrongful, objectionable, or untoward conduct on her part. Unlike the sort of "blame" we might attribute to malfunctioning artifacts or disruptive weather patterns, moral blame of persons is thought to have a characteristic "force" or "depth" that goes beyond a mere description of causal responsibility for a bad result (Wolf 1990; Hieronymi 2004). In addition it is generally agreed that *blaming* someone for something goes beyond simply judging or believing *that* she is blameworthy for it. After all, it seems perfectly legitimate to say things like "I know he is blameworthy for doing X, but I just can't bring myself to blame him for it," suggesting that blame involves something that goes beyond the simple judgment of blameworthiness (Cohen 1977). And when we forgive a person, it seems that we retain our judgment of blameworthiness but disavow certain critical responses that we would ordinarily be justified in taking toward the agent on the basis of her objectionable conduct. But what, exactly, are these "critical responses," and how do they go beyond the judgment of blameworthiness? And how should we understand their characteristic "force" or "depth"?

---

[4] Here I am influenced by Pamela Hieronymi's (2001) argument that there is an intimate tie between resentment and protest, as well as Matthew Talbert's (2012) helpful development of this idea.

One natural answer to these questions is that blame must be some sort of punitive activity we direct toward those whom we regard as morally blameworthy. If we take our cue from the criminal legal system, a judgment of moral blameworthiness might be seen as akin to a finding of criminal guilt, and moral blame might be seen as akin to criminal punishment. To blame someone, on this view, is simply to engage in negative overt behavior (such as scolding, rebuking, telling off, or ostracizing) in response to someone's objectionable conduct. According to many Utilitarian philosophers writing in the first half of the twentieth century, moral blame should be understood as a form of negative treatment whose purpose is to bring about socially beneficial outcomes; blame is justified, on this view, so long as it is possible to influence a person's future conduct or character through such sanctioning activities (Schlick 1939; Smart 1961).

While this sanction account of blame was once widely accepted in the philosophical literature, I think it is fair to say that it has now fallen decisively out of favor. Even philosophers who see close connections between blame and certain forms of punishment or unpleasant treatment generally insist that blame *itself* is distinct from any of these forms of punitive activity (Wallace 1994, pp. 55–56). One obvious problem with this account is that it does not appear to allow for the phenomenon of private or unexpressed blame. Yet we can coherently say things like "Though I never told him, I always blamed my father for neglecting me when I was growing up." Nor does it appear to allow for blame of people who are outside the reach of our sanctioning activities (either because they are now dead or are distant from us in time or space). But it also seems quite possible for us to blame people such as Hitler, Omar al-Bashir, and even the reckless driver on the highway whom we are not in a position to personally sanction in any way. Both of these objections point toward a more general objection, which is that even when blame is overt, its force seems to reside not in the outward conduct itself but rather in the negative attitude that is expressed by this outward conduct. Indeed, we generally do not think that the overt sanctioning activities directed at small children or pets count as instances of "moral blame" precisely because these activities do not express the relevant sort of moral attitudes or judgments. But if that is correct, then it seems that the sanctioning activities many people identify with blame are really just vehicles for the *expression* of moral blame, and we still need an account of what blame itself is.

The next two views attempt to provide such an account. According to what I have called the assessment view, to blame a person for something is essentially to take that thing to reveal something negative about that person's character. Defenders of the assessment view often appeal to the idea of a moral "ledger" or "balance sheet" and suggest that when we praise and blame persons we are, in effect, making additions or subtractions to our assessment of their overall "moral record" (Feinberg 1970, pp. 125–27; Glover 1970, p. 64; Zimmermann 1988, p. 38). Wrongdoers are judged to have a black mark, or a demerit, in their moral ledger, which in turn lowers our overall assessment of their moral worth. Since most of us care about whether others regard us as morally worthy or not, we care about these positive and negative evaluations of our moral standing.

One advantage of the assessment view is that it can explain how blame goes beyond a mere judgment of blameworthiness, but in a way that, unlike the sanction view, allows for the phenomenon of private or unexpressed blame. In order to blame a person, I must not only judge that she is blameworthy for something; I must also judge that *she* is diminished or disfigured or tarnished in some way in virtue of her misconduct. But I can make such an assessment without ever expressing that judgment to the person in any way, through word or action. Yet critics of the assessment view have argued that this simply does not capture what most of us have in mind when we blame someone for her misconduct. In particular it has been argued that this view cannot capture the distinctive force of blame or explain why it is anything more than "a pointless assignment of moral grades" (Scanlon 2008, p. 127). The notion that in blaming we may be dispassionately evaluating a person's moral record simply does not do justice to the emotional significance of blame and to the important role this attitude plays in structuring our moral relations with one another. Reflection on this significance and this role brings us to the third, and probably most influential, contemporary account of the nature of blame.

In his landmark essay, "Freedom and Resentment," P. F. Strawson (1962) drew attention to a set of attitudes that he argued is intimately bound up with our practices of holding one another responsible. These "reactive attitudes," as he called them, are essentially emotional reactions to the goodwill or ill will that people manifest toward us (or others) in their behavior. Strawson, and Strawson-inspired theorists such as R. Jay Wallace, put particular emphasis on the negative attitudes of resentment, indignation, and guilt as the characteristic emotional responses to perceived manifestations of ill will (Wallace 1994, pp. 29–30). According to these philosophers, these reactive attitudes are the key to understanding the nature and significance of blame (and self-blame). Blame, on this view, is not simply a negative assessment of someone's character, nor is it an explicit activity we engage in in order to sanction someone for bad behavior. Blame is a way of responding emotionally to the perceived disregard or disrespect manifested in someone's behavior toward oneself or others. These reactions, according to Strawson, "rest on, and reflect, an expectation of, and demand for, the manifestation of a certain degree of goodwill or regard on the part of other human beings toward ourselves; or at least on the expectation of, and demand for, an absence of the manifestation of active ill-will or indifferent disregard" (1962, p. 84). And these reactive attitudes, in turn, "tend to inhibit or at least limit our goodwill toward the object of these attitudes, tend to promote an at least partial and temporary withdrawal of goodwill" (p. 90). When we blame someone, then, we are emotionally exercised by what they have done, and this emotional disturbance carries with it a certain amount of hostility toward the offender. As Strawson puts it, the reactive attitudes entail "the modification . . . of the general demand that another should, if possible, be spared suffering" (p. 90).

The reactive attitude view has seemed to many philosophers to capture quite nicely the distinctive force of blame and to explain how blame differs from a simple judgment of blameworthiness. The person who says "I know X is blameworthy, but I just can't bring myself to blame him" is indicating that he does not feel the usual attitudes of resentment, indignation, or hostility toward a person who has manifested ill will. And the person who forgives can be understood as disavowing the sort of "partial withdrawal of goodwill" that would normally be justified in response to a blameworthy agent. This view clearly allows for the possibility of private or unexpressed blame, but it also gives a plausible account of what the reactive attitudes express when they are communicated to others: they express a kind of hostility toward the agent for violating the "basic moral demand" for goodwill or reasonable regard in her interactions with others. This, in turn, explains why blame plays such an important role in our interpersonal relationships, for blame and the other reactive attitudes embody at a deep level the basic expectations we hold one another to as members of a shared moral community.

Despite the apparent advantages of the reactive attitude view, various objections have been raised to this account as well. In particular both Sher (2006) and Scanlon (2008) have objected that blame does not *necessarily* involve reactive emotions such as resentment or indignation. It seems possible to blame friends or loved ones for their misdeeds, for example, without feeling any attitudes of resentment, anger, or hostility toward them. Others have objected to the apparent "retributivist" elements of Strawson's view, specifically to his claim that these reactive attitudes necessarily embody a kind of hostility or a "partial withdrawal of goodwill" (Stern 1974, pp. 78–79; Watson 1987b, p. 286).[5] Finally, it has been argued that Strawson, and those inspired by his account, have put the emphasis on the wrong aspect of his view (Scanlon 1988, pp. 160–72; Hieronymi 2004, pp. 122–25). In order to understand the special force of blame, according to these critics, what is important is not so much the emotional heat of the reactive attitudes (understood as affects) but rather the fact that blame is a way of registering a modification in one's moral relationship with another. While the reactive attitudes may be one way of registering such a modification, according to these critics, they have no privileged status in this regard. One can also register such a modification by dispassionately "unfriending" someone on one's Facebook page, for example, or by simply refusing to trust her anymore, and these too should qualify as forms of blame.

---

[5] As Justin Coates and Neal Tognazzini have pointed out to me, however, one need not interpret the reactive attitudes as retributive in this sense; therefore it is not clear that this is an objection to the most plausible interpretation of the reactive attitude theory of blame.

It seems, then, that each of the three traditional accounts of the nature of blame has certain advantages and disadvantages. The sanction account easily explains how blame goes beyond a mere judgment of blameworthiness, but it does not allow for the phenomenon of unexpressed blame, nor does it make clear the special tie between moral blame and ascriptions of moral responsibility. The assessment account easily explains the phenomenon of unexpressed blame, but it fails to capture the special "force" of moral blame and the distinctive role it plays in our interpersonal relationships. The Strawsonian account appears to solve these problems with the first two views, but in tying blame so closely to the reactive attitudes it seems to exclude genuine instances of blame that do not involve these reactive sentiments.

On the basis of this critical evaluation of the three traditional accounts of blame, then, we are in a position to identify four of the key desiderata that any successful account of the nature of blame must meet. First, the account must explain how blaming someone goes beyond simply judging her to be blameworthy. Second, the account must allow for the possibility of unexpressed blame, including blame of the distant and the dead. Third, the account must be flexible enough to accommodate the variety of attitudinal and behavioral reactions we are inclined to countenance as instances of blame. And fourth, the account must explain the special tie between moral blame and ascriptions of moral responsibility; that is, it must make clear why the responses of moral blame are appropriately directed only at individuals deemed morally responsible for their conduct.

In the next two sections, I will look at two recent accounts of blame that attempt to meet these desiderata.

3. Sher's Dispositional Account

In his recent book *In Praise of Blame*, George Sher (2006) sets out to defend a comprehensive account of blame that avoids some of the pitfalls of the traditional accounts discussed above. Sher is particularly eager to provide an account of blame that can explain why blame is so often associated with things like anger, hostile behavior, and reproach, while not being exclusively identified with any one of these things. In order to accomplish this, he puts forward the following proposal: Blame should be understood as a set of *dispositions* to have certain attitudinal and behavioral reactions, and these dispositions should be understood as traceable to a single desire-belief pair that includes (1) a belief that the person in question has acted badly or has a bad character, and (2) a corresponding desire that the person not have acted badly or not have a bad character (Sher 2006, p. 112). This results in what Sher calls a "two-tiered account of blame" (p. 138), with the core desire-belief pair forming the first tier and some collection of blame-related behavioral and attitudinal dispositions forming the second tier.

According to Sher, the core belief component of blame is the belief that a person has acted badly or has a bad character. In the introduction of his book, Sher makes clear that what he means in saying that a person has performed a "bad act" is that he has performed a wrong act for which he does not have a sufficient excuse or justification. He goes on to define bad acts as "morally defective acts that render agents blameworthy" (2006, p. 9). So the belief component of blame, on Sher's account, is the belief that an agent has performed a wrong action for which he is blameworthy.

Now, as Sher himself points out, if we are trying to give an account of what is involved in the stance or attitude of *blaming* someone, it will not do simply to identify such a stance or attitude with the belief that a person is blameworthy. For, as he puts it, "this merely returns us to the question of what, in blaming the wrongdoer, we believe him to be worthy of" (Sher 2006, p. 75). So anyone who wants to account for blame in terms of a belief cannot take the content of that belief to be simply "that the agent is blameworthy" without facing a vicious circularity. But if we add a desire to this belief and show how this desire-belief pair can make appropriate a range of attitudinal and behavioral responses to the agent, we will be in a position to say what it is that the blameworthy are worthy of. They are worthy of whatever reactions are made appropriate by this desire-belief pair in the context.

One of the really attractive features of Sher's account, as well as Scanlon's (as we will see), is that it can make sense of the fact that the type of blame that it is appropriate for any particular individual to direct toward a blameworthy agent may vary depending on that individual's relation to the agent and other specific features of the context. While the core desire-belief pair he identifies remains constant across all agents and contexts, it will make appropriate different reactions depending on whether, for example, I am myself the wrongdoer, or the victim of the wrongdoing, or a neutral third party observing the offensive action. I may feel guilt or a disposition to apologize to the person I have wronged; the victim of my wrongdoing may feel resentment or a disposition to reproach me; and a third party may feel indignation or a disposition to ignore or snub me. Any and all of these responses seem to qualify as forms of "blame," yet they are all quite different. This account can also explain why anger or hostile feelings are not necessary components of blame. In some cases, because of my close relationship to someone who has wronged me, I may not feel resentment or hostility toward her, yet I may still be disposed to confront her with her wrongdoing and to demand an apology from her. And this too would seem to be a way of blaming her. Thus Sher's account can capture the variety of things we are inclined to describe as instances of blame without identifying it exclusively with any particular attitudinal or behavioral reaction. And what allegedly allows for this heterogeneity is that all of these responses are ultimately explicable in terms of the core desire-belief pair he identifies.

The central question to be asked about his account, then, is whether this core desire-belief pair has the correct content to explain and unify the various attitudinal and behavioral dispositions we associate with blame. Since the belief component is simply the judgment of blameworthiness, what is really doing the work in his account of blame is the desire component. That component, recall, is a desire that the person not have acted badly or not have a bad character (Sher 2006, p. 112). Sher thinks the presence of this (frustrated) desire can explain all of the attitudinal and behavioral dispositions we associate with blame. As he puts it, using D to refer to the desire in question, "[T]he obvious way to invoke D to account for our disposition to become angry at those we blame is to assimilate that anger to the other negative feelings that we have when we see that we cannot get what we want. Just as obviously, the way to invoke D to account for our disposition to display hostility toward those we blame is to see our hostile behavior as a natural expression of our negative feelings toward them" (pp. 104–5). Is Sher right that the addition of this desire to the judgment of blameworthiness can capture and make appropriate all and only those reactions we associate with blame?

I think not. In fact, I think this core desire-belief pair is neither necessary nor sufficient to account for all of the reactions we are inclined to classify as forms of blame. Let's begin by looking at why the account is not sufficient. Consider, for example, the reactions of a mother whose son has been justly convicted of murder. Assume that she judges that her son is blameworthy for the crime (she does not doubt that he is guilty) and that she strongly desires that he had not committed it. She desires this because she knows that his wrongdoing will ruin the rest of his life, and she is deeply distraught by this fact. Her reactions in this case might well take the form of deep sadness, despair, or pity, and these reactions appear to be justified by her belief and desire. Yet I would not be inclined to say that these are reactions of blame. Indeed, some of these reactions (e.g., sadness and pity) seem to be the opposite of blame, yet they are perfectly understandable responses to loved ones who have behaved badly in ways that we strongly desire they had not.

Not only is this core desire-belief pair not sufficient for explaining the dispositions we associate with blame; it is also not necessary. Consider, for example, the attitudes of many Republicans on learning of Bill Clinton's ill-fated dalliance with Monica Lewinsky. I think it fair to say that a great many of these individuals *blamed* Clinton for his behavior (or at least for his lack of candor about his behavior). Is it so clear, however, that all of these individuals desired that Clinton had not behaved badly? To the contrary, I suspect most of them were quite happy to see him do wrong, yet they blamed him all the same. In fact—and this is a sad truth about us—I think it is rather common for us to relish the missteps of others, yet this in no way inhibits our tendency to blame such individuals for their misdeeds.

So what has gone wrong here? It seems to me that the desire Sher has placed at the core of his account of blame is simply incapable of capturing what is essential to this distinctive type of moral response. When we blame another, we don't simply desire that the wrong had not been done. As we have seen, such a desire is not even present in all instances of blame, and it is possible to have this desire (and the corresponding belief in blameworthiness) without reacting in any of the ways typical of blame. Sher may be correct, however, that there is something distinctively motivational at the heart of blaming reactions and that this is the key to distinguishing between merely judging someone to be blameworthy and blaming her. But if it is not a desire that the agent not have acted badly, then what could it be?

To focus the mind a bit, we might consider what is going on when we blame brutal political leaders such as Slobodan Milosevic and Bashar al-Assad for their slaughter of innocent agents. In these cases, of course, I'm sure we all do have a desire that they had not acted as they did, precisely because of the hor-rible suffering they have caused others. But *this* desire is, in a way, no different from the desire we might have that an earthquake had not hit Haiti or that a grizzly bear had not attacked campers in Yellowstone; that is, *this* sort of desire can take as its object the occurrence of natural disasters or the behavior of nonrational animals no less than the actions of morally responsible agents. If we are looking for a motivation that is distinctively connected with moral blame, then its content should be such that it would not make sense to direct it toward these sorts of regrettable "natural" occurrences. So what is special, then, about the sort of reaction we might have to a Milosevic or an Assad that differentiates it from the sort of reaction we might have to an earthquake or a grizzly bear?

I propose that we understand the distinctive motivational element implicit in all instances of moral blame as a disposition to protest conduct that we regard as wrongful or disrespectful to ourselves or others. What distinguishes moral blame of persons from the sort of regret or sadness we might feel over natural disasters is that the former embodies a disposition to repudiate, to take some kind of stand against, a certain presumption implicit in the wrongdoer's behavior: the presumption that he or she has a right to treat others in objec-tionable ways. When it is a *person* who has caused unjustified pain and suf-fering to others, we not only desire that he had not done so; we feel compelled to register in some way—in our attitudes or in our conduct—the fact that his actions are morally unacceptable, that they have violated basic norms of mu-tual respect and recognition. Our blame in these cases represents our *protest* of his actions and our repudiation of the attitudes toward others that these actions reflect.

I will say more in section 5 about how I think we should understand the element of protest embodied in all cases of blame, but I hope I have said enough to distinguish this view from the one Sher defends. The fundamental motivational element underlying all instances of moral blame, I suggest, is not a desire that a person not have acted badly or not have had a bad character, but rather a desire to protest and repudiate conduct or attitudes that manifest moral disregard. If I am correct, then this would explain why such reactions are properly directed only at morally responsible agents. Earthquakes and grizzly bears cannot show moral disregard since they are clearly incapable of recognizing the moral significance of their activities. It would thus make no sense to protest anything they "do." Creatures who have the ability to recognize, assess, and respond to reasons, however, *are* capable of expressing moral disregard through their activities and thus are appropriate targets of responses of protest. In the next section, I will try to build on this suggestion by considering another account of blame recently put forward by T. M. Scanlon.

4. Scanlon's Impairment Account

The final account of blame I will look at before spelling out my alternative account is one defended by T. M. Scanlon in his recent book *Moral Dimensions: Permissibility, Meaning, Blame* (2008). Like Sher, Scanlon finds difficulties with all of the traditional accounts of blame and seeks to present an account that explains how blame is more than a (negative) evaluation but not a form of sanction. Scanlon believes that Strawson was basically correct to place human relationships at the foundation of blame, but rather than identifying blame with the reactive emotions of resentment and indignation, Scanlon places emphasis on "the expectations, intentions, and attitudes that constitute these relationships" (p. 128). He puts his proposal as follows:

> To claim that a person is *blameworthy* for an action is to claim that the action shows something about the agent's attitudes toward others that impairs the relations that others can have with him or her. To *blame* a person is to judge him or her to be blameworthy and to take your relationship with him or her to be modified in a way that this judgment of impaired relations holds to be appropriate. (pp. 128–29)

For example, if I discover that a friend has betrayed me, I will take his action to reveal attitudes (of disloyalty, disrespect, etc.) that impair my relationship with him. His action reveals that he does not have the attitudes, dispositions, and intentions that are (ideally) constitutive of a relationship of friendship. I may respond to this judgment of impairment in any number of ways. I may do nothing at all, in which case it might be said that I judge my friend blameworthy but do not blame him. On the other hand, I may modify my own attitudes, intentions, and expectations toward my friend in response to my judgment of impaired relations. I may no longer trust him or seek his company; I may feel angry, upset, disappointed, or just sad; I may complain to him about his conduct and seek explanation or justification. In Scanlon's view, all of these possible modifications to my own attitudes, intentions, and expectations count as ways of "blaming" my friend, and what unites them is that they are all responses to a judgment of impaired relations. Like Sher, then, Scanlon thinks it is a mistake to identify blame with any single attitude or type of behavior; rather, blame can take any number of different forms depending on the nature of the relationship that is impaired, the nature of the impairment itself, and the specific relation between the agent and the one who is blamed.

Once again I think it is an advantage of Scanlon's account that it can accommodate a wide variety of reactions that we are inclined to classify as forms of blame. While he admits that the reactive attitudes are a common response to judgments of impairment (this is *one* way we can modify our own intentions, attitudes, and expectations in response to a judgment of blameworthiness), he insists that such attitudes are not necessary for blame. And this seems right: if someone that I care deeply about wrongs me in a serious way, I may feel extreme sadness rather than resentment or indignation toward her, but I may also proceed to cut off all further interactions with her and refuse to consider her requests for reconciliation. These responses too seem to be forms of blame, even if they are not accompanied by the Strawsonian reactive attitudes.

Yet there still seems to be something missing from Scanlon's account, and I submit that it is the same thing that is missing from Sher's account: namely, the element of moral protest. Consider again the case of a mother whose son has been convicted of a terrible crime. Since she does judge him to be blameworthy, we can assume that she judges him to have attitudes that impair his relations with others. And on the basis of this judgment, she might modify her own attitudes, intentions, and expectations toward him. For example, she might make an extra effort to show love and affection toward him, either as a way of compensating for the hatred others will likely direct toward him or in an effort to get him to modify his own relationship-impairing attitudes. Or she may reluctantly modify the high expectations she once had of his becoming a great artist or a successful businessman. But surely *these* modifications to her attitudes, intentions, and expectations toward him would not show that she *blames* him for his crime. While we certainly want an account of blame that can accommodate a variety of attitudinal and behavioral responses, it is clearly going too far to suggest that showing extra love and affection toward someone can count as a way of blaming him!

In response Scanlon might well protest that I am not taking seriously his claim that to blame a person is to judge him or her to be blameworthy (i.e., to have relationship-impairing attitudes) and to modify your attitudes, intentions, and expectations toward him or her *in a way that this judgment of impaired relations holds to be appropriate*. That is to say, what is crucial here is that the modification in question be an "appropriate" response to the relationship-impairing attitudes of the other. The problem, however, is that the standard of

against a moral threat in the same way that pain is a primitive reaction of protest against a physical threat.

If we understand blame as itself a form of moral protest, then, we might see it as having two distinct but related aims: first, to *register* the fact that the person wronged did not deserve such treatment by *challenging* the moral claim implicit in the wrongdoer's action; second, to prompt moral recognition and acknowledgment of this fact on the part of the wrongdoer and/or others in the moral community. But as both Hieronymi's and Boxill's quotations make clear, it is the first aim that is primary: even in cases where our protest is unlikely to prompt moral recognition from others, it still has the important function of registering a significant moral truth—namely, that unjustified disregard was shown to a morally considerable being.

If these reflections are on the right track, perhaps we can simply modify Scanlon's basic account of blame to capture this essential element of moral protest. I propose that we understand the nature of moral blame as follows:

> **The Moral Protest Account:** To *blame* another is to judge that she is blameworthy (i.e., to judge that she has attitudes that impair her relations with others) and to modify one's own attitudes, intentions, and expectations toward that person as a way of *protesting* (i.e., registering and challenging) the moral claim implicit in her conduct, where such protest implicitly seeks some kind of moral acknowledgment on the part of the blameworthy agent and/or on the part of others in the moral community.

In the rest of this section, I will spell out some of the advantages of this moral protest account of moral blame, explaining in particular how it meets the desiderata for an adequate account of blame spelled out in section 2.

First, this account gives a clear explanation of how blaming someone goes beyond simply judging her to be blameworthy. The account adopts the Scanlonian interpretation of what is involved in judging someone blameworthy: it is to judge that she has attitudes that impair her relations with others. This is a kind of "universal" judgment that anyone can make toward any agent, at any time, from any position. Whether a particular person can be said to *blame* another, however, depends on whether she goes on to modify any of her attitudes, intentions, and expectations toward the blameworthy agent as a way of *protesting* the moral claim implicit in that agent's conduct. When I say of someone, "I know he's blameworthy, but I just can't bring myself to blame him," I am confessing that I find it hard to *protest* the meaning of his actions. For example, I judge the agent who threw a pie in the face of Rupert Murdoch as he was testifying before a British Parliament committee to be blameworthy, but I cannot say that I have modified any of my attitudes, intentions, and expectations toward the pie-thrower as a way of protesting the moral claim implicit in his conduct. Murdoch's wife, however, undoubtedly both judges the pie-thrower blameworthy and blames him.

Second, this account allows for the possibility of unexpressed blame, including blame of the distant and the dead. This may be less obvious, given my earlier suggestion that we regard blame as incipiently communicative in nature and also my suggestion that blame has moral acknowledgment as one of its constitutive aims. If the target of our blame is now dead or distant from us in time or space, or if we do not outwardly express our blame in any way, aren't these communicative and constitutive aims idle? This is not, of course, a problem for Scanlon's own account, since he explicitly denies that blame is, even incipiently, a form of communication. But I have already argued that this is one of the unattractive features of his view, so I now need to say something about why the (implicitly) communicative nature of blame does not rule out private blame or blame of those with whom we are unable to communicate.

Let me start with the case of unexpressed blame toward those who are still alive. The reactive attitudes are clearly one way in which we can register our moral protest of another without outwardly expressing it in any way. Resentment and indignation, in my view, are ways of emotionally protesting the ill treatment of oneself or others. But we can also protest ill treatment privately through the modification of other attitudes, intentions, and expectations. Even if we are not in a position (for whatever reason) to make these attitudinal modifications known, I believe these reactions embody, at a deep level, both moral protest and a desire that the wrongdoer morally acknowledge his wrongdoing. Blame is *incipiently* communicative both in the sense that it registers (i.e., communicates, even if only to the victim herself) the existence of unjustified wrongdoing and in the sense that it seeks some sort of moral recognition of wrongdoing on the part of the blameworthy agent.

But what about the sort of blame we still feel *now* toward those who have committed egregious wrongs in the past? For example, when I read about the brutal history of slavery in the United States, I am inclined to say not only that I judge southern slaveholders blameworthy; I am inclined to say that I actually *blame* them for their unconscionable behavior. But can it make any sense to say that my current blame embodies a desire for moral acknowledgment or recognition? What could that possibly mean, given that these individuals are long dead and that the practice of slavery is in the distant past? Here, I think, we need to recognize a feature of protest that I have not yet said anything about. While protest primarily targets the false moral claim implicit in the behavior of a wrongdoer and seeks from the wrongdoer herself some kind of moral recognition of this fact, it can have as a secondary aim moral recognition on the part of the wider moral community. This is the sense in which blame can have a "point" even if, for whatever reason, the wrongdoer herself can never be brought to acknowledge the wrongfulness of her behavior (Talbert 2012). When we blame antebellum slaveholders, then, I think we should say that the desire in this case is for a continued acknowledgment, on the part of the moral community, of the horrible wrongs that were committed against particular members of our community in the past. By continuing to blame these distant wrongdoers rather than simply judging them blameworthy, we, as it were, sustain and reiterate our moral protest of this treatment of our fellow citizens.

The moral protest account can help explain, moreover, why it sometimes seems quite odd to say that we *blame* individuals in the very distant past for their atrocities, while in other cases, such as the one just mentioned, it does not seem so far-fetched. This connects with a feature of Scanlon's account that I have not said nearly enough about, which is the dependence of blame on relationships. We in the United States have a particular reason to continue to blame southern slaveholders (rather than merely judging them blameworthy), which has to do with our current relationships with members of our community who were deeply affected by this disgraceful chapter in our history. By continuing to blame, we continue to protest the "outrageous falsehood" that the practice of slavery embodied. It might not make sense, by contrast, for a present-day Norwegian to blame southern slaveholders, though he might well judge them to be blameworthy. Likewise I find it odd to say that I blame Genghis Khan for his atrocities (though I judge him blameworthy for them), but it might not be odd at all for a present-day citizen of Iraq, Iran, or Afghanistan to insist that he blames him. I do not have the space to adequately explore this suggestion here, but it seems to me the link between blame and protest gives us a way of explaining our intuitions about when it does, and does not, make sense to talk about blame of the distant and the dead.[8]

The third desiderata of an adequate account of blame is that it should be able to explain the variety of responses we are inclined to countenance as instances of blame. Like the accounts defended by Sher and Scanlon, the moral protest account allows for a wide variety of reactions to count as instances of moral blame and does not tie it exclusively to one sort of attitudinal or behavioral response. While the reactive attitudes of resentment and indignation are very common ways of "protesting" the behavior of others, this view would also allow for certain "dispassionate" forms of blame, so long as an agent modifies her attitudes, intentions, and expectations toward another as a way of registering her repudiation of the false moral claims implicit in the other's behavior. In addition this account can make sense of the fact that different people have reason to respond in different ways to the same blameworthy agent, depending on their relation to the agent, the nature of the wrong done, and even the status of their own moral character (Smith 2007; Scanlon 2008). The sort of protest it is appropriate for a betrayed lover to make is different from the sort of protest it is appropriate for a friend to make, which is different again from

---

[8] Here I am picking up on, and trying to flesh out, some of the suggestive claims on this topic made by Scanlon (2008) on pp. 146–47 and 169.

the sort of protest (if any) it is appropriate for an uninvolved third party to make. And if I am the betrayed lover, my very standing to protest might be undermined by the fact that I have engaged in similar acts of betrayal toward my lover in the past. The moral protest account can make sense of all of these ways in which blaming responses can vary among people, while still retaining a common element that explains why they all qualify as instances of blame.

But unlike the accounts defended by Sher and Scanlon, the moral protest account does not seem to allow for "false positives," that is, cases in which the basic conditions of blame are met but we are disinclined to classify the resulting reactions as instances of blame. In particular, this account would exclude the reactions of the sad mother and the better informed friend from counting as reactions of blame because the attitudinal modifications they engage in are not undertaken as a way of *protesting* the attitudes of others nor out of a desire to bring about any sort of moral acknowledgment on the part of the person blamed or the wider moral community.

The moral protest account has the further advantage of being able to explain why the natural response to blame is apology and why the natural response to apology (when all goes well) is forgiveness. In apology, the wrongdoer acknowledges and repudiates the false moral claim implicit in her conduct. In doing so, she removes the "threat" that her claim posed to the moral status of others. Apology is thus an appropriate response to blame since it acknowledges precisely the offensive moral claim that our blame identifies as the target of moral protest. If the wronged party accepts the apology as sincere, he may feel that he no longer has reason to continue to protest the past wrong (Hieronymi 2001, pp. 548–49). This is what makes possible forgiveness. It is less clear how apologies are supposed to function on Sher's and Scanlon's accounts. In the case of Sher, one's desire that the wrongdoer not have acted badly will still be frustrated, so it is not clear how apology can help. In the case of Scanlon, while apology may serve to show that the wrongdoer has modified her own relationship-impairing attitudes, it seems there are many other ways the wrongdoer could demonstrate such a change (ways that would not require apology specifically). For example, if the wrong in question involved a breach of trust, the wrongdoer could simply work tirelessly to demonstrate that she really is trustworthy now—by sobering up, or repaying her loans, or getting counseling. Yet it seems that apology is the uniquely appropriate response to justified blame, and an adequate account of blame should be able to explain why that is.

This brings me, finally, to what I regard as the most important advantage of this account, which is that it seems to me to capture the special "force" of moral blame, and it makes clear why it is a response that it is appropriate to direct only at individuals we regard as morally responsible for their conduct. To morally blame another is not merely to wish that he had behaved differently, and it is not merely to recalibrate our attitudes, intentions, and expectations toward that person in response to his perceived relationship-impairing attitudes. These are responses we can have to individuals and things that clearly bear no moral responsibility for their "conduct."[9] To morally blame is to protest a moral claim implicit in the conduct of others, and thus it is appropriately directed only at creatures that have the ability to make such claims through their conduct. And having such an ability is, arguably, both necessary and sufficient for being a morally responsible agent. Though there is deep disagreement over which capacities, in particular, one must possess in order to be capable of making "moral claims" through one's conduct, it should be common ground among the parties to these disagreements that having the ability to make such claims is a, if not the, essential condition of morally responsible agency. The moral protest account of blame, then, can help us to think more clearly about which capacities are really necessary in order for a creature to qualify as a morally responsible agent.

6. Conclusion

My aim in this paper has been to defend an account of the nature of blame that builds on the important recent work of George Sher and T. M. Scanlon. Sher and Scanlon have done us a great service in drawing attention to this remarkably undertheorized concept, a concept that plays such an important role both in our philosophical theorizing about morality and moral responsibility and in our day-to-day lives. Though I have argued that their accounts are incomplete in certain respects, the proposal I defend here clearly draws on many of their most important insights. In particular, I share their conviction that it is a mistake to identify blame with a single attitude or set of attitudes or with a single type of behavior. Blame can take many different forms, so we need an account that can explain both the variety and the unity to be found in these responses. Where I differ from Sher and Scanlon is in my account of the unifying feature, which I take to be moral protest. To morally blame another, in my view, is to register in some significant way one's moral protest of that agent's treatment of oneself or others. Such protest need not be outwardly expressed in any way, and it need not take the form of a Strawsonian reactive attitude. But what unites all of the behavioral and attitudinal responses we are inclined to categorize as instances of blame, I have argued, is that they share this element of moral protest. This element, in turn, is what explains how moral blame differs from the sorts of negative attitudes and responses we might have toward

---

[9] Indeed, another curious feature of Scanlon's account is that he appears to countenance the possibility of blame of pets if they are judged to have attitudes that impair their relations with us (2008, pp. 165–66). This seems to me to sever the important connection between moral blame and moral responsibility.

individuals and creatures whom we do not regard as morally responsible for their conduct. Of all of the traditional and contemporary accounts of blame on offer, it seems to me that Strawson's account comes closest to capturing this crucial aspect of these distinctively moral responses, which perhaps explains why his view has had such staying power. To the extent that it fails, it is only in placing too much emphasis on just one—albeit one very important—set of emotional reactions as the sine qua non of moral protest.

Wrongdoing and Relationships: The Problem of the Stranger

George Sher

Because the past can never be undone, it is not immediately clear why wrongdoing is thought to call for backward-looking responses such as blame, punishment, and the making of amends. However, in recent years a number of philosophers have sought to elucidate the backward-looking component of morality by emphasizing the destructive impact that wrongdoing has on people's relationships. By interposing damaged relationships between wrong acts and our backward-looking responses to them, these philosophers hope to gain access to new ways of justifying those responses. Unlike proponents of revisionist views such as restorative justice and care morality, who also view wrongdoing as disruptive of relationships but who tend to advocate novel patterns of response,[1] the philosophers I have in mind construe the disrupted relations as calling only for the standard responses just mentioned. In each case, the damaged relationship is said to hold the key to understanding why the relevant response is warranted.

But can an explanation of this sort be given even when the wrongdoer and his victim are strangers? How, in that case, can those parties have any relationship at all? And, if a wrongdoer does not even *have* a relationship with another person, then how can that person's backward-looking responses possibly be justified by the disruption *of* their relationship?

These questions are obvious, but they are also important; for if the relational approach cannot answer them, then it will fail to accommodate many—perhaps a majority—of the cases in which blame, punishment, or the making of amends seems appropriate. In this paper I will attempt to assess the seriousness

---

This paper was originally presented at a colloquium on Linda Radzik's book *Making Amends* at Texas A&M University.

[1] For discussion of restorative justice, see Johnstone (2003); McLaughlin, Fergusson, Hughes, and Westmarland (2003). On care morality, see Noddings (1984); Held (1995).

of this difficulty by examining a number of possible responses to it. To gain as broad a perspective as possible, I will consider three distinct variants of the relational approach, each of which focuses on a different backward-looking response. In each case, my argument will be that the difficulty has not been fully met.

1

In his recent book *Moral Dimensions*, Thomas Scanlon develops a relational account of blame. According to Scanlon, blame is not merely a judgment that someone has acted wrongly, nor yet a minor form of hard treatment that the wrongdoer deserves, but rather a reaction that is rendered appropriate by the very standards that govern the relationship that the wrongdoer's actions have damaged. Along these lines, Scanlon writes that

> to claim that a person is *blameworthy* for an action is to claim that the action shows something about the agent's attitudes toward others that impairs the relations that others can have with him or her. To *blame* a person is to judge him or her to be blameworthy and to take your relationship with him or her to be modified in a way that this judgment of impaired relations holds to be appropriate. (2008, pp. 128–29)

Scanlon writes as well:

> Impairment of the kind I refer to occurs when one party, while standing in the relevant relation to another party, holds attitudes toward that person that are ruled out by the standards of that relationship, thus making it appropriate for the other party to have attitudes other than those that the relationship normally involves. (p. 135)

Because different relationships have different features and are governed by different standards, the reactions that their impairment can call for are quite varied. These reactions can include withholding aid from the wrongdoer, ceasing to care as much (or at all) about his fortunes, severing contact with him, and much else. However, in each case, what justifies the reaction is the fact that the attitude it expresses is rendered appropriate by standards that are internal to the impaired relationship itself.

Because Scanlon is simultaneously proposing both an analysis of blame and a theory of why blame as so construed is justified, the cogency of his justification may at first appear to turn on the correctness of his analysis. It seems to me, however, that even someone who rejects Scanlon's analysis of blame may still accept something like his account of its rationale; for even if blame is not what Scanlon says it is, the reactions with which he identifies it will surely remain among its most important manifestations. Thus although I think there are serious problems with Scanlon's analysis,[2] I will not pursue these but will move directly to his claim that (what I will continue to call) the blame-constituting reactions are rendered appropriate by the standards that govern the damaged relationships.

To put ourselves in a position to assess this claim, let us begin by asking why it might be thought to constitute an advance over the simpler claim that what call for the blame-constituting reactions are simply the relevant wrong acts themselves. Why is it better to justify these reactions by appealing to standards that are associated with the relationships that wrongdoing disrupts than it is to justify them by appealing to standards that simply tell us how to respond *to* wrongdoing? When the question is posed in these terms, the obvious answer is that "standards" of the latter sort—that is, principles of the form "Don't help or associate with those who have wronged you or others"—would simply codify the prescriptions whose rationale we want to understand. The great promise of a view like Scanlon's is that it will not be similarly question-begging because the standards to which it appeals will be internal to, or in some other way derivable from, the damaged relationships themselves.

These observations suggest that if Scanlon's account is to do real justificatory work, it must be backed by an explanation of how standards that call for blame-constituting reactions to those who damage relationships can be built right into the very relationships that they damage. Moreover, to justify such reactions even when they are directed at strangers, this explanation must apply even to whatever "relationships" can obtain *among* strangers. If Scanlon cannot provide such an explanation—if, instead of being able to derive the standards that call for blame-constituting reactions from considerations internal to the wrongdoer's relationships, he is forced to treat those standards as freestanding moral principles that call for blame-constituting reactions whenever certain conditions are met—then the relationships themselves will simply drop out as irrelevant. In that case, our original question of why an action-guiding morality should call for such backward-looking reactions will merely reappear in altered guise.

---

[2] To cite just one difficulty that Scanlon acknowledges but I think does not fully meet, his claim that blame is a reaction to the relationship-impairing attitudes for which wrongdoing is evidence has the counterintuitive implication that we never really blame people for what they actually *do*. On Scanlon's account, the agents whom we appear to blame for acting wrongly would in reality be just as blameworthy as they now are, and would be blameworthy for just the same reasons, in an alternative situation in which they had their current attitudes but did not act wrongly because opportunity to do so did not arise. I develop similar criticisms of the related Humean view that what we are really blaming wrongdoers for are the character flaws that their wrong acts manifest in chapters 2 and 3 of my 2006.

2

The central question, therefore, is whether Scanlon's account enables him to establish a suitable internal link between relationships and standards that call for blame-constituting reactions to those who damage them. To get a sense of the possibilities, it will be helpful to discuss the elements of the account in the order in which Scanlon develops them. His strategy is first to discuss personal relations such as friendship and then to extend what has been said to less personal contexts, so I will consider his treatment of those topics in that order.

Where friendship is concerned, Scanlon begins by reminding us of certain truisms that together define the relation: we harbor intentions to help our friends when necessary, to spend time with them, to confide in them and keep their confidences, and to stay in touch; we are disposed to take pleasure in their company, to hope that things go well for them, and to be pleased when things do. Moreover, and crucially,

> [i]n a true friendship, the attitudes just described are mutual. Mutuality is not a further, independent feature of friendship but is presupposed by the attitudes that constitute it. You are disposed to confide in a friend because you suppose that he or she is disposed to keep those confidences, and also, at least as important, because you suppose that the friend cares about you and about how your life is going. Similarly, the particular kind of pleasure that you take in being with a friend presupposes that he or she takes pleasure in the interactions as well. If this is not so—if the other person is bored, or merely indulging you—then the whole thing is founded on a mistake. (Scanlon 2008, p. 133)

Thus in Scanlon's view, each person's friendship-defining intentions and dispositions are based on his beliefs about the other party's friendship-defining intentions and dispositions.

However, if this is so, then it follows that any discovery that one's beliefs about the other's friendship-defining intentions and dispositions are false will undermine the rationale for one's own friendship-defining intentions and dispositions. By extension, such a discovery will also undermine the rationale for any forms of behavior to which one's friendship-defining intentions and dispositions naturally lead. It will, for example, justify such changes in attitude and behavior as no longer trusting, and no longer confiding in, a former friend who has betrayed a confidence. But, significantly, these are precisely the sorts of alterations that Scanlon takes to constitute blame of a friend. Because he takes these blame-constituting reactions to be justified by the familiar standards of theoretical and practical reasoning as these apply to the beliefs that ground our friendship-constituting intentions, Scanlon is indeed entitled to deny that the standards that justify us in blaming false friends are freestanding moral principles.

The harder question, though, is whether he is entitled to say anything similar about the standards that justify us in blaming *strangers* who act wrongly. Can these standards too be explicated in a way that does not beg the question by relying on a freestanding principle that calls for the very reactions whose justification is at issue? Do they too represent only the application of the familiar canons of theoretical and practical reasoning to the complex intentions and beliefs that structure a particular sort of relation?

According to Scanlon, there is indeed a structured relation in which we stand to all persons, including strangers, and that is precisely the *moral* relation. He writes:

> [I]n my view, morality requires that we hold certain attitudes toward one another simply in virtue of the fact that we stand in the relation of "fellow rational beings." It requires us to take care not to behave in ways that will harm those to whom we stand in this relation, to help them when we can easily do so, not to lie to them or mislead them, and so on. A morally good person will have standing intentions to regulate his or her behavior in these ways. . . . Beyond these intentions, good moral relations with others involve being disposed to have certain other attitudes. These include, in general, being disposed to be pleased when we hear of things going well for other people. (2008, pp. 39–40)

As Scanlon presents them, the intentions that constitute this moral relation are less uniformly conditional on reciprocation than those that constitute the friendship relation. On the one hand, Scanlon suggests that the familiar conditional structure is in place when he writes that "normal moral relations . . . involve a general intention to help others with their projects when this can be done at little cost, and we need not have this intention toward those who have shown a complete lack of concern for the interests of others" (144). He also suggests that it is present when he writes, "The fact that a person has behaved very badly toward you or toward others can make it appropriate not to take pleasure in that person's successes, and not to hope that things go well for him" (p. 144). On the other hand, he suggests that it is *not* present when he writes that even persons who lack moral intentions toward others "still have claims on us not to be killed, to be helped when they are in dire need, and to have us honor promises we have made to them" (p. 142). Thus Scanlon appears to understand the moral relationship as involving two distinct sets of intentions and dispositions, the members of one of which are conditional upon others having corresponding intentions and dispositions while the members of the other are not.

Will the moral relationship, as so understood, support a justification of the blame-constituting reactions that parallels the one we have extracted from Scanlon's account of friendship? In particular, are the standards that justify us in having those reactions toward strangers who act wrongly simply the familiar standards of rationality as these apply to the conditional intentions that partially constitute this moral relationship? Doubts arise when we remind ourselves that morality's demands are universal and that the moral relationship therefore cannot be said to hold only among persons who *actually have* the relevant intentions and dispositions toward each other. As Scanlon himself writes:

> Insofar as one assumes that any relationship must, like friendship, be constituted by the parties' attitudes, this provides a . . . reason for thinking it inappropriate to say that morality defines a relationship that holds even between total strangers. But this assumption is mistaken. The conditions in virtue of which relationships exist, and the relevant normative standards therefore apply, do not always involve the parties' attitudes toward one another. (2008, p. 139)

The fact that the moral relationship can hold even among persons who do not share the attitudes that define it—the fact that it is an ideal of human interaction rather than a psychological phenomenon—does not mean that the standards that call for blame-constituting responses to strangers who act wrongly cannot be derived exclusively from the application of the familiar canons of rationality to the conditional intentions and dispositions that define that relationship. However, what does follow from the fact that the moral relationship need not involve any actual attitudes is that any such derivation must at best be indirect. Instead of viewing the withholding of easily provided aid from miscreant strangers as what rationality requires of those who actually do intend to provide such aid only to persons who display suitable concern for others, we can at best view the withholding of aid as what rationality requires of all of us in virtue of morality's demand that we all *have* this conditional intention.

But the need to retreat to this indirect derivation surely gives the game away; for if Scanlon's appeal to the moral relationship amounts only to the claim that morality calls on us to have certain conditional intentions toward all people, and that the standards that justify us in reacting to miscreant strangers in blame-constituting ways are simply codifications of the reactions that these intentions make rational, then the real work of justifying those reactions will still be done by morality itself. When a stranger steals someone's identity or runs someone off the road in a fit of rage, the deep normative force of the claim that we are required or permitted to withhold aid from him or not to take pleasure in his success will be supplied not by the principles of practical or theoretical rationality as these apply to the conditional intentions that partly define the moral relation, but rather by whatever aspect of morality calls on us to *have* those conditional intentions. Thus the net effect will simply be to replace our original question—Why should an action-guiding morality contain principles that license the backward-looking blame-constituting reactions?—with the near-equivalent question of why an action-guiding morality should require that we harbor conditional intentions the nonsatisfaction of whose conditions makes it rational *to* have these reactions. To whatever extent the first question is puzzling—and, of course, the puzzlement it evokes was precisely what got us started—the second will be no less puzzling. Thus, far from advancing our understanding of blame, Scanlon's introduction of the moral relationship will turn out to be an idle wheel.

3

I began by discussing Scanlon's version of the relational approach because I view his strategy of appealing to standards internal to the relationships that wrongdoing disrupts as especially elegant. However, even if Scanlon's account fails to resolve the problem of the stranger, it hardly follows that no other version of the relational approach can do a better job. In particular, it may still be possible to accommodate some or all of our familiar backward-looking responses to miscreant strangers by adopting the simpler strategy of first pointing out the bad effects that their wrongdoing has on certain relationships and then justifying the backward-looking responses as necessary to undo those effects.

How, exactly, might this shift enable the relational approach to block the objection that a stranger is, by definition, someone with whom one has no relationship? There are, I think, two main possibilities here. On the one hand, it can be argued that even when a wrongdoer has never met his victim, his wrong act itself *creates* a disvaluable relationship which then must be transformed or undone. Alternatively or in addition, someone might maintain that whatever relationship a wrongdoer does or does not have with his victim, his wrong act damages various *other* relationships which then need to be repaired. In the remainder of my discussion, I will consider these possibilities first as they relate to punishment, then in connection with making amends.

In a recent article, Christopher Ciocchetti has argued that "by focusing on the kinds of relationships that crime establishes and punishment alters, we can develop a viable expressive justification of punishment" (2003, p. 71). Concerning a crime's effect on the criminal's relation to the person he wrongs, Ciocchetti writes:

> A criminal act alters the relationship between the criminal and the victim so that both the victim and the criminal come to expect future crimes. If a criminal assaults his victim and is not punished, the victim takes on a vulnerable status. Even if he does not assault the victim again, his interactions with the victim will be "colored" by the history of the relationship. . . . [T]his is not *simply* a matter of prediction of crimes. How both the criminal and the victim interpret their relationship and the noncriminal actions that take place within it are also affected. (pp. 72–73)

Concerning the crime's effect on the victim's relations to others, Ciocchetti adds:

> In most cases . . . the expectation that crimes will recur is not just a matter of victim psychology. Others will often interpret a victim of a single crime as a victim in general. His actions will be understood in terms of his victim status. . . . [T]he relationships established by the criminal's actions are generalized through other relationships that the victim has, through interpretations of his statements and actions. For many, what he says or does will be said and done as a victim. (pp. 73–74)

To be thought of as a victim, Ciocchetti suggests, is to have a "perceived vulnerability" (p. 74) and to be viewed as subject to "the dominance of the criminal's will and desires" (pp. 72–73) and thus as someone over whom others may "claim superiority" (p. 74).

Although Ciocchetti's conception of a relationship is somewhat different from Scanlon's,[3] there is no denying the destructiveness of the interpersonal effects to which he calls attention. But how, when a crime has had these destructive effects, does punishing the criminal improve matters? Insofar as the damage resides in the victim's inability to trust others fully, or to relax enough to interact with others in normal ways, one obvious good effect of punishment is an increase in the victim's sense of security and confidence. However, as Ciocchetti makes clear, the more important effect is a change both in the way the criminal and others view the victim and in the way the victim views himself. Although he remains someone against whom a crime was committed, he no longer occupies the *status* of victim. After the state intervenes on his behalf, his actions can no longer be interpreted as those of someone who is vulnerable or subordinate, and his relationships are accordingly altered for the better. As Ciocchetti himself writes, when we punish, we are

> altering our interpretation of the relationship between the criminal and the victim so that generalization of the victim's status is impossible. The victim may still be vulnerable to this kind of treatment, but he or she is understood to be protected by the force of the law. Though this will likely deter some, it will certainly affect everyone's relationships with the victim and even alter the significance of any future crimes committed. (2003, pp. 75–76)

---

[3] Although Scanlon and Ciocchetti both think of relationships partly in terms of what the parties expect of one another, Ciocchetti, unlike Scanlon, does not require that the relevant expectations be either mutual or conditional. Also unlike Scanlon, Ciocchetti assigns a prominent role to the categories of thought in terms of which each party defines the other's status. Nevertheless, despite these and other differences, the concept of a relationship seems more than elastic enough to accommodate both conceptions.

When the victim's rights are thus vindicated, he is again able to relate to the criminal and others on a footing of strength and equality.[4]

Unlike Scanlon's version of the relational approach, this one does not distinguish between strangers, acquaintances, and intimates; for a stranger is no less capable than an acquaintance of treating someone in a way that leaves a legacy of fear and mistrust and that leads many to view him through the lens of victimhood. The important question, though, is whether Ciocchetti's account really works for *any* of these classes of wrongdoers. To show that we are justified in punishing either strangers *or* nonstrangers whenever they commit serious crimes, Ciocchetti would have to establish both that their crimes (almost) always have the relevant bad effects on the victim's relationships and that punishing them will (almost) always undo those bad effects. However, at least when they are understood as empirical generalizations, both claims seem remarkably implausible.

One obvious problem with the first claim is that because crime is so pervasive in our society, anyone who maintained that being victimized usually or always confers victim status would have to attribute that status to most Americans. Given Ciocchetti's view of what is so damaging about the status—that those who have it are viewed as vulnerable, subordinate, and the like—this suggestion is hardly coherent. Nor, more simply, does experience confirm the suggestions that most crime victims are left with enduring legacies of fear and mistrust, that most of them interpret their situations in light of these attitudes, that most categorize themselves primarily as victims, or that most are consigned to that category by others. Some highly "personal" crimes such as rape and assault may indeed leave many victims feeling vulnerable and afraid and may make it hard for many to live normal lives, but even these effects are far from universal, and rape and assault are in any case only a small subset of the crimes for which punishment seems appropriate. Where most crimes are concerned, common experience suggests that most victims simply shrug it off, some sooner and some later, and get on with their lives.

The second empirical claim that Ciocchetti would have to establish—that punishment very commonly relieves the fear and cancels the victim status that crime produces—is if anything even less plausible. One major problem here is that both fear and stereotyped interpretations seem far too durable to be eliminated so easily. Phobias are notoriously hard to extinguish, and a crime victim who needs psychotherapy before the criminal is convicted will almost certainly continue to need it afterward. Moreover, even when a crime does leave someone fearful, his fear generally extends to all who might commit similar crimes and so is unlikely to be much affected by the apprehension and conviction of

---

[4] For another discussion that links punishment to the aim of restoring relationships disrupted by crime, but that does so in a somewhat different way, see Bennett (2008).

his particular victimizer. Nor, finally, does the knowledge that the criminal has been punished seem likely to alter the attitudes of those who do categorize the wronged party as a victim—who view him as vulnerable, subordinate, weak, and the rest—since these attitudes are grounded more in the harm that he has suffered than in the impunity of the criminal who has inflicted it.

All this, of course, is very obvious—so obvious, in fact, as to raise the suspicion that I have misunderstood what Ciocchetti has in mind. And so perhaps I have; for these problems would not arise if we rejected the psychological interpretation of his generalizations and instead understood those generalizations as simply recording the analytical consequences of crime and punishment. Under this alternative interpretation, the claim that those against whom crimes are committed always acquire victim status will not say anything about anyone's actual beliefs or attitudes—it will not assert either that all victims actually view themselves as vulnerable, subordinate, or weak or that anyone else actually views them that way—but instead will simply equate having victim status with *having been* cast in this light by the wrongful subordination of one's rights or interests. Analogously, the claim that a person's victim status is canceled by the criminal's punishment will not assert that anyone actually responds by ceasing to regard him as vulnerable, subordinate, or weak, but rather will simply say that he is *in fact* elevated from his subordinate position by society's intervention on his behalf.[5]

Although this interpretation does not comport well with the overtly psychological nature of much of what Ciocchetti says, I see no way short of adopting it of avoiding the profusion of counterexamples to his claims about the effects of victimhood and punishment. However, and crucially, if we do retreat to a nonpsychological interpretation of Ciocchetti's claims, then the relations that wrongdoing is said to damage, and that punishment is said to repair, will turn out to have nothing to do with the beliefs, expectations, or feelings of any of the relevant parties. If what is bad about being on the receiving end of crime is that one's interests are thereby subordinated, one's rights thereby ignored, and one's vulnerability thereby demonstrated, then whether anyone actually recognizes the victim *as* subordinate or morally inconsiderable or vulnerable, and whether anyone actually alters either his own behavior or his interpretation of the victim's behavior as a result, will simply be irrelevant. Correspondingly, if what is good about punishing the criminal is that it treats the victim as morally significant and thus undoes his subordination and the previous demonstration of his vulnerability, then its good-making feature will also be independent of *its* impact on anyone's attitudes, actions, or interpretations. As so understood, Ciocchetti's defense of punishment would rest not on the principle that we

---

[5] For another account along these lines, albeit one that Ciocchetti classifies as expressive rather than relational, see Hampton (1988a, 1988b).

ought to promote and protect good human relationships but on some more abstract principle of equality or transtemporal fairness. Although it would remain appropriate to speak of punishment as replacing the unequal relation between the criminal and his victim with one of equality, the relations in question would be purely comparative and so would be no less formal than the larger-than relation that obtains between an elephant and a mouse. Thus, here again, the introduction of relations, understood as relation*ships*, would turn out to be an idle wheel.

4

The final version of the relational approach that I will consider is the view, advanced by Linda Radzik, that when someone worsens a relationship by acting wrongly, he thereby incurs an obligation to make amends in order to repair the damage. Unlike the relational justifications of blame and punishment, which focus primarily on responses by persons other than the wrongdoer, this one focuses primarily on actions that must be performed by the wrongdoer himself. Nevertheless, despite this difference, the same basic idea—that an otherwise puzzling backward-looking reaction to wrongdoing becomes intelligible when we view it against a backdrop of disrupted relationships—is clearly evident in passages like this:

> "A wrongful act distances people from one another. It tears apart social bonds. When past wrongs persist as present threats, people are separated from one another by fear and distrust. If this is the case, then to right the wrong is to repair the rupture. Successful atonement would be a matter of bringing people back together again—or reconciliation" (Radzik 2009, p. 80).[6]

Because apologies, donations, and the other gestures through which wrongdoers seek to make amends are all constructive activities, it seems intuitively clear that atonement is far better suited to repair damaged relationships than are either punishment or blame.

If Radzik's aim were either to reconstruct what those who make amends are in fact trying to accomplish or to explain why their accomplishing it is important, I would have no significant disagreement with her account. As so understood, I think what she says is perceptive and largely correct. However, as I understand her, Radzik wants to go further; for she says not only that wrongdoers who seek to make amends are in fact trying to (re)establish valuable relationships but also that they are obligated to do so. She says as well that this obligation extends to those who wrong strangers as well as intimates, friends, or acquaintances. Taken together, these two further claims confront us yet again with the problem of the stranger.

---

[6] For related discussion, see Walker (2006), especially chapter 6.

Radzik is well aware of this problem, and her response to it combines elements of those of Ciocchetti and Scanlon. On the one hand, like Ciocchetti, she takes atonement to be called for not because it will restore any preexisting relationship between the stranger and the wronged party but rather because it will (1) improve the bad relationship that the wrong act itself has created, and (2) mend the damage that has been done to other relationships (including, on her account, those between "the wrongdoer and the community, the victim and the community, the victim and herself, and the wrongdoer and himself" [2009, p. 81]). Aspects of both ideas emerge when, discussing an odd case in which a driver has somehow wronged a pedestrian by splashing him with mud, Radzik writes, "When the stranger who has splashed us with mud stops to apologize and make amends, not only is our fleeting relationship with her improved, but our relationship to the community of drivers is improved as well" (p. 80). However, on the other hand, when it comes to characterizing the crucial "fleeting relationship" between the driver and the pedestrian, Radzik does so not, like Ciocchetti, in terms of the pedestrian's fear, mistrust, or victim status, but rather as a departure from a Scanlonian form of moral equality: "The kind of reconciliation that is the goal of atonement, then, involves the restoration of a paradigmatically moral relationship. It is one wherein the parties regard one another and themselves as equally valuable moral persons" (p. 81). Thus the question we must now ask is whether an obligation to atone for wrongs done to strangers can really be grounded in the need either to restore this relationship or to improve any of the others that Radzik mentions.

There are, I think, several respects in which Radzik's relational account is better equipped to deal with the problem of the stranger than is either Scanlon's or Ciocchetti's. First, because she locates what is problematic about the stranger's relationship with the wronged party in the very attitude that informs (and often is crystallized by) his wrong act itself, she avoids the objection, advanced above against Ciocchetti's account, that the effects of wrongdoing are far too variable to call consistently for any single kind of ameliorative response. Second, because Radzik declines Scanlon's gambit of taking the moral relation to obtain even among persons who do not actually regard one another as moral equals, she also avoids the difficulty of having to explain how a "relationship" that is independent of the parties' psychological states can be damaged by anything that happens in the empirical world. Third, by stressing the stranger's dismissive attitude toward his victim, she makes it easy to understand both why their new relationship is a bad one and why a change in the stranger's attitude would be an improvement.[7]

---

[7] Indeed her account implies that this change would be an improvement for two different reasons: first, because it is intrinsically good that each person regard all others as morally valuable, and, second, because if a person continues to lack this attitude toward another, then any further interactions between them are likely to be one-sided and exploitative.

If atonement involved only a change in the wrongdoer's attitude toward his victim, there would be little doubt that strangers as well as nonstrangers are under an obligation to atone. However, as Radzik herself emphasizes, atonement is not a purely private matter. In addition to undergoing a change of heart, the wrongdoer who wishes to make amends must both communicate the change and, as far as possible, undo the harm that he has done. In Radzik's own words, "she must send the message that she now recognizes that the victim is a person of equal worth to herself, that she should not have wronged him in this way, and that she intends not to repeat this sort of offense in the future" and must also "make reparation for the other kinds of harm created, which may encompass material, physical, psychological, and relational damage" (2009, p. 86). At first glance, these public aspects of atonement may seem to dovetail neatly with Radzik's general approach since in their absence, the persons whose relationships have been damaged will have no way of knowing that the wrongdoer's attitudes have changed and so will have no reason to make any adjustments in their own attitudes.

But if the wrongdoer is a stranger, and the relation that needs to be restored between him and his victim is simply one in which each views the other as a moral equal, then why must the victim *be* convinced that the stranger's attitudes have changed? The victim's coming to believe this can hardly be a prerequisite for his viewing the stranger as *his* moral equal; for a person's moral standing neither is, nor is widely thought to be, a function of his attitudes about the moral standing of others. But why, in that case, isn't the stranger's change of heart *itself* sufficient to restore the moral relationship between him and his victim? And why, for that matter, is the victim's (or anyone else's) awareness of the stranger's change of heart required to restore any of the *other* relationships that the stranger's wrong act may have disrupted?

5

If these questions cannot be answered, then Radzik's claim that strangers who act wrongly are obligated to atone publicly in order to repair the relationships they have damaged will not be consistent with her view of the relationships that are in need of repair. Thus to assess her claim that the public aspects of atonement are always called for, we must get clearer about how these might improve the relationships that strangers damage when they act wrongly. As we saw, Radzik takes the affected relationships to involve three different (sets of) parties: the wrongdoer himself, his victim, and the wider community. Taking my cue from this, I will now ask why the stranger's demonstration of his change of heart might be needed to repair (1) the stranger's relation with himself, or (2) the victim's relations with himself or others, or (3) the stranger's relations with the victim or others.

1. *The stranger's relation with himself.* Because each person is intimately (if obscurely) related to himself, there is some plausibility to the claim that a person's relationship to himself is always damaged when he wrongs someone he does not know. However, even if we accept this claim, we cannot decide whether the public aspects of atonement are really needed to repair the damage without knowing exactly what that damage involves. There are, I think, at least three possibilities: the damage may consist either of (1) the stranger's simply not *being* someone who stands in the proper moral relation to his victim, or of (2) his inability to *see* himself as someone who stands in this relation, or of (3) whatever guilt, shame, or self-hatred his inability to see himself this way has elicited. Thus to show that the relevant communicative and reparative acts are necessary to repair the damage that the stranger's wrong act has done to his relation to himself, Radzik will have to establish that these acts are usually if not always needed either to (1) bring about or consolidate a change in the stranger's attitude toward his victim, or (2) reinforce his belief that his attitude really has changed, or (3) alleviate his guilt or shame about the attitude he previously manifested.

But quite apart from the lack of evidence for these causal claims, there is commonsense reason to doubt each one. To cast doubt on the claim that the public manifestations of atonement are needed to bring about or firm up a change in the stranger's attitude toward his victim, we need only call attention to the many familiar contexts in which internal shifts in attitude— toward the permissibility of activities such as meat eating or abortion, the desirability of maintaining turbulent friendships, the wisdom of wars we formerly supported, and so on—are more than firm enough to stand up in the absence of external reinforcement. To cast doubt on the claim that the public manifestations of atonement are needed to convince the stranger that his own attitude really has changed, we need only advert to each person's usual direct and reliable (though far from infallible) access to his own opinions and beliefs. Finally, to cast doubt on the claim that these public manifestations are needed to exorcise the guilt and shame to which the stranger's wrongdoing has given rise, we can point out several things: first, that an obligation to make amends, if there is one, will surely apply even to wrongdoers who in fact feel no guilt or shame; second, that in most instances, a wrongdoer's occurrent guilt and shame will fade by themselves as time passes and his awareness of his wrongdoing recedes into his passive memory; and, third, that, as a matter of fact, the public gestures that give evidence of our current good attitudes seem only indifferently effective at eliminating the feelings of guilt and shame whose occasions are the previous bad attitudes, and their manifestations in action, which those good attitudes have replaced.

2. *The victim's relations to himself and others.* To make the case that the public manifestations of atonement are needed to repair the damage that the stranger's wrong act has done to the *victim's* relations with himself or the wider community, Radzik must equate that damage with some kind of disvaluable change in the attitudes that members of the victim's community hold toward him or that he holds toward himself. The most obvious candidate, and the one that Radzik in fact seems to favor, is the change of coming to believe that the victim lacks full moral standing. This view of the damage is implicit in her assertions that "[i]f the wrongful act gave the community any reason to doubt whether the victim . . . is an equally valuable moral person . . ., then the wrongdoer should work to repair that impression" and that "[t]he victim will be reconciled with herself when her sense of herself as an equally valuable moral person is restored" (2009, p. 82). Thus the questions we must ask here are, first, how likely it is that a stranger's demonstration that he does not view his victim as an equally valuable moral person will evoke similar beliefs in others, and, second, how likely it is that the stranger's subsequent demonstration that he no longer holds this belief will induce those whom he has so influenced to reverse themselves.

When I discussed Ciocchetti's account of punishment, I remarked that it is a vast overstatement to say that all, or even most, of those against whom crimes are committed are subsequently consigned to "victim" status and are thenceforth viewed by themselves or others as subordinate, vulnerable, or weak. For similar reasons, I think it is a vast overstatement to say that all or most of the burglaries, assaults, and mud-splashings that are committed by strangers cause their victims or others to stop believing that the victims have full moral standing. It is indeed precisely the continued existence of this belief that standardly undergirds both the victim's own resentment and the indignation that others commonly feel on his behalf. I also think that it is, if anything, even more of an overstatement to say that demonstrations by wrongdoers that they no longer view their victims as having lesser moral status are either necessary or sufficient to reverse this effect on the rare occasions when it does occur. However, because my arguments for these claims are essentially the same as those I advanced earlier, I shall not bother to repeat them here.

3. *The stranger's relations to the victim and others.* As I noted earlier, Radzik's characterization of the moral relation as one in which each party regards the other as an equally valuable moral person does not require that either party believe that the other regards *him* as a moral equal. This means that if Radzik is to base her defense of the stranger's obligation to communicate his newly acquired belief that his victim *is* his moral equal on the need to improve his relations with the victim or others, she must somehow

explain why his (re)establishing a moral relation of the kind she originally described is not good enough. Soon after her discussion of the mud-splashing stranger, she writes that when a wrongdoer atones, "[t]he victim will have good reason to give up her resentment, fear, and distrust of the wrongdoer" (2009, p. 82). This suggests that Radzik's reason for requiring that the stranger atone publicly may be that even if his private change of heart is good enough to reestablish a *moral* relation between him and his victim, his failure to communicate the change will leave intact the bad *non*moral relations that result from fear and lack of trust.

There are, however, at least two problems with this suggestion, the first of which is that even when a person *is* left fearful or untrusting by the act of someone he has never met and about whom he knows absolutely nothing—a stranger he can identify only as "whoever stole my car"—he has a "relationship" with that stranger only in the hopelessly attenuated sense in which I also have one with the vice president of the United Auto Workers or the copyright holder for *Grand Theft Auto*. Thus although the fear and mistrust are indeed disvaluable, their disvalue appears to reside not in the unsatisfactory nature of any relationship of which they are constituents but only in their unpleasantness or broader destructive effects. This does not mean that a stranger cannot be obligated to atone publicly to eliminate the fear and mistrust that he has caused, but it does mean that if Radzik defends his obligation on this basis, then her ostensibly relational defense of the public aspects of atonement will devolve into a more orthodox consequentialist argument. Also, of course, if this is Radzik's reasoning, then she will again face the objection that persistent fear, resentment, and mistrust are not common enough effects of wrongs done by strangers, and that public atonement is not effective enough at eliminating them when they do occur, to support the conclusion that any stranger who acts wrongly is thereby automatically obligated to atone publicly to his victim.

In view of these difficulties, Radzik will evidently need some other way of grounding the stranger's obligation to atone publicly in the disvalue of his relations with his victim or others. I can think of one further possibility, and that is to ground the stranger's obligation not in the need to improve his *non*moral relations with anyone but rather in the need to establish a suitably robust set of *moral* relationships. It might be argued, in other words, that in its ideal form, the moral relation is one in which each individual not only regards each other as an equally valuable moral person, but also truly believes that this belief is reciprocated *by* each other person. This is in some ways an appealing idea, but its strong interpretation of the moral relation would obviously have to be defended in its turn. Whether a suitable defense can be produced, and if so whether it can sustain an obligation on the stranger's part to publicize his change of heart, are questions that would take us far afield, so I will end by simply flagging this proposal as one that might repay further inquiry.

6

Despite the problems we have encountered, it remains possible that some further version of the relational approach will succeed in justifying some or all of our backward-looking responses to wrongdoing in a way that resolves the problem of the stranger. However, because the views discussed here are among the best-worked-out representatives of that approach, and because each must either rely on implausible empirical claims or else retreat to a nonempirical and potentially question-begging account of the relevant relationships, I think it is safe to say that the prospects are not bright.

This does not mean that we cannot learn much that is important by attending to the relationships that wrongdoing damages. To the contrary, we clearly do learn much both from Scanlon's ingenious explanation of why we are justified in recoiling from friends who have done us wrong and from Radzik's resourceful discussion of the importance of repairing breaches that we have caused. However, what the shortcomings of the relational approach do suggest is that any adequate general account of our backward-looking responses to violations of moral norms may have to make essential reference to the violated norms themselves. If we cannot plausibly ground the demands of blame, punishment, and atonement in any facts about the relationships that a wrongdoer has damaged, then we are thrown back on the task of explaining how considerations related to those that obligated him not to act as he did in the first place can now alter the obligations and permissions that would otherwise govern our responses to him and his own responses to himself.

{ 4 }

The Expressive Function of Blame

Christopher Bennett

1. Expression and the Special Force of Blame

One of the central philosophical questions about blame is how to account for—
and, if appropriate, justify—its special force. Perhaps anyone who takes morality
seriously and thinks of persons as in some way accountable to moral standards
will have to make some sort of negative evaluation of agents who fail to meet those
standards. But we can imagine a form of moral seriousness that would have no
role for the special force of blame. For instance, an agent might respond to wrongdoing with a simple moral "grading" or appraisal. Such appraisal might involve
recognizing and appreciating the gravity of some moral failure (in some sense at
least); it might issue in behavior such as taking such steps as are prudent to limit
the bad consequences (for oneself or more generally) of that failure for the future.
It might involve making judgments of persons and their behavior as better or
worse depending on how closely they adhered to moral standards. Alternatively
an agent might respond to moral wrongdoing by verbal moral criticism, communicating the judgment that what was done was wrong in such a way that the offender can grasp the force of the reasons neglected in his action and take them into
account in the future. But something of our common reactions to wrongdoing
would be missing on these approaches. Blame involves us in a more intimate and
charged relationship with a wrongdoer than does grading or moral criticism. The
flavor of blame can be captured by seeing it as an accompaniment to the question
"How could he/she/you/I?": it brings the offender's attitudes vividly into our field
of attention and concerns us with how the offender could possibly have been
thinking (as she acted thus). And notoriously, blame often issues in some sort of
"withdrawal of goodwill" from the offender as a result of the offense.

The ideas in this paper benefited greatly from discussions at the symposium "The Apology Ritual" held
at the University of Valencia in January 2011. I would like to thank the participants at that event, in
particular Josep Corbi, Antony Duff, Jules Holroyd and Sandra Marshall. I am also grateful to Rob
Hopkins and Andrew Williams for discussions on these topics and to the editors of this volume for
helpful comments on an earlier draft.

The influential "reactive attitudes" approach of P. F. Strawson (1962) and R. Jay Wallace (1994) seeks to account for the special force of blame by seeing blame as an essentially emotional response. However, if we are interested in attempting to justify blame, the emotions may be false friends. Appeals to the emotions in normative matters raise the suspicion that an important justificatory burden is being evaded by brute psychological fact (see, e.g., D'Arms and Jacobson 2000). If, on the other hand, we insist that emotions are not noncognitive states but that they (partly) consist in, or essentially depend on, judgments, we face the problem of explaining how, even if the judgment itself is appropriate and true, that part of blame that exceeds the judgment (for instance, the way blame leads us to treat the offender) is to be justified. Why the charged atmosphere of blame rather than rational moral criticism?

In this paper I am interested in an idea that might (mis)lead us into thinking that the force of blame has to be accounted for through the emotions—namely, the thought that blame's special force is expressive. I will explore the idea that, in accounting for this force, we do not get to the bottom of the matter, normatively speaking, if we appeal to the emotions. Rather, I think, we have to begin with the observation that expressive behavior is symbolic and not merely instinctual or noncognitive but that it makes a claim to the adequacy of its symbolism.[1] That way of putting it makes it clear that if, in seeking to justify blame, we are tempted to talk about its expressive nature, a justificatory burden is not being evaded. There are justifications to be offered, but they are justifications having to do with (1) the need for a distinctively symbolic response, and (2) the adequacy of a particular set of symbols. The crucial relation of "expression," on this view, is not a mechanical one, on which behavior is pushed out of us by the force of internal emotional pressure; rather the symbolism responds to, and can seem to be required by, a way of understanding the normative demands of a situation.[2]

In developing this line of thought I will contrast it with the view of blame developed by T. M. Scanlon (2008, ch. 4).[3] Scanlon's view is in some ways similar to the view I will propose:[4] it also seeks to give a justifiable interpretation of the idea that blame is essentially bound up with an impairment of relations with the offender and a withdrawal from the offender that reflects that impairment.[5] But these apparent similarities mask some fundamental differences. I will argue that Scanlon is right to think that blameworthiness involves the

---

[1] For another view of blame that (implicitly) draws on its symbolism, see Skorupski (1999).

[2] For the underpinnings of the view I am suggesting here, see the distinction between two meanings of "expression" drawn by Richard Wollheim (1968), in particular the reference to "correspondences."

[3] See also Scanlon (1998, ch. 6); Scanlon (1988, pp. 149–216).

[4] And have defended elsewhere: see, e.g., my 2002, 2003, and 2008.

[5] For other interpretations of this influential idea, see Winch (1972); Dilman (1979, ch. 5); Morris (1981, pp. 263–71); Duff (1986, ch. 9); Gaita (1991, ch. 4); Radzik (2004, pp. 141–54).

impairment of the relationship it is possible to have with the agent blamed, where this impairment is brought about by the manifestation of some intolerable attitude to others (or indeed to the proper demands of whatever is of value). But I will argue that there are two importantly different ways of understanding "impairment." The relationship might be impaired because the person's intolerable attitudes makes the person hard to trust or hard to get on with. Or the relationship might be impaired because the person who takes seriously the values underpinning the relationship would experience that agent's intolerable attitudes as something it is necessary to dissociate herself from, so that it would appear a wrongful acquiescence in those attitudes to continue the relationship as normal. I will argue that the latter is the better way to understand impairment. However, I will argue that this is a line of thought that involves making the claim that the most adequate response to the situation is an expressive or symbolic one and hence raises a question whether some normative reasons refer essentially to expressive or symbolic relations.

2. Scanlon on Blame, Impairment of Relationships, and Withdrawal

Central to Scanlon's account of blame is the idea that wrongdoing impairs the relations it is possible to have with a wrongdoer: "[T]o claim that a person is blameworthy for an action is to claim that the action shows something about the agent's attitudes towards others that impairs the relations that others can have with him or her. To blame a person is to judge him or her to be blameworthy and to take your relationship with him or her to be modified in a way that this judgement of impaired relations holds to be appropriate" (2008, pp. 128–29). Thus wrongdoing takes place in the context of human relations: even though we might not actually have a relationship with the wrongdoer, he is someone with whom it is, other things being equal, possible to enter into a range of distinctively human interactions. Such relationships and interactions require certain sorts of mutual attitudes of respect and concern on the parts of their members. However, wrongdoing reveals that a person has attitudes that are incompatible with full membership in such relationships: the person does not give the appropriate importance to the standards of respect and concern that underpin that kind of relationship. As a result, the relations that one can have with that person are impaired. Scanlon illustrates his view with an example of friendship:

> Suppose I learn that at a party last week some acquaintances were talking about me, and making some cruel jokes at my expense. I further learn that my close friend Joe was at the party, and that rather than coming to my defence or adopting a stony silence, he was laughing heartily and even contributed a few barbs, revealing some embarrassing facts about me that I had told him in confidence. This raises a question about my

relationship with Joe. Should I still consider Joe to be my friend? This is not just a question about his future conduct. . . . The question is not just about how he will act in the future but about what happened in the past, and what it indicates about Joe's attitude toward me and about the nature of our relationship. (2008, p. 129)

As a result of what one now knows about Joe, one might consider whether his action could be interpreted in such a way that it is consistent with the basic demands of friendship. In this example, it seems one might conclude that it is not so consistent, and hence one might alter one's relationship with Joe, thinking of him and treating him differently as a result of his action and what it shows about his attitude to you: "I might, for example, cease to value spending time with him in the way one does with a friend, and I might revise my intentions to confide in him and to encourage him to confide in me" (pp. 129–30). The nub of Scanlon's view is that to judge that a person has failed to govern himself consistently with the basic demands of the relationship, and that this makes it impossible for the relationship to continue on its previous terms, is to judge the person blameworthy, and that to blame someone is to reorient (or downgrade) the relationship in accordance with this judgment.

Scanlon's central example of blame takes place in the context of an ongoing relationship characterized by shared interaction.[6] But Scanlon argues that the same structure of blame can be applied to violations of the terms of what he calls the "default moral relationship" that we are all in with one another simply by virtue of being rational human agents:

To judge individuals to be blameworthy, I am claiming, is to judge that their conduct shows something about them that indicates this kind of impairment of their relations with others, an impairment that makes it appropriate for others to have attitudes toward them different from those that constitute the default moral relationship. To blame someone is actually to hold modified attitudes of this kind toward him or her. (2008, p. 141)

The default moral relationship exists because "morality requires that we hold certain attitudes toward one another simply in virtue of the fact that we stand in the relation of 'fellow rational beings.'" It requires us to take care not to behave in ways that will harm those to whom we stand in this relation, to help them when we can easily do so, not to lie to them or mislead them, and so on (p. 140). This relationship is one we are in with "people in general not simply [with] specific individuals whom we are aware of or could specify" (p. 140). It may be odd to talk of being in a relationship with people one has never met

---

[6] For a good characterization of this conception of a relationship, see Kolodny (2003).

and will never meet or have any interaction with. But the analogy is sufficiently close to make the structure of blame relevant to both because "when we do become aware of others and are in actual or potential interaction with them, we generally assume that even if they are strangers they will manifest at least the basic elements of this ideal concern" (p. 141).

The basic structure of blame that holds in the case of friendship also holds in the case of the moral relationship, but, as Scanlon notes, this poses a problem since he believes that "the basic forms of moral concern are not conditional on . . . reciprocation. Even those who have no regard for the justifiability of their actions toward others retain their basic moral rights— they still have claims on us not to be hurt or killed, to be helped when they are in dire need, and to have us honor promises we have made to them" (2008, p. 142). Thus while it may be an option in the case of friendship sim- ply to end the relationship—and that is precisely what blame might consist in—no such thing is possible in the case of acts that undermine the moral relationship. So what can blame in this case consist in? Scanlon's answer is that we should look at that "range of interactions with others that are mor- ally important but not owed unconditionally to everyone" (p. 143), such as our having a willingness to enter into agreements and other cooperative relations of trust, to help when it will cost us little, and to hope that things will go well for the person. It is these things that may be suspended in moral blame.

3. Why Can't the Relationship Continue Unaffected after Wrongdoing?

One of the crucial moves on Scanlon's account—particularly in terms of the concerns of this paper—comes in answering the question why, if we have con- cluded that a person has violated the basic terms of some relationship, we should therefore reorient or downgrade the relationship. Scanlon answers this question by saying that the agent's own attitudes have impaired the relation- ship: "Impairment of the kind I refer to occurs when one party, while standing in the relevant relation to another person, holds attitudes toward that person that are ruled out by the standards of that relationship, thus making it appro- priate for the other party to have attitudes other than those that the relation- ship normally involves" (2008, p. 135). This way of putting it raises the question of what makes it appropriate for the wronged party to have attitudes that depart from those normal to that type of relationship. A similar question is raised by some of Scanlon's other formulations:

> At the extreme I might conclude that Joe was not really a friend after all. To conclude that this is so would be to conclude that I have reason to revise my expectations and intentions in certain ways: to decide not to rely on or confide in Joe as one would in the case of a friend, and not

to seek his company, to find it reassuring, or to have the special concern for his feelings and well-being that one has for a friend's. To revise my intentions and expectations . . . in this way . . . is to blame him. . . . [Alternatively] the relationship can continue in an impaired form. If it does, there may be changes in the ways that the injured party has reasons to behave. For example, if I have been making fun of you behind your back, then you have reason to be less free in revealing yourself to me than you would normally be with a friend. (p. 136)

This passage makes the claim that the injured party "has reason to" abandon or downgrade the relationship and that these reasons will be reasons to blame. What sorts of reasons are these? One possible answer that this passage suggests is that the reasons to change the terms of the relationship are in the final analysis prudential: reasons of self-protection. This interpretation might give us an odd-sounding view, since it might seem unlikely that our reasons for blaming others are, at least in any direct way, self-interested reasons. However, this interpretation might be supported by Scanlon's claim that it would be weak or servile or demeaning to continue being good friends with someone who never treats one as a friend himself. The person who fails to break with the abusive friend is someone who puts too little weight on her own value and hence is prepared to be a "doormat" for others to trample over (Murphy 1988; see also Hieronymi 2001).

On the other hand, perhaps a stronger interpretation of Scanlon's view is that the reasons the person has to revise his treatment of his (erstwhile) friend have rather to do with the standards of friendship themselves. After all, there are degrees of friendship, based on confidence, trust, distance, and sharing; one can change the terms of a friendship to reflect the fact that a person is simply not as close a friend to you as you had previously thought. Another way of putting this would be to say that you change the terms of the friendship because, on the basis of her actions, the person does not deserve to be treated as one of your close friends. This second interpretation ties in with Scanlon's own characterization of his theory as a type of desert theory:

My account of blame is a desert-based view, in the sense in which I believe that term should be understood. That is to say, I take blame to consist of attitudes toward a person that are justified simply by attitudes of that person that make them appropriate, and I hold that there is no need to appeal to other justifications such as the beneficial consequences of blaming or the fact that the person could have avoided being subject to blame. Like refusals of friendship, blame is justified simply by what a person is like. (2008, p. 188)

Scanlon offers us a desert theory, where desert means having relationships with others that their attitudes fit them for. In this case, desert involves including a person in those relationships in which she is fit to participate.

Scanlon effectively gives a justification for the retributive-sounding idea that one should—or at least is permitted to—treat others as they treat you, but the force of this reciprocity comes not from an independent idea of desert but from the relationships themselves. No one deserves to be treated as a friend who does not treat her friends as friends.

We should briefly note at this point that there are in turn two ways of interpreting this claim about fittingness and desert. On the first interpretation, it is the thought that one should not have friendships with those who abuse you, not simply for self-interested reasons but because such people are not the fitting objects of friendship: they have no claim on the deployment of your time and resources that is involved in friendship if they do not have the appropriate attitudes to you (they don't deserve your friendship). On the second interpretation, the thought is that the withdrawal is fitting regardless of any wider questions of how to spend one's time and resources; the point is rather that the other's attitudes make (that degree of) friendship between the two of you impossible. Given that the relationship "is constituted by certain attitudes and dispositions" parties have to one another (Scanlon 2008, p. 131), it follows that where one party changes his attitude the relationship changes. Even if you, as the victim, ignored the other's violation of the terms of the relationship and continued to treat him as if nothing had happened, the friendship would not be what it was (or what you had mistakenly thought it was). Your actions in this case would be out of line with the nature of the relationship.

I won't attempt definitively to adjudicate between these interpretations of Scanlon's desert theory of blame, except to ask what the significance of each is for the question of why we have reason to blame. The second interpretation has the advantage of restricting our reasons for withdrawal to considerations to do with the nature of the relationship rather than invoking the wise use of time and resources. But, perhaps for that very reason, on this interpretation Scanlon lacks a good answer to the question of why I have strong reasons to change my behavior toward the offender. If I fail to withdraw from one who has abused me, my actions might be out of line with the relationship. But is it a vice or a virtue to be more generous to a person than the relationship demands? If we have strong reason to blame, then, other things being equal, there must be some failing in not blaming. It is not clear that, on this second interpretation, Scanlon can explain what that failing is.

4. Problems with Scanlon's View

Assuming, at any rate, that the desert account in some shape is the correct interpretation of Scanlon's view, there are a number of problems with it. First of all, it is not clear that the desert theory can give him the conclusion that he wants. In the phrase I quoted earlier, Scanlon characterizes blame as coming about when a person's attitudes are such that it impairs the relationship one "can" have with her. It is this "cannot" that is meant to explain why relations between the two parties have to change when such attitudes are manifested. The interpretation of this "cannot" that I am offering is that, on Scanlon's desert theory, the person's attitudes show her to be unfit for friendship. However, contrary to Scanlon, being unfit for friendship doesn't make it the case that one cannot seek to have a relationship of friendship with her. One may be unwise to; it may be pointless; one may be leaving oneself open to abuse; perhaps the relationship is unlikely to be successful. But is that what is meant by "cannot"? It would have struck the wrong note if Scanlon had characterized blame as the revision of relationships that comes about when someone acts in a way that makes it inadvisable to continue to have the same relationship with her. Alternatively one might interpret Scanlon's view as saying that one is within one's rights to revise the relationship, or that, given the level of her commitment, she can have no justified complaint if one does so. However, this does not give us the conclusion that the relationship is impaired in the sense that one cannot continue as things were.

A further response to these concerns would be to turn to the second interpretation of "desert" that I offered earlier. On this interpretation, Scanlon's thought is that, because the relationship is constituted by the attitudes the parties can have toward one another, a certain degree of friendship cannot exist when one party has attitudes incompatible with that degree. And that would seem to be correct. However, this "cannot have that (degree of) relationship" is meant in turn to explain why one cannot continue to treat the person as though nothing had happened. And that it fails to do. Failing to withdraw might be out of line with the nature of the friendship. But as I said earlier, Scanlon doesn't explain what reason this gives a person to withdraw (except that it is inadvisable, unwise, pointless, a waste of time, etc. not to). Scanlon's view, then, fails to give us a satisfying account of the strength and nature of our reasons for withdrawal.[7]

Second, as Scanlon himself notes, there are problems applying this model to the default moral relationship. In the case of friendship, it might—the criticisms of the previous paragraph notwithstanding—be plausibly argued that the viable existence of the relationship is conditional on a person being in some way fit for it, where fitness will involve certain commitments to respecting and sustaining the terms of the relationship. Even if disqualification is not called for, there are degrees of friendship, degrees that are determined by

---

[7] My argument here assumes that Scanlon does indeed seek to account for our reasons for withdrawal. Theoretically he could claim that he only seeks to account for our reasons to thinking that wrongdoing impairs the relationship. But the section titled "The Ethics of Blame" suggests that Scanlon does think that a disposition to blame and withdrawal is constitutive of taking a relationship seriously: for example, "[T]he complete rejection of blame would rule out important relations with others" (2008, p. 168). My concern is that his desert theory doesn't give a good explanation of that claim.

some sense of the extent to which the parties are committed to one another. Given this, Scanlon can argue that the existence or degree of the relationship depends on the extent of the commitment. If we apply this model to the default moral relationship, we get the claim that what is owed to the person as a member of the relationship is similarly conditional on the degree of her commitment to it and that there can be degrees of what is owed in the way of basic moral respect. As we have seen, Scanlon denies this conclusion and argues that all that can change is our morally good but not required willingness to go the extra mile for someone. However, his analogy between blame in friendship and blame in the moral relationship would seem to suggest that, when someone has done a serious moral wrong, something counts in favor of making her inclusion in the default moral relationship—and hence basic moral respect—reflect the level of her commitment to moral ends, even though some other prohibition (the one that makes Scanlon unwilling to make basic respect conditional) makes it impermissible to do so. But this seems uncomfortable: on Scanlon's account we end up, in offering wrongdoers basic moral respect, treating people as if they were fit to participate in the default moral relationship even though they are not.

Third, a consequence of this second problem is that, in his account of blame in the moral relationship, Scanlon loses the ability to claim that his account respects the intuition that the degree of blame should be proportional to the seriousness of the wrong. Scanlon's friendship example appeals to a strong intuition that one should drop or at least revise one's relationship with the offender. But to what extent should the relationship be revised? The proportionality intuition that I am interested in is that the revisions one is prepared to make in the relationship reflect one's view of the seriousness of the wrong. Let us adapt Scanlon's example and imagine that a third close (mutual) friend—call her Jerry—was also present at the event and, although she did not join in with Joe, neither did she act as though what Joe had done to you should in any way affect her relationship with him. She protested a little, perhaps, but not to any great degree; she is still seeing Joe socially as a friend and has not dissociated with him to the extent that you think is necessary to the case. You remonstrate with her about her continued relationship, telling her you feel undermined by her and that it puts your own friendship in doubt. Whether that accusation would be right or wrong in this particular case, these are conversations that we often have, and they reflect our interest in proportionality of response. Scanlon can capture proportionality in a manner of speaking when he concentrates on the case of friendship. Here his desert theory would suggest that the revisions in the relationship should reflect not necessarily the seriousness of the wrong but the extent to which the wrong shows that the person is not fit for the relationship. One should downgrade one's relationship so that it reflects the degree of the other's commitment. Perhaps this view could then give us an interpretation of what is going on when we criticize one another for departures from proportionality. Too little and one could be criticized for underestimating the extent to which the wrong manifested a lack of the commitment necessary for the relationship; too much and one is overestimating. However, as we have seen, the ability to downgrade the terms of the relationship to reflect the level of the wrongdoer's commitment is lost when we move from friendship to the moral community. It's perhaps a hoary example, but there does seem something a bit strange in the view that the blame we could express toward murderers and rapists would simply take the form of not trusting them, not helping them, and not hoping things go well for them.[8]

Furthermore, this is a serious problem because proportionality between the manner in which the offender is treated and the seriousness of the wrong (or the extent to which the wrong shows a lack of commitment) is essential to the credibility of blame as an expression of disapproval. At least that is the thinking that would seem to underpin criticism of one's friend for not blaming Joe enough. Because she does not blame enough, she does not disapprove enough: she is treating it lightly, as though it were consistent with the terms of the friendship to act in that way. None of this makes sense unless we think of blame as an expression of disapproval, an expression that is called for when one is in relations with the wrongdoer and where the degree of the blame (or withdrawal) should reflect the seriousness of the wrong.

Could Scanlon deny that blame is an expression of disapproval? In fact, I think this is perhaps the position he should, in consistency, take. However, this leads to the fourth and most fundamental problem: that the view of blame as an expression of disapproval, which his desert theory fails to capture, is a natural and compelling way to think about blame. Blame, on Scanlon's view, is simply the reorientation of a relationship so that it better matches the level of commitment the person brings to that relationship. But nowhere does he canvass the natural and simple idea that the justification of blame lies in the need to disapprove of wrongdoing. However, this means that Scanlon also cannot accommodate the natural thought that to blame someone is to hold him accountable to the standards that he violated. For Scanlon, the person who blames does not assert the authority of the violated standards but rather downgrades the standards to which she thinks it appropriate for the person to be held. In some ways this sounds more like a judgment of contempt rather than blame. Blame pays the offender the compliment of asserting that the more demanding standards of the higher form of cooperative relationship are still appropriate; an account of blame should explain the sense in which it is inclusive where contempt is exclusive.[9]

---

[8] Of course, this is not to deny that other actions may be taken against murderers and rapists, such as strong verbal criticism, legal sanction (where this is not seen as an institutionalized form of blame), and so forth.

[9] The failure to capture the sense of superiority inherent in contempt is a problem with Michelle Mason's (2003) attempted defense of this reaction.

5. Disapproval and the Symbolism of Blame

The problems with Scanlon's account point us toward a more adequate understanding of blame. Like his view, this more adequate account sees blame as a
kind of withdrawal or distancing that occurs in the context of a relationship
when the terms of that relationship have been violated. But on this view the
distancing is instead experienced as a necessary part of taking wrongdoing
seriously and disapproving of it. On this view, it is in order to do justice to the
significance of some wrong that we must partially suspend the attitudes of
goodwill, respect, and concern that would normally be owed to a person with
whom we are in that relationship, and we must do so in a manner proportionate to the seriousness of the wrong. Grading judgment is unsatisfactory
because it is inadequate to the seriousness of the wrong; the special force of
blame—including the withdrawal of goodwill—is needed to reflect the seriousness of the situation. This way of justifying blame can be called expressive
since it appeals to the idea that withdrawal from the offender is the necessary
and appropriate vehicle of condemnation and that without this vehicle the
condemnation lacks meaning and hence fails adequately to distance the con-
demner from the wrong.

If blame expresses disapproval, and blame consists in partial and temporary
withdrawal from a relationship one has with the offender, then there is an obvious sense in which, as Scanlon wants to say, the wrong impairs the relationship one can have with the person. However, rather than the "cannot" being
prudential or advisory or to do with a person's "fitness" for the relationship, it
is now a distinctively ethical "cannot." One cannot continue the relationship
with the person as before except by failing to express appropriate disapproval
of his action. But failing to express disapproval of the action means condoning
it or acquiescing in it, perhaps even becoming complicit in it. That is what you
might feel toward your friend: that in continuing to have a normal relationship
with Joe she has associated herself with what he did, become part of it, taken
his side against you. Therefore, on this view, taking the demands of the relationship seriously and disapproving of what was done requires that one not
continue the relationship as before: some sort of withdrawal or blame is
required as what Feinberg calls "symbolic nonacquiescence" (1970, ch. 5). In
the face of wrongdoing, one must not simply avow that it is wrong; one must
distance oneself from it. Hence the act impairs the relationship that it is possible, consistent with proper respect for the demands of the relationship, to
have with the person.

Contrary to Feinberg's position on the symbolism of punishment, though,
we cannot see the symbolism of blame as merely conventional. In order to
explain this point, we can look again at how this view of the significance of
withdrawal differs from Scanlon's. On Scanlon's view, as we have seen, withdrawal is appropriate because or insofar as the offender has shown himself to

be unfit for the relationship. On the view I am now proposing, however, withdrawal is appropriate precisely because the offender is fit for the relationship. Withdrawal is called for in order to capture the "What did you think you were doing?"—since this is someone who should have known better. Blame is a partial and temporary withdrawal from an offender, (1) carried out because of responsible wrongdoing and (2) carried out in a way that the offender herself can be expected to understand. Because of (1) and (2), blame is a way of treating the offender as a moral agent. It asserts the authority of the violated norms over the offending agent, holds the offender accountable to those norms, and in doing so includes the wrongdoer in the moral community. Therefore in blaming we include by partially excluding. That this is what we do, however, seems no accident: it is behavior that is sensitive to the offender's moral position and the need to find a form of behavior toward the offender that is adequate to that position. This is the way we need to treat the offender because the offender is a competent member of our moral community, a community defined by an understanding of what we owe to one another on the basis of the relationship we are in together, but who has violated the basic terms of that understanding. Understood in this way, the appropriateness of the symbolism is not simply conventional (at least if we mean by that that it is an intrinsically arbitrary marker that has its place because of a mutual agreement to use it in a certain way) but instead has to do with the fittingness of the action to the situation. In blaming we display our understanding of how to translate the significance of the situation of wrongdoing into action.

What is true in the claim that such behavior is conventional is the Fregean thought that, as with any individual proposition, any piece of symbolic behavior can only symbolize by virtue of its place in a wider language that contains myriad other expressive possibilities. Unlike the mystical claim that there are hidden "correspondences" that exist between different objects, the existence of which is prior to forms of human understanding being brought to bear, symbolic relations of the sort I am interested in cannot be thought to exist independently of the human ability to trace connections, similarities, resonances. But this lack of strict mind independence need not undermine the thought that these resonances, once noticed, can be compelling.

On the view I am proposing, we might say, the right way to account for the special force of blame is in terms of its expressive power. Talking of expressive power makes it clear that the notion of expression that we are interested in is not merely the notion of an instinctual expression of the emotions. It is not simply that the expression is forced out by some inner emotional force. If there is a connection between emotion and expression in the sense I am using it, it is that the expression gives form to the emotion, or rather gives form to the sense of salience or significance that constitutes the way the person experiencing the emotion construes the situation. Just as expression, in my sense, is not instinctive, so it is not a contingently appropriate means to a further end;

we should not confuse expression either with the actions one might choose as an effective way of venting one's feelings or with the actions one might choose as an effective way of communicating one's feelings to others. Like finding an effective means of reducing psychological pressure or of communicating, finding the right form of expression is like solving a problem. But deliberating about the latter is essentially backward-looking—it has to do with finding a proportionate response to some past event that conditions the situation one is now in—whereas deliberating about the former requires an empirical investigation into how to produce some future good state of affairs. It is in order to distinguish the sense of expression I am interested in from these other interpretations that I have stressed the symbolic element of expressive action. The idea is that expressive action purports to be a symbol of the situation, where a symbol is not merely a conventional way of denoting something other than itself but is a meaningful item that bears a more intimate relationship to the thing signified. Successful symbolic action is like a successful metaphor, capturing that aspect of the thing signified that is most relevant in the context.

Clearly blaming is not the only such symbolic action. Other examples include acts of symbolic nonacquiescence such as civil disobedience, the act of marriage, expressions of gratitude, acts of grieving and mourning. Perhaps not surprisingly it is often when we are confronted with important passages from one place or state or situation to another that we reach for symbolism in an attempt to capture the importance of what we think we are going through.[10] And in all of these cases, an important parameter of appropriateness will be the proportionality of the response to the significance of the occasion. In the case of mourning, for instance, where one has lost a loved one, one might search for a way of capturing one's sense of the significance of the loss: one might feel that words are not enough and that a certain way of treating the person's body is now important, before that opportunity is irrevocably lost. Something like that thought might be the driving force behind the various forms of funerary rites that we find resonant. As with blame, there are various equally valid ways of carrying that basic impulse through, but the impulse itself, and the basic form of its symbolism, doesn't seem merely conventional.

To sum up the thesis for which I have argued in this section, blame is an expression of disapproval; it works in symbolic terms, attempting to capture or do justice to the offender's moral position as a member of a relationship who has violated the basic terms of that relationship. In more general terms, I have claimed that some acts are essentially symbolic in that they work a bit like metaphors, capturing and illuminating some aspect of the situation. The form of the behavior is not conventional or arbitrary but rather has an essential role

---

[10] For an account of ritual action that draws on this point about passage from one state to another, see Rappaport (1999). However, I do not intend the thesis here to apply only to ritual or ceremonial action.

in making the action adequate to the situation. Like a metaphor, sometimes symbolic action can seem to get the situation just right (as when, after much deliberation, one alights on just the right way to express one's gratitude for the help one has been given). Thus sometimes the symbolism of the action is compelling. Otherwise put, sometimes it is the symbolism of the action that provides the reason to do the action. Therefore a consequence of what I have argued here is that, in order to give a comprehensive theoretical account of our best understanding of morally adequate response, we need to recognize a category of essentially expressive, symbolic reasons, reasons for action the force of which has to do with the way those actions symbolically capture or do justice to the significance of the situation.

6. Scanlon on Affirming Victims and "Symbolic Value"

Having looked at some problems in Scanlon's account, I have argued that a more plausible theory of blame would see it as an expression of disapproval without which agents relevantly connected to the offense would be condoning or acquiescing in the offense. In order to justify blame we would have to argue that the symbolism of blame—specifically the enactment of a kind of distancing or withdrawal—is necessary to bring this nonacquiescence about. In this section I would like to point out that a number of the elements of this theory are to be found in other aspects of Scanlon's work. I will argue that Scanlon has the resources to accept (1) that essentially symbolic acts are necessary to bring about nonacquiescence in an offense, though he rejects (2) that withdrawal is the necessary symbolism. However, (3) he recognizes that blame essentially involves withdrawal and therefore (4) attempts to account for such withdrawal in a different way. In response I want to argue that (4) fails and that (2) is unnecessary.

In his reflections on punishment, Scanlon (2003b) is sensitive to the point that I have claimed is central to understanding blame, namely, the importance of affirming the claims of the victims of wrongdoing. He argues that "the expression of condemnation seems to be importantly connected with punishment. . . . The central function of criminal law is to protect rights whose violation makes condemnation appropriate. So punishment will not be justifiable except where condemnation, and hence the affirmation of victims' rights, is appropriate, and *just punishment will constitute such affirmation*" (pp. 231–32, my italics).[11] In this aspect of his position, Scanlon seems to accept that a

---

[11] Note that Scanlon complicates this position by arguing that the need for affirmation, though it will justify having some public forum for the recognition of violated rights, will not itself justify punishment.

failure to mark the violation of rights as such would reflect "indifference on the part of society towards the wrongs and those who suffered them" and that "the victims of such wrongs are demeaned when the victimizers are treated as respected citizens with no mention of their crimes" (p. 223). Another way of putting this point, which Scanlon makes use of, is to say that violations of rights must be given proper recognition. However, to see that this commits Scanlon to something in the way of what I have called the expressive, consider that there are two things that might be meant by "recognition," and hence by the claim that a failure to engage in certain acts of affirmation shows lack of recognition. One is that recognition consists in cognitive appreciation or understanding. If we think of recognition in this way, then Scanlon's claim is false: it is not true that a failure to engage in acts of affirmation necessarily shows either a failure to understand the gravity of the act or indifference to it. Someone might care deeply that a person's rights have been violated but think that the appropriate response is simply doing what one can to prevent such things happening again. Such a person would be unusual but not inconsistent. However, another thing that might be meant by the need for "recognition" is that the violation of victim's rights must be reflected in one's own behavior, in the sense that an essentially symbolic affirmation is called for. On this reading of "recognition," I have argued, Scanlon's claim is true: a failure to engage in symbolic affirmation is a failure to dissociate from the wrong and hence represents culpable indifference. Therefore this aspect of Scanlon's position should be understood as committing him to the necessity of something in the way of essentially symbolic understandings of "affirmation," "recognition," and "indifference."

That Scanlon can accept the importance of the expressive is also suggested by his inclusion of "symbolic value" in the discussion of the value of choice:

> In a situation in which people are normally expected to make choices of a certain sort for themselves, individuals have reason to value the opportunity to make these choices because not having or not exercising this opportunity would be seen as reflecting a judgement (their own or someone else's) that they are not competent or do not have the standing normally accorded an adult member of the society. (1998, p. 253)

For instance, he suggests that in a society in which arranged marriages are not the norm, having one's parents make the choice of marriage partner would be "demeaning" on the grounds that it would "suggest that they [the betrothed couple] are not competent, independent adults" (p. 253). Thus we could interpret his claims about condemnation on these lines: that in a society in which certain acts are normally understood as expressing condemnation for an act, failure to engage in those acts will symbolize indifference. Admittedly these brief remarks on symbolic value could be interpreted in two ways. First of all, as I suggest, they might be read as committing Scanlon to the claim that some actions have an essentially expressive or symbolic aspect and that a failure to engage in symbolically adequate acts can in itself be wrong. Or, second, they could be given a more deflationary reading: that what is wrong with engaging in behavior that has a certain symbolic value is that, given a certain audience, one thereby conveys the impression that one has certain beliefs about the person's value or standing (and giving that impression can have bad consequences, say). My reasons for thinking that Scanlon is committed to the first reading is that he does not simply say that, in a given context, depriving a person of certain choices gives the impression that the agent views the person as lacking competence or independence; rather, in this case and the case of failure to condemn, he says these actions are demeaning. As I have explained, this understanding of demeaning requires some awareness of the symbolic adequacy of our actions.

Hence I think that Scanlon has the resources to accept my claim that what makes an act obligatory can be its symbolism (and that this symbolic relation does not reduce to a more fundamental claim about bad consequences). However, what Scanlon is prepared to say about state condemnation of wrongdoing raises the question of why he does not see blame similarly as a symbolic expression of disapproval and nonacquiescence. I think the reason for this may be that Scanlon is persuaded that some sort of withdrawal or impairment of relationships is essential to blame but is also convinced that condemnation does not need the symbolism of withdrawal in order to be adequate to the gravity of the wrong. Therefore he cannot make the move I make, using symbolism to explain the meaning of withdrawal. As a result, he develops his distinctive desert theory. As we have seen, the cost of this development is that he gives up the natural thought that blame is essentially an expression of disapproval, a holding to account. Hence my claim that the stronger account of blame will be one on which the blamer sees withdrawal precisely as the necessary vehicle for the expression of disapproval.

Therefore the heart of the matter, perhaps not surprisingly, turns on Scanlon's rejection of retributivism. For I think it is this that leads him to deny that withdrawal is necessary for symbolically adequate condemnation.[12] However, I would like to conclude by suggesting that Scanlon could accept the claim I have advanced in this paper about the symbolism of withdrawal without committing himself to what is objectionable in retributivism. What leads Scanlon to reject retributivism would seem to be the thought that retributivism consists in what he calls the Desert Thesis: "that when a person has done something that is morally wrong it is morally better that he or she should suffer some loss in consequence" (1998, p. 274). However, if my account of blame is retributivist, then what it justifies is not the infliction of suffering or the valuing of that person's

---

[12] It also leads him to deny that punishment is necessary for state condemnation of wrongdoing—though this makes it harder to interpret his claim that when punishment is carried out it could constitute such condemnation. See Scanlon (2003b).

suffering or harm as such but rather a kind of cutting off or distancing. Such with-drawal may itself cause suffering; furthermore it may turn out that such with-drawal may make it permissible to cause or allow certain harms to a person that would not otherwise have been permissible.[13] But these further harms are not es-sential to the nature of blame (except insofar as blame can be characterized as a willingness to let such things happen). Blame can successfully be carried out with-out such suffering occurring (except, perhaps, the pain of remorse). Does the sym-bolic view commit me to the worrisome view that "when people's moral deficiencies are great, the proper response on our part is to see even their most basic moral claims on the rest of us as limited and qualified" (p. 142)? Not necessarily. It depends on what degree of withdrawal is proportionate to wrongs of such seriousness. Pro-portionality, it is fair to say, is not well understood in desert theories of punishment and blame. I don't have a general theory to offer, nor am I sure that one could be given (though it seems also fair to say that the possibility of social interaction requires that there be some shared basis for judging which claims about propor-tionate response are reasonable and which not). But one crucial thing to be taken into account in any judgment about proportionate blame and withdrawal is the point I made earlier in criticism of Scanlon: that the right theory of blame should be able to account for the fact that blame is inclusive as well as exclusive. We with-draw from the offender precisely because she is that extraordinary and valuable thing: an agent capable of self-government. The offender's moral status as an agent with whom we could potentially engage in distinctively human, rational, ethical interaction should be at the fore whenever we blame, as a factor informing our judgments about which blaming response is proportionate. A plausible implica-tion of this is that blaming judgments do not require us to neglect the basic human needs even of very serious wrongdoers. At the same time, on this theory of blame, we might also be able to explain that sense of discomfort, even horror, that is some-times reported by those who find themselves in the presence of evil.

7. Conclusion

I have defended two main claims in this paper. The first is that the most prom-ising way to understand—and, if appropriate, to justify—the special force of blame is to see blame as embodying the view that, in order for a response to (serious) wrongdoing to be adequate to the significance of those wrongs, one

---

[13] It is not clear that Scanlon's own position on punishment is coherent unless he accepts the same. His claim is that those who deserve condemnation can be punished for deterrent purposes. However, he presumably doesn't think that the innocent can be punished when doing so would be necessary for some important deterrent effect. Therefore Scanlon seems committed to the thought that being condemnation-worthy makes it permissible to cause you harms that would not otherwise have been permissible. See Scanlon (2003b).

must not simply say or judge that the action is wrong but must distance oneself from it. Such distancing, through withdrawal of goodwill, is what blame consists in. The second claim says that the best way to understand the first thesis is to see it as appealing persuasively to some kind of symbolic necessity, that is, to the fact that what makes it the case that one must distance oneself from wrongdoing is that such including-but-distancing behavior captures or reflects the offender's moral situation and that the fact that such behavior captures the offender's moral position makes it wrongful acquiescence or complicity to continue the relationship as normal. I imagine that objections to my argument will either, as on the view I ascribed to Scanlon in the preceding section, accept my wider claims that the symbolism of an action is sometimes the ground of our reason to do that action but dispute my claim that blame and withdrawal are necessary in order to do justice to the wrongs, or reject the idea that symbolic relations can be the ground of moral reasons at all.

I admit that the topic of the normativity of expressive action requires a good deal of further research; no doubt further argument is required to make it persuasive to many readers. On the other hand, the position for which I have argued has been, if not well understood, at least reasonably familiar in Anglo-American moral and legal philosophy since Feinberg and the Hart-Devlin debate, though it has its roots in the Romantic reaction to the Enlightenment, in Hegel's theory of action, and in Baudelaire's Symbolism. It is perhaps more often found in aesthetics than in moral philosophy, but that seems to me a mistake. In neglecting the expressive, symbolic aspects of action, or treating them as at best conventional and at worst dangerously irrational, moral philosophy deprives itself of one of our basic modes of responding to moral significance.

Interpreting Blame

T. M. Scanlon

1

'Blame' refers to a class of responses to morally faulty actions. Although experiences of blaming and being blamed are familiar parts of everyday life, it is not entirely clear what blame involves. So it is worth seeking a clearer interpretation of blame simply as a way of better understanding our moral lives. But this is also worth seeking because we need a clearer understanding of blame in order to understand, and perhaps resolve, some important philosophical puzzles.

For example, most of us are strongly inclined to think that it is appropriate to blame people who commit terrible crimes. But, on the other hand, we are also sometimes inclined to think that these people cannot properly be blamed if, as seems likely, their characters and actions are caused by factors outside of them, over which they have no control. Similarly, we are inclined to think that two drivers who are equally careless deserve the same amount of blame, but also inclined to think that if one of them kills a pedestrian then he or she should be blamed more severely than the other who, through sheer good luck, gets home without an accident. In order to resolve these puzzles we need to understand why it should seem to be the case that blame is appropriate only for things that are under an agent's control, and what kind of control is required. And in order to understand these things we need to understand what blame is.

A satisfactory account of blame should be as faithful as possible to the phenomenology of blaming and to our judgments about when it is appropriate to blame people and in what degree. But as I have said, it is not entirely clear what we have in mind in speaking of blame, and the things we are inclined to believe about blame form an inconsistent set. This is why I will refer to what I am offering as an interpretation of blame rather than an analysis, which would suggest a higher degree of clarity and specificity in the object of analysis than I believe exists. Any interpretation of blame will be in some way revisionary: accepting it will involve changing our minds about some things we previously were inclined to believe. An interpretation would be revisionary in a bad way if it involved changing our minds just in order to avoid the puzzles I have mentioned. A satisfactory response to these puzzles has to be grounded in a deeper understanding of blame, in the light of which we can see why some of the things we were previously inclined to think are in fact mistaken. A satisfactory interpretation of blame should also explain why the puzzling cases are puzzling— why it is that we are pulled in two directions in these cases.

One natural interpretation of blame is that to blame someone is just to have a negative moral assessment of what he has done and the character that this reflects. This interpretation is suggested by the frequent pairing of blame with praise. Since praise is a (positive) evaluation, blame would also be purely evaluative if it were simply the negative correlate of praise. But this interpretation of blame is unable to explain the puzzles just mentioned. If blame is merely a negative evaluation, it is difficult to see why it should seem inappropriate to blame people for characteristics that are due to factors that are not under their control. Whatever caused us to be the way we are, we *are* that way, with our particular faults and virtues. If blame is just a form of evaluation, there is no reason why causal explanations of our character and actions should undermine blame, any more than such explanations undermine appraisals of our intelligence or our athletic or aesthetic skills.[1] Similarly, if blame is merely evaluative, then moral luck cases should not be at all puzzling: it should be simply obvious that the two drivers in the case I described are equally blameworthy since their actions and character are faulty in the same way.

An alternative interpretation takes blame to be a kind of punishment. This might explain why blame requires freedom, if it is unfair or otherwise objectionable to punish people for things that they could not have avoided doing or for traits that they could not avoid having. This could also explain our puzzlement about moral luck cases, if we are inclined to think that the driver who kills a pedestrian should be punished more severely, but this thought is in tension with our recognition that that driver is morally no worse than the one who merely drove recklessly.

It is not clear, however, what punishment or penalty is supposed to be involved in our ordinary practice of blaming. Perhaps the penalty is just the unpleasantness of being subject to moral criticism. But negative assessment of our talents and skills is also unpleasant, and criticism of these kinds, for traits that we could not have avoided having, seems quite appropriate, at least if it serves some social purpose.

---

[1] Hume's interpretation of moral criticism is purely evaluative (a matter of "disinterested approval and disapproval"). This is what leads him to believe that the only lack of freedom that undermines blame is the lack of "liberty of spontaneity," which distorts the connection between an agent's action and his or her character.

Perhaps blame is not itself a sanction but rather a judgment that some sanction would be appropriate. If these sanctions are justified only if people have
had a fair chance to avoid them, this would explain why blame is appropriate
only for things that are under a person's control. But it does not seem that
whenever we blame someone we have in mind that some sanction is called for,
let alone what this sanction might be. Perhaps this is something about which
competent users of the term 'blame' can disagree. But I, at least, when I blame
someone, do not believe that it would be a good thing if they should suffer in
some way.[2]

So it is worth looking for an interpretation of blame that lies between these
two extremes: an interpretation that involves more than mere negative assessment but is not a form of punishment. In this essay I will consider three interpretations of blame that lie in this intermediate space. The first interprets
blame as the expression of a moral emotion such as resentment or indignation.
The second goes beyond this and sees blame as not only expressive but also
communicative: as a demand for justification, explanation, or apology. The
third is my own view, which sees blame as a modification of one's understanding of one's relationship with the person blamed.[3] I will present this view
in section 2 and then, in section 3, respond to some objections to it, coming
mainly from views of the other two kinds I have mentioned.

2

To explain my interpretation of blame, I will start by explaining the abstract
idea of a relationship, on which it is based. I understand a relationship as a set
of intentions and expectations about our actions and attitudes toward one another that are justified by certain facts about us. The concept of a relationship
is a normative concept specifying the conditions under which a particular relationship of this kind exists and the attitudes and intentions that parties to
such a relationship ought, ideally, to have toward each other.

Friendship, for example, involves intentions to spend time together, to stand
ready to aid each other, to share and keep confidences, to take pleasure in each
other's successes and be distressed by each other's setbacks, and in general to be
particularly concerned with each other's welfare. These intentions (and the
corresponding expectations) are made appropriate by such things as the
friends' common interests and experiences and the enjoyment of each other's
company. This abstract normative ideal of the relationship of friendship should
not be confused with the particular relationships that hold between actual

---

[2] As will become clear, I do believe that they should be treated in a way that they have reasons to
dislike, but not as a form of punishment and not *because* they dislike it.

[3] Presented in my 2008, chapter 4.

individuals who are friends. These relationships are constituted by the actual attitudes that the parties have toward one another. If these conform closely enough to the normative ideal of friendship, then they count as friends even though their relationship may be flawed as measured by this ideal.

Another kind of relationship is the kind that people stand in to one another when they share a commitment to some group, cause, or ideal. Like friendship, these relationships have preconditions: they hold only between individuals who have commitments of the relevant kind, or perhaps, in some cases, who share some properties in virtue of which they *should* have such a commitment.

I believe, more controversially, that there is also such a thing as the moral relationship that we stand in to all rational creatures. As in the case of other relationships, the normative concept of this relationship specifies, first, the conditions under which people stand in the relationship and, second, the norms governing attitudes that those who stand in this relationship should, ideally, have toward one another. As to the first, the moral relationship holds among all rational agents. As to the second, the normative concept specifies that we should have certain general intentions about how we will behave toward other rational creatures, namely, in my view, that we will treat them only in ways that would be allowed by principles that they could not reasonably reject. It also specifies other attitudes that we should have toward one another, such as being pleased if things go well for another person and regretful (and certainly not pleased) when things go badly for him.

Unlike friendship and other relationships of the kinds I have mentioned, the moral relationship does not apply only to people who know of or are acquainted with one another or who actually have certain attitudes toward one another. It holds universally, of all rational agents. It is thus, in a way, inescapable. By failing to hold certain attitudes one can fail or cease to be friends or fellow members of a political party.[4] But no matter what attitudes a person has, and no matter how badly he or she may have behaved, we still stand in the moral relationship with that person. This may seem to imply that what I am calling the moral relationship is not an actual relationship between individuals. A real relationship between two people, it might be said, is constituted by their actual attitudes toward one another. Since what I am calling the moral relationship holds independently of such attitudes, it might be said not to be a relationship at all but just a set of moral requirements. There is, it might be said, nothing in this case corresponding to the actual relationship between two friends.

---

[4] Universality and inescapability need not go together. It may be claimed, for example that members of certain ethnic groups are bound by norms of that group whether or not they choose to accept this. In many cases this claim does not seem defensible, but when it is, the relationship in question would be inescapable, although not universal.

This does not seem to me to be correct. Insofar as we hold general moral views about what we owe to others and what they owe to us, these views constitute a relationship in the abstract sense I have in mind: a set of intentions and expectations about how we will behave toward one another. We have not only intentions and expectations regarding our interactions with friends and associates but also intentions and expectations that define a relationship with other people in general. We have, for example, views and intentions about the care one should take not to injure strangers and the duties one has to aid them should we be in a position to do so. The normative ideal of the moral relationship specifies what these intentions and expectations ought to be. Our actual attitudes may fall short of this ideal, but we have them nonetheless. I recognize that this stretches the normal idea of a relationship, but I believe that enough of that idea remains for it to be a useful framework for interpreting blameworthiness and blame.

Blame and blameworthiness as I understand them are always relative to some relationship or relationships. A person is *blameworthy*, in my view, if he does something that indicates intentions or attitudes that are faulty by the standards of a relationship. Someone is morally blameworthy if his attitudes are faulty by the standards of the moral relationship. But people can also be judged to be blameworthy because their attitudes are faulty by the standards of some other relationship, such as friendship (thus impairing the person's relations with those to whom he stands in this relation).

The relationships I have mentioned as examples have been ones, like friendship, that we properly value. But I believe that there can be attitudes properly called blame relative to other relationships. For example, a Mafioso can be said to blame an associate for violating the code of *omertà*. Since, we assume, the associate has good moral reason for this violation, he is not *morally* blameworthy for it and, I would say, not blameworthy at all (that is, not blameworthy by any defensible standard). But this does not mean that his comrades' attitude toward him is not an attitude of blame, because they accept and value the relationship of which this code is a part, even if they do not have good reason to do this.[5]

A judgment of blameworthiness is a judgment that an action shows something about the agent that impairs, in various ways, his or her relations with others. The nature of this impairment will vary, depending on the ways that these others interact with that person—on which more particular relations they stand in to this person and the significance for them of that person's faults. A judgment of blameworthiness is a judgment that those others have reason to understand their relations with that person in ways other than they normally would. Like an assessment of a person's character, it is an impersonal judgment that one can make, with the same content, no matter how one is related to the person in question.

---

[5] This paragraph responds to a question raised by Jussi Suikkanen (2011, p. 572).

But blame, the response that this impairment calls for, is more personal. To *blame* a person is to judge that person to be blameworthy and, as a consequence, to modify one's understanding of one's relationship with that person (that is, to alter or withhold intentions and expectations that that relationship would normally involve) in the particular ways that that judgment of blameworthiness makes appropriate, given one's relation with the person and the significance for one of what that person has done. The modification that is appropriate will vary depending on how one is related to the person in question and to his or her action. It will depend, for example, on whether one is a member of the agent's community or a stranger and whether one is the victim of the agent's action, a relative of the victim, or a bystander.

The personal nature and hence variability of blame on the interpretation I am offering is a reflection of the fact that, like Strawson, I am interpreting blame as involving reactive attitudes—attitudes toward a person that are reactions to the attitudes toward others that are reflected in his or her actions.[6] The main difference between my view and Strawson's lies in the particular reactive attitudes that we regard as centrally important. While not discounting emotions altogether, I emphasize changes in intentions. Strawson emphasizes reactive emotions (although, I will explain later, his view involves other attitudes as well).

What I have just been doing is simply to emphasize the fact that, unlike an interpretation that sees blame as an evaluation of a person's character, a reactive attitude interpretation like mine or Strawson's can recognize that the kind of reaction that a given agent's actions and attitudes call for can vary from person to person, depending on how one is related to and affected by that person and his or her actions.

The particular modification of attitudes (the kind of blame) that is justified in a given case is determined by first-order normative reasoning: first-order moral reasoning in the case of moral blame, and in other cases moral reasoning supplemented by reasons relating to the special relationships in question. It is strength of this account that it allows explicitly for this kind of variability, since most blaming occurs between people who know each other well and stand in special relations to one another in addition to the general moral relationship.

Blame of a disloyal friend, for example, might involve suspending one's normal intentions to trust the friend and confide in him or her and assigning a different meaning to one's interactions. Blame of a fellow member of a cause or group might, similarly, involve lessened trust and decreased feelings of solidarity. In extreme cases, blame in relation to such relationships may involve writing a person off as no longer someone one is related to in the relevant way: no longer a friend or no longer a fellow devotee of the cause or a member of the group.

---

[6] A point noted by Jay Wallace (2011, p. 352).

In the case of moral blame, wholesale exclusion of this kind is not a possibility. The moral relationship is, as I have said, inescapable: the requirements of morality still apply to one's treatment of a person no matter how badly he or she has behaved and whether or not he or she takes those requirements seriously. It is a first-order moral question, therefore, what one owes to a person given the moral deficiencies he or she has displayed. I believe that most basic moral requirements, such as those not to kill or injure a person, are unconditional and are owed to a person no matter what he or she has done. This raises the question of what room there is for meaningful moral blame that goes beyond mere negative evaluation. It seems to me that there is room for this. A person's morally deficient attitudes and behavior can justify a withdrawal of the presumption of trust and of willingness to enter into relationships that require trust, such as friendships of cooperation. There is also room for decreased willingness to help a person with his or her projects and for a change in one's attitude toward how things go for the person. As I have said, it is normally a moral fault not to be disposed to hope that things go well for a person, not to take pleasure in their going well, or to take pleasure in their going badly. But if a person has behaved very badly toward oneself or others, it is not a moral fault to fail to take pleasure in that person's successes or not to be distressed at things going badly for him or her.

This change in attitude—not hoping that things go well for a person or being pleased when they do—should not be confused with the retributivist attitude of thinking it *good* that a person should suffer, given what he or she has done, or that this is less bad than that an innocent person should suffer. The difference between hoping that something will happen, or being pleased when it does, and believing it good that it should happen can be seen from the case of attitudes toward the fates of one's friends. If my friend has bought a lottery ticket, then as her friend I hope that she wins, and I will be pleased if she does. But this does not mean that, as a friend, I must think that it would be a better thing if she wins than if someone else, equally in need, gets the prize.

Failure to make this distinction may be one thing that makes it seem to many that blame is appropriate only for things that are under a person's control. If blaming someone involved judging it to be a good thing that he should suffer as a result of what he has done, then, since it seems objectionable to make people suffer for things they could not have avoided, it would be plausible to think that people should not be blamed for things that are not under their control. But, as the contrast between friends and strangers shows, we do not owe it to people generally to hope to the same degree that things go well for them or to be pleased when they do. These attitudes can vary, depending on our relations with a person. Just as being a friend, or a particularly nice person, can justify our taking increased pleasure in things going well for someone, being a particularly nasty person is adequate reason for decreased empathy of this kind. In neither case—neither in the upward nor the downward direction, as it were—is it required that the person have chosen to be the way that leads us to have these increased or decreased feelings.

This illustrates the general point mentioned earlier that it is a first-order moral question whether the responses involved in moral blame are appropriate only if the faults they are responses to are under the person's control. I believe that with respect to all of the blaming responses I have mentioned the answer is that they do not. We do not owe it to people generally to trust them, be willing to cooperate with them, or be ready to become their friends regardless of what they are like. And facts about what they are like, quite apart from whether they choose to be that way, are sufficient reason to withhold these attitudes.

This dependence of the appropriateness of blaming attitudes on the relation between the person who is doing the blaming and the person who is blamed provides an explanation of our reactions to cases of moral luck in the outcome of an agent's actions. Reactions to these cases are puzzling if we take blame to depend only on the moral seriousness of an agent's faults and the degree to which this fault and its consequences are under the control of the agent. When we think of blame as depending only on these factors, we are led to the conclusion that the two drivers in the example I gave should be blamed in the same way and to the same degree. This leaves unexplained our sense that there is some difference between the two that is related to blame.

The feeling that there is a difference can be explained by the difference in the significance of the two drivers' faults for those affected. Most obviously, these faults are of very different significance for the family of the person who was killed. It is reasonable for them to give that driver's faults more importance than those of the merely careless driver in determining their continuing relations with these people—and thus to blame the driver who caused this harm to a different degree. Our judgments of blameworthiness, as neutral observers, will reflect this difference insofar as they are judgments about the differing reactions that various others (those who are harmed and those who are not) will appropriately have to an agent's conduct. This explains the duality in our reaction to moral luck cases: the two drivers are equally faulty, but the different kinds of significance that these faults have for other people make it reasonable for those people to react to these faults in different ways.[7] (This explanation is available to any reactive attitude interpretation of blame that allows the appropriateness of reactive attitudes to have this personal character.)

The idea that the form of blame that is appropriate depends on one's relation to an agent and his or her actions may seem to lead to implausible conclusions about the possibility of blaming people with whom we have no relations and whose actions do not affect us or anyone known to us. For example, can

---

[7] This responds to a question raised by Dana Nelkin (2011b, p. 606) about how my interpretation of blame can explain both sides of our reaction to cases of moral outcome luck.

we, on this account, blame Agrippina for murdering Claudius in A.D. 54 (assuming that she did this)? We can, on my account, judge her to be *blameworthy*, since this is a judgment about the responses appropriate for others who did stand in certain relations to her. But what content could an attitude of blaming on our part have? What intentions involving her might we modify?

An interpretation of blame emphasizing moral emotions such as resentment and indignation also has difficulty with such cases. It would be odd to say that we resent what Agrippina did, since we are not affected by what she did, and it sounds odd as well to say that we are indignant about it. Indignation seems overblown because of our lack of connection to what she did. So this problem, insofar as it is a problem, will arise for any account of blame that emphasizes what I called earlier its personal character. Blame of distant agents is most easily understood as an impersonal evaluative judgment of the agent's action and character. Beyond this, there may seem to be little room for blame, as opposed to a neutral judgment of blameworthiness.

But the account I am offering does allow for another way in which blame of people in the distant past can have content. This content lies in differences in the way we react to what happens to them, the degree to which we are distressed by bad things that happen to them or pleased by their good fortune.[8] (This aspect of blame could also be captured in Strawson's account via his idea of a withdrawal of good will.) Blame of fictional characters can be understood in the same way. Fiction works in large part by engaging our natural moral tendency to be concerned with the fate of people we hear about—to hope things go well for them and to be distressed when they do not. This engagement creates a large part of the tension that pulls us along as a story unfolds. Our attitude toward the villains in a story (our blame of them), insofar as it goes beyond evaluation, lies in changes in this concern: in being less distressed, and even pleased when things go badly for them.

3

I turn now to some objections to the account of blame that I have offered. According to my account, the fact that certain attitudes, such as a complete disregard for the interests of others, are attributable to a person is sufficient grounds for blaming him or her. This may seem mistaken because it leaves out what Gary Watson refers to as the requirement that those who are subject to blame should be morally *accountable* (2011, pp. 308–9; see also Watson 1996). Psychopaths, for example, may be rational in a general sense and capable of

---

[8] I am grateful to Colin Marshall for calling this possibility to my attention in a discussion at New York University.

means-ends reasoning but nonetheless unable to understand why they have any reason to take moral requirements seriously as limits on the pursuit of their aims. If they see no reason not to kill, injure, or manipulate us when this promotes their ends, then this judgment about reasons is attributable to them. It is their considered judgment about the reasons they have. But if they are incapable of understanding why they should not hold this view, then, Watson believes, it makes no sense to demand of them that they take our interests seriously in the way that morality requires.

By this he does not mean merely that it is pointless to ask them why they hold their views and how they can defend them. Rather, he thinks that given their lack of moral capacity the requirements of morality do not apply to them, and it is senseless to blame them for failing to comply with these requirements. He writes, "I can legitimately require others to do things only if they have good reasons to act in this way because I have required it. In other words, it is normatively infelicitous to make demands of people who have no good reasons to regard the demanding as legitimate" (2011, p. 314). I take it that by "have no good reason" Watson means "are not capable of seeing that they have good reason," or that he takes the ability to see that one has a reason of a certain kind to be a necessary condition for having such a reason. I believe, on the contrary, that in the sense relevant to questions of blame a person can be blind to reasons that he really does have. This disagreement may be important to our conflicting views about psychopaths.[9]

Watson's objection to my view can be understood in two ways. Understood in the first way, it suggests that because my view interprets blame as a unilateral reaction on the part of the person doing the blaming, it does not take into account the responses that are called for on the part of those who are blamed, such as explanation, justification, or apology, and hence neglects the fact that blame is inappropriate in the case of individuals who lack the moral capacity to respond in these ways.

In response it should be said, first, that although on my account blame itself (as opposed to some *expressions* of blame) does not literally involve a demand for justification or apology, this account does explain why these responses are called for and how blame can be undermined when they are forthcoming. Blame, as I interpret it, involves a modified understanding of one's relationship with a person, which has been impaired by that person's actions or attitudes. It follows that a person who is blamed, insofar as he or she has reason to want that relationship to be preserved, has reason to respond by justifying what he or she has done (thereby denying that an impairment has occurred)

---

[9] Watson might say that at least a person who cannot see that he has a certain reason cannot be *blamed* for not seeing it. There is certainly a sense in which this is so: it is not his fault that he can't understand this reason—not his fault that he is a psychopath. But this is in my view a separate question, and in any event is not Watson's main objection.

or by offering an apology, which acknowledges the impairment and attempts to restore the relationship on a new footing.[10] To accept a justification or apology is thus to set aside the attitudes that constitute blame as I interpret it, or at least to modify these attitudes going forward. I regard it as a strength of my account that it explains the relation between blame, apology, and forgiveness in this direct way.

An account that gives central place to moral emotions such as resentment might also explain this relation, given some account of how apology makes these emotions no longer appropriate. It might be said that what makes resentment appropriate is the impairment of one's relationship caused by the person's past attitudes, and that apology undermines resentment by removing this impairment. This seems right, although one might wonder whether resentment is really undermined if the object of resentment is the person's past action and the attitudes reflected in it, which apology cannot modify. The attitudes that my interpretation of blame stresses are more explicitly forward-looking: they concern the way one intends to be related to a person in the future, given what he or she has done in the past. Insofar as one has reason to want to restore the relationship with a person on something like its former basis, that person's apology, by providing a basis for doing this, can make it the case that one has reason to modify the intentions that are central to blame on my account. I am not saying that an emotion-based account cannot explain these things, but my interpretation seems to me to have the advantage of making the connections more explicit.

It would be unreasonable literally to demand justification or apology from a person who lacks the moral capacity to understand and offer these things. As Watson acknowledges, blame, on my account, need not involve such demand. But the second, deeper form of the accountability objection holds not simply that it is unreasonable to literally demand justification or apology from people who lack moral capacity, but that it is unreasonable to demand that they comply with moral requirements, and to blame them for not doing so, since they are incapable of seeing that they have any reason to take these requirements seriously.

We are, Watson says, pulled two ways in reacting to psychopaths. On the one hand their cruel and manipulative behavior seems to make them prime candidates for blame. But on the other hand the very incapacity that explains this conduct disqualifies them as moral agents and hence from blame (Watson 2011, p. 307). Watson believes that my view is unable to account for this ambivalence about the blameworthiness of psychopaths since it seems to come down firmly on the side of saying that psychopaths are blameworthy, indeed that the

---

[10] This depends, as I have said, on whether the person has reasons to value the relationship in question. See note 4 above.

attitudes attributable to them make them prime subjects for blame. There is, however, a way in which my view can account for this ambivalence. Insofar as they lack the capacity to understand and respond to moral requirements, it is questionable whether they can be participants in the moral relationship. Like young children (but in a different way), they both are and are not members of the moral community. We owe them some kinds of moral concern and care. We may not, for example, kill or injure them at will. But they are not candidates for relations of cooperation or trust, so withholding these relationships is not a modification of a status they would have had were it not for certain particular instances of behavior and attitude. Because they are psychologically complex, psychopaths are able to *simulate* normal behavior and to use this to manipulate us. They *seem* to be, and can present themselves as, candidates for trust and hence subject to blame in the form of withholding trust. But when we understand more about what they are like we can see that this is an illusion.

This might explain the ambivalence about psychopaths that Watson describes. But is holding that psychopaths are in this sense not candidates for normal moral relationships an exemption from blame or a *form* of blame? The answer would seem to lie in whether withholding these relationships has the condemnatory aspect typical of blame. Blame as I interpret it has this aspect of condemnation because it involves withholding trust, cooperation, and so on from a person *because of* attitudes that person holds that are faulty by the standards of some relationship to which he or she is a party. It also involves withholding a relationship that he or she is seeking in trying to manipulate us. Neither of these things is true of tigers. They are not candidates for trust, which explains why refusing to trust them is not a form of blame. If there is ambivalence in the case of psychopaths, I have suggested, it is about whether they actually are candidates for moral relations at all.

Another criticism of my view has been that its explanation of the condemnatory aspect of blame is too weak. In order to do justice to what Jay Wallace calls the element of "opprobrium" in blame, he and others argue that an adequate interpretation needs to give a greater role to moral emotions.[11]

To assess this objection it is helpful to consider the parallel case of gratitude. As Adam Smith points out, blame is best understood as the negative correlate of gratitude rather than praise.[12] Praise is a purely evaluative notion. So the idea that blame is the negative correlate of praise supports an evaluative interpretation of blame, and this, as I pointed out earlier, makes it difficult to explain why it should seem to many that blame is appropriate only for things that are under a person's control. Gratitude, on the other hand, provides the model for an interpretation of blame that is more than mere negative evaluation but yet not punitive.

---

[11] See, for example, Wallace (2011), Wolf (2011), and Mason (2011).

[12] See part 2, section 1 of Smith's *The Theory of Moral Sentiments* (1759). Strawson also mentions gratitude as a reactive attitude, along with resentment. See Strawson (1962, as reprinted in Watson 2003, p. 75).

Gratitude toward a person who has done something to help you is not just a matter of thinking well of that person. It involves, centrally, a change in intention, in the form of an increased readiness to help that person in turn should the need arise and, commonly, an increased tendency to be pleased when something good happens to him or her. In cases of genuine gratitude, helping a benefactor is not seen as a way of rewarding him or her for helping you (the positive analogue of a punishment), and certainly is not viewed as an incentive to encourage such behavior in that person and others. Rather, it is simply called for by what the person has done for you—by the way your relationship with that person has been altered by what he or she has done.

It might be said, however, that gratitude is, at base, a moral emotion, a positive correlate of resentment.[13] It is certainly true that feeling grateful generally involves a warm feeling toward the person who has benefited you, in addition to the attitudinal changes I have mentioned, just as blame generally involves hostile feelings such as resentment. I do not mean to deny these emotional factors in either case. The question is what is central to the reactions in question. It seems to me that, however warmly a person might feel toward someone who has benefited him, someone who lacked any increased tendency to help this person in turn could not really be said to be grateful. Such a person would not understand what it is to be grateful. On the other hand, someone who was very glad to have been helped and saw this as a reason to be ready to help the other person in turn could properly be said to be grateful even if, because he was something of a cold fish, this intention was not accompanied by any other affective element. I am not saying that this is the normal case or denying that such a person would be odd. The question I am interested in is the relation between affective and other responses and their relative centrality.

The fact that the person I have described intends to help his benefactor in turn *because of the help that person has given him* accounts for the "positive" aspect of his gratitude just as, on my account, the "condemnatory" aspect of blame lies in withholding certain intentions because of the faultiness of a person's attitudes, as measured by the standards of the relevant relationship. The question is whether further positive or negative emotional responses are not only normal but also essential to the reactive attitudes of gratitude and blame.

To address this question it will be helpful to consider how my interpretation of blame differs from, and also resembles, Strawson's reactive attitude account. I believe that there is less difference between our views than might at first appear. The first thing to notice is that moral emotions are not the only elements of Strawson's view. There is also the element of what he calls "good will." Strawson writes, "Indignation, disapproval, like resentment, tend to inhibit or at least to limit our good will towards the object of these attitudes, tend to promote

---

[13] As Strawson suggests (1962, as reprinted in Watson 2003, p. 90).

an at least partial and temporary withdrawal of good will: they do so in proportion as they are strong; and their strength is in general proportioned to what is felt to be the magnitude of the injury and to the degree to which the agent's will is identified with, or indifferent to, it." He goes on to say that this withdrawal of goodwill involves also a "modification of the general demand that another should, if possible, be spared suffering" and "preparedness to acquiesce in that infliction of suffering on the offender which is an essential part of punishment" (1962, as reprinted in Watson 2003 p. 90). I assume that if he were to say more about gratitude as a positive reactive attitude, Strawson might have said, similarly, that it tends to promote an *increase* in goodwill and an increased *unwillingness* to acquiesce in another's suffering.

The idea of good will is left somewhat vague and unexamined in Strawson's brief remarks. But the withdrawal of good will as he understands it clearly goes well beyond mere feelings insofar as it includes a willingness to acquiesce in the infliction of suffering. As I indicated earlier, it seems to me that an answer to the first-order moral question of whether blame is appropriate only for things that are under a person's control depends crucially on how much this attitude involves—how much of what one normally owes a person is altered or suspended when one blames that person. Here there seems to me to be a significant difference between angry feelings and the infliction of suffering, and that the latter requires more by way of justification. It is one thing to say that it is simply part of our practice to feel resentment toward those who violate the norms of interpersonal relationships and that no argument is needed that the objects of these attitudes could have avoided being subject to them. But it is quite a different thing to claim this about the deliberate infliction of suffering.

I do not believe that moral blameworthiness ever means that the deliberate infliction of suffering is justified. The moral prohibition against individuals' inflicting suffering on one another seems to be unconditional. (Whether the needs of public safety can justify the infliction of suffering by the state is a separate question.) So the benefits that blame can involve withholding on my view are less weighty than Strawson seems to envisage. But it nonetheless seemed to me important, in order to explain and do justice to the thought that blame is appropriate only for things that a person could have avoided, to develop an interpretation of blame that includes more than emotional reactions.[14] In short, it seemed to me that what Strawson calls the "withdrawal of good will" is where the action is: that it is important to be clear about exactly what this involves and about what is required in order for these things to be justified.

---

[14] Since I focused on the modification of intentions because I thought that seemed, initially, more difficult to justify than emotional reactions and more likely to raise issues of freedom and control, I was surprised that Susan Wolf seems to believe the opposite (2011, p. 342). One possible explanation for this might be that, like Strawson, she takes retributive attitudes such as a willingness to acquiesce in the infliction of suffering to be part and parcel of these emotions, whereas I explicitly exclude these from the modifications of intention that I take blame to involve.

An important possible difference between my view and Strawson's concerns the relation between reactive attitudes such as resentment and indignation, and the withdrawal of good will. It is not entirely clear how Strawson understands the relation between these, and their relation in turn to a person's violation of moral demands. In the first of the passages I quoted, where he is talking about strength, Strawson seems to be claiming that violations of moral demands give rise to reactive attitudes, which in turn bring about ("tend to promote") the attitudinal changes he calls withdrawal of good will. But later on that page he seems to suggest a more intimate relation between the first of these factors and each of the other two. He says that "the making of the demand [that people comply with moral requirements] is the proneness to such attitudes [of resentment etc.]," and that the partial withdrawal of good will which these attitudes entail is the consequence of viewing the person as a member of the moral community "who has offended against its demands." This suggests that in his view taking moral demands seriously involves seeing both feelings of resentment and the withdrawal of good will as appropriate when these demands are violated (although he continues to say that this withdrawal is "entailed by" those reactive attitudes).

So there are two possible views here about the relation between moral emotions such as resentment and indignation and the modified attitudes that my account of blame emphasizes, which are parts of what Strawson calls the withdrawal of good will. On one account reactive emotions and these modifications of attitude are both justified as reactions to a person's faulty attitudes toward others, but the justification of the latter need not go by way of justification of the former. (This is compatible with the idea that the reactive emotions cannot be fully understood without reference to these other modifications of attitude—that resentment would not be resentment if it did not involve some modification of intention—as long as it is understood that these modifications of intention can be independently justified.)

This is the position I have taken. I hold that both emotional responses and changes in other attitudes can be justified by an agent's faults, but I focus on the latter changes of attitude for reasons I have mentioned. It seems to me that there can be instances of blame without moral emotions. In particular, as I said earlier, the content of blame of figures in the distant past seems to me best understood in this way.

Wallace argues that this "parallel" account is inadequate and reflects a superficial understanding of the moral emotions (2011, p. 356). He thus seems to favor an alternative view, suggested by Strawson, according to which the moral emotions explain ("promote") and even justify what Strawson calls withdrawal of good will. Wallace says (discussing the case of friendship) that the presence of emotions such as resentment gives additional reasons for other adjustments in attitude, thereby giving these adjustments a different meaning than they otherwise would have had (p. 357).

It does not seem to me that a feeling of resentment gives one additional reason for withdrawing readiness to trust, cooperate, or sympathize with a person. It is much more plausible to say that feeling resentment involves taking oneself to have reasons for these other adjustments in attitude, reasons provided by the same faults that are reasons for resentment. I do believe, as I have said, that such adjustments have special (condemnatory) meaning in virtue of being made for such reasons. Being made for these reasons seems to me sufficient to make these adjustments an instance of blame, although I would not deny that further special meaning can be given by the fact that they are accompanied by resentment, or what Wolf calls "righteous anger."

The idea that such emotions are essential to blame may be supported by examples that seem to be cases of blame in which there is no modification of intention. I am not positive that there cannot be such cases, although it seems to me that when they are looked at closely some shift in attitude, in addition to emotion, turns out to be involved. Wolf mentions the case of a daughter who borrows her mother's clothes so freely that the mother wants to put a lock on her closet door (2011, p. 336). Contrary to what Wolf says, however, this reaction seems to me to involve a shift in intention as a consequence of seeing one's relationship as impaired. The kind of mother-daughter relationship one has reason to want would involve borrowing and lending clothes with pleasure, trusting the other to exercise the proper restraint and care in doing this. Intentions and expectations of the kind Wolf describes, according to which one does not lend things gladly and take pleasure in sharing, but would prefer to put a lock on one's closet, constitute an impairment in my sense. There is a shift in attitude here that amounts to blame in my view whether it is accompanied by righteous anger or only by disappointment.[15]

To sum up my responses to these objections: It would be foolish to deny that moral emotions such as resentment and indignation are appropriate responses to actions and attitudes that are incompatible with important personal relationships and that these emotions are common elements in the reactions that we call blame. But these emotions are not all that blame normally involves. Other attitudes, such as modified intentions, are also important. They are, I believe, what gives blame its special weightiness and what gives rise to concerns about freedom of the will as a precondition for blame. In order to understand blame, and to respond effectively to these concerns, we need to focus on these reactions. In particular we need to see how they are justified directly by the way another person's actions and attitudes impair his or her relations with others, rather than viewing them merely as concomitants of, or as produced by, emotional reactions.

---

[15] I discuss a similar familial example in my 2008 (p. 73).

6

Blame and Punishment

David Shoemaker

[My] remarks on sanctions are no more than a crude
beginning to a real exploration of this territory. They treat
moral accountability as a legal-like practice, an informal institution
serving the ends of social regulation and/or of retributive and
compensatory justice. No doubt this treatment leaves out crucial
features of moral blame, and taken by itself it would give a very
distorted view. Yet it seems to me an important truth that
blame *does*, among other things, serve these functions.

—GARY WATSON, *TWO FACES OF RESPONSIBILITY*

Contrary to Watson, I do not believe that moral blame serves such functions. In this essay, I want to start to explain why by examining the most plausible recent account of moral blame—T. M. Scanlon's—to see if it involves a "legal-like" understanding of its target at all. To understand whether it does, we will need to explore the nature of punishment, which for most is just what legal (criminal) blame amounts to.[1] I hope by the end to have shown that Scanlon's account cannot plausibly be extended to cover legal blame—and that no other account is likely to be able to do so either—precisely because moral and legal blame have subtly but importantly different structures and functions. This project thus represents an attempt to undermine the nearly universal assumption in the literature of both moral and legal theorists that criminal and moral responsibility are of a piece, that the former entails the latter, and that they

I am grateful to Neal Tognazzini and Justin Coates, both for the invitation to contribute to this volume and also for their extremely insightful comments on an earlier draft of this paper. I am also grateful to those who contributed to a discussion of some of these topics on PEA Soup in May 2011, including especially Mark van Roojen, Tim Scanlon, and Victor Tadros.

[1] Michael S. Moore's hefty collection of essays laying out his grand theory of criminal law, responsibility, and punishment is entitled *Placing Blame* (1997). But curiously, beyond the title, there is not a single indexed mention of blame in the book.

differ only in terms of their specific normative content.[2] The relation between the two is actually far more complex than has previously been appreciated.[3]

1. Scanlonian Blame

An adequate theory of blame will have a wide dataset it needs to account for. It must explain not only public blame but private blame; how blame involves attitude adjustment (and not mere deployment of judgments); how its degree or force may plausibly vary in moral luck cases where different agents' characters and intentions are identical but the outcomes of their actions vary widely; how it can involve a range of attitudinal responses other than anger; how it seems importantly embedded in interpersonal relationships; why some agents may legitimately be blamed and some may not for performing the same action; why blame is an attitude worth preserving in our practices; how apologies may undermine blame; how facts about the standing of the blamer may affect the appropriateness of his or her blaming another; and how blame for actions and attitudes, which are momentary events, typically attaches to agents, which are enduring entities. Earlier theories of blame do rather poorly at accounting for this intimidating set. (I won't go into the details.) Scanlon's theory is explicitly intended to rise to the occasion more successfully.[4]

For Scanlon, blame is a response to a judgment of blameworthiness, which is a judgment that the targeted agent has revealed attitudes that impair his or her relationships to others. To blame the agent, then, is "to take your relationship with him or her to be modified in a way that this judgment of impaired relations holds to be appropriate" (2008, pp. 128–29). This recognition consists in the modification of one's attitudes and dispositions with respect to the blameworthy agent and may include, but is not exhausted by, the following sorts of responses: ceasing to value hanging out with the agent, revising one's typical intentions to confide in or trust him or her, complaining to him or her about the impairment, feeling resentment or other reactive emotions, withdrawing normally friendly exchanges with the agent, refusing to take pleasure in the agent's company, or simply writing the agent off and not dealing with him or her again (see, e.g., pp. 129–30, 132, 134, 137, 140–46). What counts as the appropriate response among these many possibilities depends on the precise

---

[2] For a recent representative sampling of theorists working under this assumption, see Tadros (2005), Duff (2009), Morse (2008), and Husak (2010).

[3] In what follows, I will be focusing exclusively on *holding* responsible in both realms, whereas in "On Criminal and Moral Responsibility" (Shoemaker forthcoming), I focus on the differences between moral and criminal responsibility with respect to *being* responsible.

[4] And I believe it does so more successfully than the other most interesting and important recent account of blame, the one put forward by George Sher (2006). Unfortunately I lack the space here to discuss Sher's view or why I think it stumbles over a few entries in the dataset.

nature of the relationship that has been impaired, for such impairments are violations of the norms defining specific relationships. The view thus takes very seriously the importance of relationships to blame, recognizing the distinctive *meaning* impairments of these relationships have for us.

Scanlon takes one of the distinct advantages of his view to be how it accounts for varying reactions in moral luck cases (2008, pp. 128, 147–52). In the standard presentation, Tom drives home recklessly in two different scenarios; in the first he reaches home safely, but in the second he kills a little girl who runs out into the street. His behavior and psychology are the same in both cases, but blaming reactions are likely to be much different in each. For Scanlon, Tom's reckless driving impairs his relations with us (his neighbors, say) in both scenarios, insofar as he endangers us each time he's out and about. But his reckless driving has a special meaning for the parents of the girl he kills in the second scenario. They have a reason to treat Tom in the two scenarios differently, despite the identical nature of his character, intentions, and behavior in each. He has a fault in both scenarios, but the fault's *significance* is multiplied for the parents, given its causal outcome. Consequently, the response rendered appropriate for them by his actions is very different (pp. 148–50).

I find this account of blame deeply insightful. It does very well with the other features of our moral practices articulated in the dataset as well, especially the notions of private blame and blame *sans* anger. But while it is explicitly pitched as a general account of the nature of blame, full stop, in illustration and defense Scanlon's view draws solely from examples of blame in interpersonal morality, and it is most at home in detailing responses from within friendships and other close personal (moral) relationships. I find the theory to be enormously plausible here. But blame is obviously not restricted to the moral realm; it is also central to the criminal realm. Our question, then, is whether Scanlon's theory may plausibly account for criminal blame as well.

2. Meaning and Criminal Blame

Legal punishment is a response to a judgment of the defendant's (criminal) blameworthiness, involving "the imposition of something that is intended to be burdensome or painful, on a supposed offender for a supposed crime, by a person or body who claims the authority to do so" (Duff 2008). In other words, it is a coercive restriction of his freedom in response to a verdict of guilt, a response presumably rendered appropriate by that verdict.[5] This construal may seem tightly analogous to, if not a direct instantiation of, Scanlonian

---

[5] It is in virtue of its being rendered appropriate by a particular verdict that, at least in part, distinguishes legal punishment from mere coercive detention.

essential to blame. Criminal blaming is simply a response to people who have violated the law without justification or excuse. If their reasons for acting don't acquit them, then they are simply shunted aside as irrelevant to the sort of response the state appropriately has. Consequently, if Scanlonian meaning is found only in one's reasons for acting, and these reasons are irrelevant to the state's response to wrongdoing—punishment—then it looks as if Scanlonian meaning is indeed irrelevant to criminal blame.

This conclusion is too quick, however, for it depends on what turns out to be an unduly restricted understanding of "meaning." To this point, I have taken it to consist in the reasons on which the agent acted. But Scanlon himself suggests a wider understanding in a parenthetical remark: "The agent's reasons for acting (*and the fact that other considerations did not count for him as reasons against so acting*) are what constitute his attitude toward others, and what have the implications that blame involves, in the account I am offering" (2008, pp. 152–53, my emphasis). This addition would seem to make my thesis much less defensible, for if the considerations against my performing some criminal action simply didn't count as reasons for me when I performed it, then punishing me for that offense would seem straightforwardly to count as punishing me in response to the meaning of my action, a response independent of the reasons on which I *did* act advanced in any of my defenses. As Tadros has put it, "The definition of any offence must include a feature that, in the absence of a defence, renders perpetrating it impermissible all things considered. And in fulfilling the conditions of the offence, in the absence of a defence, the defendant must at least have failed to give due weight to this feature."[11] If this is right, then failure of this sort would constitute Scanlonian meaning on the parenthetical amendment, and so punishment for such an offense would be a response to the meaning of the defendant's action, placing it squarely under the rubric of Scanlonian blame after all.

Nevertheless, I don't think this is right. Consider what might at first seem a good illustration of Tadros's objection, namely, rape statutes, which typically specify that the prosecution establish that the defendant acted either knowingly or recklessly with regard to the victim's lack of consent.[12] This lack of consent is thus a reason some defendant might ignore, and if so, perhaps it would count as a good example of Scanlon's parenthetically amended notion of meaning. To the extent the state punishes such a defendant, it would seem to be doing so in response to his ignoring a consideration crucial to making what he did illegal.

---

[11] See Tadros's comments on May 23, 2011, at 10:28 p.m. on PEA Soup: http://peasoup.typepad.com/peasoup/2011/05/scanlon-on-blame-part-3-criminal-blame-and-meaning.html#tp.

[12] See, e.g., California Penal Code § 251.1: http://law.justia.com/codes/california/2009/pen/261-269.html.

Nevertheless, all that's established in such cases is *mens rea*, and to establish *mens rea* is merely to establish that a criminal action properly attaches to an agent, not that there is some particular meaning attached to that agent's actions. It establishes, in other words, *that* someone performed the action in question, not *why* he did it. This way of putting it points to aspects of a distinction between different conceptions of responsibility I have defended elsewhere, namely, *attributability* and *answerability* (Shoemaker 2011). To be attributability-responsible for A is, roughly, for A to flow from or reflect one's character as a practical agent. Typically this will involve A's causal dependence on some motive with which the agent is identified (e.g., a motive depending on the agent's cares, commitments, or evaluative judgments). Attributability is solely about *structure*, about the way actions are tied to agents, warranting the move from evaluation of actions (momentary events) to evaluation of agents (persisting entities) in virtue of those actions expressing the agent's practical self. To be answerable, on the other hand, is for one to be able to cite the evaluative reasons one took to justify A, and the aim of an answerability demand (in both morality and the law) is to hear and evaluate those reasons. Answerability is thus solely about *content*, about the nature of the reasons relevant to one's acting, so it is obviously one's answers to this demand that will reveal meaning. Consequently, even if one thought that actions were attributable to agents only in virtue of their issuing from the agent's reasons, this would not yet create a tight connection between attributability and meaning, simply because the fact that some action flows from one's reasons remains entirely distinct from the fact of what those reasons turn out to be.[13]

Return, then, to the issue of *mens rea* as it pertains to ignoring certain reasons. "Astuteness to consent" may indeed be a critical condition for not being a rapist,[14] but the fact of a defendant's failure of astuteness in sexual matters only provides prosecutors with one of the tools to show jurors that the crime can be attributed to him. The crime must be reflective of his practical identity in order to be his in the way that grounds punishment. Now *that* the crime flowed from his practical agency (he wasn't sleepwalking or brainwashed into performing it, say) doesn't yet tell us a thing about the first aspect of Scanlonian meaning, namely, the reasons he actually performed *the-action-now-attributable-to-him*. But more to the point, it also doesn't tell us anything about the second (parenthetical) aspect, for while attributing a rape to a defendant does require making reference to the fact that lack of consent didn't count for him against his sexually penetrating the victim, the relevant reasons he must have failed to consider in order to make punishing him for the rape count as Scanlonian blame would have to be instead the *reasons against the rape.*

---

[13] Thanks to the editors for pressing me to address this distinction in more detail.
[14] For this phrase, see Gardner 2007, pp. 26–27.

In other words, the fact that he failed to consider the available reasons regarding the victim's lack of consent was, in part, what *made* his action fall under the criminal rubric of "rape," and so what also, in part, made that criminal action (the rape) properly attributable to him. But Scanlonian blame (in its parenthetical aspect) is explicitly supposed to track a different fact, namely, the fact that the defendant failed to consider the available reasons *against rape*. It is only this last fact that pertains to the agent's attitudes and thus the meaning of his action. It is what the perpetrator is blamed for in the realm of interpersonal morality. But it is not what the perpetrator is punished for in the realm of criminal law. Instead, in that realm, he is punished *for the rape*. The reasons he performed *that* action, or the fact that he failed to consider reasons against it, would seem to be irrelevant to that extent.[15]

What all this comes down to is whether *motive* matters to criminal punishment, as it clearly does for Scanlonian blameworthiness. My answer is obviously no, most generally because I think the reasons at the root of criminality and the reasons at the root of immorality have different structural relations to the fundamentally different values on which they each rest, as well as to the values and aims in each set of responding practices. Start with morality. Scanlon's own account of morality is contractualist, but the reasons he cites for us to do what morality requires ostensibly rest on a valuable relation that many noncontractualists also believe underlies morality, namely, "a relation of mutual recognition" (1998, p. 162). There is great value in living with others on terms of equal regard, a kind of "mutual concern that, ideally, we all have toward other rational beings" (Scanlon 2008, p. 140). And it is this relation that, for Scanlon, gives rise to various moral proscriptions: one ought not do those things that impair this relation; that is, one ought not *fail to regard* one's fellows in the appropriate way. This is clearly a guideline about the *attitudes* one ought to have toward one's fellows, and it makes the normative connection between mutual regard, immorality, and blame very tight. The reasons against various sorts of interpersonal treatment derive from the lack of regard expressed by such treatment, so to the extent I am blamed for such an act, I am

---

[15] But aren't the reasons he ignored regarding the victim's lack of consent just *the same as* the reasons he ignored against rape, such that to establish attributability here just is to establish the relevant sort of meaning? No. Suppose this agent were considering raping someone. This amounts to considering whether to sexually penetrate someone where the victim's lack of consent would be either discounted or ignored. Were he to engage in this act, he would be ignoring reasons regarding the victim's lack of consent. That's what (in part) would make it rape. But in considering whether to perform this action, he could be weighing an entirely different set of considerations, perhaps including a variety of prudential reasons against raping people. And some of these considerations will be reasons specifically about ignoring or taking seriously the more particular reasons regarding the victim's lack of consent. To perform a rape (voluntarily), therefore, will indeed include ignoring or discounting certain reasons about the victim's consent, but the issue of meaning, as I understand it, must go to whether one ignored or discounted the reasons there were *against ignoring or discounting these reasons about victim's consent*. (I expand on this point in the section on hate crimes.)

blamed *for this failure to regard*, that is, for my poor attitude. In other words, the only way to violate the key value at the root of interpersonal morality, on this picture, is via one's poor motives. This is why I may be blamed even where I haven't performed an injurious act, just in case my motive in doing what I did still embodied the relevant lack of regard.

For most criminal theorists, however, the value giving rise to criminal proscriptions is *harm reduction*. Furthermore, the normative connection between harm, criminalization, and punishment seems very indirect and loose, for a few reasons. Consider first the relation between criminalization and harm. Instead of criminalizing X because X causes harm, by far the more sensible justification is to criminalize X because the *failure* to do so will cause harm.[16] For example, John Gardner argues that the best case for why rape is illegal is that failing to criminalize it would increase violations of people's rights to sexual autonomy, and this would harm both those who were sexually violated (and aware of it) and those whose level of fear about not being protected from such violations would increase (2007, pp. 29–30). But this justification allows that someone still performs a criminal action even when his raping someone involves no harm whatsoever. Such a possibility is illustrated by Gardner's case of "pure rape," where the victim is forever oblivious to what occurred (perhaps she was voluntarily intoxicated to the point of unconsciousness) and so never felt violated, was physiologically aroused at the time (so no physical injuries occurred), the rapist wore a condom, and the events never came to light. The victim was therefore rendered no worse off, either physically or psychologically, than she otherwise would have been; her life was not changed at all for the worse (pp. 5–8).[17] What this means, though, is that the reason(s) against someone's performing this variation of the criminal action cannot directly or even ultimately be derived from the value grounding its criminality: *that it will be harmful* is no reason against committing a harmless rape. Furthermore, someone could be guilty of this criminal act regardless of whether he in fact paid attention to the specific reasons grounding its *being* a criminal act

---

[16] Gardner makes a powerful case for this view of the relation between harm and criminalization in "The Wrongness of Rape" (2007, ch. 1).

[17] Gardner notes the rarity of such a case, as well as the fact that it would never be brought to court (as it would, by stipulation, never come to light), but this is a way to drive home the point: surely such an act would still be wrong. The hard question is why, absent harm? As noted, Gardner's answer is that it is a violation of the victim's right to sexual autonomy. One could of course still insist that such rights violations are harmful in and of themselves, but this is to lean on a very capacious understanding of harm, one that defenders of harm-grounded criminalization themselves don't even typically advocate. Think about it in another, perhaps analogous, case. It is plausible to think that the wrongness of trespassing is ultimately grounded on property rights violations. It seems to stretch the term beyond recognition, though, to say that when I cut through your property without you or anyone knowing it—and so trespass—I have *harmed* you thereby. Nevertheless, failure to criminalize trespassing would surely involve a variety of harms worth preventing.

(i.e., that failure to criminalize would increase harm—indeed how could one even pay attention to such reasons?). Consequently, punishing someone for rape would not legitimately be a response to his ignoring the relevant values underlying the law or the specific reasons grounding criminalization of the act he performed, contrary to how blame for the rape would be tightly tied to the rapist's disregard for the victim in the world of interpersonal morality.

This disconnection between the reasons for criminalization and the reasons against performing the criminal acts is found throughout the law. Note the following introduction of a criminal statute against the theft of motor fuel in Illinois: "It is the public policy of this State that the substantial burden placed upon the economy of this State resulting from the rising incidence of theft of motor fuel is a matter of grave concern to the people of this State who have a right to be protected in their health, safety and welfare from the effects of this crime."[18] The motivation and justification for this law is to ease the economic burden on the state (given citizens' "grave concern" about it). This is the reason sufficient to render the immoral action of fuel theft illegal; that is, it is the reason citizenry rights in this morally loaded zone are deemed worthy of legal protection. Do we think the punishment of a defendant found guilty of fuel theft who failed to take seriously these economic considerations would be a response to that failure? It seems obvious that the answer is no. That a fuel thief discounted or ignored the economic consequences of lots of people stealing fuel would be irrelevant, both to a determination of his guilt for the offense and any punishment response to that guilty verdict. If these are the reasons being ignored, therefore, and there are no additional reasons for avoiding the action the ignoring of which is something to which the state responds, then its response won't be a response to any sort of meaning. (I will address whether there are in fact no additional reasons for avoiding the action momentarily, though.)

Returning to the contrast between the interpersonal morality and the law with respect to the normative connections between its key features, consider second the loose relation between criminalization and punishment. As Tadros points out, on any plausible construal of criminalization, given that some criminal regulation is just, it will be in the interests of the state that people adhere to it. The state thus must also have an interest in responding to breaches of that regulation, for otherwise it would have had no business making the regulation criminal in the first place (see Tadros 2011). But there seems to still be a gap here between the state's interest in regulating X and its interest in punishing for breaches of that regulation. After all, the aim served in regulating X, and thus in trying to get as many people as possible to adhere to the regulation, may not be served by individual cases of punishing for breaches of

---

[18] 720 ILCS 5/, Criminal Code of 1961, http://www.ilga.gov/legislation/ilcs/ilcs4.asp?DocName=072 000050HArt%2E+16K&ActID=1876&ChapterID=53&SeqStart=46300000&;SeqEnd=47200000.

that regulation. One might think this is because criminalization and punishment are grounded on two very different sorts of justifications, but I think instead that, regardless of the reasons for the state interest in regulating specific sorts of conduct, justice demands that all citizens are equally subject to its purview. In other words, equality before the law requires that prohibited conduct is prohibited for all. So the reason for the prohibition per se is quite distinct from the reason for the *universality* of the prohibition. The fact, then, that the state has an interest in people's adhering to its regulations won't necessarily be the same interest it has in responding to their individual breaches, for the latter might simply be a requirement of upholding equality before the law, and this requirement may be met in punishment even in the absence of setbacks to the interests the state had in criminalizing the relevant conduct in the first place. If so, then the reasons defendants have or ignore relevant to their criminal breaches may be quite irrelevant to the state's reasons for responses to those breaches. Once again, this is very different from the extremely tight structural relations between wrongness and the aims of Scanlonian blame in the interpersonal moral realm, where blaming responses are rendered appropriate only in virtue of the offender's violation of relationship norms where this violation crucially reveals the lack of regard impinging the value at the foundation of morality.

Our final question, then, is whether there might still possibly be some overarching reason against criminal breaches, the ignoring of which constitutes the Scanlonian meaning of one's actions to which the state could be responding in punishing someone. There are two types of possible reasons here: prudential and moral. The former can quickly be dismissed as irrelevant, given that failing to count some purely prudential consideration as a reason against performing the crime wouldn't express any meaning for one's relationships with *others*. Considering only moral reasons, then, the most plausible contender would be a general reason of regard. Specifically, the reasons against breaching the criminal law, we could say, most fundamentally boil down to paying insufficient regard to the interests of others.

I don't think this possibility works, however, primarily because it is not the sort of reason that can be codified in the law. It is too vague to be a realistic target of investigation in criminal trials. How could we possibly determine the threshold for "insufficiency" in regard, for example? And even if we could articulate a determinate threshold, it is quite conceivable for criminal activity nevertheless not to cross it, to be compatible with sufficient regard. I could, for instance, take extremely seriously your interests in doing what you want with your property but still steal from you because I weigh my own interests as slightly more important than yours. Finally, there is a significant body of criminal law to which the notion of regard of this sort doesn't even seem to apply, namely, regulatory offenses like tax fraud. Here there may be no "interests of others" at all that were disregarded, as the obligation to pay the amount of taxes one owes doesn't necessarily require paying attention to *anyone else's* interests, so punishment for it couldn't (uncontroversially) count as a failure of the relevant sort of regard.

The main worry, however, is this: to punish for insufficient regard for the interests of others is, at the end of the day, just to require *sufficient* regard, that is, to make it part of the criminal code that citizens must pay attention to a certain class of reasons, at least when they are considering criminal breaches. This would be an outrageous demand, however. It can be no legitimate business of the state what actual attitude we have toward one another in interacting; rather its demands for our interactions cannot go beyond requiring that we behave toward one another *as if* we had sufficient regard. It is only our failing to *act* in this way that provides legitimate targets for state punishment.

To conclude, then, criminal blame (punishment) is not a response to the defendant in virtue of his attitudes; it is instead a response to him solely in virtue of what he has done—his performance of the action properly attributable to him—and the response may well be for reasons drawn from values independent of those at the root of criminal wrongness (e.g., reasons drawn from the value of equality before the law rather than harm prevention). In Scanlon's account, however, blame is a response to the agent in virtue of her attitudes, and its appropriateness is tied directly to the values underlying her relationship impairment. Scanlonian blame, therefore, is not criminal blame.

3. An Objection: Degrees of Murder and Hate Crimes

It may be thought that my analysis, while plausible for a significant chunk of the criminal law, nevertheless stumbles over some pretty obvious cases of state punishment in response to criminal attitudes, namely, those attitudes reflected in varying degrees of murder and, most obviously, hate crimes. Regarding murder by degrees, as Scanlon has put it in responding to an early version of my arguments in this paper, "Distinctions between various crimes, such as manslaughter, first degree murder and second degree murder are a matter of the agent's attitudes. This strongly suggests to me that criminal penalties are, among other things, expressions of blame [in] the sense I describe."[19] Even more so, it would seem, with hate crimes, which are precisely a matter of the defendant's motives in action, motives involving the targeting of certain people because of their various hated aspects. While my initial instinct was to note these cases as exceptional, I now think showing why they are actually included under my rubric serves to illustrate the overall points here quite nicely.

---

[19] T. M. Scanlon, on May 19, 2011, at 9:51 a.m., on http://peasoup.typepad.com/peasoup/2011/05/scanlon-on-blame-part-3-criminal-blame-and-meaning.html#tp.

Start with the degrees of murder. The difference between murder and man-slaughter is typically put in terms of only the former's involving "malice afore-thought," where this has come to be primarily about the agent's deliberate intent: where you deliberately intend to kill or inflict grievous bodily harm on someone, it is murder; where you kill someone unlawfully but without delib-erate intent to do so, it is manslaughter. And the difference between first- and second-degree murder is a matter of the deliberateness and goal of the inten-tion: if the action was squarely aimed at ending the victim's life, it is usually of the first degree; if some brutality was done to the victim where it was likely the action would end the victim's life, it is usually of the second degree. It may thus clearly seem that these distinctions are among types of *attitudes*, such that punishing for their commission is punishing for their meaning.

Not so, however, for the various types of unlawful killing are really being distinguished here in terms of their specific types of *intentions*, alongside the amount and type of planning that went into them. In other words, they are distinguished in terms of the conditions of *mens rea*, the crucial component in the categorization of the specific action performed that makes it properly at-tributable to the defendant. If I kill someone, what specific kind of killing gets attached to me for purposes of the trial and subsequent punishment depends on the precise nature of my intention and the role my deliberations played in its formation and execution. But my *motive*, the reasons I performed the ac-tion (or the fact that I ignored certain reasons against it), is not relevant to whether that action is truly mine and so could not justly be the object of the state's sanctioning response.

But are motives really never relevant to attributability? To the extent that what *counts* as an intention is determined in part by the reasons motivating the agent, they surely are (see, e.g., Tadros 2005, p. 218). But all that matters with respect to attributability is *that* there is a motive fixing the aim of the intention on which the relevant action depends. The nature of that motive, however—what the precise reasons making up the motive consist in—is irrelevant to the establishment of the attributability relation. Consider an example. You and I are arguing, and you insult my mother, so I form the intention to punch you in the face. What explains and motivates my intention (i.e., my aim or objective) is my reason for doing so: the fact that it's worthwhile to defend her honor, suppose. But when I punch you, this action is attributable to me solely in vir-tue of its flowing from my intention (which, to make this a case of robust attributability, is endorsed by my "deep self," let us say). The precise nature of my reason for punching you (my motive), though, is irrelevant to whether this structural attributability relation obtains; it could have obtained if my inten-tion to punch you were rooted in any of a wide variety of reasons (e.g., I really wanted to smash that mosquito on your nose, or I cannot stand the way you say "muddah"). So the existence of motives is relevant to the establishment of attributability, but the nature of motives is not, and it is their nature that matters for Scanlonian meaning and blame, whereas only attributability matters for criminal punishment.

This point is actually—surprisingly—brought out more clearly in the case of hate crimes.[20] Here motives are indeed explicitly tracked: Did the defendant assault some victim *because* he or she fell into some class of persons deemed worthy of protection by the state? Nevertheless, the motive here too is relevant only to a determination of *mens rea*, which, again, is about the attribution of the action to the defendant via the defendant's intention (in the standard case). If the defendant's intention was rooted in the specific motive of hate (or, more precisely, of targeting a member of a certain class of citizens *qua* member of that class), then the action we attribute to him counts as a hate crime thereby. But then to punish him for the *meaning* of that action would have to be to punish him in response to his reasons for performing (or ignoring relevant reasons against performing) *the hate crime* that has thereby been attributed to him. His motive for *that* action, however, is once again irrelevant to either attribution of or punishment for it.

4. Punishment and Authority

One response to the host of differences I have articulated between Scanlonian and criminal blame would be to say that Scanlon's account of blame is just importantly incomplete. I would like to explore another response instead, which is that perhaps the functions of criminal blame are just different from the functions of interpersonal moral blame, given the different kind of relation that obtains between blamer and blamed in each. This suggests that there could in fact be multiple *conceptions* of blame. Scanlon, then, is perhaps best construed as offering an account of only one such conception, namely, interpersonal moral blame.

What would make moral and criminal blame so different? The basic idea is this: legitimate sanctioning as the primary function of a practice sensibly takes place only within the context of an asymmetrical authority relation, a relation that obtains in the criminal realm but not in ordinary interpersonal morality. To see what I mean, consider examples of nonstate sanctioning. The paradigm

---

[20] The phrase "hate crimes" includes a grab bag of statutes, some of which criminalize threats, injuries, and damages because of actual or perceived "race, color, religion, ancestry, national origin, disability, gender, or sexual orientation" (California Penal Code § 422.6), whereas others merely allow sentence enhancement for actions motivated in this way. These latter are viewed as offenses involving "aggravating circumstances." In what follows I am exclusively concerned with the former. While the latter might make it seem as if punishment in such cases is a response to the meaning of the criminal's action, this is true only about the *amount* or *degree* of punishment, not about the fact of punishment itself. To know what that involves, we must look to the nature of the criminal offense, which is its target.

cases of punishment in our nonstate dealings with one another take place in the family, between parents and children. Parents punish their children—by spanking, grounding, and/or issuing time-outs—for violations of the rules of the household. Their doing so is grounded in their authority *over* their children, who themselves are proper subjects of that authority. This relation is asymmetrical: children do not have the authority to punish their parents, even when their parents violate the rules of the household. Punishment in this world is done in response to a judgment of wrongdoing, and the response has as its fundamental aim a sanction of some sort *for* that wrongdoing.[21]

There are other nonstate arenas in which this sort of sanctioning takes place: in the military, where soldiers are made to "drop and give me twenty"; in schools, where students are suspended or expelled; on the job, where workers may be fired or suspended; and on sports teams, where the rule-violating players have to run laps. But what all of these cases have in common with the parent-child case is an asymmetrical authority relation: someone is in charge of others who are legitimate subjects of that authority and are thus legitimately subject to that authority's sanctions. And most important, the authority's responses have as their fundamental aim those sanctions. True, the sanctions may have a communicative element—expressing the authority's anger about or disapproval of the subject's conduct—but that's not a necessary component of them. Sometimes they are just what the subjects get for breaking the rules (e.g., having to run laps for being late to practice).

Contrast these sorts of cases with paradigm cases of interpersonal moral blame. Suppose I discover that you, someone I thought was my friend and ally, have been making fun of me behind my back to my enemies. In blaming you, I will likely confront you, expressing my anger and hurt, calling you names and swearing off seeing or dealing with you again. However, what I cannot legitimately or even sensibly do, it seems, is *punish* you in any sense akin to the cases above. I simply lack the authority to spank you, ground you, give you a time-out, or make you run laps or do push-ups. You are not my subject, in other words. We are instead moral equals, bearing a symmetrical relation to one another within the moral community. So while I may have the authority to make certain demands of you as a fellow member of that community, I don't have the requisite authority *over* you to legitimately carry out anything more if you fail to comply.[22] I lack the standing to coercively enforce the rules of

---

[21] Notice also that this response doesn't necessarily track the *meaning* of the child's conduct either.

[22] Locke is instructive here. According to him, it is only in the state of nature "where one man comes by power *over* another," specifically the power (and right) to punish those who violate the laws of nature (*Second Treatise of Government*, ch. 2, para. 8; my emphasis). This is one of the key rights we give up to the state when entering a civil society, though, such that we no longer have such power over others. On the notion of equality in the moral community and the authority at least to make demands, however, see Darwall (2006).

friendship by depriving you of anything to which you would otherwise have rights.[23] (You don't have a right, for example, to my being pleasant around you or my not getting upset with you.) So while I may rail and pout and bluster and cry and condemn, I simply have no authority to punish.[24]

One might resist this conclusion by pointing out that, in liberal democracies, for example, the authority-over relation grounding legitimate punishment is actually derivative from the authority-between-equals relation central to interpersonal morality. As with the military, we might say, the authority-over relation has been at least tacitly granted, and thereby grounded, by those subject to that authority, so that it is generated by the wider governing authority-between-equals relation. Punishment therefore could still count as *indirectly* meted out and undergone by moral equals, as it is an authority-over relation nevertheless created by and subject to the demands of authority-between-equals.

I believe something like this story is actually true. All it does, though, is reaffirm my general point, insofar as it identifies a subset of interpersonal morality that has been created to operate in a fundamentally different way from the rest of interpersonal morality. Specifically, on this story, we have created pockets of moral interaction in which we have agreed that some of the ordinary relations and interactions of morality don't apply: we have agreed, as equals, to be unequal in certain arenas. But like autonomously giving up one's autonomy, there is no (autonomously) going back: once the relevant (criminal) zone has been entered, the ordinary rules governing day-to-day equal interaction are no longer applicable. Even if its justificatory roots are in democratic agreement, then, punishment is no legitimate part of blame between moral equals.

Hurting often seems to be, though. If I attack you with a golf club after discovering numerous texts on your phone revealing that you've been cheating on me, I aim to hurt you in response to your infidelity. Why wouldn't this count as sanctioning of the relevant sort? While admittedly this sort of response often occurs within personal relationships and it is perfectly understandable, it is nevertheless illegitimate because immoral. As Scanlon himself points out, "Even those who have no regard for the justifiability of their actions toward others retain their basic moral rights—they still have claims on us not to be hurt or killed, to be helped when they are in dire need, and to have us

---

[23] For this understanding of punishment, see Bedau and Kelly (2010).

[24] Aren't there some interpersonal moral exchanges that involve an authority-over relation? Aside from those indirect exchanges to be discussed next, what about something like promising, wherein it might seem that a promisor bestows some sort of authority-over relation on a promisee, such that the promisee has justification for punishing the promisor for his noncompliance? I don't believe this example is promising. All that a jilted promisee has in such a case is the authority to *demand*, but not *exact*, restitution (or belated performance).

honor promises we have made to them" (2008, p. 142). For one member of the moral community to deliberately aim suffering at another is to violate the target's legitimate claims, something no individual member of the moral community has standing (i.e., authority) to do. To the extent that sanctions generally, or punishment specifically, are legitimate, then, they could only be made so by the aforementioned authority-*over* relation alongside a compelling justification (e.g., self-defense, deterrence, retribution, character building, or something else).

Nevertheless, *anger* (or resentment) is surely an appropriate response, isn't it? And if so, why isn't that alone sufficient to constitute a punishment? After all, most of us suffer when others are angry at us. And blame can definitely include deprivations: when I blame you for violating the terms of our friendship, I may deprive you of my company, trust, and cheery disposition. Consequently, you may well *take* my blame as punishment, as a sanction. So why isn't it?

First, and most important, neither anger nor blame in and of itself requires any expression at all. I may merely simmer with resentment behind your back or be quietly disappointed with you without your being any the wiser. To the extent both are responses to, and are rendered appropriate by, my judgments of your blameworthiness, they both count as (Scanlonian) blame. But insofar as you are not aware of my blame, you will have no reason to take what I am doing as a sanction.

What, though, of *expressions* of anger, of what Angela Smith calls "active blame" (2007, p. 470)? Granted, it will be only when I express my anger to you that you suffer, that you take my expression as punishment, but isn't that sufficient to put it on a par with criminal blame in at least these instances? No. There is a crucial tripartite distinction about relevant aims and functions to pay attention to here. First, there is what the function of active blame consists in. Second, there is what the target of active blame (the blamed) takes its function to consist in. Third, there is what the blamer takes the function of her active blaming to consist in.[25] I am here interested only in the first, and I will come back to what I think it is shortly. The second and third may diverge wildly, though, from the actual function of active blame itself, depending on the sensitivities or pathologies of each of the parties. While anger may be appropriate in response to your actions, in expressing it I may wield it like a club, yelling and screaming, aiming to really hurt you for what you did; alternatively I may wield it like a shiv, hissing a quick and devastating slice of sarcasm, perhaps, aiming to unsettle you or undermine your confidence; yet again, I may spew it petulantly, aiming at currying your favor with my moxie or simply garnering your attention. And regardless of these aims, you may take my active

---

[25] I am grateful to the editors for pressing me to make these distinctions explicit.

blame in a variety of respects as well, believing my anger is meant to hurt you, sure, but also possibly believing my anger is meant to unsettle you or curry your favor, and without these beliefs necessarily being at all in sync with my own aims in expressing it.

So what is the function of active blame? As blame itself is simply an appropriate response to a judgment of blameworthiness, the function of active blame must be to be a *communicative* response rendered appropriate by such a judgment. And what is being communicated? Most generally it would seem to be a communication of the basic moral demand, the claim we have on one another for goodwill (or at least no bad will).[26] Anger, remonstration, writing the other off: these are all—often emotional and dramatic—ways of stating to the target, reminding the target of, or shoving the target's face in the basic norm for reasonable regard that we judge him to have violated. Now the targets of such expressions may indeed suffer as a result. But that is not the function of the expressions, for a very simple reason: if successful, forceful communication of the basic demand for regard could occur without inducing such suffering, the point, the intelligibility, of such expression would nevertheless remain intact. Indeed this may be how to categorize the cases Gary Watson mentions of Gandhi and King, those who held their oppressors to account without any of the more "retributive sentiments" that many have taken to be sanctions (2004, pp. 257–58).

This is not true of punishment, however. Even if communication is an essential part of its function (e.g., it expresses citizens' condemnation of and to defendants), it is a kind of communication that is in actuality inseparable from the deliberate causing of suffering constitutive of punishment in the first place. Indeed, in the criminal realm, to say that punishment has a communicative function is just "to say simply that certain forms of hard treatment have become the conventional symbols of public reprobation" (Feinberg 1970, p. 100). It is only via the infliction of suffering that the message of public condemnation can currently be communicated, on this story. But given that there is no such similar suffering attached to communication of the basic demand for goodwill in the interpersonal moral realm, hurting via expressed anger is purely incidental to its function, and in fact may often be, as already noted, immoral.

5. Conclusion

Scanlon's account of moral blame does not extend to criminal blame, which must first and foremost be about the infliction of punishment (or sanctions generally) in response to judgments of guilt. The diagnosis of this disanalogy

---

[26] See, e.g., Watson (2004, pp. 225ff) and McKenna (2012). For a very insightful alternative Strawsonian story (one where the fundamental aim of reactive attitudes isn't in fact communicative), see Deigh (2012).

is, I believe, found in the distinct fundamental functions of the two realms, functions defined and restricted by the importantly different relations that obtain between blamer and blamed in each realm. While there is a kind of authority operating in both, in the moral realm the authority relation is between moral equals and so restricts appropriate (active) blaming to the addressing of demands to one another, whereas in the criminal realm the relation between state and citizen is an asymmetrical authority-*over* relation, one that is necessary to generate the possibility of appropriate punishing or sanctioning. I believe these distinct relations and functions serve to prevent moral and criminal blame from being analogous, therefore, in the way most have assumed they are.

I have thus suggested that two different conceptions of blame may be operative here. In the criminal realm, it consists in punishment—the infliction of suffering—and it is meted out legitimately only by those who stand in the requisite authority-over relation to the defendant. In the interpersonal moral realm, blame (at least on Scanlon's highly plausible account) is a response to relationship-impairing attitudes, responses that cannot legitimately involve the infliction of suffering insofar as they are responses by moral equals and are restricted by our moral claims on one another. To the extent moral blame is active, it has a communicative function with no necessary tie to any associated inflicted costs on its target, whereas in criminal blame the associated sanctions just are the method by which any communicative purpose is carried out. Finally, moral blame is a response to the meaning of an agent's actions, whereas criminal blame is not; it is instead merely a response to criminal wrongdoing. These differences strongly suggest we are simply working with two distinct conceptions of blame in each realm.

Of course, I have examined only one theory of blame, and so it might well be possible still to construct a unifying account for both realms. At this point, though, I have no idea what such an account would look like, and I suspect that, because of these myriad differences between the criminal justice system and our interactions within the moral community, it will at the very least not be easily forthcoming.

7

Directed Blame and Conversation

Michael McKenna

What is blame's nature, and what are its norms? In what follows, I shall answer these questions by reference to a conversational theory of moral responsibility. According to this theory, blame—at least a distinctive kind of blame—can be accounted for in terms of its communicative role in an interpersonal exchange between members of a moral community. The view I defend is broadly Strawsonian insofar as a restricted class of emotions plays a pivotal role. Ultimately I shall offer an account of blame's norms that makes room for the familiar thought that blame is *deserved* by one who is blameworthy.

1. The Challenge of Theorizing about Blame

Despite the pervasiveness of the phenomenon in ordinary life, blame is an elusive notion. It is maddeningly hard to nail down a theory that gets the extension even close to right. This is shown by the diversity of strikingly different views about its nature. On some views, to blame is just to engage in a kind of punishment (Smart 1961). On others, to blame is most fundamentally to register a criticism of an agent's free conduct (Zimmerman 1988) or, instead, of how she exercised her judgment-sensitive capacities (Smith 2005). On yet others, it is a matter of altering one's relationship with the blamed party in light of that party's wrongful impairment to the relationship (Scanlon 2008). Another option has it that to blame is to believe that a person has acted badly or has a bad character and to desire that this not be so (Sher 2006). On a similar proposal, to blame is to perceive that a person acted wrongly and with ill will, and to do

I would like to thank Justin Coates and Neal Tognazzini for their hard work in putting this volume together and for inviting me to contribute. My treatment of blame in this essay is built on work done in my recent *Responsibility and Conversation* (2012). I have framed things slightly differently here, since in this case blame is the immediate focus, whereas in my 2012 it was part of a larger discussion of moral responsibility. For helpful comments, I would like to thank the editors as well as Derk Pereboom and Guido Pincione.

so from the standpoint of caring about morality (Arpaly 2006). Then there is the view that blaming is a matter of reacting to the one blamed with a pertinently charged emotion, such as resentment or indignation (Strawson 1962). This list is far from exhaustive.

The task of accounting for blame is made all the harder given that there are different notions of responsibility. It's not just that there are different theories of what responsibility is; it's that there are different kinds of responsibility to theorize about and a multiplicity of theories directed at these different kinds. Blame, as one member in the family of responsibility concepts, is caught up in this mix. So it is especially challenging to get focused on the proper range of phenomena and the attendant concept(s) of blame.

There is, furthermore, a wide variability to the permissible modes of manifesting blame. This complicates matters even more. You and I might both be entitled to blame a colleague for some bit of scandalous conduct, and yet we might fittingly do so in ways that are wildly divergent. How, then, might one get an account of blame up and running?

I shall proceed by focusing on prototypical cases of blame, which I shall characterize in terms of *directed blame*. I'll seek a means of explaining just these and will forgo any attempt at an exhaustive account of blame. Nevertheless, the central cases of blame I will focus on are, I think, representative of what many have in mind when reflecting on the nature and norms of blame. My hope is that other cases of blame—cases within, so to speak, the extension but closer to the periphery of the concept—can be explained at least in part by reference to my treatment of the prototypical cases. I'll begin by calling attention to several points on a conceptual map.

2. Some Preliminary Considerations regarding the Nature and Norms of Blame

Consider first responsibility. I am interested in blame only as it bears on questions of moral responsibility, as opposed to, say, legal responsibility. As for moral responsibility, many philosophers have argued that there is more than one sort (e.g., Haji 1998; Fischer and Tognazzini 2011; Scanlon 1998; Shoemaker 2011; Watson 1996; Zimmerman 1988). Here, I wish to focus just on moral responsibility in the accountability sense. Moral responsibility in this sense involves the possibility of holding an agent to account for her conduct, and thereby seeing her as properly responsive to our demands and sanctions. Such an agent is one who can be expected to acknowledge and comply with others' moral expectations. When she falls short, she is taken to be justly liable to burdensome modes of response from those who are warranted in holding her to account.

Now consider blame. Moral blame as it bears on accountability involves a negative evaluation of, for instance, an agent's action in a manner that is in some way linked to the appropriateness of holding her to account for so acting. The natural thought, when focusing on this sort of blame, is to attend to cases in which a person is held directly to account by another who openly blames her as a direct means of making moral demands, expressing expectations, reprimanding, or something similar. But care needs to be taken at this point, since accountability-blame is *not* limited to such cases. We often blame others—in the pertinent sense—in their absence. Also, we sometimes conceal our blame from everyone.

It is useful to distinguish between *private blame, overt blame*, and *directed blame*. Private blame involves adopting a blaming attitude toward someone but concealing the outward behavioral manifestations. Overt blame involves adopting such an attitude and making it manifest in one's conduct. This can be done in the absence of the blamed; obvious examples involve blaming the dead. *Directed blame* is a form of overt blame manifested in the presence of the blamed party. Indeed it is outwardly directed *at* the blamed party.[1]

Instances of directed blame are relatively rare by comparison with instances of private blame and overt blame that is not directed. Or, at any rate, that is my impression. Nevertheless I wish to focus just on directed blame. In my estimation, it's the more fundamental notion. Hence, despite the relative rarity of directed blame, I believe it is best to treat such cases as prototypical and then seek to explain other cases, such as cases of private blame, by reference to our understanding of the more fundamental cases.

Thus far I have engaged in preliminary conceptual spadework in the service of getting clear on the question of blame's nature. But what of its norms? Here we can distinguish three questions. The first concerns the normative warrant for an agent's being to blame. What justifies its being the case that an agent ought to be blamed? The second concerns the standing or license one has who is rightly positioned to blame the party who is blameworthy. What makes it permissible (or obligatory?) for this person or that, but not some other, to do the blaming? While the first of these two questions naturally points to the agent who is to blame, the second points to the one who does the blaming. A third question concerns the normative force of blame—the sting it putatively ought to have when directed at one who is blameworthy. Why and how ought a blamed person regard as burdensome the blame directed at her? In my estimation, this question naturally points at the (potential) relationship between the blamer and the blamed. The first of these questions we can call the question of *normative warrant*; the second we can call the question of *normative*

---

[1] Note that directed blame, in the technical sense I have assigned to it here, is second-personal. So it is most fitting to focus on cases in which one blames *another*. Self-blame seems ill-suited for this model. Despite this appearance, I do not think it is. As I understand it, self-blame, like other forms of blame that are not directed, is to be accounted for by reference to cases of one directly blaming another. In this essay I'll not attend to self-blame. But see chapter 3, section 3 of my 2012.

standing; and the third we can call the question of *normative force*. In this paper I'll direct my attention just to the topic of normative warrant.

As to the question of normative warrant, it will be granted on all sides that one pertinent norm is a matter of veracity. Is the agent who is blamed for something or other in fact blameworthy for it? Did she, for example, perform the action, or did someone else do it? Was what she did morally wrong or instead morally objectionable along some other dimension, or is this instead a matter of dispute? Did she do it under duress or in some other manner that compromised her freedom? Was she nonculpably ignorant in doing it? In considering whether an agent ought to be blamed, these questions of fact need to be settled. The relevant norm of veracity is that, at least as a pro tanto consideration, an agent ought to be blamed only if she is in fact blameworthy. The more challenging topic as regards the question of normative warrant is why, once it is settled that an agent is blameworthy, there is reason to blame that agent. This will figure prominently in subsequent discussion.

3. Blame as a Response to Quality of Will

I turn in this section and the next two to an account of blame's nature. P. F. Strawson (1962) remarked that we care a great deal for the regard that others have for us, especially when that regard is revealed in how they act toward us. He then proceeded to account for the phenomenon of blaming in terms of responding to such regard. On the Strawsonian view I endorse, blaming another for something she has done is primarily, albeit not exclusively, a matter of responding in a distinctive fashion to the perceived morally objectionable quality of an agent's will as manifested in her blameworthy behavior.

What is meant by the expression 'quality of will'? On my view, it is *not* about identifying a distinct faculty, a will, and attending to some particular features of it. It's rather a matter of the value or worth of an agent's regard for another, or other salient considerations (McKenna 2012, pp. 57–63).[2] This value can be good, ill, or indifferent. It can also be further qualified as moral or nonmoral. So understood, the moral or nonmoral worth of an agent's regard for another can be manifested in the content of her intentions or her reasons for action. But it also can be revealed by her failure to show due regard for someone who, or something that, she should have, and thus in her failure for this to figure in her intentions or reasons at all.

One important factor in assessing the moral quality of an agent's will has to do with the moral status of her action—for instance, whether the agent acted

---

[2] The qualification "other salient considerations" is meant to allow for morally objectionable behavior that involves not necessarily harm to another person but instead to, say, nonhuman animals, or the environment, or perhaps a value or ideal.

morally wrongly and so violated a moral obligation. Another is whether she did so freely. A third is whether she did so either knowingly or from nonculpable ignorance. Note that we have here three variables. One concerns some moral evaluation of the nature of the agent's action. A second concerns a control or a freedom condition. And a third concerns an epistemic condition. Each can contribute to an assessment of the moral quality of an agent's will. Although controversial, I do not think these factors are always sufficient to discern the quality of an agent's will as it bears on blameworthiness. In many cases they will be. But it is possible to imagine cases in which an agent freely and knowingly does something morally wrong and yet she does not act from a morally objectionable quality of will. Suppose, for instance, that she is acting in the context of a moral dilemma. (Think of Sophie from *Sophie's Choice*.) Or she might be acting under some sort of duress that does not exempt her from her obligations or take her freedom from her. In these kinds of cases, she might very well not act from any objectionable lack of regard for moral considerations. Indeed she might be pained by the thought of acting as she does. If so, I contend, she is not blameworthy (McKenna 2012, pp. 14–20).

As the preceding discussion shows, blameworthiness involves different sorts of evaluative considerations. As a form of moral appraisal, one evaluative ingredient of blameworthiness is focused on *the action* performed by the blameworthy agent.[3] This is settled by, for instance, determining that the agent acted morally wrongly. Here the evaluative focus is on the *object* of moral responsibility. But a distinct evaluative ingredient, I contend, is focused on the *agent* in relation to her action. Her regard for others and for salient moral considerations (such as the fact that she does moral wrong) is a *further* evaluative ingredient. In this case, the focus is on the *subject* of moral responsibility. Note that modifiers of 'good,' 'ill,' or 'indifferent' as pertaining to an agent's will are axiological not deontological terms. And of course, insofar as the value or worth of an agent's regard for her manner of acting also casts light on the nature and character of the agent, there is, at least potentially, an aretaic dimension as well. Hence, appraisals of blameworthiness can be evaluatively complex, encompassing deontic, axiological, and aretaic judgments.

This is an essay about the nature of blame, not the nature of blameworthiness. So, granting the preceding point, why is it important as regards blame? Because blaming is most fundamentally a response to perceived blameworthiness. It is useful to get a clear sense of what it is to which blame is sensitive. Indeed there is an important lesson about blame close at hand: variability in the fitting modes of blaming is liable to be a function of the variability in the evaluative cocktail that is embedded in a judgment of blameworthiness.

---

[3] Of course, omissions or consequences of actions or omissions are also candidate objects of blameworthiness. I restrict attention here just to action solely for ease of exposition.

As for the evaluative component of blameworthiness involving the object of responsibility, some contend that moral blameworthiness is limited in its potential objects to morally wrong action (and omissions), and so to violations of moral obligations. In this way, it is thought that what an agent can be blameworthy for must be limited to the sphere of deontological evaluations (e.g., Darwall 2006; Wallace 1994). Naturally, on this view blame is limited accordingly.[4] Although I wish to remain officially neutral on this point, my impression is that this is unnecessarily restrictive. Consider, for instance, the category of the suberogatory. Why are actions that can only be negatively evaluated in axiological or instead aretaic terms not even potential objects of blameworthiness? I fail to see why exactly a person cannot be blameworthy for acts that involve no violations of any moral obligations and so are not, strictly speaking, morally wrong, but are nevertheless morally bad, or instead unvirtuous. It may be that the mode of blaming that is fitting as a response to such acts is different. Perhaps it is weaker than that which is called for when an agent does something that is straightforwardly morally wrong. But as I see it, blameworthiness for such acts, and thus the prospect of blame directed at the agents who perform them, should be left open as a theoretically live option.

4. The Mode of Response Constitutive of Directed Blame

Grant, as I have argued in the previous section, that blaming is primarily a matter of responding to the morally objectionable quality of an agent's will as manifested in her behavior. Grant also that blameworthiness is evaluatively complex and that blaming is liable to be sensitive to that complexity. The question remains, what sort of negative response is constitutive of blaming? More specifically, what sort of negative response is constitutive of directed blame? Is it primarily a matter of belief? Desire? Some combination? Along with other Strawsonians, I contend that it is most useful to understand moral responsibility and its cognate notions, blame being among them, by reference to a range of morally reactive attitudes. A reactive attitude is an attitude in response to the perceived attitude of another.[5] The reactive attitudes at issue are not (merely) cognitive or conative but are affective; they involve emotions, in this case *morally* reactive emotions, and they pertain to the stance of holding morally responsible. Central to the current topic are those morally

---

[4] Some (e.g., Haji 1998; Zimmerman 1988) deny that blameworthiness requires moral wrongdoing, but they do so in a manner that preserves a conceptual connection between blameworthiness and wrongness. On this sort of a view, moral blameworthiness involves acting with the belief that one is doing something that is objectively morally wrong.

[5] There are as well reactive attitudes that are self-referential, such as guilt. Here I shall focus on reactive attitudes had by one that are directed at others.

reactive attitudes directly implicated in blaming. These particular reactive emotions are best understood as a species of moral anger, picked out by the terms of sentiment 'resentment' and 'moral indignation.'[6]

R. Jay Wallace (1994, pp. 25–33) made an important contribution to the reactive-emotions account of blaming by developing a normative interpretation whereby we can make good sense of a reactive emotion's being appropriate or inappropriate or, perhaps put more cautiously, fitting or unfitting. The idea is to understand the emotional dimension of a phenomenon like blaming not merely in terms of a disposition to have and act from an emotion of a certain sort, but in terms of when it is apt or fitting to have one, and so when it is apt or fitting for one to respond to another in a blaming manner motivated by such an emotion. As Wallace noted, these attitudes have certain propositional objects at which they are directed. This allows us to make sense of how it is that these attitudes might be misdirected.

Wallace limited the relevant propositional objects to beliefs involving failures to comply with obligations or expectations. A blaming attitude of moral indignation, for instance, is inappropriate when the one at whom it is directed did not after all fail to comply with any obligation to which the one blaming held her. Or instead it is inappropriate when it is unfair to hold such a person to an expectation of this kind (perhaps she is severely mentally retarded and is just incapable of grasping or complying with such demands). While I agree with Wallace's strategy regarding the normative interpretation of these reactive emotions and their place in blaming, I prefer a more inclusive and open-ended treatment of the range of propositional objects that bear on considerations of propriety or fittingness. By restricting the relevant morally reactive attitudes to beliefs about obligations, Wallace explicitly limits the domain of moral responsibility, and so the domain of blame's target, to the deontic sphere of moral right and wrong (1994, p. 63). On my view, it is better to characterize the reactive attitudes of resentment and moral indignation so that they are sensitive to the belief that a person acted in a manner that is subject to *some* sort of moral criticism in deontological terms, but also, at least possibly, in axiological or aretaic terms.

On the view I propose, the species of moral anger distinctive of resentment and moral indignation is directed at a more complex sort of propositional object as in comparison with Wallace's fairly lean, and admittedly more elegant, proposal. This species of moral anger, I contend, is aptly responsive to all of the following: the belief that an agent acted freely; the belief that an agent acted knowingly or from nonculpable ignorance; the belief that an agent's act

---

[6] There is some disagreement as to how exactly resentment and indignation differ. As I see it (McKenna 2012, p. 66), resentment is at play when one is oneself the person wronged or harmed or is in some manner directly affected or targeted by the objectionable behavior eliciting the emotion. Indignation is at play when it is another who is wronged, harmed, or in some way affected by the eliciting behavior.

was morally criticizable in some manner (was morally wrong, morally bad, or vicious); and, *most prominently*, the belief that an agent acted from a morally objectionable quality of will, either by acting with ill will or by acting in the absence of a sufficiently good will.

Strawson himself (1962) discussed the reactive attitudes in the context of their central role in adult interpersonal life, and most notably in our complex web of social practices. This emphasis is highlighted by Gary Watson's (1987b) observation that for Strawson, holding someone morally responsible means something in practice. Blaming via resentment or indignation reveals itself in the altered means of interacting with the one blamed. Normal courtesies are withheld, patterns of conduct are changed, expected social plans and arrangements are altered, and particular means of expressing one's moral anger in word and deed are found to be common in ways that are sometimes fitting and sometimes not. Although those discussing Strawson's work often note this point, in my opinion it has not been fully appreciated. A focus *just* on the range of emotions and their aptness invites the misleading thought that what matters most fundamentally in the affective dimension of a phenomenon like blaming is the feeling part that can be privately experienced and concealed. In my estimation, this is backwards. As I have argued elsewhere (McKenna 2012, pp. 69–72), the conceptually more fundamental cases of emotions like resentment and moral indignation are those that encompass their characteristic behavior manifestations in ways that reveal their place in our interpersonal lives. We are able to understand privately experienced resentment, for example, by reference to the public cases.

To help illustrate the way these emotions are manifested in practice, I have focused on a simple case of blame between two friends and coworkers, Daphne and Leslie, who meet at a local shop for an afternoon coffee (McKenna 2012, pp. 68–69). In response to what she took to be an offensive racist joke about Hispanics, Daphne becomes morally indignant toward Leslie, angrily tells her she does not welcome the remark, and then storms out of the coffee shop. Daphne then alters future plans with Leslie, not inviting her to a lunch date with another coworker, who is Hispanic, and in various other ways makes fitting alterations to her means of interacting or not interacting with Leslie. Further, as I set up the case, Daphne takes there to be limits to the modes of blaming Leslie. For example, she does not let it affect her judgments about whether to offer Leslie some extra work. The point of calling attention to these details is to help show that these different ways that Daphne acts, from her angry verbal confrontation to her altered lunch plans, are not distinct from and so simply caused by her blaming Leslie; they're constitutive of her blaming Leslie. They express her moral indignation and so are not *merely* motivated by her moral indignation. The role and presence of the emotion is infused in the altered social practices themselves, giving them a salience or meaning that they would otherwise not have.

Watson (1987b) has claimed that the morally reactive attitudes are incipiently forms of communication. This is dead right. It is shown especially by focusing on cases of directed blame like the case of Daphne and Leslie. When the focus on the morally reactive attitudes is on their manifestation in our social practices and as directed at those blamed, we can see how it is that an episode of resentment or indignation can communicate moral demands and expectations. It can, as well, communicate an altered regard for the one held to blame and an indication of the likely means of future treatment, further expectations about means of redress, moral atonement, compensation, and so on.[7]

5. Directed Blaming and Conversation

On the conversational theory of moral responsibility I defend, the actions of a morally responsible agent are potential bearers of a species of meaning, *agent-meaning* (McKenna 2012, pp. 92–94). As bearers of agent-meaning, such actions function as (fallible) indicators expressive of the quality of will with which agents act. When one directly blames another, she responds to the agent in light of this species of meaning. Her blaming response, via an overt manifestation of a pertinent reactive attitude such as resentment, communicates her regard for the blamed agent and that agent's action in light of the quality of will that is presumed to be manifest in it.

Just now I characterized actions as being bearers of a species of meaning and of expressing quality of will. I also wrote of directed blaming via the morally reactive attitudes and altered interpersonal practices as playing a communicative role. But I have proposed a bolder thesis (McKenna 2012, ch. 4). The notions of meaning, expression, and communication do not fully capture the distinctive interanimation between blameworthy agent and those blaming, at least when the kind of blame is directed. More mileage can be gotten out of Watson's insight that the reactive emotions as manifested in practice have a communicative role. The relation between a morally responsible agent and those who hold her to account for her blameworthy conduct, I contend, can be usefully illuminated on an analogy with a conversation. When a blameworthy agent acts, she understands that her actions are liable to interpretations in which members of the moral community might assign a salience or meaning to her mode of acting as indicative of one kind of quality of will or other. As a morally responsible agent, when she acts, she is aware that her actions can take

---

[7] One wrinkle I have not taken in this section but have elsewhere (McKenna 2012, p. 25) has to do with the prospect of one's holding morally responsible another who is blameworthy in cases in which one does not experience an episode of a morally reactive emotion at all. As Wallace has noted (1994, pp. 76–77), we can still hold a person morally responsible for a blameworthy act in those cases where, for whatever reasons, we just cannot muster the emotion.

on meaning. Hence, when her acts are pertinently morally charged, we can understand her *as if* she were introducing, or risking the possibility of introducing, a meaningful contribution that is a candidate for a conversational exchange with others. I have called this stage *Moral Contribution*. When one holds another morally responsible by blaming her, on the theory I have proposed, what she communicates can be understood on analogy with engaging in a conversation with the agent who initiated that exchange. This second stage, the stage wherein one blames, I have called *Moral Address*. It is then open to the blamed agent to extend the "conversation" further by means of offering an excuse, a justification, an apology, and so on. This third stage I have labeled *Moral Account*. It is then open to those holding morally responsible by blaming to extend the conversational analogue further, by, say, forgiving, or punishing, or simply ending the exchange and moving on, and so on. This dynamic, which we might call a *moral responsibility exchange*, is modeled on analogy with a conversational exchange between competent speakers of a natural language.

Understood in this light, moral responsibility is shown to be a dynamic process that is *essentially* interpersonal. It relates those who are and those who hold morally responsible in a fashion structurally analogous to the sort that unfolds between competent speakers of a natural language when involved in a conversational transaction. The nature of blaming, and specifically directed blaming, is a distinctive move in that kind of social practice. The conversational role of particular instances of blaming will arise against the backdrop of, or put differently, within the framework of, patterns of social life wherein variation from expectations will have a certain salience; for example, were Leslie not typically involved in lunch outings with Daphne, Daphne's failure to invite her could not take on the meaning it does in the case as I have set it out.

Theorizing about moral responsibility in general and blame in particular as I have here has a payoff in terms of extending the analogy with features of literal, linguistic conversational exchanges. Speakers of a natural language engaged in the give and take of conversational transactions rely on complex expectations of shared background assumptions of a sort that allow for successful implicatures and related modes of conveying meaning that cannot be captured simply by attending to the strict semantic content of what is said between interlocutors. Innuendo, sarcasm, things discretely not said or not even indirectly mentioned, all figure into our understanding of the delicate interactions of individuals engaged in felicitous (and infelicitous) conversations with each other. Pragmatic context takes center stage here. A structurally analogous point applies to the nature of blaming understood as functioning like a move in a conversation. An altered pattern of behavior by one person as a means of manifesting her indignation could very well be taken to have a salience by a blamed party that it would not and could not have for another person. That other person's interactions and relations with the blamed party might be quite different, or might involve different roles (say, boss or spouse rather than mere acquaintance or casual friend). Hence, there is a sufficiently complex web of social interrelations between persons to make sense of something analogous to phenomena like implicatures in the modes of blaming that are available to members of a moral community. This helps to explain an observation made early on: that two individuals might very well blame another in ways that are equally warranted and fitting, but do so in wildly divergent ways.

Before turning in the next two sections to the norms of blaming, I pause to comment on two points about blame's nature which show where I part company with other Strawsonians. The first has to do with the modal status of claims about the relation between blaming and the morally reactive emotions. What I take to be *essential* to moral responsibility is that it is deeply interpersonal. It relates those who are morally responsible agents to those who hold morally responsible. This relation is essential to the nature of being morally responsible. This is in contrast to, for example, a ledger theory (e.g., Zimmerman 1988; Haji 1998). On a ledger theory, being morally responsible is, so to speak, metaphysically settled irrespective of any of the phenomena related to holding morally responsible. So I contend (McKenna 2012, pp. 80–88), along with other Strawsonians, we cannot make good sense of being morally responsible in the absence of some understanding of the standpoint of holding morally responsible. (Just as we cannot understand competent speakers of a natural language without understanding the nature of the audience to whom such speakers address themselves.) But are emotions required for this? Well, that depends on how strongly we understand the modal force of 'required.' Is it a metaphysical or a conceptual necessity that blaming involves some reference to an episode of a reactive attitude like resentment or indignation? I think this goes too far and is unnecessary to account for the phenomenon at hand. It seems to me to be at the very least a conceptual possibility that there could be beings who engage in social practices that are like ours, who hold each other to account for their morally significant conduct, and so on, but are emotionless beings altogether. Of course, qua agents who act at all, they would be *motivated* beings; they'd have a conative structure but would be devoid of affect.

It could be countered on behalf of Strawsonians that any essentialist claim about the place of the reactive attitudes is indexed to beings like us, to human persons. Rigidly designating humans, the claim might be, the morally reactive emotions are essential to accounting for moral responsibility in general, and the nature of blaming in particular. A yet weaker claim involves rigidly designating not humans, but instead just our practices—moral responsibility as we understand it—and then claiming that it is essential to those practices and this way of life that the moral emotions play a role. Perhaps this is correct, but I see no motivation to make any of these fairly strong modal claims, even the weakest of them. Why can't the relation between these emotions and the social practices I have highlighted here be contingent but nevertheless deeply embedded, so much so that we just would not get a credible theory of blame without attending to the role of these emotions? At any rate, as I see it, the morally reactive attitudes need only be thought of as contingently related to the nature of blaming (McKenna 2012, pp. 110–14). Regardless, they are deeply embedded in our blaming practices, and we would not understand our blaming practices, such as they are, without reference to them.

Here is the second point. Strawson (1962) and most Strawsonians (e.g., Bennett 1980; Wallace 1994; Watson 1987b) contend that the nature and norms of holding morally responsible are more fundamental than the nature of being morally responsible. The latter is not to be thought of as having a metaphysical standing to which the former must comply, but rather vice versa. I disagree. This is shown by how I have approached the topic of blame's nature in this and the two preceding sections. To get clear on blame, I have first attended to what it is to which blame is a response. Thus, I have focused on features of the agent who is morally responsible (by attending to quality of will considerations) as a way of helping to understand blame as a mode of holding morally responsible. It might be thought that I am forced into the opposing camp of those who would regard being morally responsible as the more basic or fundamental thing. But on my view, the mistake is to think that either is more basic than the other (McKenna 2012, pp. 50–55). There is a relation of mutual dependence that cannot be eliminated, much as we cannot make sense of what it is to be a competent speaker of a natural language without reference to the standpoint of a speaker's audience of potential interpreters who seek to understand what the speaker means to convey.

6. Directed Blaming and the Question of Normative Warrant

I turn now to the question of the normative warrant for directed blaming. What justifies its being the case that a blameworthy agent ought to be blamed? Also, how ought an agent to be blamed? There are at least two identifiable norms that bear on these questions. One, as previously noted (section 3), has to do with veracity. Is it true to the facts that the alleged blameworthy agent acted freely? Did she act with knowledge or culpable ignorance in doing what she did? Was what she did morally wrong, bad, or unvirtuous? Did she act from a morally objectionable quality of will?

A second norm arises naturally out of a conversational theory of moral responsibility. It has to do with meaningfulness or intelligibility—what makes sense as a sort of conversational response to the agent in light of her blameworthy action (McKenna 2012, p. 90). Just as in literal conversational transactions between competent speakers of a natural language, so too with blaming: there can be more and less sensible or intelligible responses to a meaningful contribution. In literal conversations, some conversational replies are infelicitous, complete nonstarters. This happens when, for instance, there is a breakdown in communication, perhaps because one misheard what another said or did not pick up on an intended implicature. But other contributions can be felicitous and still be, on a scale, more fitting or apt than others. Sometimes, as in comparison with another conversationalist, one knows "just what to say," and even here, there's no reason to think that there was, literally, just one correct way to contribute to or continue the conversation. I contend likewise for blaming. Some modes of blaming are infelicitous; they miss their target altogether and just do not make sense as a fitting response to one who is taken to be blameworthy. But as for those that do make sense, that are meaningful ways of communicating with a blameworthy party, there is no regimented way this must be done. Daphne blamed Leslie in, we can grant, a fitting manner by manifesting her moral indignation as she did. But we can equally well imagine that she could have done so by other means that made just as much sense—that is, that were just as conversationally meaningful. Here again we have a further explanation of why quite different modes of blaming can be regarded as equally suitable.

Norms of conversational intelligibility or meaningfulness also help call to attention a further feature of the permissible variability of blaming. In literal linguistic conversations, a contribution by an interlocutor is often pregnant with meaning so that there are different aspects or dimensions to what the speaker means. It is open to another conversing with the speaker to carry the conversation in a range of different ways, depending on which aspects of the original contribution this interlocutor wishes to focus on. Likewise for blaming as a "conversational" response to the perceived agent-meaning of a blameworthy party's act. Recall that judgments of blameworthiness are evaluatively complex. They can encompass deontological, axiological, and aretaic ingredients. If so, then it is open to one who replies to the blameworthy agent to attend more to one than another element in this evaluative cocktail.

As I have argued elsewhere (McKenna 2012, pp. 150–54), the two norms just countenanced—the norms of veracity and conversational intelligibility—are not adequate to account for the normative warrant of blaming. They're necessary but not sufficient. Directed blaming is liable to harm, and the norms canvassed thus far do not account for why it is that it is at least permissible to harm by directly blaming those who are blameworthy. What further norm will fill this bill? To answer this question, we need a clearer sense of just what about blaming constitutes the harm in it. Here we first must settle on what is meant by 'harm' and then return briefly to the topic of (directed) blame's nature.

As for the matter of harm, I follow Joel Feinberg in thinking of harm in terms of a setback to one's interests (1986, pp. 33–34). Feinberg held that the many different kinds of interests available to persons can be sorted into two general categories: welfare interests and ulterior interests. *Ulterior interests* concern aspirations and ultimate goals of the sort that figure in writing a novel or seeking a cure for cancer. *Welfare interests* are those more fundamental interests that serve as a foundation for one's pursuing ulterior interests. Among these welfare interests Feinberg listed continuance of one's life into the future, physical health, integrity and functioning of one's body, absence of absorbing physical pain and grotesque disfigurement, emotional stability, the capacity to engage normally in social intercourse and enjoy and maintain friendships, minimal income and financial security, a tolerable social and physical environment, and a certain amount of freedom from interference from others (p. 37).

Now return to directed blame's nature. Due to blame's communicative and conversational role, it is liable to impose on the one blamed in particular ways.[8] Anger, shunning, and alienation as expressions of morally reactive attitudes are often conveyed in blaming, and there is an expectation that the one blamed ought to reply by offering an apology or an explanation, revising modes of behavior, and so on. This can be emotionally taxing. It can compromise a person's welcomed relations with others. It can also cost her in terms of psychic energy and the freedom to live her life without having to pay the interpersonal costs of altered relationships and unpleasant demands and expectations put to her by those holding her to account. These conversational burdens placed upon her—even if she wishes to shrug them off—come at a cost to her, or at least they are liable to do so for all but the most hardened and indifferent among us. But notice that these costs are restricted to just *some* of the welfare interests Feinberg mentioned, in particular:

- The capacity to engage normally in social intercourse and enjoy and maintain friendships
- Freedom from others' interference
- Emotional stability

So, in directed blaming, a distinctive, albeit limited, class of welfare interests is liable to be compromised. A setback to these interests constitutes the unique harm(s) in directed blaming (McKenna 2012, pp. 134–41).

One further point about blame's nature before returning to the matter of blame's norms: On the conversational theory I endorse, and in opposition to how many others understand the issue,[9] blame is distinct from punishment in a number of ways; it is not merely something like informal or "mini-punishment." For one thing, on the conversational theory I endorse, punishment is better thought of as having a distinct communicative and conversational role as in comparison with blaming, and so as coming at a distinct stage in a moral responsibility exchange. Blame occurs at the stage Moral Address and precedes the stage Moral Account. Punishment is suited for a stage that follows the stage Moral

---

[8] My treatment in what follows of the harm and also the normative warrant for blaming shares affinities with an especially penetrating treatment of the topic by Christopher Bennett (2002).

[9] See, for example, Bennett (2002), Feinberg (1970, p. 68), and Sidgwick (1874, bk. 3, ch. 5), who think of blame as just a species of punishment.

Account. At the stage Moral Account, the blamed agent is afforded the opportunity to offer some explanation, justification, apology, and so on. Punishment follows as a further response. But more to the immediate point of concern, the harms constitutive of punishment include a much greater range of setbacks to a person's welfare interests, including a compromised physical environment and a loss of greater freedoms (confinement), on some views, physical harm (corporal punishment), loss of life (capital punishment), and certainly the prospect of financial insecurity (fines and penalties). The harm in blaming, limited to the distinctive class of welfare interests as I have set it out, is also limited in how much it can harm. Unlike the potential range of harms in punishment, the harm in blaming does not expose the blamed to the kind and degree of suffering that is at least available for various modes of punishment. The point is important since it bears keeping in mind when reflecting on what sort of warrant is called for to justify the harms in blaming. Some are against the practice of blaming because they conflate the harm in blaming with the harm in punishing, and then, thinking that the potentially extreme harm in punishing cannot be justified, draw the same conclusion about any normative warrant for the harm in blaming.[10]

So in light of these considerations, what further norm might account for the warrant to harm in ways that are distinctive of directed blaming? One way to distinguish between different approaches to this question is in terms of whether it is good to harm a blameworthy person by blaming her. Some contend that it is no part of their account of the normative warrant for blaming that it is in any way *good* that the blameworthy person be harmed by way of blaming her.[11] Others contend that it is. Call the former *nondesert theorists* and the latter *desert theorists*. Of those advancing desert theories, some contend that the ground for this goodness issues from more basic normative considerations.[12] This would be analogous to what in the sphere of distributive justice Rawls (1971, p. 104) called postinstitutional desert. On such a view, the goodness of the harm in blaming would flow from some sort of consequentialist or contractualist proposal, perhaps. Others advancing a desert theory contend that the pertinent

---

[10] There is yet another distinction between blame and punishment that appears to make justifying blame easier than doing so for punishment. In order to punish, one must intend to harm. But this is not so for blaming (McKenna 2012, pp. 144–46). All one must intend, in cases of directed blaming, is that one communicate one's altered regard for the blamed agent in light of the quality of her will. One might thus intentionally harm the one blamed or instead just do so knowingly without intending to so harm her. (For a convincing treatment of the distinction between intending, intentional, and knowing, see Mele and Sverdlick [1996, pp. 273–74].) Some object that certain theories of punishment are objectionable due to their connection with the vengeful intention to cause harm to those who are to be punished. Even if this were grounds for indicting those theories of punishment, it would miss its mark if targeted to similar theories of blame.

[11] See Scanlon (1998, pp. 293–94; 2008) and Wallace (1994, p. 60).

[12] This seems to be the view that some, such as Ayer (1954), Hobart (1934), and Schlick (1939), endorsed. A more refined version, and an especially plausible one, as I read him, is found in Lenman (2006).

ground does not derive from more basic normative considerations; its desert claim is basic.[13] The goodness of harming one who is blameworthy by the very activity of blaming her is a matter of its intrinsic or noninstrumental value.[14] It is grounded just in the very fact of its being a distinctive kind of fitting response to the one blamed. Call these *basic desert theories* and *nonbasic desert theories*.

I find promise in efforts to account for the normative warrant to blame *either* by way of a nondesert theory *or* by way of a nonbasic desert theory (McKenna 2012, pp. 154–64). Each has merit and is worth exploring. In my view, those inclined to dismiss these strategies, taking them to be on their face inadequate to the task of accounting for moral responsibility, are mistaken to do so. Others, such as Pereboom (2009), far more cautiously acknowledge that these approaches offer accounts of bona fide senses of moral responsibility. They take these senses to be worth cultivating, but they reject the accountability senses of responsibility and blame that are in dispute in areas such as the free will debate. I disagree (McKenna 2012, pp. 171–72). I think it is a live option to argue that one can get the normative warrant for the pertinent sort of blaming and responsibility (the accountability sense) by way of some strategy other than appeal to basic desert. Nevertheless, I also think that, relying on the conversational theory, formulation of a defensible basic desert thesis for blame's warrant is a live option (p. 172). Space does not permit consideration of the full range of theoretically live options. Because many take a basic desert thesis to capture a widely held conviction about moral responsibility's normative warrant, in what follows I'll devote my attention just to the articulation of a basic desert thesis for blame.[15]

---

[13] For example, see Bennett (2002), Pereboom (2001), and Sher (2006). Of course, as is well known, Kant endorsed a version of this view.

[14] I prefer the term 'noninstrumental' rather than 'intrinsic' despite the fact that many, such as Wallace (1994, p. 60, n. 13), are careful to use the term 'intrinsic.' Why the more inclusive formulation? On a narrow understanding of 'intrinsic,' in contrast with 'extrinsic,' something does not have intrinsic value but instead extrinsic value if its value is dependent on its relation with other things. (Example: a flower's being valuable because rare depends on whether there are others like it.) Things with extrinsic value can still, however, have value that is not instrumental—is not in the service of other things. I wish to leave it as an open theoretical possibility that on a basic desert theory for blame, the harm in blaming has extrinsic value (insofar as it depends on its relation to "conversational" dynamics of moral responsibility relations), but that this value is nonetheless noninstrumental. (I am indebted to conversations with Piers Rawling and Mark Timmons on this point.)

[15] Justin Coates and Neal Tognazzini have raised an especially insightful question about my proposal thus far. I granted above that the norms of veracity and conversational intelligibility are insufficient to account for the normative warrant to harm by way of blaming. And I have turned to the question of whether an appeal to desert can bridge that gap. But why doesn't the conversational norm already have a consideration of desert built into it? The norm would be of the following sort: It's not conversationally fitting to blame one who does not deserve it. This is a nice question. And I suppose one could contend that we could get at least this much commitment to desert from my conversational proposal. But note here that the appeal to desert is meant to do no more than function as a defeater to the claim that it would be warranted to harm a blameworthy person. Appeal to desert is not here doing the work of providing a positive justification for why, in responding in a conversationally meaningful way, it would be at least permissible to engage in a practice that is liable to harm the one blamed. I am interested in what might account for this more robust justificatory question.

7. Directed Blaming and Basic Desert

In the previous section, to draw the distinction between desert-based and nondesert-based theories, I formulated the desert thesis in axiological terms. But this was slightly misleading. There is some discrepancy as to whether a basic desert thesis ought to be formulated in axiological terms or instead in deontological terms. Some, such as Feinberg (1970), Sher (2006), and Zimmerman (1988), characterize a basic desert thesis for blame in terms of what is required, right, or instead permissible. Others, such as Bennett (2002) and Scanlon (1998), do so in terms of what is good. A useful proposal, which I will adopt here, joins the two.[16] Here is a formulation of a generic and modest basic desert thesis that draws on both axiological and deontological ingredients:

GD: Because it is a noninstrumental good that a wrongdoer is harmed, it is permissible to harm her.

Why is GD generic, and why is it modest? It is generic because it is not tailored to blame in particular and so could be used in a justification for punishment as well. It is modest because it does not add further content that many retributivists take to be essential to basic desert, such as a requirement of proportionality for deserved punishment, as well as some consideration of answering a harm with a deserved like harm (e.g., an eye for an eye). Its modesty is also a function of its deontic status, which commits to no more than permissibility, as opposed to a stronger version that would be expressed in terms of obligation. To the extent that these further desert theses make justifying basic desert more difficult because they command harsh(er) treatment for wrongdoers, or instead impose greater burdens on others, GD is by comparison more modest. It makes room for the possibility that it might be good and so permissible to harm a wrongdoer by harming her in ways that are in no way as great as was the sort of harm she caused. It avoids any connection to barbarisms of the sort associated with taking an eye for an eye. And it also does not *require* of others that they harm wrongdoers.

On my view, the claim of noninstrumental goodness is to be understood in terms of cross-world differences. Consider two worlds exactly alike in every respect as regards their histories and as regards two qualitatively indistinguishable agents, each of whom do something morally wrong. The worlds now differ in just the following way: In one world the wrongdoer is harmed in response for her wrongdoing. In the other she is not. In the former, due to her wrongdoing, she is made worse off than she otherwise would be. In the latter she is not. According to those who would advocate a thesis like GD, or some stronger variant, the former world is noninstrumentally a better world in

---

[16] Wallace formulates a desert thesis in this manner, treating retributivism as "the view that it is intrinsically good that wrongdoers should suffer harm, and that we therefore have a positive moral obligation to inflict such harms on them" (1994, p. 60, n. 13).

comparison with the latter. Put simply, in the former world, the wrongdoer gets something that she deserves.

As it is, GD needs developing. It does not distinguish between culpable and nonculpable wrongdoing. For example, some who are wrongdoers might not have done so freely, or instead might have done so from nonculpable ignorance. Furthermore GD restricts the desert thesis to wrongdoing, which some might contend is problematic. But set these concerns aside since our interest here is in a more refined version of a desert thesis that is more specifically about blame and the harms distinctive of blame. The reason to begin with the more generic GD is just to call to attention that, as a general point, one that is not unique to the advancement of a theory like my conversational theory of blame, desert theses of the sort that apply to both blame and punishment can be fairly modest and so can avoid the more excessive commitments that are often the target of critics' most damning objections to claims of basic desert.

So now let us apply these considerations to the distinctive characteristics of directed blame as I have characterized it. Consider, then, this principle:

> DB: Because it is a noninstrumental good that one who is blameworthy is harmed by the communicative practices constitutive of directed blaming, it is permissible to harm her by directly blaming her.

Like GD, DB also needs further development. For instance, some qualification is needed to accommodate considerations of normative standing. It might be amended to read, "it is permissible for those with proper standing to blame her." We might also amend DB by making perspicuous that the mode of directed blaming that harms is by way of a conversationally intelligible or meaningful reply to the agent's blameworthy conduct. But considerations such as these aside, DB will suit our current purposes.

Apply the same thought experiment about cross-world differences to the claim of noninstrumental goodness in DB. Consider the case of Daphne and Leslie. Would it have been a better world had Daphne not blamed Leslie as she did when Leslie made that racist remark? Would it have been a better world if Daphne had not responded in a conversationally apt way to Leslie about the meaning of her (Leslie's) remark, and so had not expressed her moral demands and expectations? And would it have been a better world had Daphne's taking that stance and engaging in those practices not harmed Leslie in just the following specific ways? (1) Leslie was emotionally upset and hurt by Daphne's withdrawal of her goodwill toward Leslie and her (Daphne's) expressed anger. (2) Leslie's personal freedom from interference was strained by virtue of the social pressures Daphne placed on her. These pressures were to acknowledge the morally objectionable meaning of her remark and the quality of her will reflected in it and to respond to Daphne's mode of blaming her. And (3) Leslie's capacity to maintain and enjoy friendships with Daphne and other coworkers was diminished by virtue of how Daphne communicated her regard toward Leslie in her (Daphne's) withdrawal from normal, friendly personal interactions.

It is open to those advocating a desert thesis for blame as expressed by DB to contend that these distinctive harms to Leslie are noninstrumentally good. It would be a worse world were Leslie not to have been harmed in just these very special ways. Of course, it is open to those who argue against a desert thesis to dispute this. They might ask why it would not be an even better world if Daphne and Leslie were to be engaged in the sort of conversational analogue I have highlighted but Leslie were not harmed in that process. As regards this manner of resisting a basic desert thesis for blame, first, bear in mind that all I have attempted to do in this and the preceding section is *articulate* a basic desert thesis for blame. I have not attempted to argue for it.[17] But, second, note also that this claim about cross-world comparisons has to be assessed in terms of what sort of agents we can expect the likes of Daphne and Leslie to be. Were we all closer to angels, then we might hope for modes of communicating our blaming regard in ways that are not liable to harm at all, and we might hope that those blamed are not disposed to experience these sorts of harms while nevertheless remaining open to the moral entreaties of others. But given that we are the kinds of creatures we are, it is not clear how we could engage in these practices at all and how they could have the kind of meaning for those blamed they have without their also carrying the characteristic sting associated with them. Nor is it clear how those doing the blaming could with sincerity communicate and engage with those blamed while fully suppressing the emotional springs that often motivate the likes of mere mortals like us. So in making the cross-world comparisons currently under consideration, great care has to be taken in thinking about whether, at pertinent worlds, we are departing far too much from the kinds of creatures that in fact we are, and in fact we are able to be.

The modest desert thesis, DB, when developed within the framework of a conversational theory of moral responsibility, has a considerable theoretical payoff. Some philosophers committed to one species or other of moral responsibility skepticism have made their task far too easy. They have presumed that the moral responsibility at issue concerns claims of basic desert, and then they have ramped way up the dramatic nature of what is or potentially could be deserved, especially as regards the blameworthy. Galen Strawson (1994), for instance, executes his impossibilist argument for moral responsibility by contending that genuine responsibility of the sort that, he contends, is not metaphysically possible but is nevertheless presupposed by our moral responsibility practices, requires that we at least be able to make sense of heaven and hell

---

[17] For such an argument, see my 2012 (pp. 164–71).

responsibility—which includes hell's eternal torments and suffering. Others, such as Derk Pereboom (2009), make far less dramatic claims but still maintain that the kind of moral responsibility that implicates basically deserved blame is liable to license excessive means of acting on one's moral anger in ways that can lead to violence and other forms of extremely harsh treatment. As should be clear, the basic desert thesis DB, as applied to the conversational theory of moral responsibility, has no such implications. If the accountability sense of moral responsibility, the sort at issue in the free will debate, really does require a commitment to basically deserved blame, then these moral responsibility skeptics might have made clear why excessive versions of desert theses should be rejected, but they have not told us enough to explain why the claims of goodness and permissibility constituting DB, constrained as they are by a conversational theory, are to be rejected.

8. Concluding Remarks

In this essay I have drawn on the conversational theory of moral responsibility to offer an account of the nature and the norms of blame. I have done so by limiting the relevant notions of blame and of moral responsibility just to the accountability sense, and then to prototypical cases of blaming in the form of what I have called directed blame. I shall close by commenting briefly on a few points that I was not able to attend to in detail in the preceding discussion.

One dimension of directed blame's nature has to do with its relation to the voluntary. Curiously, few critics of emotion-based theories have raised worries about the control a blamer can be expected to exercise over her blaming. But there is a worry here that needs addressing. For the most part, except in fairly esoteric contexts, the mere experiencing of an emotion is not thought to be under an agent's direct voluntary control.[18] If so, it looks like emotion-based theories of blaming risk the objection that one who blames is not in a position to settle freely on whether or not to blame. This objection need not be developed in terms of a blamer's having *no* control over whether she experiences an episode of a blame-constituting emotion. There is the notion of nonvoluntary control of the sort competent rational agents exercise in belief formation and retention. An agent who resents someone for wrongdoing can, for instance, exercise *rational* control over her emotion. She can do so to the extent that she can assess the truth as to whether, for instance, that agent really did wrong. But this being the case, she is not able to simply choose or decide directly whether, with these factual matters settled, she undergoes the emotion. Agents can't control their emotions directly in the requisite way.

---

[18] Of course, there are indirect methods. One can avoid conditions in which she might have occasion to experience the emotion, or can have a stiff drink ready at hand, and so on.

If those advancing an emotion-based theory of blame were not able to say more about the control an agent can exercise in blaming, this would create problems accounting for the relation between the nature of blaming and its norms. Some of these norms concern questions of whether an agent ought to be blamed, and not just whether it is true to the facts that she is blameworthy. But if merely by having an episode of a pertinent reactive emotion, one does blame, it appears that one cannot comply with relevant judgments about whether, all things considered, an agent *ought* to be blamed. As might be expected, the way out for the emotion-based theorist is by tending to features of blaming that are within an agent's voluntary control. The outward manifestation of blaming practices in modifications to interpersonal relations involves acts and omissions that, it can be argued, *are* within a blamer's control. Here we have further reason to attend to the (I say) more fundamental prototypical cases of blame outwardly directed at the blamed. Doing so makes clear that the relevant norms of blame—and more particularly the expectation that blamers can comply with them—are not defeated merely by the fact that blame's nature has an emotional and so nonvoluntary dimension.

I close with one final comment about the methodology I have adopted. Some will be disinclined to a conversational theory, or more generally any communication-based theory, because it seems too easy to generate counterexamples to it. There are cases in which an agent is morally responsible for some act, being either praiseworthy or blameworthy for it, and there is no conversational analogue that takes place. Or instead, it will be protested, in cases of private blame or blaming the dead, we have blame but no communication at all. So a theory such as the one I have advanced and a treatment of blame by reference to it is just inadequate. It tends to some special range of cases but not others. Scanlon, for instance, has objected to Watson's contention that blame is to be understood in terms of its communicative role. Why? Because a person can blame while not communicating anything (Scanlon 2008, pp. 233–34, n. 54).

My reply to this objection is that it assumes that a proper theory of moral responsibility should be cast in terms of necessary and sufficient conditions à la proper classical analysis. But I reject this way of proceeding. Phenomena such as blaming are too diffuse in their extensions, and our intuitions about them are too contested in a wide range of cases, to hope that we can get anything like a proper analysis of the full extension of these concepts. Rather, it is best to proceed by focusing on central cases, ones that are of immediate concern as regards questions of normative warrant, standing, and force. If we can account adequately for the nature and norms of these, then the other cases can be explained by reference to these prototypical cases. My conversational theory of moral responsibility attends most directly to our adult interpersonal relations with each other, and the ways these do alter, and give good reason to alter, our moral standing with those who are capable of morally significant action. It does so by finding meaning in the actions of morally responsible agents and in the means of conversationally engaging with them in ways that communicate moral demands and expectations. I propose that blame, at least the sort that bears on moral responsibility in the accountability sense, is best understood by adopting this strategy.

8

Taking Demands Out of Blame

Coleen Macnamara

1. Introduction

There are multiple accounts of the nature of blame. For example, according to George Sher, blame is a set of behavioral and attitudinal dispositions that have their source in a belief-desire pair: the belief that someone has acted badly and the desire that the one blamed not have done what she did or not have the character traits she has. Thomas Scanlon argues that to blame is to change one's comportment toward another in acknowledgment of the fact that she has done something to impair your relationship with her. A third account finds its origin in Peter Strawson's seminal work "Freedom and Resentment" and has since been widely endorsed by theorists such as R. Jay Wallace, Susan Wolf, and Stephen Darwall. On this view, I blame another when I respond to her conduct with resentment, indignation, or disapprobation; that is, I blame another when I respond to her wrongdoing with a negative reactive emotion. This view, the reactive attitudes account of blame, is the focus of this paper.

Anyone who takes even a cursory look at the reactive attitudes literature would be struck by how frequently theorists discuss *demands*. Strawson told us that the reactive attitudes "are associated with," "involve," "express," and "rest on and reflect" demands (1962, pp. 84, 85, 90). Those inspired by Strawson have taken up this theme with a vengeance. Gary Watson suggests, "The negative reactive attitudes express a *moral* demand, a demand for reasonable regard" (2004, p. 229). According to Darwall, "Resentment doesn't represent its object as simply contravening one's will, but as contravening some justified demand" (2006, p. 81). And Margaret Urban Walker

My sincerest thanks to Christina Hollowell, Elisa Hurley, Justin Coates, Neal Tognazzini, Zac Bachman, Dan Ehrlich, Chris McVey, and Philip Swenson for their helpful feedback on earlier versions of this paper. Thanks also to Monique Wonderly for discussion on these issues and invaluable research. I owe special debts of gratitude to Maggie Little and Joshua Hollowell for countless conversations on the issues discussed in this paper and for reading and commenting on numerous drafts.

claims, "When we express and direct our resentment or indignation at a norm violator, we demand some rectifying response from the one who is perceived as out of bounds" (2006, p. 26). These remarks represent only a small sample of the demand language that pervades the reactive attitudes literature.[1]

The idea that demands are a key constituent of any analysis of the negative reactive attitudes is rarely challenged, enjoying a freedom from scrutiny uncommon in philosophy. The literature on the negative reactive attitudes proceeds as if their connection to demands is too obvious to merit skepticism.

I think this is a deep mistake, and in this paper I press on this orthodox view. I argue that there are, broadly speaking, three ways in which the term 'demand' is used in discussions of the negative reactive attitudes; each, I argue, is problematic. First, theorists of blame link the negative reactive attitudes to demands understood as a model or metaphor for the standing requirements of morality. In so doing they suggest that the negative reactive attitudes are at home in the deontic but not evaluative realm. This picture is problematic. Second, theorists put the term 'demand' to its other paradigmatic use: demand as a particular kind of speech act. 'Demand' is used in this way when it is claimed that to feel or express resentment, indignation, or disapprobation is to implicitly demand something. I show that this view is untenable. Third, the term 'demand' is used loosely or figuratively to point to the fact that the negative reactive attitudes seek a response. This use of 'demand' is, to my mind, correct so far as it goes. Nonetheless I argue that it is infelicitous in this context.

I conclude by showing how little we have to lose by taking demands out of the attitudes associated with blame. To so reject demands is not to deny that the negative reactive attitudes are forms of moral address, or that demands can serve to hold responsible, or that wrongdoing warrants a unique response from the moral community.

2. From Demands to Morally Untoward Actions

Many theorists have emphasized the relationship between the reactive attitudes and demands understood as a model or metaphor for the requirements of morality. For example, Strawson tells us that when we respond to another with a negative reactive attitude we "view him as a member of the moral community; only as one who has offended against its demands" (1962, p. 90). Watson suggests that "the negative reactive attitudes come into play only when the basic demand has been flouted or rejected" (2004, p. 234). He also tells us that

---

[1] For other examples, see Hieronymi (2004), McGeer (2011), McKenna (1998), Shoemaker (2007, 2011), Smith (2008b), and Wallace (1994, 2007, 2008, 2010, 2011).

the "reactive attitudes depend upon an interpretation of conduct. If you are resentful when jostled in a crowd, you will see the other's behavior as rude, contemptuous, disrespectful, self-preoccupied, or heedless: in short, as manifesting attitudes contrary to the basic demand for reasonable regard" (p. 223). Consider also the following comments from Wallace, keeping in mind that for him the terms 'moral demand,' 'moral obligation,' 'moral requirement,' and 'moral expectation' are all used interchangeably (1994, pp. 22, 38). The negative reactive emotions are "focused emotional responses to the violation of moral obligations that we accept" (p. 69). The content of the negative reactive attitudes "is given by the thought that a person has violated moral requirements that we accept, requirements that structure our interactions with people in the social world" (Wallace 2010, p. 323). Given that, for Darwall, to violate a moral obligation is to violate a moral demand (2010b, pp. 151, 156; 2010a, p. 35), he too links the negative reactive attitudes to demands: "The connection between the concepts of moral obligation and wrong (on the one hand) and the reactive attitude of blame (on the other) is then this: What is morally wrong is what is blameworthy—that is, what is warrantedly blamed, if the action is done without an excuse" (2010b, pp. 142–43).

For Wallace, then, a negative reactive attitude is a "response" to a violation of a moral demand. Watson and Strawson add that the negative reactive attitudes depend on or involve "an interpretation" of another's conduct or "viewing" the person as having violated a moral demand. The negative reactive attitudes are not, that is, knee-jerk responses to another's wrongdoing; rather they involve cognitions, and more specifically they, like all emotions, involve a construal of their object under an evaluative guise.[2] Just as fear of the ice involves a construal of the ice as dangerous and feeling pride about passing the bar exam involves construing one's passing as reflecting well on oneself, so too do resentment, indignation, and disapprobation involve construing another as having violated a moral demand.[3]

Though there are a number of different accounts of the relationship between an emotion and its corresponding construal, for many contemporary emotion theorists, including Wallace, the relevant construal is at least partly constitutive of the emotion.[4] For Wallace, the negative reactive attitudes are in part constituted by one's construal of another as having violated a demand. What's more, once we have in hand the conceptual content of the negative reactive emotions, we also have in hand their warrant or fittingness conditions.

---

[2] See, for example, de Sousa (1987, 2004), Helm (1994), Nussbaum (2001), Roberts (1988), Sherman (1997), Solomon (1973), Stocker and Hegeman (1996), and Taylor (1985).

[3] The fear of ice example is from Stocker (1983, 1987), and the bar exam example is borrowed from Elisa Hurley.

[4] See, for example, Solomon (1973, 2004), Nussbaum (2001), Stocker and Hegeman (1996), Goldie (2000), Greenspan (1981), de Sousa (1987, 2004), Roberts (1988).

An emotion is warranted or fitting just in case it construes the world as it actually is. (One's fear of the ice is warranted if the ice is in fact dangerous, and one's pride about passing the bar exam is fitting just in case passing the bar exam reflects well on the person.) The resentment, indignation or disapprobation one feels toward another is thus warranted just in case that person has in fact violated a moral demand. If she has not violated a demand—that is, if she is innocent of wrongdoing—resentment and the like are not fitting.[5]

Thus far I have been at pains to distinguish the various ways in which demands understood as standing moral requirements have featured in discussions of the negative reactive attitudes. Such reactive attitudes have been described as a response to, as involving a construal of, and as being warranted by the violation of a demand. I have drawn these various distinctions not because the difference among these claims is of the utmost importance but rather to illustrate that theorists' commitment to the tight relationship between the negative reactive attitudes and demands runs deep. The plurality of claims made sends a clear message: demands qua standing moral requirement are the kind of normative material with which the negative reactive attitudes are concerned.

For all that, I think it is a misguided impulse. When theorists use the term 'demand' as a model or a metaphor for standing moral requirements, they are using it to pick out what it is *wrong* to do. The reason is easy to see: demands *understood as speech acts* are a ubiquitous part of everyday life, and they, where legitimate, make it the case that the target, absent exculpatory justification, is wrong not to do as demanded. In other words, where legitimate, demands qua speech act place on their target a deontic burden. For just this reason, many

---

[5] Wallace makes one more claim that is worth noting. For Wallace, the connection between resentment, indignation, and so on and the demands of morality is essential to understanding what it means to have an attitude of holding others morally responsible. He explains, "[T]here is an essential connection between the reactive attitudes and a distinct form of evaluation, or quasi-evaluation, that I refer to as holding a person to an expectation (or demand)" (1994, p. 19). Here Wallace is not directly describing the negative reactive attitudes; rather, he is explicating the attitude or stance that leaves us susceptible to them, that is, the stance of holding someone to a demand or moral requirement. According to Wallace, to adopt this stance just is to be susceptible to the negative reactive attitudes when that person violates the relevant moral requirement.

This attitude is perhaps easiest to isolate when we think of cases in which we decide to forgo it. Imagine your partner routinely forgets your birthday. For the first few years of the relationship you held her to the norm of remembering one's partner's birthday, thus feeling and perhaps expressing resentment each year as your birthday came and went without notice. But as the years went on, you decided to spare yourself the inevitable birthday emotional distress and quarrel. Your partner, you concluded, is lovely in every other respect; it is in your best interest and that of the relationship to let go of this one. Letting go did not mean that you rid yourself of the *belief* that she ought to remember your birthday; you believe that she should. Rather letting go amounted to jettisoning the attitude of holding her to the norm of remembering your birthday. With this attitude discarded, you are no longer susceptible to feeling and thus expressing resentment when she forgets your birthday. As a result, your birthday now comes and goes in relative peace.

use the term 'demand' to refer to moral requirements understood as the deontic burdens of morality.

What's more, theorists, especially Darwall and Wallace, use the term 'demand' not just to indicate the morally deontic but specifically to contrast the deontic with the evaluative. For both Darwall and Wallace, the moral realm is rich, including not just morally right and wrong actions but also good and bad actions—the morally commendatory and discommendatory. When they use the term 'demand,' they are invoking the distinction between the deontic and evaluative realms, indicating a shift out of the broader realm of moral value into the narrower domain of the *required*, the *forbidden*—the *wrong* (Darwall 2010a, pp. 31, 35; Wallace 1994, pp. 37, 38).

When theorists link the negative reactive attitudes to demands, then, they are identifying them as creatures of the deontic and not of the evaluative realm. But while it is certainly true that resentment, indignation, and disapprobation are responses to, involve a construal of, and are warranted by moral wrongs, is it really that obvious that the same cannot be said of these attitudes and moral bad?

Consider, for example, the following scenario: You are a graduate student and you have a paper due in exactly twenty hours. Your plan is to stay seated at your desk typing away until the paper is finished. It just so happens that you have three library books due today, and though it would not be the end of the world if you failed to return them on time, your roommate, another graduate student, is headed to campus. You ask her if she will return your books for you. She says no. She refuses, not because she won't be near the library and her day is jam-packed, but simply because she doesn't feel like it. You react with resentment: you bite your tongue, but you think to yourself, "What a jerk!"[6]

Given the details of the case, it does not seem that this is a favor the roommate is *required* to do; that is, it is something of a stretch to characterize the roommate's refusal as, strictly speaking, *wrong*. At the same time, her refusal is far from morally neutral: it certainly comes at a cost to both the roommate relationship and more broadly to the moral relationship of mutual regard. And while this cost is not the sort to render the refusal wrong, it arguably renders it bad. But if this is right, and if resentment in this case is apt—as it certainly seems to be—then this vignette speaks against the claim that the negative reactive attitudes live exclusively in the deontic realm.

But we need not rely on these intuitions to show that the negative reactive attitudes have a place in the evaluative realm. Reflection suggests that we should *expect* moral bad to have an interpersonal footprint—a pragmatic upshot in our moral psychological states and attitudes. Whatever else we say

---

I address how the argument of this section affects our understanding of the stance that leaves us susceptible to the negative reactive attitudes in note 11.

[6] I borrow this example from Driver (1992).

about morally bad actions, it is clear that they have moral significance for us. Add to this the fact that it is via our moral psychological states and attitudes that creatures like us take up or register matters of moral import, and it becomes natural to expect the moral bad to have a pragmatic upshot.

Wallace would be the first to admit this, but on his picture the moral emotional reactions associated with bad are not resentment, indignation, and disapprobation; rather they are moral sentiments of some other kind (1994, pp. 63–64). As far I can tell, his only reason for thinking this is that he has antecedently defined the negative reactive attitudes in terms of the deontic. And he has done this because for him the negative reactive attitudes are key components of our practices of holding responsible, and these practices, he contends, are intuitively about the concepts of moral obligation, moral right, and moral wrong (p. 52). But absent the intuition that holding responsible is exclusively about the deontic, Wallace's position on the moral sentiments associated with bad seems unmotivated.

What's more, reflection on the nature of bad and wrong in conjunction with Wallace's own (and, I would argue, correct) description of the negative reactive attitudes suggests that the fit between these attitudes and bad is as tight as that between these attitudes and wrong. Morally bad and morally wrong action share a core element: both thwart the values at the heart of morality.[7] To be sure, determining when the thwarting of moral values warrants the label of 'bad' as opposed to 'wrong' is a difficult, complicated matter. Nor is it immediately clear what difference the distinction between bad and wrong makes from the perspective of the moral agent deliberating about how to act. I myself endorse Margaret Little's (forthcoming) view that while wrong action necessarily betrays some weak will, deficiency of discernment, or difficulty in deliberating on part of the agent, bad action need not. But the fact that the distinction between bad and wrong brings to the fore deep and difficult philosophical questions should not obscure the point that concerns us here: namely, that bad and wrong action are bad and wrong because they thwart values at the heart of morality. With this in mind, consider Wallace's apt description of the reactive attitudes:

> To respond to wrongdoing with one of these reactive emotions is a way of being exercised by immorality, taking it to heart that the values around which our common social life is organized have been flouted or undermined. A disposition to respond emotionally to immorality in these ways is a sign that one cares about the values at the heart of morality. One does not merely acknowledge that it is valuable to relate to people on a basis of respect and regard; one values this way of relating to people, with the emotional vulnerability that is characteristic of the broader phenomenon

---

[7] I borrowed the lovely phrase "values at the heart of morality" from Wallace (2010, p. 324).

of valuing on occasions when what one cares about has been damaged or insulted in some way (2010, pp. 323–24).

According to Wallace, we are susceptible to the reactive attitudes in virtue of caring about the values at the heart of morality, and the negative reactive attitudes are simply our way of taking to heart, or becoming exercised by, the fact that the values we care about have been thwarted in some way. But if this is a correct description of the negative reactive attitudes, and if it is true, as I suggested earlier, that both morally wrong and morally bad actions thwart the values at the heart of morality, then the negative reactive attitudes are properly thought of as responses to both morally wrong and morally bad actions.

To be sure, one might continue to insist that negative reactive attitudes have a privileged connection to demands and thus wrong. Some, for example, reject the existence of moral bad. If one holds that bad exists in other normative realms, the aesthetic or epistemic, for instance, but not in the moral realm, then it is obvious that the *moral* negative reactive attitudes live solely in the deontic realm. They have, as it were, nowhere else to go.

Or one might be led to the view that negative reactive attitudes are warranted only in the case of wrongdoing because one construes these attitudes as being heavy-handed in some way. As I will explain in detail in the next section, Darwall maintains that reactive attitudes are tacit demands qua speech act. For Darwall, then, resentment, indignation, and so on are heavy-handed insofar as they are an exercise of authority over another. For Darwall, this is an authority we simply do not possess unless another's action rises to the level of wrong. But one need not think the reactive attitudes are tacit demands to think that they are heavy-handed. The tendency in the literature is to model the reactive attitudes on sanctions—and sanctions are weighty in their own right.[8] If reactive attitudes are sanctions, then arguably to deserve such a punitive response one must act in a way that is wrong and not just bad.

But it is far from clear either that the above metaethical view is correct or that the negative reactive attitudes are in fact heavy handed. The claim that there is no moral bad is a controversial metaethical claim. And the view that the negative reactive attitudes are properly modeled on either demands qua speech act or sanction is far from obviously true. I object to the demand qua speech act view in the next section. Thus, for now it suffices to notice that there is something deeply counterintuitive about construing the *unexpressed* reactive attitudes as sanctions. In "Two Faces of Responsibility," Watson expresses this sentiment in a question: "[H]ow is being subject to a blaming attitude a sanction?" (1996, p. 238).[9] Perhaps it makes most sense to move away from modeling the reactive

---

[8] Those who construe the reactive attitudes as sanctions include Strawson (1962), Watson (1996), and Shoemaker (2011).

[9] Also see Shoemaker (2011, p. 617).

attitudes on punishments and sanctions and address them in their own right: as the moral psychological phenomena that they are.[10] Doing this might reveal them as having, metaphorically speaking, a rather light touch.

None of this is to say that at the end of the day one might not reasonably conclude that the negative reactive attitudes have a privileged connection to demands and thus wrongdoing. My point here is simply that absent some prior controversial theoretical commitment, this claim appears unmotivated. From the perspective of moral psychology, it seems highly plausible that the negative reactive attitudes are connected to the morally untoward in general and not exclusively to violation of demands.[11]

3. Demands qua Speech Act

Another way in which theorists have linked the negative reactive attitudes to demands takes us into the territory of speech acts. It's a familiar idea that we can do many things with words: we can *ask a question, warn* our hiking companion of the tree branch falling toward her head, *invite* a friend to a party, *assert* that a tree branch is falling, and, most important for us here, we can issue *demands*. To my children I bark, "Clean your room!" To the stranger on the bus, "Get off my foot!" Demands are among the many kinds of speech acts we perform.

In *The Second-Person Standpoint* and subsequent writings, Darwall frequently draws on speech act theory in the course of discussing the reactive attitudes (see, e.g., 2006, pp. 3–4, 52–54, 75–76, 265–66). More specifically, he identifies the reactive attitudes as forms of moral address, meaning that they are speech acts or "quasi speech acts," and in particular that they are implicit demands:

---

[10] I have argued elsewhere that when we start with the idea that the reactive attitudes are emotions we are led to the view that both the expressed and the unexpressed reactive attitudes are at bottom modes of recognizing another as having done something good, bad, right, or wrong. This view of the reactive emotions is not incompatible with the idea that they are responses to both wrong and bad. See Hurley and Macnamara (2010) and Macnamara (forthcoming).

[11] Recall that Wallace is unique insofar as he brings our attention to the stance that leaves us susceptible to the negative reactive attitudes—what he describes as the stance of *holding someone to a demand*. I agree that there is a stance that leaves us susceptible to the negative reactive attitudes and that this stance is a crucial component of the moral psychology of our practices of holding responsible. However, insofar as there is reason to think that the negative reactive attitudes are warranted by the entire class of morally untoward actions, there is room for skepticism about Wallace's *description* of this stance. If the negative reactive attitudes are plausibly construed as responses not just to violations of *deontic* normative material but also to *evaluative* normative material, then the stance of holding another to a *demand* will not leave us susceptible to the negative reactive attitudes in all the cases in which they are warranted. If I hold John to the deontic burdens he faces and not similarly to the evaluative burdens, then while I will be susceptible to a negative reactive attitude in cases of wrong action, I will not be similarly susceptible in cases of bad action.

What gives Strawson's discussion of reactive attitudes its special relevance to the issue of free will is that reactive attitudes invariably address demands, and, as Gary Watson notes, there are "constraints on moral address" that must be presupposed as felicity conditions of addressing a demand (Watson 1987b: 263, 264). . . . [T]he capacity to recognize and act on second-personal reasons is, I am claiming, a felicity condition of moral address's having its distinctive "illocutionary force" (that is, making it the distinctive speech act it is) (Austin 1962). (Darwall 2007, p. 120)

On Darwall's account, then, the negative reactive attitudes, whatever else they might be, are implicit demands. For Darwall, this holds for both the expressed and unexpressed reactive attitudes: "If you *express* resentment to someone for not moving his foot from on top of yours, you implicitly demand that he do so" (2006, p. 76, my italics), and "in *feeling* resentment or moral blame toward someone for stepping on your feet, you implicitly demand that he not do so, answer for having done so, and so on" (2010c, p. 219, my italics).

While there is strong evidence that Darwall regards both the expressed and the unexpressed negative reactive attitudes as implicit demands, his view on the propositional content of these demands is not similarly clear. It is not clear what he thinks the negative reactive attitudes are demands *for*. He never explicitly takes up questions about propositional content. Perhaps this is because his broader project of arguing for the second-personal nature of morality requires only that the reactive attitudes make demands—not that they make this or that particular demand.

But the quotes above are suggestive; there are two views on propositional content that Darwall might seriously entertain. The first is what I will call the "standing moral requirement" view, the second, the "acknowledgment of fault" view. Both of these views have some initial plausibility.

We can easily remedy this problem by broadening Wallace's description of the stance. If the negative reactive attitudes are warranted by the entire class of morally untoward actions, then the stance that leaves us susceptible to these attitudes is not the stance of holding another to a demand but rather the stance of holding another to the range of normative material the violation of which renders an action morally untoward.

What's more, Wallace is inclined to refer to the stance that leaves us susceptible to the reactive attitudes not just as the stance of holding someone to a demand but also as the "psychological stance of demanding" (1994, p. 22). But if the stance that leaves us susceptible to the negative reactive attitudes is the stance of holding another to the range of normative material that renders an action morally untoward, then it is infelicitous to refer to this stance as the psychological stance of demanding. We need a more inclusive term.

My inclination is to use the term 'normative expectation' to refer to the stance that leaves us susceptible to the reactive attitudes. Wallace uses the term 'normative expectation' to refer to standing moral requirements (1994, p. 22), thus I am urging a use that diverges from his. One point in my favor is that my use honors, in a way that Wallace's does not, the fact that 'normative expectation' is in the first instance a psychological term.

The standing moral requirement view piggybacks on the idea that the negative reactive attitudes are intimately connected to demands understood as standing moral requirements. As we saw in the previous section, theorists claim that resentment, indignation, and disapprobation are responses to, involve a construal of, and are warranted by the violation of a demand qua standing moral requirement. The standing moral requirement view of content merely pushes the connection between a negative reactive attitude and the moral requirement with which it is correlated one step further: it claims that the negative reactive attitudes, as it were, give voice to or issue the demand that underwrites them. Most precisely, on this view the content of the demand constitutive of the negative reactive attitude mirrors the content of the standing moral requirement whose violation prompted it. To be sure, the fact that resentment, indignation, and disapprobation are responses to, involve a construal of, or are warranted by a particular demand qua moral requirement does not *entail* that they themselves issue a demand, let alone a demand with the same content. But the already tight connection between the negative reactive attitudes and standing moral requirements renders this view of content plausible.[12]

On the acknowledgment of fault view, a negative reactive attitude is a tacit demand that its target acknowledge her fault, where this includes both feeling guilt and expressing it via apology and amends.[13] The plausibility of this account of the content comes into view when we remind ourselves that there is a certain sort of propriety in the target of a demand doing as the propositional content directs. Thus to say that the negative reactive attitudes demand that their target feel guilt and express it via apology and amends is to suggest that it is in some sense appropriate for the target to respond in this way.

This sentiment finds considerable support in the literature. For example, Walker (2006, pp. 125, 138) and Shoemaker (2007, pp. 91, 100) join Darwall in countenancing this idea. What's more, it is quite intuitive. There is, after all, nothing as satisfying as having one's blame met with a sincere apology and reparations. Such a response tends to dissipate even intense feelings of resentment or indignation. Further, wrongdoing creates rifts in relationships, straining and tearing the fabric of the moral community. If we are going to stay together, these rifts need to be repaired. Repair happens when those who have done wrong take up and make good on their faults by feeling guilt and expressing it via apology and amends.[14] The fact that acknowledging one's fault has the potential to catalyze moral repair certainly suggests that there is a propriety in a negative reactive attitude being met with this response.

---

[12] For evidence that Darwall holds this view see Darwall (2010b, p. 155; 2006, p. 76; 2010c, p. 219).

[13] For evidence that Darwall holds this view see Darwall (2006, pp. 71, 79, 85–86, 112; 2010a, p. 37; 2011, p. 331).

[14] See Walker (2006) for a thorough treatment of the concept of moral repair.

But while both the standing moral requirement and acknowledgment of fault views have initial plausibility, they do not, I will argue, stand up to scrutiny. More broadly, in the remainder of this section I identify a number of problems for the idea that the negative reactive attitudes are tacit demandings. I argue that problems arise at three different levels: first at the level of the bare claim that they are speech acts, second with the claim that they are a specific kind of speech act—namely, a demand—and third at the level of propositional content. Importantly, these critiques hold even if it is correct to confine resentment, indignation, and the like to the deontic realm.

Let's start with the claim that the negative reactive attitudes are speech acts. This first point is a simple one. While it certainly seems right to characterize *expressions* of resentment, indignation, and disapprobation as speech acts, the same cannot be said of *unexpressed* resentment, indignation, and disapprobation. It is difficult to see how an emotion that remains buried in one's heart can be appropriately characterized as a speech act. To be sure, Darwall calls them "quasi speech acts," but to identify them as such is simply to mark the awkwardness of identifying them as speech acts; it does nothing to explain it away.

A second strike against the demand qua speech act view is that the ethics of negative reactive attitudes and demands come apart: the former do not require authority and the latter do. Imagine that you promised to meet your friend for dinner on Friday night, but that before Friday rolls around someone you have had your eye on for *forever* asks you out on a date: dinner and a party Friday night. It just so happens that this dreamy date and your engagement with your friend fall on the same night, so you tell your suitor that you will probably be able to go but that you need to make sure. You quickly call up your friend, tell her your exciting news, and ask her to release you from your promise. You say, "We can do dinner some other time. You know how much this date means to me!" To your surprise your friend, for no good reason, refuses to release you. You are quickly besieged by resentment—resentment that seems, given the history of the friendship and the importance to you of the event, to be warranted. You know your friend has every right to refuse, but this date means a lot to you. You can have dinner with her on Saturday night; it's not as if Friday night is her birthday or something. But while you think your resentment is fitting, you know you do not have the authority to demand that she release you from your promise. This is simply part of the logic of promising. Once you make a promise, the promisee is in charge of whether you will be released or not. It is not for you to decide and certainly not for you to command.

Consider another case. You are on a crowded train and you witness the following: An elderly couple enters the car, clearly anxious at the thought of not sitting together. Seeing only scattered single seats, they politely ask a passenger a few rows in front of you if he would be willing to move so that they can sit together. He says no. He is polite enough, but no is his answer. Witnessing this scene fills you with indignation—indignation that, given the elderly couple's predicament, you think is warranted. "What a jerk," you think. "What is wrong with people!" To be sure, moving would be an inconvenience, but only a small one, and it would be a great help to the elderly couple. But just as you know that indignation is warranted, you know that you do not have the authority to demand that he move. It is, after all, his seat, his to give or keep. He sat in it first, and on the train it is first come, first serve. If you got up and demanded that he move, he would likely respond by saying, "Who the heck do you think you are? You can't demand that I move. This is my seat!" And you know he would be right.[15]

In both these cases unexpressed negative reactive attitudes seem in order and demands do not. If you share my intuitions about these cases it is likely because you take the reactive attitudes seriously as *emotions*. Let me explain.

When Mary legitimately demands that Sarah φ, she makes it the case that Sarah must φ *because she said so*. In other words, in legitimately issuing a demand to Sarah, Mary normatively subordinates Sarah's will to her own. But to do something like this is to exercise a normative power. This sort of power requires normative authority—precisely the kind of authority that the sergeant has with respect to his soldiers but you arguably lack in the promise and train cases.

Emotions, in contrast, do not require normative authority, and the reason is easy to see. Emotions are not first and foremost about subordinating another's will to one's own; rather they are, as we saw in the previous section, modes of recognizing a feature of the world under an evaluative guise. Modes of recognition simply do not require normative authority.

Of course, this is not to deny that emotions are subject to various norms of correctness. It is widely agreed that emotions can be assessed in terms of a variety of norms. First there are what one might think of as internal norms, that is, norms that are indexed to the kind of thing the emotions are: forms of recognition. Emotions are assessed as fitting or not or as warranted or not, where this just tracks whether or not the emotion recognizes the world as it actually is. Our emotions, though, are open to a further level of assessment. They, like our actions and character, are subject to moral and prudential norms.[16] Warranted emotions are not, then, necessarily beyond reproach. For example, one's amusement at an objectively funny racist joke is fitting, but nonetheless morally untoward due to its racist content.[17] Your resentment toward someone who has in fact done wrong may nonetheless be morally

---

[15] I borrow this example from Driver (1992).

[16] It is also true that legitimate demands can violate moral and prudential norms. Though the sergeant may possess the authority to demand that his solider drop and give him fifty, it would be morally inappropriate for him to issue this demand when he is a guest at the soldier's wedding. I am indebted to Maggie Little for this example.

[17] This example is from D'Arms and Jacobson (2000).

untoward because of your hypocrisy, that is, because you are an unrepentant violator of the precise norms to which you are holding your target.

On my view, to take reactive attitudes seriously as emotions is to see them as sharing key features with emotions in general. Importantly, this involves seeing the reactive attitudes as subject to the same standards of correctness as all other emotions. But if this is what it means to take reactive attitudes seriously as emotions, we can see why doing so leads to the conclusion that in the above scenarios resentment and indignation are appropriate even though you lack the authority to demand. What is relevant to the assessment of your resentment and indignation is, first, whether their target has in fact done something wrong (or bad) and, second, whether your resentment and indignation square with moral and prudential norms.[18] In both respects, your resentment and indignation fit the bill: your friend and the man on the train have both done something wrong (or bad), and there is no indication that your emotions violated a moral or prudential norm.[19]

Just as unexpressed resentment, indignation, and disapprobation do not require authority, so too with *expressions* of these emotions. The promise case is an excellent illustration of this. It seems appropriate for you not only to feel resentment toward your friend but also to express this resentment to her—despite the fact that you clearly lack the authority to demand.

The train case may seem different. While it seems perfectly appropriate for you to feel indignation, expressing it is another matter. But while the inappropriateness of both demands and expressing indignation seems to speak against my view, reflection suggests otherwise. To turn this apparent difficulty into a solid objection would require showing that expressing indignation is inappropriate because you lack the authority to express it and not for some other reason—say, because you should mind your own business or, to put it another way, because expressing indignation here would violate a norm of privacy.

We can see that it is the norm of privacy rather than lack of authority that renders your expression of indignation inappropriate by considering a variation on the train case. Imagine that the man who refuses the elderly couple is a good friend of yours. In this case, expressing indignation could very well be appropriate. We often legitimately call out our friends for just this sort of infraction. At the same time, though, friendship does not alter the economy of authority. It is still his seat to give or keep.

---

[18] To be clear, when I say that the negative reactive attitudes do not require authority, I do not mean to imply that they do not require *standing*. They do. On my view, to say that the negative reactive emotions require standing is simply a shorthand way of claiming that they can be warranted or unwarranted and that in feeling them we can violate various moral and prudential norms.

[19] This brings out the fact that to identify negative reactive emotions as demands is to identify them as subject to modes of assessment to which no other emotions are subject. To my mind, this is an awfully big bullet to bite. To be sure, the reactive emotions are special—they are special insofar as they are key constituents in our practices of holding responsible. However, they can be special in this way without running roughshod over their status as emotions.

It should not be that surprising that expressions of the reactive attitudes do not require the authority distinctive of demands. Demands are a unique kind of speech act. As I emphasized earlier, demands make it the case that their target must do as demanded because it was demanded. To demand is to make another's will an instrument of your own. There are countless other speech acts—invitations, pleas, assertions, and conjectures, to name a few—that are not heavy-handed in the way that demands are and thus do not require the authority that demands do. The above scenarios merely point to the fact that on matters of authority, expressions of the reactive attitudes join most other speech acts.

My final critique of the demands qua speech act view draws on a point made earlier, namely, that there is a certain sort of propriety in the target of a demand doing as the propositional content directs. We can now put this point more precisely: demands seek compliance, which is simply to say that demands are fully successful as the kind of thing they are just in case their target does as demanded because she was so demanded. To be sure, there are what one might think of as diminished forms of success. For example, if I demand that my children clean their room, and they do so for some other reason than because I demanded it, then my demand is partially successful. Technically put, in this case my children have conformed to but not complied with my demand. And it is true that conformity falls short of rendering a demand fully successful even if the demander herself is perfectly satisfied with conformity. What satisfies the demander is one thing, and what satisfies the demand is another. While I may want my children to clean their room—not caring one bit about their reasons for doing so—my demand is not so laid back: it, as it were, wants my children to clean their room and do so *because it was demanded* (Searle and Vanderveken 1985, p. 14).

But if this is what demands want, then both the moral requirement view and the acknowledging fault view of content are problematic. The former suggests an implausible account of the response sought by the negative reactive attitudes, and the latter suggests that the negative reactive attitudes make an unintelligible demand.

Recall that on the moral requirement view, the content of the demand constitutive of a negative reactive attitude mirrors the content of the standing moral requirement that underwrites it. This implies that a negative reactive attitude is fully successful just in case the target of that attitude complies with the demand the flouting of which prompted the attitude. To see why this is a problematic account of the success conditions, consider the following example. Imagine that I intentionally trip you, and you feel resentment and express that resentment to me. When I trip you, I violate a moral requirement: Don't intentionally trip others. On the moral requirement view of content, when you feel and express your resentment, you, as it were, give voice to this moral requirement. Your resentment makes a demand with the same content as the demand I violated. When you resent me, you are, in essence, demanding that I not intentionally trip you. What this implies is that your resentment will be fully successful just in case I respond by not intentionally tripping you because you so demanded.

But when you consider the fact that I have already tripped you, options for complying with your demand are rather limited. I cannot comply with respect to the offending action, since it is already in the past; it is not as though I can change the past so that I never tripped you. Future compliance, of course, is possible; I can refrain from tripping you in the future. But while we can agree that this would be a good thing, such forbearance is not a satisfying account of the response resentment seeks. It is highly implausible that my merely not intentionally tripping you in the future renders your expression of resentment successful. If you take me to task for tripping you and I respond simply by saying "Okay, I won't trip you in the future," my guess is that you would be taken aback. What about the fact that I have already tripped you? Resentment is a response to a past wrong, and whatever else we say about the response it seeks, it needs to be at least in part about this past wrong. An account of the content of the demand constitutive of the negative reactive attitudes that entails that the success-constituting response is as thoroughly forward-looking as "Okay, I won't intentionally trip you in the future" is hard to swallow. The defining response to resentment must involve a backward-looking element.[20]

This critique of the moral requirement view points us directly toward the acknowledgment of fault account of content. If the negative reactive attitudes demand that their target feel guilt and express it via apology and amends, then these attitudes are fully successful when their target feels and expresses guilt because it was so demanded. This response *is* suitably backward-looking. When we feel guilt and express it via apology and amends we appropriately redress the wrong that gave rise to resentment, indignation, or disapprobation.

But while the acknowledgment of fault view plausibly captures the response sought by the negative reactive attitudes, it fails because it implies that these attitudes are constituted by an unintelligible demand.

As we saw earlier, an agent issues a felicitous demand only if she possesses the requisite authority. The mugger's demand that I hand over my wallet is infelicitous because the mugger lacks the requisite authority. But, strictly speaking, not all infelicities stem from a lack of authority. A demand can be infelicitous because the target of the demand is incapable either of understanding or of complying with the demand. These are, to use Watson's phrase, "constraints on moral address" (1987b, p. 229). When a demand is infelicitous because the target is incapable of understanding or complying with the demand, the demand is said to be unintelligible.

The emotional component of acknowledging one's fault—that is, feeling guilt—is simply not the sort of thing that can be intelligibly demanded of another.

---

[20] See Talbert (2012) for another objection to the moral requirement view of content.

To comply with a demand, one must do as directed because it was directed. But feeling guilt is not something we can do at the direction of another. We can no more bring it about that we feel genuine guilt on command than we can bring it about that we digest our food on command. With guilt we can, as it were, go through the motions; feigning guilt is possible, of course, but *feigning* guilt is not what is demanded of us. We can also work to develop our capacity for and sensitivity to guilt; emotions are susceptible to this sort of "indirect" control. What we cannot do is will the genuine feeling of guilt as a response to another's authority.[21]

But perhaps the demand view is salvageable. What if we simply take guilt out of the equation? Perhaps the negative reactive attitudes demand not that their target feel guilt and express it but rather that they simply apologize and make amends. No guilt, no problem.

This, I want to urge, is not a suitable solution. The key reason is that on this view, the negative reactive attitudes are fully successful when they receive an insincere apology. To be sure, sometimes the person who feels resentment, indignation, or disapprobation would find even an insincere apology satisfying. Likewise it certainly seems true that a negative reactive attitude has achieved a degree of success in eliciting an insincere apology. But as we saw earlier, what a demander finds fully satisfying is one thing, and what fully satisfies the demand is another. And again, partial success is one thing and full success another. For the demand view of the reactive attitudes to succeed, it needs to be true that the negative reactive attitudes are *fully* successful when they are met with an insincere apology (and amends); this, though, seems implausible. To say that an apology is insincere is to mark it as hollow, that is, as defective in some way. And if the reactive attitudes are at all successful when they meet with a defective apology it is hard to see why they would not be more successful when they receive the real deal.[22]

Thus once we take seriously various features of demands—that they are speech acts, that they require authority, and that they seek compliance—we see that the demand qua speech act view of the negative reactive attitudes faces far more serious problems than were immediately apparent.

4. Seeking a Response

As we saw in the previous section, identifying the negative reactive attitudes as demands qua speech act implies that they seek a response. But as with any implication, the denial of the antecedent does not entail the denial of the consequent. The negative reactive attitudes need not be demands—or even

---

[21] For additional objections to Darwall's characterization of the reactive attitudes see Wallace (2007).

[22] For an excellent analysis of apologies see Smith (2008).

for that matter speech acts at all—to be the sort of thing that seeks a response from their target. 'Demand' is used in its third and final way to point to the fact that the negative reactive attitudes seek a response.

In this section I argue that Walker uses 'demand' in precisely this way.[23] Consider the following quotes: "When we express and direct our resentment or indignation at a norm violator, we demand some rectifying response from the one who is perceived as out of bounds" (Walker 2006, p. 26). "Resentment and indignation in particular express a finding of *fault* of others and a *demand* on them for an appropriate response" (p. 25).[24] It is tempting to read Walker as simply echoing Darwall's position, that is, as endorsing the demand qua speech act view. But examination of these quotes in the context of her work as a whole gives us strong reason to resist this temptation. First, as I mentioned in the previous section, one of the main reasons to attribute the demand qua speech act view to Darwall is his frequent invocation of speech act theory. But Walker's work makes no mention of speech act theory. Second and more important, Walker does not exclusively or even predominantly use the language of demands when discussing the reactive attitudes and their sought response.

Consider the following passages from Walker: "[R]esentment not only sends a message but *invites* a response" (2006, p. 114, my italics; see also p. 134). "[R]esentment both expresses a sense of wrong and *calls out* to others for recognition and a reparative response" (p. 136, my italics; see also p. 138). "It is surely correct that resentment of serious wrong, experienced or expressed by victims or others, *requires* a response" (p. 138, my italics). "Resentment at serious wrong, then, *deserves* responses from wrongdoers" (p. 138, my italics).

It is clear from these passages that Walker holds that there is a crucial relationship between the reactive attitudes and their responses—a sentiment that, interestingly enough, is championed throughout the reactive attitudes literature.[25] But while Walker unquestionably takes the negative reactive attitudes to

---

[23] Strictly speaking, Walker holds that the negative reactive attitudes seek a response not just from their target but also from the wider community. While numerous theorists posit a relationship between the negative reactive attitudes and a response from their target (see note 26), Walker stands alone in positing a relationship between these attitudes and the wider community. Since I focus on Walker primarily because she is representative of a broader trend in the literature, I focus solely on her claim that the negative reactive attitudes seek a response from their target.

[24] For additional passages in which Walker speaks of resentment's demands see her 2008 (pp. 140, 143, 149).

[25] Some theorists employ precisely the locutions Walker does. Smith, McGeer, and Darwall all characterize the reactive attitudes as "calling for" or "calling upon" the target to respond (Smith 2008b, p. 281; McGeer 2011, p. 303; Darwall 2006, pp. 145, 170). But theorists such as Darwall, Shoemaker, and McGeer also deploy other terms. Darwall describes the reactive attitudes as *seeking* a response (2011, p. 331). Shoemaker tells us that a reactive attitude is "an emotional address, *urging* the wrongdoer to feel what I feel as a result of his wrongdoing and then subsequently to feel the guilt or remorse (at having caused that feeling) which I expect to motivate him to cease his wrongdoing" (2007, p. 51). And according to McGeer, the reactive attitudes "serve to elicit a response," and their "aim is to elicit such responses" (2011, pp. 304, 316).

be importantly connected to a response from their target, it is not yet clear what she thinks this connection amounts to. What, in other words, is she getting at when she says that the negative reactive attitudes "demand" or "invite" or "call for" or "require" or "deserve" a response?

I propose that Walker is claiming that the negative reactive attitudes are fully successful just in case they elicit a response from their target. Each of the terms she uses to describe the relationship between the reactive attitudes and their defining responses can be read as pointing to this sentiment.

Start with "reactive attitudes *deserve* a response." Read most broadly, this means that there is a certain sort of propriety in the reactive attitudes' receiving a response or that there is something normatively correct in the target's replying. Insofar as success carries with it the notion of propriety or normativity, the phrase "reactive attitudes deserve a response" is simply a more general way of putting the claim that negative reactive attitudes are fully successful just in case the target responds.

The claims that the reactive attitudes "demand," "call for," and "require" a response also point to the idea of success conditions. Each of these terms can be used to indicate that one thing is in need of another: parenting demands patience; trees require sunlight; philosophy calls for dedication. Walker arguably uses these terms in much the same way to suggest that the negative reactive attitudes are "in need of" a response—that is, that they need a response for success.

But there is another way to interpret the claims that the negative reactive attitudes "demand," "call for," or "require" a response. This second interpretation, like the first, points to the idea of success conditions, and this interpretation has the added benefit of being equally illuminative of the claim that "the reactive attitudes *invite* a response."

The terms 'demand' and 'invite' can be used to refer to two distinct speech acts. But while it is one thing to demand and another to invite, both of these speech acts are of the same general kind: both are directives, that is, speech acts that aim at getting another to do something. 'Require' and 'call for' can also be used to refer to a speech act; these terms, though, refer to directives generically rather than particular kinds of directives. Thus 'require' and 'call for' are often used interchangeably with one another and with 'demand' and 'invite.'

Thus we might read Walker as suggesting that, figuratively speaking, the negative reactive attitudes issue a directive. In other words, she might be, as it were, anthropomorphizing the negative reactive attitudes. It is when we consider the point of this anthropomorphization that we see the connection to success conditions. The fact that Mary demands that Joe ϕ is a reliable indicator that Mary aims for Joe to ϕ. This is just an instance of the broader point that people's actions are often reliable indicators of their aims. What this suggests is that anthropomorphizing something by characterizing it as acting in various ways can serve to convey the anthropomorphized object's aim. Just as we can read a person's aims off her actions, we can read the aims of the anthropomorphized object off its actions. It is possible, then, that in depicting the negative reactive attitudes as demanding, inviting, calling for, and requiring a response, Walker is trying to convey that they aim at a response. But this leads us directly to success conditions. If the negative reactive attitudes aim at a response, then they are fully successful as the kind of thing they are only if they receive the response aimed at.

If this last interpretation of Walker is correct, then like Darwall, she uses 'demand' to refer to a speech act. But unlike Darwall, she is using the term figuratively, and for her, 'demand' is simply a stand-in for a generic directive. Darwall, in other words, is using the term 'demand' literally and specifically, in contrast to Walker's figurative and generic usage.

To my mind, there is nothing illicit, strictly speaking, about Walker's use of 'demand.' In fact, I endorse the claim that negative reactive attitudes are fully successful just in case they receive a response from their target. That said, I do think it is infelicitous to use the term 'demand' to express this important point. The phrase "reactive attitudes demand a response" does not convey this point with an optimum level of precision and clarity. And while this would not be a decisive strike against a turn of phrase in most contexts, it approximates such a strike here, insofar as this context renders "reactive attitudes demand a response" ripe for misinterpretations. And these points hold even if I have misinterpreted Walker's position on the relationship between the negative reactive attitudes and their response. Whatever relationship the phrase "the negative reactive attitudes demand a response" is pointing to, there is bound to be a more precise rendering and, more important, a way of expressing it that does not invite misinterpretation.

5. Conclusion

Even those who find what I have said thus far compelling may be reluctant to take the demands out of negative reactive attitudes in the ways I have suggested. There are those who may be committed to the idea that the negative reactive attitudes are forms of moral address, or to the idea that demanding is a way of holding responsible, or to the idea that wrongdoing merits some unique response from the moral community. These theorists may worry that taking the demands out of the negative reactive attitudes will require them to abandon these strongly held beliefs. I conclude by showing that these concerns are unwarranted.

Let's start with moral address. The negative reactive attitudes can be forms of moral address even if they are not demands qua speech act. To see this, we simply need to bring to mind the fact that many kinds of speech acts constitute forms of address: questions, invitations, hails, recommendations, and entreaties all fit the bill. It is possible that the expressed negative reactive attitudes are aptly assimilated to one of these speech acts. In fact, I have argued elsewhere that they share quite a bit in common with the hail. Whereas a hail— "Hi, Mary" or "Hello, Joe"—recognizes its target as Mary or Joe, an expressed negative reactive attitude recognizes its target as having done something wrong (or bad) (Macnamara Forthcoming).

What's more, much depends on what being a form of moral address consists in. Address is arguably a functionally specified concept, such that something is a form of address if it seeks a response. If this is the case, then the negative reactive attitudes need not be speech acts at all to count as forms of moral address. It need only be the case that we can't understand the negative reactive attitudes as the kind of thing they are without understanding that they are successful just in case they receive the reply they seek.[26] If the unexpressed reactive attitudes are forms of address in this sense, they are forms of moral address in much the same way as an unsent invitation.

Turn now to demanding as a way of holding responsible. To reject the demand qua speech act view is not to reject the claim that demanding that another do as she ought is a way of holding her responsible. It is possible that the negative reactive attitudes and their expressions constitute one way of holding responsible, and demanding constitutes another. In fact, I have elsewhere argued for precisely this view (Macnamara 2011). On my view, our practice of holding another responsible has both a backward-looking face that includes the negative reactive attitudes and their expressions and a forward-looking face that includes demanding that another do as she ought. We demand that another do as she ought not in response to actual moral violations—this is the domain of blame—but rather in response to threatened infractions. Sometimes we anticipate that someone might flout a moral requirement, and when we do, we might hold her responsible before wrongdoing commences.

To see what I am getting at, consider the following. In college my housemates and I decided that we would not buy household food; each person agreed to buy her own food and not to dip into the others' stashes. Even though everyone was well aware of the food rules, incidents of late-night looting were commonplace, and leftover pizza was the most vulnerable foodstuff. One night my roommate Norah was up late studying and ordered a pizza—a large pizza in fact, specifically with the intention of having the leftovers for breakfast the next day. As Norah was going to bed, worrying about whether her pizza would be in the fridge in the morning, she decided to take control: she put a Post-it note on her pizza box that read "NO TOUCHY." In her own clever way Norah demanded that we, her roommates, do as we ought: she demanded that we

---

[26] See Kukla and Lance (2009) for an example of an argument for this view of address.

keep our late-night looting hands off her pizza. On my view, in doing this she held us responsible, not in response to a violation but to forestall one.

Finally, one can concede that negative reactive attitudes are connected not just to wrong but also to bad and still hold that violations of deontic normative material warrant a unique response. Arguably the negative reactive attitudes and their expressions are not the only form of blame. On my own view, for example, there are the negative reactive attitudes and their expressions on the one hand, and what I would call "enforcement blame" on the other. Enforcement blame is like demands qua speech act and unlike the negative reactive attitudes in that it involves an element of subordination and thus requires authority. Enforcement blame is, then, demand-like but not strictly speaking a demand. Enforcement blame, on my view, is connected exclusively to the deontic realm: it is the distinctive pragmatic upshot of wrongdoing.

The point of this concluding section is, of course, not to convince you that moral address is a functionally specified concept, or that there exist two distinct forms of blame—one at home in both the evaluative and deontic realms and the other limited to the deontic—or that blaming another is one way of holding responsible, and demanding that someone do as she ought is another way. Rather, the point is simply to show that there is conceptual space between the claim that demands are an essential element of any analysis of the negative reactive attitudes and claims about moral address, holding responsible, and blame's relationship to the deontic realm.

{ 9 }

Civilizing Blame

Victoria McGeer

Introduction

The phenomenon of blame, understood most broadly as a distinctive class of negative reactions prompted by wrongdoing and directed toward wrongdoers, has lately received a great deal of attention from moral philosophers. Perhaps this is not surprising. Certainly blame, by anyone's reckoning, is a pervasive feature of our moral experience. Rightly or wrongly, happily or unhappily, human beings are the kind of creatures that go in for blaming one another for perceived wrongdoing, where wrongdoing involves not just doing a bad thing but doing something *wrong*—that is, doing something that the perpetrator knows, or ought to know, is a bad thing without any justifying or exculpating excuse. Of course, the wrong thing in question need not be a moral offense. I may blame you for failing to pay a bill on time, or weakly accepting an invitation I know you have good reason to turn down, or forgetting to take the dog out for its morning walk. Yet as Bernard Williams points out, even in such cases the wrongdoing (act or omission) has "some kind of ethical dimension to it"; that is to say, "for blame to be appropriate, there must be some generally reprehensible characteristic involved in the explanation: the agent must have been careless, or lazy, or self-serving, or something of the sort" (1995a, p. 40). Such cases shade by degrees into those more centrally associated with what might be called 'moral blame,' where blamers perceive the perpetrator's wrongdoing as demonstrating a morally significant measure of disregard or disrespect toward themselves or toward others whom the perpetrator wrongs.

It is blame in this moral sense that has attracted the attention of an impressive array of moral philosophers, including (among others) Nomy Arpaly (2003,

Previous versions of this paper have been presented at a number of colloquia and workshops, and I am very grateful for all the challenging questions and comments I have received on these occasions. I owe a particular debt of gratitude to those who have provided me with more extensive comments, including Pamela Hieronymi, Daniel Kelly, Owen King, Nicola Lacey, Philip Pettit, Jesse Prinz, Tamar Schapiro, George Sher, Seana Shiffrin, Michael Smith, Manuel Vargas and, last but not least, the editors of this volume, Justin Coates and Neal Tognazzini.

2006), Pamela Hieronymi (2004, 2007, 2008), Gideon Rosen (2006), T. M. Scanlon (2008), George Sher (2006), Angela Smith (2007, 2008a), Jay Wallace (1994, 2011), Gary Watson (2004), and Susan Wolf (2011). One specific reason for this focus derives from a basic tension. On the one hand, because moral community depends for its existence on relations of mutual respect and goodwill, upholding the norms that constitute such relations—and so reacting negatively toward transgressors—seems part and parcel of what we owe to one another. On the other hand, the negative reactions characteristic of blame often have an angry, punitive edge that many theorists find morally distasteful, not least because of the range of painful, even destructive behaviors it so often motivates. In other words, there seems to be an unacceptable normative tension between recognizing the importance of blame as a negative response to wrongdoing and acknowledging various features or aspects of it that appear to be part and parcel of the way blame is expressed or enacted by real people in their everyday interactions. The consensus among moral philosophers is that this tension must be resolved if blame is to be condoned as playing an appropriate normative role in responding to wrongdoing.

The broader philosophical project that drives much of this work on blame is therefore one of showing how it can be a normatively acceptable, even valuable response to wrongdoing. I call this the project of 'civilizing blame' and agree with moral philosophers that it is an important one to pursue, but not, I claim, at the expense of taking the bile out of blame. In my view, this contravenes a constraint that any satisfactory account of blame must meet—that it should direct us to a psychologically plausible phenomenon, however unsavory, that answers to our ordinary conception of blame: it satisfies the ordinary connotations of the term, including connotations of resentment and anger and the desire for payback. The challenge is to accept this constraint while showing that blame may nevertheless be a normatively fitting response to wrongdoing.

I argue for an account in this paper that can, I believe, rise to this challenge. It is psychologically realistic in taking blame to be a phenomenon that displays the negative profile (warts and all) that is typically associated with blame. Yet it satisfies the normative constraint by explaining how this affective complex, unsavory as it undoubtedly is, can still do valuable normative work so long as it is constrained by social and institutional practices that support its more constructive features. I present and defend that view in the second and third sections of this paper. However, before coming to that argument, I lay out the rather different approach to civilizing blame that is adopted by many of the moral philosophers I named earlier. On their version of the project, civilizing blame amounts to sanitizing it—in effect, to purifying blame of what they take to be features they find normatively problematic; thus, by my lights, it is a psychologically unrealistic theory. Defenders of the sanitizing approach think, further, that this psychologically purified version of blame is normatively satisfying so far as certain features are eliminated. I say they are wrong on this count too. In rushing to reform the psychology of blame, they actually misrepresent what is normatively problematic about those features and so end up with an account of blame that fails to meet either psychological or normative desiderata.

The paper is in four sections. In the first, I look at the sanitizing approach, situating the question addressed, setting out the concerns that motivate it, and raising my critical worry that this approach is psychologically unrealistic—and, for that reason alone, must be normatively unsatisfying. In the second section, I argue in support of my contention that it is psychologically unrealistic to identify blame with the purified phenomenon that sanitizing theorists target. In the third section, I show that the warts-and-all psychological phenomenon in which blame consists has, despite its problematic features, a rich normative role unmatched by the sanitizing counterpart. And then in a short conclusion, I advertise a further benefit of my approach, showing that the argument points to a plausible project in the institutionalization of blame; broadly, it supports something like the restorative approach to issues of criminal justice. This conclusion drives home the idea that any sensible prospect for civilizing blame lies not in transforming (*per impossibile*) the psychology of blame but rather in supporting better practices of blame in both formal and informal contexts.

1. The Sanitizers' Approach to Civilizing Blame

There are two distinct projects that can be discerned in the philosophical work on blame—projects that are related but can nevertheless be distinguished. The first of these is a project of "metaphysically justifying" blame: showing that there is no metaphysical bar to satisfying an essential condition of warranted blame—namely, that individuals may be genuinely culpable for the wrong that they do. Though important, this project is not the focus of this paper, and I hereby put it aside. My concern is with a project that, by contrast, simply presupposes individuals can be culpable in a way that is metaphysically unproblematic.[1] This project—civilizing blame—is focused on a different kind of question—namely, is there something in the nature of blame *itself* that makes it a morally objectionable response to (culpable) wrongdoing? Philosophers who want to civilize blame aim to show how and why this is not the case.

As I said at the outset, I am sympathetic with the fundamental goal of this project but object to a standard way of pursuing it. The standard strategy aims to develop or defend a plausible account of blame that preserves its normative powers while purging its unsavory characteristics. It is a strategy of "sanitizing blame." And though I concede it has some initial appeal, I claim it will ultimately prove forlorn.

To understand its initial appeal, consider two questions that philosophers must address in pursuing their work on blame: (1) a conceptual question—What exactly

---

[1] Some might say these projects bear on one another in important ways, so should be tackled together. I don't dispute their interconnection (discussed further in the current section, see also McGeer 2011) but still claim we gain some analytic clarity by pulling these enterprises apart.

is blame?; and (2) a normative question—Is this phenomenon, so understood, morally defensible? The challenge, as they construe it, is this: if giving an intuitive or folk-psychological answer to the conceptual question seems to push toward giving a negative answer to the normative question, then defending a positive answer to the normative question will require giving a (somewhat) revisionist answer to the conceptual one. Specific theorists differ as to how revisionist an account of blame must be in order to pass normative muster, but none can go too far without vitiating the whole enterprise. After all, if the proposed account of 'blame' fails to connect in substantial ways with our ordinary understanding of what is involved in that phenomenon, then this is tantamount to agreeing with those who want to claim that blame as normally experienced has no positive normative standing; hence, it should be banished (to whatever extent is possible) from our moral-psychological repertoire (see, e.g., Smart 1961; Pereboom 2001).[2] Thus philosophers whose aim is to civilize blame by way of sanitizing it face two distinct challenges. First, they need to argue that their preferred account of blame is not *too* revisionist: it captures the central or, indeed, "essential" features of blame as a moral-psychological phenomenon, even if that means cleaning up the ordinary conception to some degree; that is to say, their preferred account passes psychological muster. Second, they need to argue that blame understood in their preferred sense is indeed "fairly" or "properly" directed at a wrongdoer in light of the wrong he or she has done; that is to say, their account passes normative muster as well.

Jay Wallace gives a nice illustration of this balancing act in his recent work on blame.[3] In his estimation, the philosophical project (civilizing blame) should take the form of "find[ing] space between two extremes for a defensible form of blame to occupy" (2011, p. 348). At one extreme is a weakly evaluative view that sees blame simply as a matter of sizing up a wrongdoer's moral short-comings as displayed in his or her acts and attitudes. Blame, on this view, is nothing more than a form of judgment, coolly registering facts about the wrongdoer independent of any response the blamer might make to the facts so registered (for defenders of this view, see, e.g., Smart 1961; Arpaly 2003).[4] But despite some dissenting opinions, most philosophers would agree with Wallace that such an account misses blame's "characteristic (if elusive) quality of

---

[2] It should be noted that, for many philosophers—Smart and Pereboom among them—the primary reason for denying that blame has any positive normative value stems from the metaphysical conviction that no person is genuinely blameworthy for their actions; hence, to blame them for what they do (in any deep moral sense) is manifestly unwarranted.

[3] This paper (Wallace 2011) is largely a critical response to Scanlon's view on blame, which, in Wallace's estimation, errs on the side of being too revisionist. See also Wolf (2011). I am largely in agreement with this aspect of Wallace's insightful paper (including his emphasis on the affective dimension of blame). Nevertheless I regard Wallace and Scanlon as pursuing (importantly different) variations on a fundamentally similar theme.

[4] Arpaly herself now acknowledges that this purely cognitive (or doxastic) account of blame is not fully adequate to everyday phenomena. See Arpaly (2006).

opprobrium" (2011, p. 348). In other words, they hold that judging someone blameworthy and actually blaming them are important to distinguish on both psychological and normative grounds. To judge a person blameworthy is certainly to find fault with them, maybe even moral fault. But to make such a judgment requires only that the judger assess that person's acts and attitudes in a way that is sensitive to the requirements of norm-governed behavior; it does not imply having any reaction to *them* as a blameworthy person. So, for instance, a therapist or parent may judge her patient or child to be blameworthy in a purely fault-determining sense, without thinking it right to blame him. To blame someone, by contrast, is to have in addition some kind of negative reaction to them as a blameworthy person—a feature that many would say makes blame a normatively more problematic phenomenon, although much will depend on what blame is supposed to add to the phenomenon of merely judging someone to be blameworthy.

This brings us to the other extreme: an essentially punitive or retributive view that equates blame with punishment, or at least pictures blame as a hot motivational prompt for a variety of sanctioning behaviors. Again, in many philosophers' estimation, this analysis seems to miss its psychological target. As Wallace says, "[W]e can blame someone without undertaking to punish them or to impose unpleasant sanctions of some kind" (2011, p. 348). But even should this view have some psychological traction, it is certainly not one that moral philosophers would happily endorse. As Wallace representatively insists, an essentially punitive account of blame "deprives . . . [it] of its legitimacy as a form of interpersonal behaviour" (p. 348). He adds, "[M]ost of us would feel some discomfort about acting with the aim of punishing or imposing sanctions on individuals for their moral transgressions. This is not, one wants to say, an appropriate way for autonomous individuals to interact with one another" (p. 348).

Now I grant that neither of these extremes does justice to the rich phenomenon of blame. But despite the ingenuity of various philosophical accounts, I doubt we can come to a satisfactory compromise between psychological realism and normative acceptability by trying to occupy an elusive middle ground in the analysis of blame, preserving its "quality of opprobrium" while stripping away its unsavory features, identified in particular with the angry punitive face of blame. In my estimation, a realistic assessment of the psychology of blame suggests that it is a robust human phenomenon with many unattractive features—for instance, often entraining a desire to hurt or get back at the wrongdoer. Furthermore though the significance of this fact is disputed (see, e.g., Scanlon 2008; Sher 2006), blame is typically emotionally toned, manifested in a variety of expressive behaviors that will often be experienced *as* punitive by those to whom it's directed. We are, after all, emotionally reactive creatures, feeling hurt and even attacked by the angry or indignant emotions of others, even when those emotions are in some sense merited or deserved and notwithstanding how blamers come to reveal such emotions to us (running the gambit, as it may be, from cold withdrawal or the silent treatment all the way through to verbal recriminations or physical threat; indeed sometimes a nasty or condemnatory look can be enough to make a wrongdoer suffer).[5] The question is how to take all this on board without giving up on the overarching project of civilizing blame.

The remainder of this paper addresses this problem. In section 2 I set out a hypothetical, naturalistic account of the psychology of blame, arguing that emotion is intimately connected with blame and cannot be analyzed away. In section 3 I address two distinct worries that I see as implicit in the concerns of sanitizers about such an approach and defend the view that we can be naturalistically realistic about blame and yet see an important normative role that it plays. In section 4 I look briefly at institutional developments in criminal justice and related areas that would build constructively on this naturalistic understanding of blame.

2. Excavating the Complex Psychology of Blame

2.1 IS BLAME EMOTIONALLY TONED? WHAT A NATURALISTIC APPROACH CONTRIBUTES TO CONCEPTUAL ANALYSIS

Blamers characteristically experience a range of negative emotions toward those whom they blame: anger, indignation, resentment, outrage, irritation, frustration, hurt feelings, distress. To what extent are these negative emotions part and parcel of blame? There are those who favor a cooler account of blame, insisting that, while such emotions are often associated with blame, they are not essential to it (Scanlon, Sher). Others argue that blame would not be *blame* (at least as we ordinarily understand it) absent such emotional reactivity, especially absent the core emotions of anger, indignation, and resentment (Rosen, Wallace, Wolf). How is this dispute to be resolved?

Here is one argument that proponents of cool blame offer in favor of their position: Despite the fact that certain emotions are often, even characteristically,

---

[5] This argues for taking a more encompassing view of sanctions according to which they are many and various, distinguishable in terms of a number of cross-cutting dimensions—for example, formal versus informal, substantive versus symbolic, material versus psychological. And though adults may judge it inappropriate to sanction one another in certain ways (they cannot tell one another to go stand in a corner), this still leaves a wide array of possibilities open to them. Indeed it is a sign of maturity that adults are susceptible to a variety of more subtle forms of sanction (the angry look, the cold withdrawal of friendly feeling). Hence though philosophers may be tempted to take a narrower view of 'sanction' (say, one that is material or substantive in certain key respects), I think that is psychologically unrealistic, and not just from the perspective of the one who is sanctioned but also from the perspective of the sanctioner (see also Sripada 2005). As P. F. Strawson (1962) points out, we are too invested in the goodwill of one another not to understand the chilling force of its withdrawal, and can use such withdrawal to powerful sanctioning effect (i.e., *as* a form of social regulation).

associated with blame, this is not invariably the case. Blamers may feel atypical emotions—or no emotions at all. Yet even in cases of "dispassionate" blame, where the blamer has no affective reaction to the wrongdoer as such, it seems intuitively obvious (at least to some) that the blamer fully blames the wrongdoer for something she has done. For instance, it seems intuitively obvious (at least to some) that we might fully blame a distant third party for some egregious act without any flutter from our amygdalas, as when we read about some crime in the morning newspaper. But, the argument continues, this implies that negative affect has no critical role to play in a philosophical account of blame. After all, philosophical analyses attempt to delineate the essential features of such phenomena. And since negative affect is not present in every legitimate instance of blame, it could not be an essential feature. Hence, philosophers should put it to one side in their attempts to specify what precisely blame involves.

In my view this argument is misguided, encouraging accounts of blame that are psychologically distorted. However, my resistance to it does not depend on contesting the claim that there may be genuine instances of dispassionate blame or instances of blame wherein the blamer has an atypical affective reaction to the person blamed (intuitions clearly differ on this point, for reasons I think will become clear in a moment). My concern is rather to challenge the guiding assumption that a proper analysis of blame should focus on identifying so-called essential features (features present in every legitimate instance of blame), discounting those that are "merely characteristic." While this is a standard move in analytic philosophy, it can be overdone, showing insensitivity to the fact that characteristic features can be of two very different types. They can be features whose contingent association with the phenomenon in question is of no criterial significance. Call such features, 'kind-associated features.' Or they can be features that have criterial significance in the following sense: they account for our interest in identifying a kind as such, even though things belonging to the kind do not invariably manifest the feature in question. Call such features 'canonical features' (Jackson and Pettit 1995).

Consider how we come to identify the kind 'heart.' Whether natural or artificial, hearts are canonically the kind of things that pump blood. A heart deserves to be called a heart only so far as it is a thing of *that* (instrumental) kind. But, of course, this doesn't mean that all hearts are able to pump blood. Things of that kind sometimes malfunction. Or consider how we come to identify the color kind 'red.' Things that are red in color are canonically the kind of things that produce a certain visual sensation in visually unimpaired human beings under normal lighting conditions. Something gets to be called 'red' only so far as it a thing of *that* (visual) kind. But, of course, this doesn't mean that all red things invariably produce the requisite visual sensation. Viewing conditions may be atypical in various exogenous or endogenous ways. And here is one final example, perhaps more relevant to the phenomenon in question. Happiness is canonically the kind of psychological state that is affectively toned in a particular way. A person is only characterized as 'happy' so far as he or she is in a state of *that* (psychological) kind. But, at least if great writers are to be believed, there are occasions when individuals can be happy (and even know they are happy) without the canonical affective experiences. Jane Austen gives us a nice example of this at the dénouement of *Pride and Prejudice*, when, against all odds (including her own initial and well-articulated antipathy), Elizabeth Bennett has finally accepted Mr. Darcy's hand in marriage:

> The evening passed quietly, unmarked by anything extraordinary. The acknowledged lovers talked and laughed, the unacknowledged were silent. Darcy was not of a disposition in which happiness overflows in mirth; and Elizabeth, agitated and confused, rather knew that she was happy than felt herself to be so; for, besides the immediate embarrassment, there were other evils before her. She anticipated what would be felt in the family when her situation became known; she was aware that no one liked him but Jane; and even feared that with the others it was a dislike which not all his fortune and consequence might do away.

In keeping with these examples, I suggest that blame constitutes a moral-psychological kind, a canonical feature of which is its emotional tone. One of the attractions of this view is that it's commensurate with a more general functionalist approach in the philosophy of mind. According to functionalism, folk-psychological concepts like 'blame' are best understood as designating states or attitudes that typically play a certain causal role in the cognitive economy of (typical) human beings (Lewis 1980; Armstrong 1980). In the case of blame, it is a state that is apt for being caused by perceived wrongdoing and apt for producing certain behavioral effects. (I will say more about these behavioral effects below.) Now on a functionalist approach, the fact that blamers characteristically experience a range of core emotions that color their blaming acts and attitudes (anger, indignation, resentment, outrage) strongly suggests two things. First, the state that typically plays the causal role of blame in human beings is an affective state, though perhaps not invariably so; there may be various deviating background conditions in place, as in the happiness example given earlier. Second, the emotional character of the state is not incidental to the causal role it typically plays; on the contrary, emotions are motivational drivers in human beings, reliably and involuntarily priming certain action tendencies. Moreover, because of this, or so I shall argue, their presence transforms the meaning of the actions thereby produced, giving those actions a particular normative cast.[6]

The approach I take in this paper is thus avowedly functionalist—and more generally naturalistic. I cite a number of advantages in the following pages. But

---

[6] Cf. Wallace (2011) for a compelling conceptual defense of this point.

one at least is this: it helps tip the balance on a hotly disputed issue as to whether emotional reactivity is a constitutive feature of blame. By making sense of the fact that exceptional cases are beside the point, it lends credibility to the conceptual point that blame would not be blame absent the characteristic presence (and effect) of certain core emotions: anger, indignation, and resentment. Of course, as we know from everyday experience, the intensity of these emotions may vary widely, running the gambit from mild irritation all the way through to burning outrage. And the duration of these emotional episodes may vary as well, from relatively fleeting to unhappily persistent. Such variability surely depends on a number of factors: the type of wrongdoing; the frequency of the wrongdoing (does it represent an established pattern?); the wrongdoer's own attitudes and subsequent behavior; the blamer's own position vis-à-vis the wrongdoer; and so on. Yet even amid such variability, what I am calling the emotional tone of blame—the anger, resentment, indignation—remains relatively constant. So this naturalistic approach suggests a more fundamental question: Why is blame emotionally toned in this way? That is, why is the negative emotion canonically associated with blame some species of anger rather than, say, sadness (*pace* Scanlon)? This in turn leads to a more general question: Why is blame emotionally toned at all? What function does this serve?

These questions point up the need for thinking about blame in the wider context of understanding the role of emotions in human cognition and behavior. While this is a broad topic, philosophical work on the emotions has become increasingly interdisciplinary in recent years, deriving considerable insights from evolutionary biology, cultural anthropology, cognitive neuroscience, and experimental economics (see, e.g., Griffiths 1997; DeLancey 2001; Prinz 2004). Leaning on such work, I turn now to developing and defending a hypothesis that accounts for why anger is a characteristic feature of blame and, more broadly, why blame should have the kind of complex profile we see in everyday life—a profile that encompasses both problematic and positive normative characteristics. This account involves dipping into our evolutionary heritage, understanding that such reactions can be deeply embedded in human nature but still have a psychological complexity that is characteristic of a brain that has evolved in part by adapting old functions to new uses.[7] While the evolutionary account I offer is provisional, allowing for considerable refinement and revision in its detail, it serves to make plausible my basic thesis that blame has certain elemental or primitive features on which later evolving cognitive sophistications have been built. More to the point, it serves to underscore how these features are inextricably intermingled, making sense of the everyday phenomenology of blame, while ultimately putting paid—as I shall argue—to the sanitizers' strategy for civilizing blame.

---

[7] For a similar kind of approach aimed at evaluating the role of disgust in moral judgment, see Kelly (2011).

2.2 BLAME AS AN EVOLVED PHENOMENON:
ELEMENTAL FOUNDATIONS

I begin with some preliminary remarks on the nature of anger. There are many theorists who contend that anger is a "primary" or "basic" emotion (along with fear, happiness, disgust, sadness).[8] Basic emotions are distinctive so far as they appear to be universally shared among human beings, with cross-cultural patterns of eliciting conditions, physiological manifestations, facial expressions, and behavioral responses (Ekman 1972, 1992). This suggests that they are, at least in part, innately programmed responses to stereotypical situations in the world of relevance to individual survival and/or well-being. Such responses are rapid and involuntary, recruiting areas of the midbrain in the absence of, or at least prior to, any higher cortical activity; hence they are not cognitively mediated in a reflective or judgmental sense. Even so, they involve a *backward-looking element of appraisal*: they are triggered by various events only so far as those events are coded (i.e., perceived) as situations of the relevant emotion-inducing type. And they involve a *forward-looking action-priming element*, disposing agents to behave in ways that, in situations of the relevant type, had an overall tendency to enhance individual fitness in ancestral populations. For instance, thanks to our evolutionary heritage, we have an innate fear response triggered by looming objects. The response is rapid and involuntary, involving a noncognitive appraisal that looming objects are potentially dangerous and simultaneously priming a suite of defensive behavioral reactions (ducking, protecting vulnerable body parts, turning away, fleeing). This same general pattern applies to anger, only here the kind of situations that involuntarily provoke the emotion are coded (i.e., perceived) as something like "an offense to me or mine," and the response thereby provoked is a suite of aggressive behaviors aimed at defending whatever it is that's threatened by the offense.[9]

With these general observations in mind, I turn now to the question of why anger is involved in our blaming acts and attitudes. The first thing to note is that blaming anger is often triggered by something more specific than "an offense to me or mine"—namely, norm transgressions of one sort or another. Why should this be the case? An evolutionary approach would suggest that early hominids were subject to selective pressures that favored the policing of social norms. And indeed many theorists argue that large-scale human cooperation could emerge only with the development of social norms, supported

---

[8] While different theorists often give a more extensive list of basic emotions, differing considerably on what should be included, they generally agree on the five listed here. For discussion, see Griffiths (1997); Prinz (2004).

[9] For discussion, see Prinz (2004), especially chapter 3.

and defended by cognitive/affective mechanisms specifically recruited to this task (Nichols and Mallon 2006; Henrich and Henrich 2007; Boyd and Richerson 2005; Sripada and Stich 2007; Nichols 2002). Of course, various emotions might lend themselves to such recruitment; for instance, disgust is argued to be importantly involved in supporting social norms (Kelly 2011). Still, there can be little doubt that anger, and the suite of aggressive behaviors it entrains, should play a major role in this process, perhaps particularly with regard to supporting those norms involving fairness and harm (Sripada and Stich 2007).

In support of these evolutionary speculations, consider a convergent line of research from behavioral economics. A number of game-theoretic studies involving norms of social exchange demonstrate that punishment, and the threat of punishment, stabilizes cooperative interactions, especially when there is a tendency in the population toward "altruistic punishment" (the punishers are bystanders who have not been directly affected by the transgression) (Fehr and Gachter 2002; Fehr and Fischbacher 2004a, 2004b). Yet from the economist's perspective, the emergence of such a tendency is somewhat mysterious. After all, punishment is costly, not only using up valuable resources but also potentially incurring the costs of reprisal. So why would self-interested agents go in for such a thing, especially if it were not to benefit them directly? Robert Frank (1988) suggests the answer lies in our emotions (and specifically here in our blaming anger). On his account, thanks to the pressures of natural selection, human beings are not simply (or primarily) rational agents in a narrow calculative sense; we are also *passionate* agents—agents whose short-term behavior can serve broader rational goals when driven by forces that do not depend on more narrowly circumscribed reasoning processes. In Frank's terms, these forces—that is, emotions—not only prime us to act in ways that serve our broader rational interests; they operate as "commitment devices," making credible to others the overwhelming likelihood of our acting in such ways. Hence, the fact that human beings respond emotionally to things not only has an important action-priming function; it also has an important *signaling* function, a feature I will return to below.

The relatively simple story of blame that emerges from taking a broadly evolutionary perspective can thus be summarized as follows. At the most elemental level, blame is a quasi-autonomous, emotionally mediated response to others that is specifically prompted by, and targeted on, behavior that transgresses personally or socially valued norms. Despite its quasi-autonomous (nonreflective) character, this blaming response has both a backward-looking appraisal dimension and a forward-looking regulative dimension. The backward-looking appraisal dimension consists in coding—that is, perceiving—others' behavior as (offensively) transgressive; the forward-looking regulative dimension consists in an aggressive (punitive) response aimed at changing or inhibiting such behavior.

2.3 BEYOND ELEMENTAL BLAME

But is this simple story adequate to our everyday experience of blame? On the one hand, it certainly accounts for what appear to be the cruder features of blame, even in its contemporary guise. (Consider, for instance, the power and immediacy of "road rage"—the angry blame one feels at being cut off in traffic.) Yet, on the other hand, it seems to miss certain respects in which blame can function as a more reflective and nuanced response to wrongdoing, open—to some degree—to reflective criticism and control. For instance, we are generally well able to withhold or suppress our blame when we judge (for any of a number of reasons) that someone does not deserve such a response despite his or her transgressive behavior. How, then, to account for the more sophisticated ways in which our blaming emotions operate?

The answer, I believe, lies in our higher-order *mentalizing* capacities, the fact that we understand what others do in terms of a wide variety of mental states (beliefs, desires, intentions, emotions, and so on). Such capacities dramatically transform how human beings are able to experience blame, both as individuals who do the blaming and as individuals who are the targets of blame. They make sense of how a more primitive system of blaming anger could have been recalibrated, not simply in terms of the kinds of situations that would elicit it, but also in the kinds of responses to which it would naturally give rise.[10] Nevertheless, recalibration is not wholesale replacement. Recalibration works by co-opting basic features that are already in place. Thus we might expect that such developments in the cognitive anatomy of blame would simply have built on its more elemental foundations. And this implies that blame remains, at root, an emotionally mediated response to another's behavior, structured in terms of a backward-looking appraisal dimension *and* a forward-looking regulative dimension.[11] How, then, has this two-dimensional focus of blame been transformed by our mentalizing capacities?

Consider, first, the backward-looking appraisal dimension. I take it to be undeniable that when we blame others it is principally for something they *do*: for their transgressive behavior. Yet as mentalizing creatures, it is also undeniable that we care deeply about the underlying attitudes that motivate and thereby explain what others do. We care about this not just because it tells us more about how to code some particular instance of behavior—to determine

---

[10] For a suggestive account of how basic emotional systems become recalibrated by way of higher-order cognitive processes, see Prinz (2004).

[11] Fully acknowledging this forward-looking dimension of blame has the potential of removing a philosophical puzzle that seems to drive a lot of the work on blame: understanding the peculiar force or power of blame to do something more to the wrongdoer than give negative evaluation of his or her behavior. In my estimation, this force largely resides in the regulative dynamics of blame, which dynamics many philosophers are resistant to acknowledge because of what I shall argue are misplaced normative concerns.

if it was genuinely a transgressive act, as opposed to, say, an accident (e.g., he stepped on my foot deliberately, not just because he didn't see it). We also care about a person's underlying attitudes because we take these to be reliable indicators of *patterns* of behavior—that is, how that person is likely to act toward others, or again toward ourselves. It is thus our mentalizing capacities that explain P. F. Strawson's insightful observation that our blaming emotions—resentment, indignation, anger—are acutely sensitive to the *attitudes* that others manifest in their behavior, whether what they do displays a "good will, its absence, or its opposite" (1962, pp. 76–77). The focus on attitude explains, indeed, why Strawson calls our blaming emotions "*reactive* attitudes," insisting that, even though we experience such attitudes when others do something transgressive, we generally endorse our reaction only when that behavior betrays some attitudinal deficiency on their part that has more general significance for their interpersonal activities (cf. Strawson's long discussion of excusing and exempting conditions, pp. 77–80).

Of course, such attitudinal deficiencies may be many and varied. In blaming, we might judge others to be lazy in their interpersonal concern, unthinking, indefensibly ignorant, neglectful, uncaring, disrespectful, mean, or downright malicious—or even some combination of these. Yet if my general thesis about the foundational structure of blame is right, the attitudinal focus in our experience of these blaming emotions should have both the backward-looking appraisal dimension *and* a forward-looking regulative dimension. That is to say, we should certainly care about what attitudes individuals manifest in their behavior. But if those attitudes are interpersonally deficient in some way, we should care equally about seeing a change in those attitudes, working to promote this change first and foremost through our blaming reaction. Indeed I think this is just what we find.

The two-way dimensionality of our attitudinal concern is made manifest, in my view, by thinking about what makes our blaming emotions go away, not in a purely psychological sense but rather in a normative sense—that is, what makes our blaming emotions feel "properly addressed" (so that if, psychologically speaking, we have any lingering remnants of anger or indignation, we judge these feelings to be misplaced or inappropriate).

On the backward-looking appraisal end of blame (to which moral philosophers have given most of their attention), our blaming emotions are appropriately modified if it turns out that the attitudinal deficiency we think we detect in someone's transgressive behavior is not in fact present. For instance, the person had a reasonable excuse for what she did: it was an accident, or she was compelled by circumstances beyond her control, or she was under great strain and did not mean to show any disregard or ill will, and so on. We feel mollified then, and our blaming emotions naturally tend to die away.

But equally, on the forward-looking regulative end of blame, these emotions are normatively answered—and naturally tend to die away—when wrongdoers admit that their actions did display a bad attitude (that they were lazy in their concern, uncaring, disrespectful, mean, or even malicious); that such attitudes were, and are, inappropriate; that they are therefore responsible for the injury they caused; and, more important, that they take responsibility for not so harming again by changing or regulating the attitudes that led to the offensive behavior.

But how could wrongdoers convincingly show all this? In part, I claim, by their own reactive emotions of guilt, shame, and remorse and the activities such emotions tend to generate. These are themselves *reactive* emotions (or attitudes) because they react to the blaming emotions of others and, indeed, importantly invite a reactive response in turn—for instance, when all goes well, the blamer's mollification, understanding, and even forgiveness. Now I do not mean to suggest that this process is typically easy or straightforward and oc-curs in the blink of an eye. My point is rather to highlight a dynamic trajectory of unfolding events, orchestrated back and forth between blamer and wrong-doer, which we recognize as having a normatively appropriate, even desirable structure because of the potential power it has to develop the moral under-standing of all parties in a normative dispute—most importantly, the offend-er's, but often as well the moral understanding of those who would call the offender to account. Importantly, this structure, which I have elsewhere called 'reactive scaffolding' (McGeer 2011), is enabled and enhanced because we are emotionally sensitive creatures, attuned to the way others are speaking to us in large part by way of their emotional responses. (I return to this point below.)

Understanding this feature of our psychology paves the way for restoring the credibility of the sanctioning face of blame; in particular, it gives us the necessary resources for responding explicitly to the kind of worries that may drive the sanitizers' quest to transform blame into something rather more civ-ilized at the psychological level. In the following section, I explicitly identify and discuss two such concerns, aiming to show that they are fundamentally misguided, however well motivated they may be. My conclusion will be that somehow we must search for resources outside the head if we are ultimately to succeed at the task of civilizing blame.

3. Replies to the Sanitizers' Normative Concerns

The account of blame I offer in the previous section has two distinct goals. The first is to remain true to the complex psychology of blame as experienced in everyday phenomenology. The second is to give some account of that psy-chology within a broadly naturalistic framework. These two desiderata are met, I believe, by understanding how blame could be an evolved reaction to transgressive behavior (as it undoubtedly is, no matter what the correct details of such an account), with more nuanced reflective features (courtesy of our mentalizing capacities) that build on a more primitive foundation. I leave any further defense of this account to another occasion.

My purpose now is to consider why the moral philosophers discussed in section 1 might find the nature of this bricolage somewhat disturbing, for, if I am right, the persisting elemental features of blame here identified are precisely what give rise to their deepest normative concerns. There are two concerns in particular that are likely to worry them. The first and most important of these underwrites their deep resistance to the sanctioning face of blame; I label it the 'anti-regulation concern.' According to this concern, a civilized form of blame cannot aim at the regulation of behavior without becoming an essentially conditioning enterprise in which the blamer fails to treat the one who is blamed with appropriate moral respect (i.e., fails to acknowledge his or her moral personhood appropriately). The second normative concern is less widely shared but tends to be articulated in addition to the anti-regulation concern, perhaps because of how blaming emotions so often motivate explicit sanctioning activities. I call it the 'anti-emotion concern.' According to this concern, while blame is often associated with angry, punitive emotions, these emotions are dangerous and surely not essential to a more civilized form of blame. After all, a civilized form of blame would simply consist in making a normatively appropriate response to wrongdoing—that is, a response that, however specified, is essentially nonsanctioning (in keeping with the anti-regulation concern). Why can't this be accomplished in an affectively neutral way? I try to address these two concerns in this section and use my responses to build up the naturalistic picture of blame introduced in the previous section.

3.1 THE ANTI-REGULATION CONCERN

The anti-regulation concern gives expression to the worry that there is something essentially disrespectful about blamers working to regulate a wrongdoer's behavior; hence a morally defensible account of blame cannot take such regulation to be an essential feature of blame. Why should this be the case? Here is a line of reasoning that may be driving the concern: To view blamers as working to regulate the behavior of wrongdoers is to see the blamers as engaging in an essentially disrespectful engineering enterprise, strategically undertaken to control the behavior of those who offend against them.[12] In other words, it involves treating the targets of blame not as moral agents in their own right but as objects of behavioral conditioning and control—in Strawson's

---

[12] This concern is explicitly voiced by Philip Pettit (2001). His solution to this problem is somewhat different from my own; it appeals to a notion of tacit consent to be so regulated by others. I go a somewhat different route, but our paths run parallel to the extent that we claim that discursive modes of affecting others' attitudes are essentially nonmanipulative; hence blame will be nonmanipulative to the extent it legitimately counts as a discursive mode of behavioral regulation. I come to this argument shortly.

terms, it is to take an "objective attitude" toward wrongdoers. But, so this reasoning continues, it is part of the very essence of our blaming activities that we treat wrongdoers as responsible moral agents in their own right. After all, if in appraising what someone does, we come to see them as out of their minds, or out of control in some way that demonstrates a compromised capacity for responsible agency, we think our blame—our blaming emotions—are misplaced. (These are the exempting conditions that Strawson emphasized.) So, as blamers, we cannot do any regulative (i.e., conditioning or engineering) work with our blame without undermining or betraying the very feature of our practice that makes such blame appropriate: treating wrongdoers as responsible agents in their own right, deserving the respect of moral address even if the content of that address is to express our anger or distress at their moral shortcomings.

I have two responses to this anti-regulation concern. The first relies on what I think is a fairly uncontroversial point and clears up an important ambiguity in the reasoning presented above. Some practices may have an underlying functional rationale such that we would surely give them up if they failed to fulfill that function. Nevertheless, fulfilling that function may not be what we explicitly aim at when we engage in the practice. Fulfilling that function may be an essential and, indeed, explicitly recognized by-product of the practice in question; yet it is not, perhaps cannot be what practitioners aim at without spoiling the functional efficacy of the practice in question.[13] This familiar observation is what lies behind the hedonistic paradox: happiness is not something we can or do achieve by directly seeking it; yet we often engage in particular practices that aim at something else because we recognize that they make us happy, and we would give them up if they did not. So too it may be with the practice of blame. Blaming is something we do not with the explicit aim of regulating others' behavior. Nevertheless, in cases where we know blame can have no such effect, it loses its appeal as an appropriate or fitting response to wrongdoing (as when we say "It's no good blaming Jones; she's out of her mind"). This would make regulating others' behavior essentially a by-product of the practice of blaming, indeed one we explicitly recognize when we regard genuine insensitivity to the demands implicit in blame as a telling sign of the kind of problem (e.g., mental disability) that appropriately exempts others from our blaming attitudes and activities.

The "essential by-product" response shows that a regulative account of blame need not flout the normative prohibition against treating others in an essentially disrespectful way—that is, in a way that fails to respect their status as responsible agents. Strawson himself emphasizes this point in the final passage of "Freedom and Resentment":

---

[13] The notion of some feature being essentially a by-product of a practice (i.e., not one that can be intentionally or explicitly aimed at) comes from Elster (1983).

It is far from wrong to emphasize the efficacy of all those practices which express or manifest our moral attitudes, in regulating behaviour in ways considered desirable; or to add that when certain of our beliefs about the efficacy of some of these practices turn out to be false, then we may have good reason for dropping or modifying those practices. What is wrong is to forget that these practices, and their reception, the reactions to them, really are expressions of our moral attitudes and not merely devices we calculatingly employ for regulative purposes. Our practices do not merely exploit our natures, they express them. Indeed the very understanding of the kind of efficacy these expressions of our attitudes have turns on our remembering this. (1962, p. 93)

Still, while this passage clearly endorses a view of blame according to which behavioral regulation can be an essential (and recognized) by-product of a normatively appropriate practice, I think it also suggests a stronger, more controversial view that I am inclined to take. So here is my second response to the anti-regulation concern. I claim there is nothing per se incompatible about consciously and explicitly aiming at changing (i.e., regulating) others' behavior and fully respecting them as persons—as responsible moral agents in their own right. What makes these things compatible or incompatible is the *means* one chooses to change or regulate the behavior in question.

Let me demonstrate this point first by way of considering an analogy. Suppose I believe that p is true and I want you to come to believe it too. (Of course, I may have a variety of motives for wanting this, but I don't think this potential variety affects the point I want to make.) Suppose, further, that there are a variety of means by which I could accomplish this goal: hypnosis, drugs, neural tinkering, or the good old-fashioned method of offering you what I take to be compelling evidence and/or argument in favor of p. Now even though I am consciously and explicitly aiming at getting you to believe that p, when I offer you evidence and argument to the best of my ability, no one would claim there is something essentially reprehensible in what I am doing, whereas if I adopted one of these other means, there certainly is. The difference is clear. In the argument case, I respect your own capacities as a reasoner to form (what to my mind are) true beliefs; I respect you as a reasoning agent. In these other cases, I treat your state of mind as something to be *engineered*, short-circuiting your own powers of reasoning to arrive at the truth of p. Note too that when I adopt such means, it does not matter whether my motives are evil or benign. Either way, there is something I am failing to respect about you *qua believer*—namely, your own capacity to track and evaluate the reasons for belief, a capacity that is central, as most would agree, to your autonomy and moral dignity as a person. Thus even were I concerned to act in your own best interest, I could not take the engineering approach to altering your beliefs without thereby compromising those interests. This is what makes the engineering approach morally reprehensible.

In sum, to be respectful of you qua believer is to be respectful of you qua reasoning agent. But in order to be respectful of you in this way, it does not matter that I explicitly aim at getting you to change your beliefs; what matters is that I choose a means whereby your own rational faculties are the proximate cause of the change in your beliefs. That is to say, I must offer you argument and/or evidence in favor of p. Of course, there may be ways in which I can fail to be normatively appropriate in offering you my arguments. (I use rhetorical tricks, I don't give you all the evidence at my command, and so on.) Nevertheless because *you* are the final arbiter in how you respond to my arguments (believing p or not), though I may mislead I do not directly and explicitly compromise your status as a reasoning agent. One significant and important test of this fact is that you not only have the power to withhold your belief, but you have the power to challenge my arguments and my evidence, thereby exposing me to the very same process and possibilities to which I expose you—specifically the possibility of changing *my* mind as to the truth of p in light of your argumentative response. Call this the 'dialogical test' on a normatively acceptable means for altering a person's beliefs.

Does this provide a good analogy for thinking about the case of blame? Specifically, can we use such reasoning to lay to rest the more direct version of the anti-regulation concern which holds that, in blaming others, we cannot explicitly and consciously aim to regulate their behavior in blaming them without disrespecting them as persons, as responsible moral agents in their own right? I think we can. To see this, recall first the mentalizing point: that what invokes our blaming attitudes is not transgressive behavior per se but the attitudinal deficiencies we take such behavior to display. Hence in blaming others, though we may aim to alter (or regulate) their behavior, it is by way of changing their attitudes—or, more precisely, by way of rectifying what seems to us a *deficiency* in those attitudes. Moreover, we may aim to change others' attitudes by way of communicating certain things to them through our blaming emotions, thereby stimulating their own capacity to track what is required of them as responsible agents. Specifically, our anger and distress communicates to others how we are interpreting what they have done, what it reflects about them, and that we don't find it acceptable. Further, by treating them as fitting or appropriate targets of our blame, we communicate to others that we regard them *as responsible agents*—hence that we have a right to expect better of them, both now and in the future, and that they will remain fitting targets of our blame absent reparative action or change on their part.

Now some philosophers may regard these blaming emotions not as a powerful communicative tool but rather as a brutally regulative stick. After all, ill will is not something that individuals enjoy having directed at them—indeed, as I emphasize in note 5, they can experience these attitudes as deeply punitive. This is simply the consequence of being (in Strawson's terms) reactively sensitive creatures, involuntarily disposed to react to the good or ill will of others, particularly when that good or ill will purports to comment on the quality of one's own actions and attitudes. Still, this psychological fact, so far from making putative wrongdoers prey to the engineering control of those who blame them, draws them into an exchange about the precise meaning of what they have done. Moreover, because such exchanges have the power to make a blamer's blame feel properly addressed, this is—consciously or unconsciously—what blamers are asking, maybe even demanding wrongdoers to do: to explain and justify themselves and, failing that, to apologize or make other reparation and to rectify their actions and attitudes going forward.

This is just what makes the belief case an apt analogy. On the account I offer, the point and power of blame is to draw wrongdoers into a kind of exchange where they are perforce challenged to exercise their capacities as responsible agents, to reflect on what they have done, whether or not it is legitimate, and if it is not, to *take* responsibility for what they have done and for what they will do in the future. Thus despite the fact that such a process aims to change a person's actions and attitudes, it is not by means of the blamers' exercising engineering control. In the first place, this process aims to change wrongdoers' attitudes and actions by way of challenging them to better exercise their own capacities as a responsible agent: via the demand for explanation, justification, reflection, and reform. But in the second place, drawing putative wrongdoers into such an exchange, and thereby fully crediting them with the capacities of responsible agency, opens blamers themselves to being challenged on the legitimacy of their blame: it opens them to explaining and justifying their normative expectations and how they think those expectations have been unjustifiably disappointed by the targets of their blame. In other words, reactive exchanges of this sort are invariably dialogical: they invariably work to develop the normative understanding of the putative wrongdoer, the blamer, or both. Hence this process—which I have elsewhere called 'reactive scaffolding' (McGeer 2011)—passes the dialogical test on a normative acceptable means for attitudinal and behavioral regulation; indeed, it is because it passes this dialogical test that it is a particularly effective form of such regulation. To quote Strawson once again, "[O]ur practices do not merely exploit our natures, they express them. Indeed the very understanding of the kind of efficacy these expressions of our attitudes have turns on our remembering this" (1962, p. 93).

3.2 THE ANTI-EMOTION CONCERN

Finally, I return to the anti-emotion concern, which now may be put like this: Suppose the foregoing account is on the right track. Blame works to instigate a process of normative reflection on the appropriateness or inappropriateness of what someone has done, with the aim of shaping or improving the actions and attitudes of a genuine transgressor—a process that, by its nature, exposes blamers themselves to the potential normative review of their blaming actions and attitudes. But now, if this is what accounts for the normative force of blame, why can't this process be carried forward, perhaps more effectively, without the coloring of a lot of (or indeed any) angry emotion?

There are two ways of interpreting this question. The first is a question about psychological reality: Is it possible for creatures like us to engage in such a process under the burden of perceived injury without feeling or expressing angry emotions, however mild these may be? My response to this is brief. Perhaps it is possible, at least for the saints among us. But however much we may suppose this is a preferable state of affairs, I doubt it is practically available to the common run of humanity. And this must pose a serious challenge to any philosophical theory that recommends it.

Still, for the sake of exploring the shape of our normative commitments, it may be worth posing this question in a second, more theoretical vein. Suppose we could dispense with the emotional concomitants of blame. Wouldn't this be a normatively preferable state of affairs? After all, we are all well-versed in the dangers of angry emotions. They can be highly destructive, leading to cruel and excessively punitive behavior. They can also be self-destructive, leading to unpleasant ruminations, loss of trust, loss of more general goodwill, loss of a capacity to appreciate the better things around us. They can get in the way of listening to what others have to say. They can generate downward spirals, where one person's anger begets what may seem to others justified anger and resentment in turn, refueling the anger originally felt and encouraging more anger in return. The list goes on. Hence even if the goal is unreachable, we should still work hard at tempering or repressing the angry concomitants of blame.

I concede all these dangers and do not want to downplay the difficulties of dealing with blame as an emotion-laden psychological phenomenon. Indeed, as I will emphasize in my next and concluding section, this is part of my motivation for writing this paper. Nevertheless, I claim that, dangerous as indignation, resentment, or outrage may be, the state of affairs in which such emotions are missing or absent from blame should not be recommended on normative grounds. In order to establish this point, I advert once again to the kind of creatures we are, for in my view, it is psychological reality that makes emotionless blame not just practically unavailable but also a misguided normative ideal. My claim turns on a premise I have defended in response to the anti-regulation concern: that, as a matter of psychological fact, emotions constitute for us a powerful form of communication. Here I up the ante by arguing that emotions constitute for us a *uniquely* powerful form of communication, the specific features of which militate against any normative recommendation that we should suppress them (to whatever extent possible) in contexts that make blame appropriate. I offer two considerations in support of this claim.

The first consideration focuses on how emotions make salient for us the communicative contents of what they convey. I have already stressed that, as reactively sensitive creatures, we are involuntarily disposed to react to—that is, both detect and *care about*—the good or ill will that others manifest toward us. And this will be so, perhaps even more strongly so, when that good or ill will is itself a *reactive attitude*—that is, when it is directed toward us in virtue of how we have treated others (or more precisely, in virtue of how they judge that we have treated them). Such emotional reactions are attention-grabbers for us, providing a form of triangulation that draws our attention both to the person manifesting the attitude and to the behavior—whatever it was—that prompted the attitude. The attitude itself is usually self-intimating: we are very good at reading the emotional reactions of others, including—in the case of blame— the opprobrium it conveys. But that someone should have such a reaction draws our attention to *her*—perhaps in a way we had not given it before; it draws our attention to her not just as a particular person but as a creature that can be hurt by what we say and do and, as such, is deserving of our regard. Furthermore, while I have said others' blame directs our attention to our own behavior, it may not be obvious to us why our behavior should prompt such a reaction. Nevertheless, our own emotional reactivity makes this an issue we cannot easily ignore. Of course, we may resist their review of our behavior, getting angry or indignant in return, thereby conveying to the blamer that she has misjudged us or somehow reacted inappropriately. But even as we offer such resistance, we are willy-nilly drawn into an exchange with her about the meaning of our behavior, the nature of appropriate expectations, the shape of prevailing norms, and so on. And as I have repeatedly emphasized, we are drawn into this content-rich exchange precisely because of the quality of our own emotional reactivity to the emotional-laden communications of others.

The second consideration digs more deeply into why we should be so reac-tively sensitive to (i.e., particularly affected by) the emotional reactions of others, both from an evolutionary and a game-theoretic point of view. The suggestion is that emotions are what biologists call 'expensive signals': they are hard to gen-erate under conditions that do not naturally prime a person to experience them; equally, they are hard to fake (Frank 1988). Blaming emotions thus have a special communicative (and evidential) power. Since they are hard to generate under conditions wherein blamers do not genuinely perceive an injury, they convey to transgressors both how seriously blamers regard the offense and their sincerity in pressing their normative demands. Furthermore, from the blamers' point of view, it is the emotional quality of the transgressors' reactions that conveys how seriously they are taking the blamers' complaint, as something to which they are sincerely paying attention (whether they accept that complaint by way of guilt, shame, or remorse or repudiate it by way of their own indignant anger). As Jay Wallace points out, emotions have the power to transform the meaning of our various communications; the suggestion here is that this is because emotions are not normally or straightforwardly under our voluntary control.

Taking these points together, we reach a conclusion that may not seem entirely satisfactory: although the anti-emotion concern is based on valid normative considerations, these should not be trumping considerations. If we do not wear the costs of angry blame, then we cannot reap its considerable rewards. This is not a wholehearted endorsement of what blame has to offer by any means. But it is to insist that we cannot—and, more to the point, should not—deal with these normative concerns by recommending that we try (as I think, *per impossibile*) to take the emotional guts out of blame.

4. Civilizing Blame: Sketching a New Way Forward

I began this paper by identifying what seems to be an unacceptable normative tension between recognizing the importance of blame as a negative response to wrongdoing and acknowledging various features or aspects of it that appear to be part and parcel of the way blame is expressed or enacted by real people in their day-to-day interactions. The bad news of this paper is that this tension is irresolvable, at least at the psychological level. While there is some reason to regret the anger characteristically manifested in blame, and while we as individuals may try to repress or overcome its more punitive dimensions, we are fighting against a very deep feature of human psychology—a feature, moreover, that (in its more constructive guise) plays a critical role in regulating behavior by way of making salient the demands that shared norms place on our actions and attitudes. Hence, I conclude, the sanitizer's strategy for civilizing blame is not only psychologically forlorn; it is normatively misguided. If this project is not to be abandoned tout court, we need to find a new way forward.

The alternative I propose does not involve reshaping the psychology of blame, but it does involve thinking about how that psychology is given expression though our social institutions and practices of blame, some for better, some for worse. The guiding idea here is that, despite our liabilities, we are at least an engineering species, able to develop practices and institutions that serve our various ends in light of our shared human tendencies. Hence in pursuit of the normative goal of civilizing blame, it makes sense to ask which practices and institutions best serve the end of capitalizing on blame's more sophisticated regulative characteristics, while checking, or reining in, those characteristics that have an unsavory and potentially destructive punitive edge. I call this the strategy of *domesticating* blame. And while I think it may be pursued with some profit in a number of different domains (both public and private), the criminal justice system provides a particularly compelling site for this inquiry, since it is here that blame receives one of its most powerful and communally sanctioned forms of institutional expression. I therefore close with some very brief and sketchy remarks on what this strategy for civilizing blame might recommend, as well as caution against, in the field of criminal justice.

Recall that, in my view, what makes blame a normatively acceptable, even valuable response to wrongdoing is that it is no longer just a primitive punitive response but one that builds onto this crude regulative structure a cognitively sophisticated *dialogical* dimension. Blame *responds to* something a wrongdoer has done and it *calls for* something from the wrongdoer in return: namely, that the wrongdoer appropriately address the blamer's sense of being wronged.[14] Of course, how this response should go is something of an open question. Blame (in its most constructive guise) will be satisfied by a variety of responses, including a discussion of fault, the offering of excuses or exculpating explanations, a recognition of the blamer's right to better treatment, remorse, apology, restitution, commitment to reform, and so on. These things constitute a family of suitable responses to blame by taking account of who was wronged and how, while at the same time reinforcing our shared commitment to the norms that make for moral community. Hence blame (in its most constructive guise) aims to generate a normatively valuable dialectic, both from the point of view of repairing the variety of wrongs done by any transgression (to the victim, to the stability of shared norms, to a sense of security, and so on)[15] and from the point of view of regulating behavior going forward. More important, I claim, what makes blame particularly apt for generating this dialectic is that it is the sort of phenomenon to which wrongdoers, as reactively sensitive creatures, are emotionally primed to respond. But could such features, which seem to require a more immediate form of encounter between blamer and wrongdoer, be given any true institutional support in the area of criminal justice? And even if they could, is this indeed a normatively desirable state of affairs?

In response to the first question, there is a family of initiatives going under the banner of "restorative justice" that appear to be doing just that.[16] Although restorative justice practices take a variety of forms, what makes them distinctive is a nonadversarial form of sentencing in which the various parties or "stakeholders" involved in or otherwise affected by the crime are brought together in a conference.[17] This includes the offender, the victim, supporters of each the offender and victim (often family members or friends), and often other representatives of the community affected by the crime. The formal purpose of the conference is to discuss the effects of the crime (in particular the nature of the harms done) and what can be done by the offender (materially and symbolically) to repair or make amends for such harms. And while the

---

[14] This dialogical conception of blame amounts to denying the common philosophical thought that blame is essentially something that individuals feel and do, as it may be in the privacy of their own hearts. On the dialogical conception, it is a constitutive feature of blame that it *aims* to engage the wrongdoer in a certain kind of conversational exchange, a fact that explains why blame is characteristically (though not invariably) enacted in social space.

[15] For an importantly nuanced discussion of the complexity of moral repair, see Walker (2006).

[16] While there is a vast and growing literature on restorative justice, good introductory discussions can be found in the following: Johnstone and Van Ness (2007), Menkel-Meadow (2007), Zehr (2002), Van Ness and Strong (2010), Braithwaite (2002).

[17] The guilt of the offender is typically established before a restorative process begins, and sometimes restorative practices are used in a mitigating way after standard sentencing is under way.

offender is expected to take responsibility for his or her offense, in part by coming to a deeper understanding of how his or her behavior has affected others through directly encountering their personal accounts of how they experienced the crime, the focus on repair is meant to serve the larger (forward-looking) goal of establishing or reestablishing a sense of shared community—encompassing, in particular, the victim and the offender, but in which all participants feel they have a stake in upholding communal norms.

Empirical research has yet to establish with full certainty the effectiveness of restorative practices across various dimensions. But initial studies are promising with respect to two significant measures, as compared with outcomes from more traditional trial and sentencing procedures: (1) greater offender and victim satisfaction from the perspective of perceived fair-dealing—victims in particular had a greater sense that justice had been done; and (2) a reduction in recidivism rates, at least for crimes not associated with addiction.[18] From the perspective of this paper, these results are not surprising insofar as restorative practices support a psychologically meaningful trajectory of reactive exchanges such as discussed in section 3. In particular the dynamics of a restorative conference are such that the victim is given the opportunity of expressing how the crime has affected him or her (psychologically as well as materially); the offender, likewise, of explaining how he or she came to commit such a crime. In the course of such exchanges, the offender often comes to recognize the harm caused to the victim in a new way, and the victim comes to appreciate that recognition, often because of the contrition the offender naturally displays.

In sum, restorative justice practices reflect central points that have been argued for in this paper. Under restorative justice initiatives, offenders are not treated in a crude consequentialist way as nonagential targets of rehabilitation and/or deterrence; they are assumed to be fully responsible agents that are appropriate targets of moral address and thus appropriate targets of our blaming acts and attitudes. Yet those acts and attitudes are given a more constructive outlet than merely ensuring that the offender receives appropriate payback (in the form of punishment) for the wrong he or she has willfully done: a goal that is considered normatively appropriate on a more retributive model of criminal justice. Instead offenders are encouraged to *take* responsibility for their wrongdoing by coming to see themselves not only as agents of crime but, more important, as agents both of restitution and of recommitment to the standards of moral community. While such restitution may be legally

---

[18] One of the more extensive empirical studies to date is the Re-integrative Shaming Experiment (RISE) conducted in Canberra, Australia, from 1995 to 2000 (discussed in Strang 2002; see also Ahmed, Harris, Braithwaite, and Braithwaite 2001; Sherman, Strang, and Woods 2000). Further corroborative work is discussed in Sherman and Strang (2007), Robinson and Shapland (2008), and Shapland, Robinson and Sorsby (2011).

required and enforced, what cannot be required are the reactive emotions that victims, offenders, and other stakeholders often feel in the context of a restorative justice conference as they try to come to grips with their own experiences of the crime and the meaning it should have in their shared community. And yet it is this reactive dynamic—in particular, specific trajectories of reactive exchange—that seems to correlate most nearly with genuine recommitment to the standards of moral community, at least as this recommitment is measured in terms of recidivism rates as well as a general feeling among all the stakeholders that justice has been served.[19]

I turn now to my second question: Even if restorative practices go some way to capitalizing on the dialogical aspects of blame, is this really a normatively desirable initiative to be advocating in the field of criminal justice? Or are there further normative demands deemed appropriate in this domain that restorative practices cannot address? A fully developed answer to this question must survey in depth what sort of demands are articulated by the two dominant traditions in criminal justice: namely, (as mentioned above), the consequentialist tradition (broadly associated with welfare-maximizing utilitarianism) and the deontological tradition (broadly associated with retributivism). The question, then, will be to what extent restorative practices meet such demands and, where restorative practices fall short, whether or not the relevant demands are in fact normatively misguided. I cannot hope to undertake such a survey here, but I close by indicating, in a highly abbreviated way, how I think such a discussion might go.

To begin with the consequentialist tradition, I assume there would be broad support for restorative practices so far as they actually do a better job than current trial and sentencing procedures in delivering on what, in their view, the justice system should be aiming at: protection of the community and the prevention of crime through rehabilitation and deterrence. Moreover, so far as such practices promote morally valuable goods such as individual moral capacity, dignity, and autonomy, they should only prove more attractive than traditional responses to crime. Indeed, while it is a standard criticism of consequentialist theories of punishment that advocates are forced to make trade-offs in the promotion of various moral goods (e.g., between successful deterrence and respecting the offender's moral autonomy), embracing restorative practices as a preferred response to crime may provide a way of silencing such criticisms.

But what about deontological retributivists? To what extent would they endorse restorative practices as a normatively fitting or even desirable initiative in criminal justice? It might seem as if they would have a normatively compelling objection. After all, in the retributivist view, the primary aim of the criminal

---

[19] Cf. Braithwaite and Braithwaite, chapter 4, in Ahmed et al., (2001).

justice system should be one of delivering just deserts (or moral payback) to the offender for his or her crime, and this is what punishment—and only punishment—serves to do (see, e.g., Duff 2001). Of course, rehabilitation or deterrence may be a happy side-effect of society's punishment practices, but no such practice should be promoted simply in virtue of furthering such consequentialist desiderata. Is there anything more to be said from the perspective of this paper against the retributive position?

I have two short responses, to be developed at length elsewhere. The first response is intended to cast a psychological shadow over the bright intuitive light that shines as a beacon in the retributivists' normative field of vision. If what I have said about blame is correct—that the psychology is built on a primitive foundation of punitive payback—it would not be surprising to find considerable intuitive support for the retributivist position. And so far as human intuitions are held to be a central and important guide to the design of a normatively appropriate criminal justice system, we can expect there to be a powerful pull toward some kind of retributive system. But, of course, the question remains: Should such intuitions be accorded such normative importance, especially if we can trace their origin to the more primitive features of our social psychology? The answer is not straightforwardly no, but nor is it straightforwardly yes, as retributivists must surely hold.

My second response is intended to cast doubt on a central normative plank in the retributivist approach to criminal justice. According to its proponents, while punishment is considered the normatively appropriate response to crime, the whole focus of retributive theory is on giving the offender his or her just deserts—no more and no less. Hence one of the main justifications of retributivism as a normatively appropriate response to crime is that it provides a *built-in* check on the amount and kind of punishment inflicted on an offender—specifically that such punishment be proportionate to the crime. According to retributivists, this built-in check is entirely lacking in other approaches to criminal justice, and that is a major normative strike against them. However, if what I have said about the moral psychology of blame is correct, this apparent advantage of retributive theory is deeply illusory.

Here is why. On the account I offer, though blame is built on a primitive foundation of punitive payback, it has certain sophisticated dialogical features that simply will not be satisfied by way of satisfying the more punitive aspects of blame. However, if these more sophisticated dialogical features go unsatisfied, then a blamer's blame is likely to persevere even in the face of delivered punishment, supporting a persisting conviction that justice has yet to be done. But now, if justice can be served only by delivering punishment or hard treatment, as retributivists aver, the only viable option will seem to be one of calling for more severe sentencing practices. In other words, the retributive call for delivering just deserts, so far from ensuring proportionality in response to crime, may, under certain circumstances, produce a powerful ratcheting-up effect in people's estimation of how much punishment is in fact deserved.[20] Hence ironically it is retributive theory that is most in danger of breaching the moral constraint of proportionality in criminal justice—a danger it courts by failing to come to grips with the complex nature of human moral psychology. So far as this argument has merit (deriving support, as needs be, from various empirical studies),[21] it points to an important moral—and the takeaway message of this paper: No normative theory worth its salt can afford to ignore the real empirical nature of the sort of beings to which it is meant to apply.

---

[20] In support of this point, it is worth noting that, especially in the United States, there has been a dramatic upswing in sentencing severity in the past thirty years or so—an upswing that is concomitant with retributive theory regaining ascendency as an intellectually respectable doctrine in both legal and policy contexts. No doubt there are many causal factors that explain this increase in sentencing severity (for discussion, see Lacey 2008, ch. 2). However, despite its much-vaunted enshrinement of a just deserts moral framework, it is no surprise that this upswing has been in no way checked by the promulgation of retributive principles. In part this is due to a feature of retributive theory noted even by its defenders: that, even though the principle of delivering just deserts ensures ordinal proportionality in response to different types of crime, there is no "natural" proportion between crime and punishment that serves to anchor the cardinality of the sentencing scale (i.e., there is no internal criterion by which to set an upper and lower bound of the appropriate amount of punishment delivered) (Von Hirsch 1986). Still, this feature alone does not explain why politicians' call to be tougher on crime plays so well in certain democratic arenas and translates so immediately into stiffer sentencing practices. Again, as Lacey argues, there will be a constellation of factors that account for this phenomenon. I merely suggest that the peculiarity of our moral psychology plays no small role in creating the perfect storm conditions that lead to devastating outcomes like the "three strikes" law in California.

[21] In partial support of this point, I cite a fascinating psychological study by Carlsmith, Wilson, and Gilbert (2008) investigating the affective consequence of punishment on those who inflict it. Using a free-rider paradigm, subjects of the study were encouraged to play cooperatively with three other players in an investment game in order to achieve an optimal group outcome. Nevertheless, players could improve on this monetary outcome by individually defecting while others cooperate (i.e., by free riding). Almost all subjects played cooperatively. (Defecting subjects were not considered in the final experimental result.) Unbeknown to the subjects involved, the three other players with whom each of them played were actually computers: two of these were programmed to play cooperatively (tit for tat); the third was programmed to free ride. Predictably, the free rider did significantly better than the other players.

At the end of the game, subjects were randomly assigned to one of three groups. One group (the punishment group) was given the opportunity to punish the free rider monetarily by using some of their own earnings; other groups were not. Almost all subjects in the punishment group chose to punish the free rider. Subjects in a so-called forecaster group were not given the opportunity to punish but were asked instead to predict how they would feel had they been given the opportunity. Subjects in a third control group just went on to the next step, a ten-minute filler task that was completed by all three groups. After completing the filler task, all subjects were asked to rate their subjective affective state (negative or positive on a 7-point scale) and how much they were still thinking about the free rider (1–7 rumination scale). Here is the startling result: punishers both felt significantly *worse* and were ruminating *more* about the free rider than subjects in either of the nonpunishment groups. In other words, punishers did not experience the sense of psychological closure they (or the forecasters) anticipated punishment would bring. The question is why not?

There are a number of possible explanations for this result (see, e.g., the discussion in Carlsmith et al. 2008), but it is certainly congenial with my own account of angry blame. At its most elemental level, blame motivates the desire to strike back at wrongdoers. But at a more sophisticated level, blame aims at changing or regulating the wrongdoers' attitudes. Hence blamers will not be satisfied at the simple infliction of punishment—there is business left undone. Thus I contend that even though psychological closure may come with a sense of justice being served, we do not really feel that justice has been served unless and until wrongdoers are brought to a recognition of their wrong and, indeed, a change of attitude. More empirical work needs to be done to determine if this hypothesis is correct.

10

Free Will Skepticism, Blame, and Obligation

Derk Pereboom

1. Free Will Skepticism and Blame

A central concern in the historical free will debate is whether the sort of free will required for moral responsibility of a central kind is compatible with the causal determination of our actions by factors beyond our control. Since Hume ([1739] 1978) this concern has prominently been extended to whether this sort of free will is compatible with indeterminacy in action. On the skeptical view I endorse, free will, characterized in this way, is incompatible with this type of causal determination but also with the kind of indeterminacy of action that Hume envisioned (Pereboom 1995, 2001, 2007). It is crucial, however, to recognize that the term 'moral responsibility' is used in a variety ways and that the type of free will or control required for moral responsibility in some of these senses is uncontroversially compatible with the causal determination of action by factors beyond our control, which have therefore not been at issue in the debate between compatibilists and incompatibilists. It is potentially open to the free will skeptic to affirm that we are morally responsible in these other senses.

The particular variety of moral responsibility that has been at issue in the historical debate is set apart by the notion of *basic desert*. For an agent to be morally responsible for an action in this sense is for it to be hers in such a way that she would deserve to be the recipient of an expression of moral resentment or indignation if she understood that it was morally wrong, and she would deserve to be the recipient of an expression of gratitude or praise if she understood that it was morally exemplary. The desert at issue here is basic in the sense that the agent, to be morally responsible, would deserve to be the recipient of the expression of such an attitude just because she has performed the action, given sensitivity to its moral status, not, for example, by virtue of consequentialist or contractualist considerations. One might be the recipient of the expression of such an attitude when this expression is either covert or

Thanks to Michael McKenna, Dana Nelkin, Philip Robichaud, Carla Bagnoli, Justin Coates, and Neal Tognazzini for valuable comments.

overt. Moral responsibility in this sense is presupposed by our attitudes of resentment, indignation, gratitude, and moral praise, since having such an attitude essentially involves the supposition that the agent in question basically deserves to be the recipient of its expression. It is thus the variety of moral responsibility that P. F. Strawson brings to the fore in his "Freedom and Resentment" (1962).

The free will skeptic will call into question any blaming practice that presupposes that the agent being blamed is morally responsible in the basic desert sense. Since much actual human blaming has this presupposition, any skeptical account of blame will be revisionary. At the same time there are a number of recent analyses of blame and blameworthiness that incompatibilists would not regard as conflicting with determinism and that the free will skeptic can take on board (Pereboom 2009). For instance, in George Sher's account, blame is essentially a certain belief-desire pair: the belief that the agent has acted badly or that he has a bad character and the desire that he not have performed his bad act or not have the bad character (2006, p. 112). The free will skeptic can, without any inconsistency, endorse such beliefs and desires about badness. One might object that if we gave up the belief that people are blameworthy in the basic desert sense we could no longer legitimately judge any actions as good or bad. But denying basic desert blameworthiness would not threaten axiological judgments of moral badness, and likewise, denying basic desert praise- or creditworthiness would not jeopardize such assessments of goodness. Even if we came to believe that a perpetrator of genocide was not blameworthy in this sense due to some degenerative brain disease, we could still legitimately maintain that it was extremely bad that he acted as he did. So far, then, the free will skeptic can accept blame on this analysis. Sher does maintain that blame involves a set of affective and behavioral dispositions, and at this point one might think his account conflicts with free will skepticism. But he does not contend that any such dispositions are essential to blame but rather only that they are connected to it in a weaker sense. Given the looseness of this tie, the free will skeptic can endorse blaming on Sher's specification. She might not endorse all of the affective dispositions that might be associated with blame, in particular not those dispositions to expressions of moral resentment and indignation justified in virtue of basic desert. Still, two dispositions to which Sher draws our attention, "to apologize for our own transgressions and vices and to reprimand others for theirs" (p. 108), are compatible with the free will skeptic's conviction.[1]

---

[1] This is not to say that I accept Sher's theory as a complete skeptical account of blame. For further critical review of Sher's account from other perspectives, see McKenna and Vadakin (2008), Reis-Dennis (2010), and Hobbs (2012).

In Thomas Scanlon's analysis, to blame an agent for an action is to judge that it reveals something about the agent's attitude toward oneself and/or others that impairs the relations that he can have with them and to take one's relationship with him to be modified in a way that this judgment of impaired relations justifies as appropriate (2008, pp. 128–31). Whether blame defined in this way is compatible with free will skepticism depends on how the appropriateness to which this characterization refers is understood. If it is taken to introduce basic desert, then the resulting notion of blame would be called into question. But there is an epistemic or evidential interpretation that is consistent with free will skepticism. One of Scanlon's examples illustrates this reading. You trusted Bill, but you then noticed that he repeatedly behaved in an untrustworthy manner, as a result of which it is now appropriate for you to take your relationship with him to be impaired to the degree that reflects this diminished trust. Here the justification is evidential. You believed Bill was trustworthy to a high degree, but you then acquired good evidence of reduced trustworthiness and hence a good reason to judge that an attitude of his was relationship-impairing. You now make this judgment and take your relationship with him to be impaired to a degree that it justifies as appropriate. All of this is unobjectionable to the free will skeptic. But let me note that blame in human relationships would seem only seldom linked with a judgment of relationship impairment. A fair proportion of blame is directed toward children by parents and teachers in the process of moral education, and only in a small minority of cases does such blame involve a judgment that a relationship has been impaired.[2]

Although Sher's and Scanlon's notions of blame can be accepted by the free will skeptic, I hope to secure a notion of blame that has a more pronounced forward-looking aspect. Free will skeptics like Joseph Priestley (1788) and their revisionary compatibilist cousins such as Moritz Schlick (1939) and J. J. C. Smart (1961) claim that given determinism, a kind of blame that can be retained is indeed forward-looking: the justification and goal of such determinism-friendly blame is to moderate or eliminate dispositions to misconduct. The dispositions addressed already exist and are manifested in past actions and are reasonably assumed to persist unless corrective measures are taken. Such blaming, then, addresses past misconduct as a means to targeting such a standing disposition (Hieronymi 2001).[3] Thus when an agent has acted badly, one might ask him, "Why did you decide to do that?" or "Do you think it was the right thing to do?," where the point of asking such questions is to

---

[2] This sort of criticism of Scanlon's proposal is developed by Wolf (2011) and Hobbs (2012); for further criticisms, see Nelkin (2011b) and Wallace (2011).

[3] Pamela Hieronymi (2001, p. 546) argues that resentment is best understood as a protest: "[R]esentment protests a past action that persists as a present threat." Although resentment is not a feature of the forward-looking notion of blame I set out here, in this view a core function of blaming someone is to protest a past action of his that persists as a present threat.

have him recognize and acknowledge a disposition to behave immorally. If the reasons given in response to such questions indicate that he does have such a disposition, it then becomes apt to request an effort to eliminate it. Engaging in such interactions will be legitimate in light of how they contribute to the agent's moral improvement. This model is a variety of the *answerability* sense of moral responsibility defended by Scanlon (1998) and Hilary Bok (1998).

Michael McKenna (2012) has recently developed a view that turns out, with some revision, to be amenable to these goals; he calls it a *conversational* theory of moral responsibility. In his conception, the actions of a morally responsible agent are potential bearers of a species of meaning insofar as they are indicators of the quality of will with which agents act (pp. 92–94). My blaming someone is an expression of a sentiment or attitude such as resentment or indignation, and its function is to communicate my moral response to her in the light of the indicated quality of will. When a morally responsible person acts, she understands that members of the moral community might assign such a meaning to her action. When her acts are morally charged, she appreciates that she might be introducing a meaningful contribution to such a conversational exchange with others. This initial stage McKenna calls *Moral Contribution*. The second stage, in which that agent is blamed by a respondent, he calls *Moral Address*. In the third stage, *Moral Account*, the blamed agent extends the conversation by offering an excuse, a justification, or an apology, for example. The respondent might at this point continue the conversation, perhaps by forgiving or punishing. In a further stage the blamed agent may be restored to full status in the moral community. This *moral responsibility exchange* is modeled on analogy with an ordinary conversational exchange between speakers of a natural language. Not all blaming fits this model; blaming the dead, for example, does not. Here McKenna invokes— plausibly, to my mind—a paradigm-similarity model for the meaning and extension of the concept (Rosch 1972, 1973). The blame conversation is the central case of blame, and examples of other sorts count as blaming because they are sufficiently similar to the central case.

Some modification to this picture is in order.[4] When overt blame is at issue, in the first stage it will often be the case that an action that can reasonably be interpreted as immoral is performed. But this is not so in all cases in which an agent is overtly blamed, since frequently agents are blamed due to mistaken reports of having acted wrongly, or to negligent or deliberate misinterpretations of actions, or to outright fabrication. Now McKenna envisions that blame proper occurs at the second stage, while some theorists—Feinberg, for

---

[4] McKenna is open to some of these amendments (in correspondence; cf. McKenna 2012, pp. 90–91), but it is essential to his proposal that at the second stage the respondent adopts a blaming attitude, which might be defeated in the third stage. My view is that even though in practice people often do adopt a blaming attitude at the second stage, doing so typically involves moral error.

example—propose that blame is a form of punishment, which in McKenna's model occurs at some stage after the third. Overt blame might in fact occur at either juncture, that is, either prior to or subsequent to a request for excuse, justification, or some other type of exonerating explanation. But if it occurs prior to such a request, it is very often in moral error. If at the second stage excuse or justification is significantly epistemically possible, an address that communicates that the agent acted badly and without excuse or justification— that is, an accusation—will typically be morally erroneous. If an accusation is made at the second stage, and a valid justification or excuse is offered, an apology on the part of the respondent is clearly in order. But even if it was significantly epistemically possible that the agent had a valid excuse or justification but in fact had none, a prior accusation would have been a moral mistake. In the normative case, if it is evident at the second stage that the agent did perform the action in question, the respondent will inquire whether he has an excuse or justification, and if it is not obvious that the agent has performed the action, the respondent will attempt to determine whether he did.

If at the third stage the agent admits to having performed the action without excuse or justification, then at the next stage the respondent might address the agent by saying to him "What you did was wrong!" in a way that expresses moral resentment or indignation. This would arguably be a form of blame that counts as punishment because it involves an intention to inflict psychological pain in response to a perceived wrong done (cf. Wallace 1994, pp. 51–83; Nelkin 2011a, pp. 31–50). If the agent does not admit to having performed the action, but it is nevertheless clear that he has done so, and without excuse or justification, the respondent might accuse him of having done wrong. This accusation would be a form of blame, and if it is communicated in a way that expresses a reactive attitude of resentment or indignation, it would again arguably count as a form of punishment. But the respondent might also address the agent by expressing disappointment or sadness, without at *the same time* expressing resentment or indignation, and she might also counsel apology and reform, and this would not conflict with the claims of the free will skeptic.

As I said, the free will skeptic can endorse an answerability notion of moral responsibility, and she can accept an amended version of McKenna's more specific proposal insofar as it avoids an appeal to basic desert and to expressions of the desert-involving reactive attitudes. McKenna argues, convincingly, that his general model is compatible with both endorsing and rejecting basic desert. I propose, consistent with free will skepticism, to ground this model for blame not in basic desert but in three non-desert-invoking moral desiderata: protection of potential victims, reconciliation to relationships both personal and with the moral community more generally, and moral formation. Immoral actions are often harmful, and those who are potentially harmed have a right to protect themselves and to protect others from those who are disposed to behave harmfully. Such behavior can also impair relationships, and we have a moral interest in undoing such impairment through reconciliation. And since we value morally good character and resulting action, we have a stake in the formation of moral character when it is plagued by dispositions to misconduct.

Blaming on such a conversational model can have a role in realizing each of these aims. Suppose someone acts badly, say by disseminating defamatory fabrications about his political rivals. One might then confront him by asking him what good evidence he has for his allegations, and supposing he cannot produce it, one might point out to him that his behavior is immoral and that he should cease to be disposed to it. As McKenna points out, citing Feinberg, this process might be harmful to the wrongdoer in various ways; it might cause psychological pain, for instance (McKenna 2012, p. 125; Feinberg 1970, pp. 60–74; cf. Zimmerman 1988, p. 155). But inflicting this harm is justified first of all by the right of the defamed to protect themselves and to be protected from this type of aggression and its consequences. In addition, one might have a stake in reconciliation with the wrongdoer, and calling him to account can function as a step toward realizing this objective. Finally, we also have an interest in his moral formation, and the moral address described naturally functions as a stage in this process. Blame grounded in this way is essentially forward-looking since its aims are future protection, future reconciliation, and future moral formation. The immediate object of blame is often a past action, but insofar as the purpose of blame is protection and moral formation, the past action will be addressed as a means for correcting a persisting disposition to act badly. Insofar as the goal of blame is reconciliation, the past action will also be addressed for its own sake.[5] There may be cases in which an immoral action has been performed but without a persisting disposition so to act, and blame can still have the point of reconciliation in such a case.

In accord with the conversational model, it is the agent's rationality that is engaged in the envisioned process. At the stage of moral address, we ask for an explanation with the intent of having the agent acknowledge a disposition to act badly, and then, if he has in fact so acted without excuse or justification, we aim for him to come to see that the disposition issuing in the action is best eliminated. In the standard sort of case, this change is produced by way of the agent's recognition of moral reasons to make it. Accordingly, it is an agent's responsiveness to reasons (cf. Fischer and Ravizza 1998), together with the fact that we have a moral interest in our protection, his moral formation, and our reconciliation with him, that explains why he is an appropriate recipient of blame in this forward-looking sense.

McKenna contends that there is a close tie between blame on the conversational model and basic desert. In his view, the connection is illuminated

---

[5] Thanks to Dana Nelkin for making this point.

by the following principle: "It is a noninstrumental good that, as a response to the meaning expressed in an agent's blameworthy act, that agent experiences the harms of others communicating in their altered patterns of interpersonal relations their moral demands, expectations, and disapproval. Because this is a noninstrumental good, it is permissible to blame one who is blameworthy" (2012, p. 150). The harms upon being blamed include the emotional pain of engagement in the moral conversation and the alteration for the worse of interpersonal relationships. McKenna proposes three respects in which such harm might be understood as a noninstrumental good and, as a result, basically deserved. For each, my sense is that the good on offer turns out to be only instrumental to realizing some further good and thus not basically deserved. The first is the good "located in the blameworthy agent's commitment to membership within the moral community." On the basic desert view, it is a good that the blameworthy agent is harmed in the ways indicated just because he has knowingly done wrong, and in the context of the debate, this is what it is for such a harm to be a noninstrumental good. Harm aimed at the good of membership in a moral community would, by contrast, be instrumental, since the harm is not envisaged as a good in itself but instead as serving the good of such membership. The second respect draws on Sher's view that "when one blames someone, her desire that a person not have failed to live up to morality's counsel is explained by her caring for these aspects of morality quite generally" (McKenna 2012, p. 168). McKenna contends, "[W]e can say that conversing with a wrongdoer by blaming is motivated out of a commitment to morality. This is to be valued; it is a good" (p. 168). But here again the harm is instrumental, since it is not conceived as a good in itself but rather as serving the commitment to morality. Even if the good of morality is a noninstrumental good, the harm motivated by a commitment to morality will be an instrumental good since it will be instrumental relative to the commitment to morality. The third respect McKenna cites is that "the goodness of the activity of blaming . . . concerns the noninstrumental value of a process that begins at one end with a wrong done, that then conversationally answers that wrong by way of some blaming practice, and that invites an extension of the unfolding conversation in a manner that values sustained bonds of moral community" (p. 169). There are two ways that this explanation can be construed as adducing harm as an instrumental good. One is that the claimed noninstrumental good at play is not the harm but rather the conversational process; the harm should then be understood as a good instrumental to the larger good of the overall process. The other is that harm serves the noninstrumental good of the sustained bonds of the moral community, but then again the harm turns out not to be a good in itself but rather as serving the good of these bonds. The free will skeptic can endorse each of these ways in which harm incurred by overt blame is a good instrumentally relative to a further good; each can be understood as a way in which blame can serve the good of moral formation.

McKenna replies by contending that the harm of blame is partially constitutive of the various noninstrumental goods he adduces and thus not merely instrumentally valuable (in correspondence; cf. McKenna 2012, pp. 123–24, n. 18). But while it is plausible that certain kinds of obvious goods, such as mental and physical health, are partially constitutive of a noninstrumental good such as human flourishing, it is at least typically less credible that harms—as harms—are partially constitutive of noninstrumental goods, and for this reason count as noninstrumental goods themselves. Vaccination may be a prerequisite of physical health, and health constitutive of flourishing, but it's not plausible that the pain of vaccination is constitutive of flourishing, by contrast with being instrumentally required for it. So my sense is that the proposed connection between moral responsibility on a conversational model and harm as a noninstrumental good hasn't been substantiated, and that thus no close tie between responsibility on this model and harm as basically deserved has been established.

2. Blame and Obligation

Against this skeptical account one might object that for an agent to be blameworthy even in this forward-looking sense requires that she ought not to have performed the action, and this in turn requires that she could have avoided the action, which is incompatible with determinism. While my free will skepticism does not endorse determinism, it leaves open determinism as a serious possibility. And according to the consequence argument, determinism is incompatible with being able to do otherwise, at least in one salient sense, and on this understanding I find the argument attractive (van Inwagen 1983; Ginet 1990, pp. 95–117). So this objection poses a threat to my view.

Here is Dana Nelkin's version of the argument that fuels the objection:

N1. If S is blameworthy for A, then S ought not to have done A.
N2. If S ought not to have done A, then S could have refrained from doing A (from Ought Implies Can [OIC]).
C. So, if S is blameworthy for A, then S could have refrained from doing A. (Nelkin 2011a, pp. 100–101; cf. Copp 2008)

In assessing this argument one must tread with caution, since 'ought' has a range of correct uses, and it may be that not all are linked to the same OIC requirement, and that some are not associated with such a requirement at all. First, Ruth Barcan Marcus (1966), Lloyd Humberstone (1971), and Gilbert

Harman (1977) distinguish between an 'ought' that applies to action and one that applies to states.[6] An 'ought to do,' Harman proposes, "implies that an agent has a reason to perform an action, whereas an 'ought to be' evaluates a state of affairs and does not by itself imply that any particular agent has a reason to contribute to bringing about that state of affairs" (p. 87; cf. Humberstone 1971; Manne 2011). But as James Hobbs (2012) points out, certain 'ought to be' claims will have implications for reasons agents have to act. He suggests the following diagnosis: If X *ought to be* the case, then agents to whom the relevant considerations apply have a reason to act in ways that respect the value of X. He contends, plausibly to my mind, that this assumption about reasons for action does not imply a route, accessible to the agent, to the realization of what ought to be. But if, by contrast, an agent *ought to do* something, that agent has a reason to do it, and there is such a route to what she ought to do. In a similar vein, Nelkin (2011a) argues that 'ought' propositions that specify what an agent ought to do are essentially action-directed, so that if 'S ought not to do A' is true, then as a matter of the meaning of 'ought' propositions, or of the essential nature of obligation, S is thereby directed to refrain from doing A, and this entails that S can refrain from doing A. One way to think about this distinction is that an 'ought to be' is an 'ought' of *axiological evaluation*, or sometimes of *axiological ideality*, which does not (at least directly) entail a 'can' claim, while an 'ought to do' expresses a demand of an agent in a particular circumstance, which does entail that the agent can perform the indicated action (cf. Humberstone 1971; Manne 2011). One might call this second type an 'ought' of *specific agent demand.*

Hobbs's more precise proposal for the ability entailed by an action-directed 'ought' is that if a person ought, all things considered, to do something, then she has the physical and mental ability, the skill, and the know-how needed, and she is in circumstances appropriate for doing that thing. However, she may not have the motivation required to do it.[7] Accordingly if an agent, all things considered, ought to do A, then she can do A in the sense that doing A is compatible with her abilities and her opportunities but not necessarily with how she is in fact motivated. Significantly, in his view determinism implies that doing otherwise is incompatible with the full range of causally relevant

---

[6] Cf. Manne (2011). In Mark Schroeder's (2011) characterization, the *deliberative* sense of 'ought' expresses a relation between an agent and an action, where an action is a property of an agent, while the *evaluative* 'ought,' as in "Larry ought to win the lottery," where Larry has been subject to a series of undeserved misfortunes, expresses a relation to a proposition, in this case *that Larry wins the lottery.* Manne argues that it is important to see that the evaluative 'ought' applies not only to nonagential states of affairs but also to actions.

[7] In Hobbs's account (2012), S has a basic ability to do A if and only if S is intrinsically such that if S were sufficiently motivated to do A and S had an opportunity to do A, then S would be relatively likely to do A (taking into account the difficulty of doing A).

features of a situation. But that an agent ought to perform an action, all things considered, implies only that her performing this action is compatible with her abilities and opportunities, not with the remaining crucial and causally relevant feature, her motivation. Hence 'S ought not to do A' can be true in a deterministic situation in which S performs immoral act A because he is not appropriately motivated.

Hobbs tests his account with the objection that the relevant 'ought' claim in fact places a stronger demand on an agent, one that it would be unfair to impose without being more sensitive to how an agent could possibly be motivated. He responds by arguing that it is not exactly clear what this stronger sense of 'ought' is supposed to be:

> [T]he practical, action guiding 'ought to do' claims I have in mind very often express obligations, and the only sense in which 'ought' could express some stronger normative claim, one for which it might be unfair to fail to consider motivational obstacles, is one that is tied to blameworthiness, such that 'A ought to Φ' more or less entails that A would be blameworthy if he failed to Φ. This is not a use of 'ought' that I am familiar with or that I find particularly useful. (Hobbs 2012, p. 67)

But it's my sense that if causal determinism precludes alternative possibilities for motivation and hence for action, there is a core sense of 'ought to do' that will be compromised. If I know that at some time an agent could not have avoided lacking the motivation required for performing some morally exemplary action, it would be unfair, and I think mistaken, for me to claim that she ought to have performed that action at that time.

Still it might well not be unfair for me to recommend to that agent that she perform an action of that type at some future time, given that it is epistemically open that she will develop the requisite motivation by then, and in particular if the recommendation might plausibly contribute causally to producing the motivation. And to recommend the action to her I might tell her that she ought to perform the action at the future time, and do so appropriately and without making any kind of mistake. The sense of 'ought' invoked here is thus plausibly distinct from the 'ought' of specific agent demand. I propose that, given determinism and that determinism precludes alternatives, when one tells an agent that she ought to perform an action of some type in the future, it is not the 'ought' of specific agent demand but rather an 'ought' of axiological evaluation or ideality that would need to be invoked, but in a way that uses it to recommend the action to the agent. Such a use of 'ought' proposes to an agent as morally valuable a state of affairs in which she performs an action of a certain sort and recommends that she perform this action. We might call this the 'ought' of *axiological recommendation*. Given determinism and that determinism rules out alternatives, the use of the 'ought' of specific agent demand could be correct and fair only if the agent is in fact causally determined to perform the action and one is reasonably sure that she is, which would be typically untrue, while the 'ought' of axiological recommendation would not be similarly undermined. Like the 'ought' of specific agent demand, the 'ought' of axiological recommendation necessarily concerns agents and actions they might perform. But as for all claims about what ought to be, this use of 'ought' should not be understood as presupposing a route accessible to an agent, via reasons for action, to her acting in some relevant way. One might be unsure about whether such a route is accessible, while the use of 'ought' is nevertheless legitimate.

So supposing that this world is deterministic, and given that determinism does preclude the relevant alternative possibilities and we typically don't know how agents will be motivated, a correct and fair use of the prospective 'ought' of specific agent demand would be compromised. Yet the 'ought' of axiological recommendation would often be in the clear. Further, this use of 'ought' meshes nicely with the forward-looking notion of blame grounded in the goods of protection, reconciliation, and moral formation. If the 'ought' in

N2. If S ought not to have done A, then S could have refrained from doing A

is read as the 'ought' of specific agent demand, then I, like Nelkin, accept N2. But this does not rule out the legitimate prospective use of 'ought' claims of axiological recommendation in cases where it turns out that due to determinism the agent could not have performed the act specified at the time she failed to do so, in particular if there was reason to believe that the agent could develop the requisite motivation, and especially if the articulation of the 'ought' claim could reasonably have been expected to contribute to producing it.[8]

How do these reflections bear on the relation between blameworthiness and 'could have done otherwise'? Here again is Nelkin's argument:

N1. If S is blameworthy for A, then S ought not to have done A.
N2. If S ought not to have done A, then S could have refrained from doing A (from OIC).
C. So, if S is blameworthy for A, then S could have refrained from doing A.

First, since I defend Frankfurt examples against an alternative possibilities requirement for moral responsibility, I reject the conclusion on one key reading

---

[8] That said, it might at times be misleading to use such 'ought to do' formulations under these conditions, since they are reasonably interpreted as specific agent demands. Formulations that are more clearly expressions of axiological recommendation, such as "It would be good of you to do A," would preclude misinterpretation. Still, as Neal Tognazzini and Justin Coates point out (in correspondence), in "You know, you really ought to do A," 'ought to do' would seem to have axiological import.

(Pereboom 2001, forthcoming).[9] Specifically, I deny that in the basic desert sense of blameworthiness, if S is blameworthy for A, then S's blameworthiness will be explained per se by the fact that she could have refrained from doing A. But I accept the second premise, N2, on the specific agent demand reading of 'ought.' As a result, I'm forced to reject the first premise, N1, given the basic desert sense of blameworthiness and the specific agent demand reading of 'ought.'

How might this be explained? When an agent is tempted to perform immoral action A, one might say to him, using the 'ought' of specific agent demand, "You ought to avoid doing A!" Suppose he does A anyway. If the source incompatibilist defender of Frankfurt is right, and I argue that he is (Pereboom 2001), then an agent can be blameworthy in the basic desert sense if he is the appropriate kind of indeterministic source of his action even if he could not have avoided the action. The 'ought' judgment, however, directs him to the avoidance of A, and in my view to do so would involve a mistake and would be unfair if he could not have avoided A. So for the source incompatibilist Frankfurt defender, the general claim

N1. If S is blameworthy for A, then S ought not to have done A

will be false, supposing blameworthiness in the basic desert sense and the 'ought' of specific agent demand. Following Ishtiyaque Haji (1998), the advocate of this position can endorse

N1*. If S is blameworthy for A, then for S doing A is bad

as an alternative account of the relation between basic desert blameworthiness and immoral action. N1* specifies an axiological prerequisite for blameworthiness and not, as in N1, a deontological constraint. That it is bad for S to have done A does not require that S could have done otherwise.

But the source incompatibilist free will skeptic can endorse N1, and the soundness of the subsequent argument, if it is read as invoking the 'ought' of axiological recommendation together with blameworthiness in our forward-looking sense:

N1'. If S is blameworthy for A in the forward-looking sense, then it is appropriate for a relevantly positioned respondent T to tell S that he ought, in the sense of axiological recommendation, not perform actions of A's type.

---

[9] In Frankfurt examples (Frankfurt 1969), an agent considers performing some action, but an intervener, say a neuroscientist, is concerned that she will not come through. So if she were to manifest an indication that she will not or might not perform the action, the neuroscientist would intervene. But as things actually go, the neuroscientist remains idle, since the agent performs the action on her own. The idea is that even though the agent could not have avoided the action she performs, she is still intuitively morally responsible for this action.

N2′. If it is appropriate for T to tell S that he ought, in the sense of axiological recommendation, not to perform actions of A's type, then it is open for T that S could, in the future, refrain from performing actions of A's type.
C′. So, if S is blameworthy for A in the forward-looking sense, then it is open for T that S could, in the future, refrain from performing actions of A's type.[10]

I accept the argument set out in this way. Blameworthiness in the forward-looking sense licenses the right sort of respondent to tell the agent who has acted badly that he ought not to act this way, where 'ought' has the sense of axiological recommendation, which in turn requires that it be epistemically open for the respondent that the agent can comply with this recommendation. While it's plausible that an agent's blameworthiness in the basic desert sense for an action is not explained per se by the fact that he could have avoided it, for an agent to be blameworthy for an action in the forward-looking sense it must be open that he refrain from performing actions of this type in the future. The Frankfurt defender can accept this conclusion. It's intuitive that the agent in a typical Frankfurt example is blameworthy in the basic desert sense, but also in the forward-looking sense. But such an agent will then retain a general ability to refrain from performing the action at issue (Smith 2003; Vihvelin 2004; Fara 2008; Nelkin 2011a, pp. 66–76), even though due to the intervention setup he cannot exercise that ability at the time (Clarke 2009). This leaves it open that he will exercise that ability in the future. When a Frankfurt case is constructed so as to permanently preclude the exercise of this ability (Pereboom 2001, pp. 27–28), then it is evident that the agent is not blameworthy for performing the action in the forward-looking sense.

3. Blame without the Reactive Attitudes

What form will blame take, absent the basic desert-presupposing reactive attitudes, such as moral resentment and indignation, and will it be effective? It is often supposed that blaming behavior would be morally optimal only if it involves these reactive attitudes. I argue, first, that there are alternative attitudes that do not presuppose basic desert that can be as effective morally as these reactive attitudes, and second, that in certain important respects blame

---

[10] One might ask whether, on the resulting view, there are any genuine moral requirements for agents. Perhaps the answer is negative, since legitimate 'ought' judgments will turn out to be axiological recommendations. A skeptic might then deny we are ever obligated, in the sense of specific agent demands, to do anything and instead defend a purely axiological ethics. Alastair Norcross (2006) proposes such a view, one that rejects any deontology, even the maximization demand of the classical utilitarian position. Instead, accessible states of affairs are ranked in accord with value, and in moral practice agents are encouraged to act with the aim of realizing a state of affairs reasonably high on the list.

without these reactive attitudes is to be preferred (Pereboom 2001, 2009; cf. Honderich 1988).

Let us combine the negative basic desert-involving reactive attitudes under the heading 'moral anger.' One might note that moral anger plays an important communicative role in our personal and societal relationships and object that if we were to strive to modify or eliminate this attitude, such relationships might well be worse off. But when someone is mistreated in a relationship, there are other emotions typically present that are not threatened by the skeptical view, whose expression can also communicate the relevant information. These emotions include feeling disappointed, hurt, or shocked about what the offender has done, moral concern for him, and moral sadness and sorrow generated by this concern when the harm done is serious (Pereboom 2001, 2009). Parents might feel intensely sad, and not angry, that their son has driven his car while intoxicated and injured a pedestrian and be concerned about his moral commitment. Ordinary human experience indicates that communicating such sadness and concern can be an effective way to motivate avoidance of future misbehavior. Often communicating anger is not required in addition to secure this effect. Feigned moral sadness is sometimes used to manipulate others, but what I have in mind is the genuine version. The alternatives to moral anger are not aggressive in the way that anger can be, and all by themselves they do not typically have anger's intimidating effect. If aggressiveness or intimidation is required, a strongly worded threat, for instance, might be appropriate. It is thus not clear that moral anger is required, or optimal, for communication in interpersonal relationships.

Shaun Nichols (2007) contends that sadness is an inadequate substitute for moral anger in personal and social relationships. His justification begins with the claim that moral anger can be shown, by way of empirical studies, to be beneficial to human relationships in certain crucial respects. He then argues, also on the basis of empirical work, that sadness will be much less effective in achieving the benefits. The essential elements of my response are, first, that Nichols's argument is remiss in not counting the cost of moral anger in comparison with the proposed substitutes, and second, that the studies he cites fail to show that adult human beings, with education and resolve, would not benefit overall from these substitutions in their personal and social relationships.

First, Nichols argues that while there is ample evidence that moral anger discourages cheating, defecting, and mistreatment, sadness tends to produce no behavior at all. Here he cites Richard Lazarus, who claims, "In sadness there seems to be no clear action tendency—except inaction, or withdrawal into oneself" (1991, p. 251). The evidence Lazarus cites is from infancy research, according to which "infants show individual differences in their propensities to feel sad or angry when blocked from attaining a desired end—some babies are more likely to feel sad, others to feel angry" (Nichols 2007, p. 420). Nichols also argues that "researchers have found that when infants show sadness as their predominant emotion, this is associated with giving up (Lewis & Ramsey 2005, 518), and it seems to be akin to learned helplessness (Abramson et al. 1978)," and that, "by contrast, infants who respond with anger are more likely to try to overcome the obstacle (Lewis & Ramsey 2005, 518)."

In response, the point I want to make about the appropriateness of sorrow and sadness as a substitute for moral anger concerns adults, not infants. It is not surprising that infants would not have developed the capacities to have thoughts like "I'm sad about what my brother has done to me, and now I will try, diplomatically, to improve this relationship." Thoughts of this sort are available to adults. Consider cases of adult sadness, in the absence of anger, about states of affairs that could not have been prevented, such as a hurricane devastating one's town or a severe illness of a child. It's clear that adults can take action, and typically do, under such circumstances by way of these kinds of motivating factors. Similarly, when a parent is too intensely sad to be angry about her son's intoxicated driving and hitting a pedestrian, experience indicates that this attitude can motivate her to take measures to cause him to change his behavior. My claim is that for adults, moral sadness and sorrow— accompanied by a resolve for fairness and justice or to improving personal relationships—will serve societal and personal relationships as well as moral anger does.

A further point, due to Carla Bagnoli (in correspondence), is that a distinction can be drawn between sadness as a form of moral address and sadness that does not have this role. When infants are sad about some state of affairs, it's dubious that their sadness could be intended to have the role of addressing another agent for his bad behavior and immoral dispositions. Infants have not reached the level of cognitive development to be capable of such moral address. Rather, it's like the sadness that we might feel when we've had to cancel the picnic due to rain or we have to miss the important game due to illness. When one's sadness is a form of moral address, it is directed toward an agent in virtue of his misbehavior, and this sort of sadness, I would venture, can clearly be effective in eliciting reform and reconciliation.

Nichols (2007) considers my proposal to supplement sadness with resolve, but here he argues that it is unlikely that resolve will provide sufficient motivation for most people. "After all," he says, "many teenagers think that they risk going to hell if they have sex, yet this often provides insufficient motivation for abstinence" (p. 421). He also cites the Marxist thought that "working hard will generate benefits for the state which will in turn benefit everyone," which he thinks "turns out to be naively optimistic about the plasticity of human motivation" (pp. 421–22). He places the proposal to replace the reactive attitudes with sadness and resolve in the same camp. Nichols may be right that desires for sex and personal material incentives for work are not evenly matched by resolve together with alternative motivations or attachment to abstract principles. (Notice that in his teenage sex example, not even the threat of the most severe punishment imaginable proves especially effective.) But we have reason to believe that we can effectively oppose behavior that hinders good personal and social relationships with a resolve to make the world more fair and just or to improve one's personal relationships, together with attitudes other than moral anger and measures other than punishment driven by such anger. Mahatma Gandhi and Martin Luther King are often cited as exceptionally successful at resisting injustice without expression of moral anger (Nelkin 2011a). In many parts of the world, children are raised and taught with much less expression of moral anger than they were a century ago and earlier. Life in primary schools in the nineteenth century, as described by Charles Dickens, for example, featured a far greater incidence of expression of moral anger than it does today, with results that are at very least no worse. One should also note that for many centuries now human beings have developed communities in which training and teaching methods are employed to diminish moral anger and to develop moral and religious excellence by other means; Buddhist and Christian monastic societies and radical reformation groups such as the Amish come to mind. It's especially important that we examine such communities to see whether these alternative methods can be successful.

My second contention is that in certain respects blame without moral anger is preferable. I have argued that destructive anger in relationships is nourished by the belief that its target is in this sense blameworthy for having done wrong. The anger that fuels ethnic conflicts often results partly from the belief that an opposing group deserves blame for some atrocity. Free will skepticism advocates retracting such beliefs because they are false, as a result of which the associated anger might be diminished and its expressions reduced (Pereboom 2001). In addition, expression of moral anger is more likely to occasion destructive resistance than is expression of moral concern and the moral sorrow that such concern is apt to generate. Sacha Sullivan (in conversation) points out that trainers of powerful animals are especially wary of expressing anger since the reaction is so dangerous and less effective than available alternatives. One might reasonably believe that the analogous claim is true for relations among humans (Pereboom 2009). (Note that trainers' ability to avoid expressions of anger counts against the concern that we lack the general ability to avoid such anger in human relationships.)

But in addition, blame fueled by moral anger arguably renders it particularly susceptible to errors that threaten to undermine the integrity and effectiveness of the moral conversation. We see that parents who become angry with children when their actions produce bad consequences are disposed to believe that these consequences were intentionally caused even if it is open that they are merely accidental, that when we are angry with politicians whose views we find despicable we too readily believe reports that they've behaved immorally, and that human beings too easily come to believe accusations against members of groups with which they are angry for perceived past immoral behavior. In the past several decades, impressive experimental evidence that blaming behavior is widely subject to problems of these kinds has been mounting (Nadelhoffer 2006). Surveys conducted by Mark Alicke and his associates indicate that subjects who spontaneously evaluate agents' behavior unfavorably are apt to exaggerate agents' causal control and any evidence that might favor it while de-emphasizing counterevidence (Alicke, Davis, and Pezzo 1994; Alicke 2000; Alicke, Rose, and Bloom 2011). Alicke calls this tendency 'blame validation.' Studies designed by Joshua Knobe (2003) and Thomas Nadelhoffer (2004a, 2004b) indicate that subjects are much more likely to judge that a bad side effect was produced intentionally than they are to judge that a good side effect was produced intentionally in an otherwise structurally similar case. A survey conducted by Nadelhoffer (2004b) provides evidence that initial judgments concerning the blameworthiness and praiseworthiness of an agent have similar influences on ascriptions of intentionality.

One might question whether moral anger has a significant role in producing the sorts of fabrications indicated by these surveys. Studies might be designed to determine whether this is the case. My hypothesis is that this is indeed often so, while other impulses, such as a desire to disempower or dominate, or sheer glee at another's being blamed and punished, might well also result in these kinds of effects. Still, my sense is that often moral anger has the key role. Evidence for this includes the fact that when someone blames in a way that expresses anger, we are typically on guard that he will attribute to its target intentions and efficacy skewed in a way that would serve to justify the blame. It stands to reason that such effects would be diminished if such anger were replaced by genuine moral concern for the agent and the moral sorrow such concern would generate if the offense was especially serious. It is noteworthy that in the various surveys in which such effects are indicated, a substantial percentage of those surveyed does not display the sort of fabrication targeted. It would be interesting to determine whether members of this group are less subject to moral anger or are capable of overcoming it by way of some rational or affective technique.

4. Final Words

To this account one might object that unless a response to bad behavior expresses the reactive attitudes of resentment or indignation it is not genuine blame (Wallace 2011). In response, when a parent points out to a child that what he did was immoral and recommends that he not perform similar actions in the future, but does so without indignation but only disappointment, it seems clear that no linguistic error is made when we say that under such conditions the child is being blamed. Let me note again that probably most of the blame that occurs in this world is blame of children by parents and teachers and that in many contemporary contexts such blame does not feature moral anger. Most parents are morally angry only in cases in which the misbehavior is especially serious.

Moreover, consonant with the phenomenon of blame validation and its connection with the reactive attitudes, we seem often to make errors about intention and causation when moral anger is involved in blaming. Certain kinds of children's stories sometimes feature parents whose expression of moral anger is never or infrequently accompanied by such error, but my sense is that this is the stuff of fiction. I suspect that children have a keen awareness of this problem and as a result are likely to discount the reasonableness of overt blame when it expresses reactive attitudes. They might be intimidated by anger-expressing blame just as they would be by a threat of physical violence, but this departs from the model of a rational moral conversation. As a result, we are apt to think that parents who express indignation whenever they believe that their children have misbehaved even in relatively minor ways fall short of the ideal in a significant respect.

At the same time, some types and certain degrees of moral anger are likely to be beyond our power to affect, and thus even supposing that the free will skeptic is committed to doing what is right and rational, she would still be unable to eliminate these attitudes. Nichols (2007) cites the distinction between narrow-profile emotional responses, which are local or immediate emotional reactions to situations, and wide-profile responses, which are not immediate and can involve rational reflection. As free will skeptics we should expect that we cannot avoid some degree of local and immediate moral anger. But in the long term, we might well be able to take measures that would moderate or eliminate moral anger, and given a belief in free will skepticism, we would then do so for the sake of morality and rationality.

11

Valuing Blame

Christopher Evan Franklin

1. Introduction

Blame is a puzzling phenomenon. Given the atrocities and crimes we daily witness, it seems like a mistake to wholly forswear blame, yet it often remains obscure why this is: What, if anything, is good or valuable about our blaming practices? Why wouldn't it be better to wholly reject the punitive practices of blame, especially in light of their often corrosive and divisive effects, and instead embrace an ethic of unrelenting forgiveness and mercy?[1] Aren't sadness and disappointment more enlightened responses to blameworthiness than resentment and indignation? The senses of goodness and rightness at stake are all things considered good and right rather than just good or right in this or that respect. Moreover, the question is not metaphysical but moral. The skepticism stems not from doubts about our status as free and morally responsible agents but from doubts about the value of these practices.[2] The "blame curmudgeons," as I will call them, reject blame, arguing that there is nothing good or right about blaming, or that whatever aspects of blame that are good and right are insufficient to justify the practice in light of both its harmful effects and our possessing myriad alternative, more enlightened responses to blameworthiness.[3] It is to this objection to blame that I aim to

---

An earlier draft of this paper was presented at the University of California, Riverside, Agency Workshop. I am grateful to the participants for their insightful and constructive feedback, especially Justin Coates, John Fischer, Ben Mitchell-Yellin, Philip Swenson, and Neal Tognazzini. I am especially grateful to Coleen Macnamara, who has provided invaluable feedback throughout this paper's many variations.

[1] Watson (1987b) raises this important question and offers Martin Luther King Jr. and Gandhi as examples of persons who forswore blame.

[2] Smart (1961, pp. 305–6) betrays an ambiguity on this point. It is unclear if his objection to the kind of blame that is "bound up" with metaphysical freedom is that we are not free and thus this kind of blame is unfair or inappropriate, or rather that this kind of blame is inherently morally problematic. Then again, perhaps he has both objections in mind. For metaphysically based objections to blame see Double (1991), Pereboom (2001), Smilansky (2000), Strawson (1986).

[3] See Seneca (1995).

respond. I will therefore assume that agents are sometimes blameworthy.[4] The challenge is to show that and explain why it is ever, all things considered, good or right to blame blameworthy agents.[5]

So is blame ever required? Consider the following case reported by Dostoevsky's character Ivan Karamazov:[6]

> There was a general at the beginning of the century . . . who [felt] all but certain that his service [had] earned him the power of life and death over his subjects. And so one day a house-serf, a little boy, only eight years old, threw a stone while he was playing and hurt the paw of the general's favorite hound. . . . It was reported to [the general] that this boy had thrown a stone at her and hurt her paw. "So it was you," the general looked the boy up and down. "Take him!" . . . The general orders [the serfs] to undress the boy; the child is stripped naked, he shivers, he's crazy with fear, he doesn't dare make a peep. . . . "Drive him!" the general commands. The huntsmen shout, "Run, run!" The boy runs. . . . "Sic him!" screams the general and looses the whole pack of wolfhounds on him. He hunted him down before the mother's eyes, and the dogs tore the child to pieces . . .! I believe the general was later declared incompetent to administer his estates. ([1880] 1990, pp. 242–43)

What is your reaction to this story? Mine is a sense of outrage, not just at the cruel murder but also at the failure to treat this crime seriously. Now admittedly further details of this case must be made explicit. Perhaps there were extenuating circumstances that mitigated the general's responsibility. (Perhaps he was insane.) But for the sake of argument, suppose that there were no such considerations. I find myself no less outraged at the general's cruelty than at the legal system's failure to take seriously the child's life and to demonstrate the people's commitment to him as a person of worth.

Now my topic in this paper is blame, not punishment, and its proper setting is morality, not the law. Nevertheless this case suggests some important facts that we must come to terms with when seeking to understand blame. First, not only is it fair sometimes to blame; sometimes it is also good. This needs explaining. What is it about blame, something that seems so unpleasant and potentially divisive, that can render it such a valuable part of our moral practices? Second, and this is a corollary of the first point, it would be wrong to

---

    [4] I take 'worthiness' in 'blameworthiness' merely to indicate that blame is permissible rather than required.
    [5] From hereon I will leave the qualifier 'all things considered' implicit.
    [6] Apparently this story appeared in the *Russian Herald*, no. 9 (1877) and was entitled "Memoirs of a Serf." See Dostoevsky ([1880] 1990, p. 785).

wholly forswear blame, as the above case of homicide illustrates.[7] What explains this?

The seeds of an answer are scattered throughout the philosophical landscape: namely that blame is connected to value.[8] Yet while many have suggested that blame is connected to value, few have either elucidated or defended this claim. Two important exceptions, however, are George Sher (2006) and R. Jay Wallace (2011), both of whom offer detailed accounts of the connection between blame and value. But while these accounts move us forward in understanding the value of blame, I argue in section 2 that both are problematic. Sher's account justifies only a very weak form of blame, failing to address the value of more severe blaming responses, such as resentment and indignation. Wallace's account fails to show that blaming is *essential* to valuing what we ought to value, leaving it unclear why we should not substitute sadness and disappointment for resentment and indignation. In order to substantiate the value of blame, in sections 3–5 I will provide a defense of the connection between value and blame that shows that blame is an essential way of valuing objects we ought to value. The connection holds, I argue, in virtue of the significance of free action and the standards governing how we ought to value objects of moral value, among which are the requirements that we defend and protect these objects. Sadness is not an apt substitute for blame because sadness cannot defend and protect these objects; only blame can play this role. Let us refer to this account of the relation between value and blame as the "value account of blame." On the basis of this account of the nature of blame we will be able to explain why we should not wholly forswear blame: if I fail to be outraged or censure the perpetrators of some crime, I fail to properly value its victims. Blaming, given the existence of blameworthy agents, is a mode of valuation required by the standards of value, and thus to forswear blame is to fail to value what we ought to value.

2. Blaming and Caring about Morality

In his recent book Sher (2006) offers an extensive treatment of blame. Two of his main contributions on this topic are his defense of a unique account of blame and his providing an ingenious argument that a commitment to blame and morality stand and fall together. According to Sher, "To blame someone . . . is to have certain affective and behavioral dispositions, each of which can be

---

[7] I will consider these points and questions, as much as possible, from a theory-neutral perspective. Thus I do not assume a Kantian, consequentialist, virtue ethical, or other theory. Because of this I allow for the possibility that the good and the right can come apart in both directions: what is best may not be right, and what is right may not be best. The account of blame I offer will allow us to link the evaluative with the deontic as I will attempt to ground the rightness of blame in its goodness.

[8] Duff (1986, p. 55); Feinberg (1970, p. 103); Hampton (1988b, p. 125); Murphy (1988, p. 18); Scanlon (2008, pp. 130, 144); Sher (2006, pp. 128–29); Walker (2006, p. 26); Wallace (1994, p. 69; 2011, p. 367).

traced to the combination of a belief that the person has acted badly . . . and a desire that this not be the case" (p. 115).[9] The affective and behavioral dispositions that the desire-belief pair gives rise to include anger, resentment, censure, and rebuke. Crucially it is only a contingent fact that the desire-belief pair gives rise to these dispositions (p. 137). So according to Sher, to blame Jones for failing to keep his promise is to believe that in so doing Jones has acted badly and to desire that Jones not have so acted and to be contingently disposed to affective and behavioral dispositions toward Jones, such as anger, indignation, and censure.

On the basis of this account of blame, Sher constructs a fascinating argument to show that caring about morality requires a commitment to blame.[10] Given the existence of many differing conceptions of morality, Sher constructs his argument solely on the basis of the formal features of morality—namely its being practical, universal, omnitemporal, overriding, and inescapable. His argument runs, roughly, as follows: a person who is committed to morality must desire not to violate its principles (given that morality is practical), desire that others not violate these principles (given that morality is universal), desire that no one in the past has violated these principles (given that morality is omnitemporal), and be disposed to certain affective and behavioral dispositions (given that morality is overriding and inescapable). The 'must' here is not psychological, but conceptual (Sher 2006, p. 124). Part of *what it is* to be committed to morality is to possess this universally and omnitemporally directed desire—namely the desire that for any bad action, the agent not have performed that action. But this just is the desire component of blame. Therefore, to give up blame would be to give up our commitment to morality: "[T]he cases for living as morality requires and for blaming those who do not must stand or fall together" (p. 135). We now have a potential answer to the question of whether blame is good or right: insofar as a commitment to morality is good and right, and surely it is both, then blame is also good and right.

What Sher's argument does not establish is striking: the argument does not establish that the affective and behavioral dispositions, such as dispositions to resentment and rebuke, are conceptually tied to a commitment to morality. Rather, the argument, at best, establishes that the desire that someone not have acted badly is conceptually tied to a commitment to morality. Recall that the desire that someone have not acted badly only *contingently* gives rise to these dispositions. There is no conceptual tie between blaming dispositions and a

---

[9] I omit Sher's claims about blame for character traits here and throughout, as my focus will be limited to blame for actions and omissions. 'To act badly' is a technical phrase for Sher, meaning a morally defective act that renders the agent blameworthy (2006, p. 9). Hence if an agent's action φ is bad, then the agent is blameworthy for φ.

[10] The sense of commitment that Sher has in mind is, or at least includes, valuing: to be committed to morality is to value morality (cf. Sher 2006, pp. 128–29).

commitment to morality, and in this way Sher has left these dispositions unde-fended.[11] This is not an oversight on Sher's part. He is skeptical that these affective and behavioral dispositions are good or right, and he concludes his book by way of raising doubts about whether we should retain these practices (2006, p. 138).

Sher's defense of blame boils down to a defense of the desire that people not violate morality. But this, I submit, leaves our original questions about blame unanswered. Part of what is driving our present inquiry is the negative and harsh side of blame, which includes attitudes such as resentment and indigna-tion and overt responses such as rebuke and censure. This observation natu-rally leads one to wonder whether Sher's account of blame accurately captures the phenomenon. Doesn't it make perfect sense to say, "I believe you acted badly and wish you hadn't, but I don't blame you for it"? To borrow a phrase from Wallace, albeit in a different context, Sher's account seems to "[leave] the blame out of blame."[12] But we need not settle this dispute here. Perhaps there are different species of blame, and perhaps Sher accurately captures one such species. However, there is a different species of blame, blame in the "reactive attitude sense,"[13] according to which, to blame someone is to experience re-sentment, indignation, or guilt because one perceives or judges that someone (including oneself) has violated a standard of conduct that one accepts, and these attitudes, in turn, essentially give rise to behavioral dispositions such as rebuke and censure. It is blame in the reactive attitude sense that fuels our present inquiry. And Sher's account offers no reason to believe that blame, in *this* sense, is ever good or right; indeed, he calls such claims into question.[14]

Sher's failure is instructive: his account failed because he defended only a contingent connection between a commitment to morality and the reactive attitudes. If we can show that blame (in the reactive attitude sense)[15] is *concep-tually* tied to a commitment to morality, just like the species of blame that Sher identified, then we will have shown that blame should not always be forsworn. Moreover, considering Sher's account helpfully focuses our attention on the sense of blame that is at stake for us, directing us toward the reactive attitude

---

[11] Consider: "Because the relation between the desire-belief pairs and the dispositions is merely contingent, it would not be inconsistent for someone to acknowledge both the moral importance and the unavoidability of the desire-belief pairs but to deny either the moral importance or the avoidability of the dispositions to which they standardly give rise" (Sher 2006, p. 137).

[12] Wallace (2011, p. 349) levels this charge against Scanlon's (2008) recent account of blame.

[13] This conception of blame is derived from Strawson (1962). Proponents of this account of blame include Fischer and Ravizza (1998) and Wallace (1994).

[14] Hampton (1988a) also falls prey to this worry. Although her topic is punishment, not blame per se, she is seeking to offer a defense of retributive responses to wrongdoing. She argues that punishment is essentially "the experience of defeat at the hands of the victim (either directly or indirectly through a legal authority)" (p. 126). However, she believes it is possible to "punish" someone in this sense without causing him any pain (p. 126). Thus her defense, like Sher's, fails to show that it is ever good or right to engage in the harsher side of blame or punishment.

[15] From here on let 'blame' be understood to mean 'blame in the reactive attitude sense.'

sense of blame. Before developing an account of blame that builds on these insights, I will consider Wallace's recent defense of blame, which improves on Sher's account but, as we will see, fails for similar reasons.

Wallace (2011) offers a sustained critique of Scanlon's (2008) recent account of blame, a central objection being that Scanlon fails to make the reactive attitudes essential to blame. In the final section of his paper Wallace turns to the question "Why does it matter that we have [the reactive attitudes as a] distinctive response to immorality in our repertoire?" (2011, p. 366). He argues that "the disposition to blame is a way of taking to heart the values at the basis of morality that is peculiarly appropriate to the relational character of those values" (p. 368). For Wallace, like Sher, there is an intimate connection between morality and blame, but unlike Sher, this claim has relevance for us, since blame here is blame in the reactive attitude sense. Morality is based on, or reflects, a range of values, salient among which is the value of a distinctive kind of interpersonal relationship: namely the relationship of mutual recognition and regard.[16] Wallace rightly points out that caring or valuing involves a level of emotional engagement and vulnerability. If I care about my wife, then I will be disposed to rejoice in her successes and be sad at her failures. To be disposed to blame, also a kind of emotional response, is a way of valuing the values at the heart of morality. Wallace concedes (mistakenly, I believe), that it is "possible for someone to care about mutual recognition and regard without the tendency to feel resentment when they have been wronged by actions that flout the norms that constitute such relationships" (p. 369). He contends that valuing X does not require that we be disposed to blame the person who disvalues X; rather valuing requires only that we have some emotional attachment to X, such as sadness when X is harmed. But this concession seems to play directly into the blame curmudgeons' hands. If blame is simply one emotional response constitutive of valuing out of many, then should we not jettison blame in favor of more enlightened responses? To restate the worry: on Wallace's account, blame is not a *required* way of valuing what we ought to value but simply one way of valuing out of many. And so, one might argue, there is no reason that we must or should continue to engage in our blaming practices.

Wallace is aware of this objection and responds by arguing that blame is a "peculiarly appropriate" way of taking to heart the values at the center of morality. It is for this reason that it is important to have blame in our repertoire of responses to blameworthiness. The burden of this reply is on Wallace's claim of unique appropriateness: What is it, and is it important enough to silence our worries about blame? Wallace's claim of unique appropriateness is based on two further claims. First, resentment, indignation, and guilt are all relational in

---

[16] This relationship serves as the basis for the conception of morality offered in Scanlon (1998).

a way that sadness is not. To resent someone is to feel that she has wronged *you*; for you to feel guilt is for you to feel that you wronged someone else; and for you to feel indignation is for you "to be exercised on behalf of another person" (2011, p. 369). Second, resentment, unlike sadness, is available only as a form of response to the person wronged and thus highlights the relational character of the values at the heart of morality. It is in these two ways that blame is peculiarly appropriate to the relational character of the values at the heart of morality.

But this defense of blame falls short of showing that it is ever good or right to blame. The main source of difficulty for Wallace is that it is unclear why blame's supposed unique appropriateness renders blame something worth engaging in. Why does unique appropriateness matter? And if it does matter, is its value great enough to outweigh the undesirable effects of blame? Wallace is silent on these issues; he gives us no reason to think that unique appropriateness is important enough to silence our worries about blame's unpleasant and corrosive effects. Since we can value the values at the heart of morality by being disposed to feel sadness when others flout these values, and since it is unclear that there is anything of importance in the nature of blame's being a uniquely appropriate response, Wallace's account fails to respond to the blame curmudgeons.

Wallace's defense of blame fails, but, like Sher, offers us important insights. First, he rightly claims that blaming is a way of valuing objects of moral value, and this suggestion will play a central role in my own account of blame. Wallace's mistakes are also instructive. His defense of blame fails for the same reason that Sher's did: he failed to show that blame is essential to an activity that is good or right. Although blame is a way of valuing the values at the heart of morality, Wallace does not show that it is essential to valuing these values, but only that it is one way among others, and thus his defense leaves the blame curmudgeons' argument untouched. We can shore up the problems that ensued from this concession by showing that blame is essential to valuing what we ought to value.

3. Valuing and Morality

To understand why sadness is not an apt substitute for blame we must first understand more generally the nature of valuing and the standards that govern how we ought to value. Importantly, we will see that we *must* value certain objects, and that part of what it is to value them is to defend and protect them. In sections 4 and 5 I will argue that blame is essential to defending and protecting the objects that give rise to moral values, and thus blame is essential to *valuing* them. Blame turns out to be good and right because it is essential to valuing objects of moral value.

Let us begin with some familiar territory. We need first to distinguish valuing something from judging it to be valuable. To value something is to have a complex set of attitudes and dispositions toward it, governed by a distinct set of norms—norms that indicate the proper way to think, feel, and act in light of the value (Anderson 1993, p. 2). In addition to the existence of a plurality of valuable objects, there is also a plurality of proper ways to care about objects of value: the proper way to care about persons differs from the proper way to care about music (pp. 4–5). Each distinct object of value will, in virtue of its nature, give rise to a distinct set of norms concerning how we ought to value it: how we ought to think, feel, and act in light of it (cf. pp. 10–11; Dillon 1992, p. 110). But this plurality notwithstanding, we can offer some general remarks about the nature of valuing. First, to value an object is to devote one's time to it in a substantive way. A nature lover is someone who spends a significant amount of time in nature, but more than that, he appreciates and enjoys nature, studies it, seeks to understand it, protects it, and enhances it. All of these actions are "modes of valuation," ways of valuing nature. Second, to value nature, as Wallace noted, is to be emotionally invested in it: being disposed to be joyful at its celebration, saddened and (I will argue) indignant at its destruction.[17] In addition to emotional engagement, valuing involves deliberative engagement: to value nature is to see it as a source of practical reasons (Seidman 2009). Importantly, it is to "see" the object of value as a source of practical reasons, though not necessarily to judge it so. We can value what we judge to be of no value, and we can see an object as a source of practical reasons even if we judge that it is no such thing. However, normally we will not only see what we value as a source of practical reasons but also believe it to be so. The nature lover will be disposed to see certain considerations as reasons for action: he will be inclined to see the fact that it is a nice day as a reason to go hiking and the possibility of new condominiums in the wildlife reserve as a reason to write his congressman.

To value an object is to be subject to a set of norms that specify, in virtue of the nature of the object, the kinds of emotional and deliberative dispositions one must possess. The perceived reasons involved in valuing are pro tanto reasons. If we value nature, we will see the fact that we can invest time in it by hiking and protecting it as a reason to do so. But these reasons can be defeated: we also value our children, and this will curtail the time we invest in nature. And just as our reasons to care about nature must be balanced against other reasons, so also our emotional engagement with nature will be curtailed by our emotional engagement with other objects of value. If we have just lost a child, then the destruction of a large portion of the rainforest may not greatly affect us. Normally such indifference to nature would show one was failing to abide

---

[17] Cf. Anderson (1993, p. 11): "Romantic love involves feeling grief when the beloved dies, despondency at her lack of reciprocation, exultation at her confession of reciprocal love, jealousy when her affections are turned to another, alarm at her being harmed." I will argue that we should add "and resentment when the beloved is freely disvalued."

by the norms of valuing nature. However, in our case, our emotional detachment is not at odds with our care for nature so long as we are *disposed* to a high level of emotional engagement.[18]

To value X, then, is to have a complex attitude constituted by a set of deliberative and emotional dispositions, specified by the norms that govern how to properly value X. In contrast to the person who values nature is the person who merely judges nature to be valuable, judges that it would be proper to have this complex attitude, but does not exemplify it himself. In this way we can judge objects to be of value without actually valuing them.[19] To judge that something is valuable without actually valuing it does not, arguably, signify a failing on the part of the agent; there are simply too many valuable things for us to value them all. I believe that an understanding of current cosmological theories is valuable, although this is not something I value myself. I have instead devoted myself to the pursuit of other valuable activities. Valuing X and judging X to be valuable are constituted by distinct attitudes and dispositions: valuing involves an amount of devotion to and emotional engagement with the object valued, while judging valuable requires only the recognition that such devotion and emotional attachment is appropriate or intelligible or worthwhile.

My focus in this paper, however, is with objects that give rise to moral values, and valuing these is not optional. The objects at the heart of morality are categorical in that they set ends for us. While much of what we value depends on unique, contingent features of the valuer—her preferences, circumstances, and so forth—objects that give rise to moral values demand our respect simply in virtue of our being rational agents capable of valuing. Thus to fail to value these objects is to fail to value what we *ought* to value. This is the first plank in my defense of blame. Some objects must be valued. The second plank concerns the proper way to value such objects. As mentioned earlier, the proper way of valuing an object depends on the nature of that object. Valuing persons ought to differ, in certain respects, from valuing nature. However, all objects that give rise to moral values require that we defend and protect them. The importance, centrality, and inescapability of moral values demand that we take these objects seriously, and part of what it is to take them seriously is to defend and protect them.[20]

Therefore, we must possess the complex attitude, constituted by emotional and deliberative dispositions, proper to valuing objects of moral values. And among the norms that govern how to properly care about morality is the requirement that we defend and protect moral values: we must stand up for and

---

[18] I return to this point at the end of section 4.

[19] Judging valuable and valuing can come apart in both directions: we can judge something to be valuable and not care about it, and we can care about things that we judge to be of no value. Cf. Seidman (2009) and Watson (1987a).

[20] Cf. Raz (2001, p. 167), who argues that we must respect everything of value, where this includes defending and protecting these values.

safeguard moral values against those who flout them. With this understanding of the nature of value and valuing in hand, let us return to our query about the value of blame.

4. The Value Account of Blame

We must value objects of moral value, and so doing requires that we defend and protect them. What exactly are the objects at the heart of morality is a substantive, first-order, ethical question. I will assume that humans, nature, and animals are among the valuable objects at the heart of morality. The reason for making this assumption is to afford us concrete examples by which we can further understand the value account of blame.[21]

To value persons is to be disposed to experience a range of emotions in response to how their lives go and to see certain considerations as reasons. If I value persons, I will see the unavoidable misfortune of some as reason to help them. I will see reason to protect those who cannot protect themselves and to afford them opportunities to direct their lives in accordance with their hopes and aspirations. If I value nature, I will be disposed to experience joy when new laws are passed to secure its protection and sadness when a precious forest is lost to fire. And according to the value account of blame, we must be disposed to experience and express blame in response to those who *freely* disvalue objects of moral value. This is the heart of the value account of blame: blame is a required mode of valuation in response to free disvaluations. I will elucidate the condition of free disvaluations in a moment, but let us first consider the details of this account more closely.

First, on my account, the connection between valuing and blaming looks in the opposite direction as familiar Kantian accounts of the value of blame.[22] Kantians often maintain that we should blame agents for acting wrongly, for otherwise we would fail to take the blameworthy agent seriously and in this way would fail to value the blameworthy agent.[23] This is a powerful claim, but I believe that it is a mistake to place it at the heart of an account of the value of blame, for it looks in the wrong direction. Our primary concern should be the victim, not the blameworthy agent, and consequently, it would seem that if blame is of value, we should be able to explain this on the basis of valuing the victim and not only the wrongdoer. To clarify, I am not denying the Kantian

---

[21] Thus, nothing I say turns on any of the specific values I identify. The reader is encouraged simply to replace any of the values on the list with the values she judges to be at the heart of morality.

[22] Thanks to Ben Mitchell-Yellin for pointing this out to me.

[23] Bennett (2008), Korsgaard (1996), and Scanlon (2008, pp. 167–68) all emphasize the importance of blame for taking the wrongdoer seriously.

thought; indeed I am inclined to accept it. However, I am denying that this thought should be the only or even the central explanation of the value of blame.

According to the value account of blame, the standards of value play a dual role with regard to blame: they specify both who is blameworthy and how to respond to the blameworthy agent. It is by freely violating the standards of value that one becomes blameworthy. This much is familiar in accounts of blame.[24] Part of what is distinctive in my theory is that the standards of value also specify how we ought to respond to the blameworthy agent: according to the standards of value we should be disposed to experience blame toward the agent who has disvalued an object of moral value and be disposed to take there to be pro tanto reason to express blame. Consequently, in failing to blame the murderer, we (all things being equal) fail to value the victim. It is not just that these responses are one way of valuing out of many; rather, one who fails to care for such objects in these ways fails to value these objects. To fail to blame, then, sometimes constitutes a form of disvaluation. It is in this sense that it can be right to blame: blaming is a necessary way of properly valuing moral values. But it is also good to value such objects, and consequently, as blame is essential to valuing them, blame is good. Therefore, it would be wrong and bad to forswear blame.

There are three main components to the value account of blame. First, on this account, blame is a required mode of valuing objects of moral value. Second, blame is a response to free disvaluations of objects of moral value. Third, the standards governing how to value such objects specify who is blameworthy and how to respond to such disvaluations. But why think the standards of valuing make blame a required response? Why do they require that one go beyond sadness and grief to the dark attitude of blame? I believe that the answer lies in understanding the significance of free actions and the specific requirements of the standards of value. Our proneness to the reactive attitudes in response to free disvaluations is rendered good and right partly by the fact that free actions function as, or express, value judgments. In freely throwing my trash on the ground in Yosemite National Park, I am, whether or not I intend to, making a value claim about Yosemite in particular and nature in general. I am claiming that nature is not altogether that valuable, if valuable at all, and so it really does not matter whether I drop my trash here or a few feet away in the trashcan. The person who destroys a Picasso painting because the owner will not sell it to him expresses value judgments about the painting, himself, and the owner. He expresses an extreme narcissism, making it clear that the frustration of his desires is not to be tolerated. Embedded in this action is a bloated view of his own value relative to other persons. He takes his happiness to be much more important than that of others and that the owner deserves little to no consideration. Moreover, he fails to respect the

---

[24] See especially Murphy (1988) and Hampton (1988a).

value and beauty of the painting, subjecting its worth to the whims of his fancy. Free actions therefore have meaning and serve to express a take on what is valuable.

It is because free disvaluations challenge the status of an object as valuable (or its degree of value) that we are to respond with blame, for the standards of value require that we acknowledge, defend, and protect what is of value. In freely insulting your wife, I am expressing a judgment about her worth. In freely disvaluing her, I am claiming that she is not to be valued. Blame (or guilt) serves both to acknowledge the wrongness of my action and to counteract my claim because it too plays an expressive role. In experiencing and expressing blame toward me for insulting your wife, you too are expressing a judgment concerning her value. In particular you are standing up for your wife and defending her value in the face of a challenge, making clear that you value her and that my actions are inconsistent with her value as a person. Moreover, by responding in this way, you are protecting your wife's value. You are making it clear to her and others that she is of value, and this is the first step in protecting her from further mistreatment. Disvaluing a person can lead the blameworthy agent, the victim, and third parties to doubt the victim's value; such disvaluing can lead (perhaps unconsciously) to a sense that the person is not valuable after all or that valuing her is consistent with treating her in this insulting fashion. Such beliefs can lead to further disvaluing. In experiencing blame you register the act's inconsistency with your wife's value and resist the subtle growth of contempt for her. You make it clear that you will not stand for or allow such treatment of her. In expressing blame, you make a case for her value to others. To fail to blame me would be to fail to take your wife seriously, implying that what I did was "no big deal." It is for reasons such as these that failing to blame me would be to fail to value your wife.

We now have the beginnings of a defense of the value account's main contention, namely that blame is a mode of valuation required by the standards of value. The connection between blame and value obtains because of (1) the significance and status of free action and (2) blame's being essential to how we defend and protect moral values. We will further explore these claims in the remainder of the paper.

5. The Meaning of Free Action and Blame

As Scanlon (2008, pp. 122–31) insightfully points out, free actions carry the significance they do because of their connection to reasons: free actions are (among other things) actions performed for reasons. A free action's significance varies with the reasons for which it was performed. My burning a Picasso painting because of a dare carries a very different meaning from my burning a

Picasso painting because of how cruelly it represents women. Free actions, moreover, constitute a take on what is of value—what is valuable, the degree and importance of the value, and so on. For example, my destroying the Picasso painting because of its misogynist overtones suggests that a proper appreciation of women is more valuable than the beauty of the painting's composition. Moreover, my action expresses that appreciation of the value of women is more important than whatever pleasure museum-goers might glean from viewing it. Indeed, our actions are so saturated with meaning that it will often be impossible to fully appreciate their significance.

Free actions constitute takes on what is of value, although they do not necessarily represent an agent's deepest commitments or all things considered view of what is of value. Our free actions can represent a take on value that we ourselves repudiate. This is exactly what happens in cases of weakness of will. A person's cheating on his wife suggests that fidelity to his wife is less important than his own sexual gratification. It represents this take on value even though he does not judge this to be the case. Instead he succumbs to temptation, acting weakly. The significance of free actions that we are concerned with does not obtain in virtue of free actions revealing the agent's "true self."[25] Frequently our free actions constitute a specific take on what is of value that we, all things considered, reject, and it is precisely this failure to live up to what we care about that is a cause for guilt and remorse.

Many nonfree actions also constitute such a stance. A young child or a person born addicted to methamphetamines can perform actions that represent objectionable takes on value. All intentional action appears to constitute such value judgments. Nevertheless, because these actions are not free, the standards of value do not require us to respond with blame. Blame is limited to free actions because only these actions both carry the relevant significance and have the status of belonging to the agent in a way in which it is *fair* or *appropriate* to hold the agent responsible for the action. In this context, "free action" is action for which it is appropriate or fair to hold the agent responsible.[26] Thus blaming is a fitting response to free disvaluations in light of the latter's significance and status.

Blame is a fitting response to free disvaluations partly because of the meaning expressed in those actions. However, according to the value account of blame, blame is not simply a fitting response but a required one. The following is a promising line of defense of this claim. First, the standards of value

---

[25] I am not denying that free actions can have meaning because they represent our true selves. Rather, I am attempting to locate a different sense of the meaning of free actions than others have emphasized. Notable examples of philosophers who offer theories along this other line are Frankfurt (1971) and Watson (1975).

[26] One might offer an additional rationale for limiting blame to freedom: namely that only free actions represent an agent's take on what is of value. I will not argue for this stronger claim.

require that we defend and protect moral values. Second, only blame plays these expressive and functional roles. Therefore, blame is a required mode of valuation. That the standards of value require us to be disposed to defend and protect moral values is clear. The notion of defense here is forensic: to defend moral values is to make a defense of the object's status as a moral value. Blame responds to challenges to an object's status issued in the free disvaluation and makes a case for its value. To fail to stand up for the moral value can involve you in a kind of complicity: your failure to act can be a form of acquiescence to the judgment expressed in the free disvaluation. To fail to stand up for the value also shows a failure of recognition: it is precisely our understanding of the importance of the object of value and the significance of the free disvaluation that moves us to experience and express blame. Moreover, to defend moral values involves expressing our condemnation of the act: by standing up and defending moral values we make it clear that we disagree with and will not stand for that kind of action.

The standards of value also require that we protect moral values. Protection can of course take many forms. We can, for example, protect humans by passing legislation forbidding mistreating them or requiring provision of certain goods necessary for their flourishing. The nature of the protection afforded through blame is more informal. The unpleasant side of blame is especially important here as it imposes a kind of sanction on the blameworthy agent, subjecting him to the unpleasantness of being the object of scorn or rebuke. However, in a more constructive mood, blame can help move the blameworthy agent to a realization of the value he flouted, bringing him to feel remorse and eventually to repent of his wrongdoing (cf. Bennett 2008). The hope is that this transformation will lead him to avoid disvaluing the moral value and thus enhance its protection. Moreover, publicly blaming the agent can serve to bring others to a recognition of the value of the object in question or to sustain the beliefs of those who already recognize it as valuable. As Jean Hampton rightly observes, we protect what we value (1988b, p. 141). Disvaluations challenge the value status of an object, and this challenge can raise doubts in the minds of the person disvalued as well as those who witness the wrong. Blame counteracts and can protect against these false beliefs. It is a way of declaring to others that this form of behavior is not to be tolerated and thus can help people to recognize the moral status of the object or sustain their true beliefs in the face of a challenge.

One might object that the justification offered here applies only to expressed blame, offering no reason to think that it is good to experience *unexpressed* blame. But this objection has little to recommend it. First, even unexpressed blame can serve to defend and protect moral values. Blame helps to undergird our own beliefs about moral values in the face of challenges. Just as expressed blame makes a case to others for the value of the object, unexpressed blame makes a case to ourselves for the value of the object. We often wonder whether, doubt that, or reject the claim that an object is of value. Blame can weigh in and direct us in this line of inquiry. These comments are especially applicable when blame is self-directed: guilt defends the status of the object to and protects against further mistreatment of the object by ourselves. According to many accounts of the nature of emotions, blame (or anger) is a particular mode of construing a situation that renders certain facts salient, such as that a wrong has been committed, that someone has been freely disvalued, and that this needs to be recompensed (cf. Roberts 2003, p. 203; Hurley and Macnamara 2010). Second, if one grants that the actions characteristically motivated by the emotions that constitute blame (resentment, indignation, and guilt) are good and right, it is hard to envision how one might still find the emotions themselves objectionable. I cannot imagine what would be the basis for endorsing the characteristic activities of blame while rejecting their characteristic motivations.

The blame curmudgeons will likely grant my first premise, that valuing entails that we must protect and defend moral values, and yet deny my second premise, that the only way we can do this is by blaming. That is, they will argue that we can defend and protect objects that give rise to moral values through alternative means. But can we really value, for example, persons and yet not be disposed whatsoever to blame those who wantonly disvalue them? Or fail to see any reason whatsoever to rebuke these blameworthy agents? Or always fail to express our indignation to the person disvalued so as to affirm her status as valuable? I find such ideas hard to square with my experience of value. It is precisely because people value things so much that they are likely to become especially exercised when these objects of value are freely disvalued. Part of what it is to *recognize* that some object is of value is to be disposed to blame those who freely disvalue it and to take there to be reason to express this blame.

But can't sadness play the same expressive role? Two features of sadness—what it responds to and what it expresses—prevent it from playing the same role as blame. Sadness is fundamentally a response to the loss of or harm to an object we value, whereas blame is a response to the object's being *freely* disvalued. We respond with sadness when an object we care about is lost or harmed, regardless of the cause of the harm; the harm may have been brought about by a nonrational agent (such as a storm), by a rational agent albeit through an accident (I tripped and knocked over your wine rack), or by a rational agent who freely disvalued the object (I purposely knocked over your wine rack because of jealousy). Sadness *only* tracks the fact that loss or harm occurred; it is not a response to free disvaluation qua free disvaluation and so cannot protect and defend moral values in the ways identified above.

Sadness also, and most important, does not have the dimension of condemnation required for defending and protecting moral values. This is because sadness does not indicate that anyone has violated the standards of value. It indicates only that an object of value has been harmed, but not all harms are disvaluations. One can feel saddened as a result of an action that one judges to be right. We can imagine a father grief-stricken over a child's incarceration, even though he recognizes this to be the right thing to do. The sadness of the father is responding to the loss of the child, not to a disvaluation of the child, since, as the father himself recognizes, there is no disvaluation in this case. It is clear that the grief is a response to the loss of the child not the value judgment expressed in the imprisonment.[27] Experiencing and expressing sadness does not indicate to others that an object of moral value was treated in an objectionable way and thus does not help to safeguard the value against further mistreatment.

One of the difficulties with discerning that sadness cannot play the requisite roles is its deep connection with blame. Whenever blame is appropriate, so is sadness. This is because blame responds to free disvaluations and disvaluing is a kind of harm, thus rendering sadness also appropriate. Nevertheless, sadness is not an apt substitute for blame since it does not carry the condemnatory aspect embedded in blame. Sadness expresses our care and is a response to loss. Blame expresses the value of the object and is a response to free disvaluation.

I have argued that the standards of value require that we be *disposed* to experience and express blame when we become aware of or perceive a free disvaluation of an object of moral value. But to fail to experience or express blame in such circumstances is not always a form of disvaluation. This point is nicely captured by Sir Walter Scott's Francis Osbaldistone, who has just discovered both that he must leave the woman he loves forever and that his father's livelihood is in peril. Francis reflects:

> I was deeply grieved at my separation from Miss Vernon, yet not so much as I should have been, had not my father's apprehended distresses forced themselves on my attention; and I was distressed by the news [of my father's ruin], yet less so than if they had fully occupied my mind. I was neither a false lover nor an unfeeling son, but man can give but a certain portion of distressful emotions to the causes which demand them, and if two operate at once, our sympathy . . . can only be divided between them. (Scott [1815] 1995, p. 209)

Scott's point is not simply descriptive but normative. Francis claims that, in light of human limitations of the store of emotions, the fact that he neither felt as distressed at the prospect of losing his lover nor the ruin of his father is not evidence that he is failing to properly care for these persons. In normal circumstances his failure to experience these emotions with greater intensity would be such evidence. But in this case, his emotions are rightly divided and

---

[27] Or if it is a response to the value judgment expressed in the imprisonment, this is because the parent recognizes the validity of the judgment, and this is additional cause for sadness.

thus inevitably lessened. Similar remarks apply to blame. If I have just received a phone call informing me that my wife has been in a horrific car accident and is being airlifted to a hospital with a specialist, then the fact that I fail to respond with or express blame to the person who has just made an extremely rude comment is pardonable. These reflections drive us toward two conclusions. First, the standards of value do not entail that we must *always* respond to free disvaluation with unexpressed and expressed blame. Rather they require that we be disposed to so respond. Second, the standards do entail that not any reason for omitting to blame will do. If I do not express blame at the person who freely insulted your wife simply because I do not feel like getting involved, then (all other things being equal) I have failed to value your wife. I have placed my own time and comfort over her worth.

We need not always stand up for what is of value when it is challenged. The vicissitudes of life will often focus our attention in a single direction, making it understandable that we do not take on the cause of standing up for certain items that are of value. But a life wholly devoid of blame will be a life that fails to take seriously what is of value, and such a failure will itself be a form of disvalue. Blame, then, is not to be neglected.

6. Conclusion

I have sought to articulate and explore a distinctive understanding of the connection between value and blame in hopes that this connection would serve as a basis for a response to the blame curmudgeons. According to the value account of blame, blame is an essential mode of valuation, and I argued that it is blame's constitutive connection to value that makes it good and right, for if we fail to blame when blame is appropriate (all things being equal), we fail to value what we ought to value. This account of the connection between value and blame remedies deficiencies in Sher's and Wallace's accounts by making blame *essential* to valuing. I offered the beginnings of a defense of this account that appealed to the expressive nature of free action and blame, as well as the standards of value (among which are requirements to defend and protect moral values), in order to render intelligible why there exists this connection between blame and value. It is, I argued, because free action and blame express takes on what is of value that blame is such a fitting response to free disvaluation. And it is because blame is essential to defending and protecting moral values that it is not merely a fitting response but also a good and required one. Sadness cannot replace blame in this expressive role since sadness is a response to loss, not to free disvaluation. Although more must be said to substantiate these claims, I offer the value account of blame as a promising line of response to the blame curmudgeons.

12

Rightness and Responsibility

R. Jay Wallace

There is a traditional debate in ethical theory about the relation between moral rightness and motivation. Internalists, as they are sometimes called, hold that there is a nonaccidental connection between these things. According to this position, sincere judgments about what is morally required are necessarily motivating (or necessarily motivating insofar as the person who makes them is rational or reasoning correctly). Externalists deny this claim, maintaining that one can fail to be motivated in accordance with moral thought and that such failures do not necessarily entail irrationality or other departures from correctness in reasoning. One thing that is at stake in this debate is the question of the constraints to which philosophical accounts of morality are answerable. If internalism is correct, then a theory of morality should aim to make sense of the noncontingent connection that is postulated between moral thought and motivation. A theory that fails to meet this constraint will be prima facie inadequate, and its acceptance would involve a revisionist understanding of the phenomenon that it attempts to account for.

In this paper I want to explore an analogous question about the relation between morality and responsibility: Is moral rightness necessarily connected to responsibility relations between people, or is the connection between these things merely contingent? Internalism about responsibility, as I understand it, is the view that rightness and responsibility are noncontingently connected. The principles that determine what it is morally permissible to do must also be suited to structure and to ground relations of responsibility among the members of a moral community. My aim in this paper is to offer a sympathetic statement of this position, exploiting the analogy with internalism about motivation to mount a modest defense of it.

The discussion divides into four parts. In the first, I offer a brief account of internalism about motivation, explaining its rationale on the interpretation

I received valuable feedback on predecessors of this paper from audiences at the 2011 conference of the Northwestern University Society for the Theory of Ethics and Politics, at the 2011 Hegel-Kongress in Stuttgart, at a meeting of the Bay Area Forum for Law and Ethics, and at the University of Wisconsin in Milwaukee. I profited especially from written comments by Coleen Macnamara, Niko Kolodny, and Cory Michael Davia and from discussion with Marcus Willaschek.

that I favor. In section 2 I draw on my discussion of internalism about motivation to develop an analogous version of internalism about responsibility. In section 3 I refine my statement of internalism about responsibility, focusing on the issue of the significance of agents' attitudes for our responsibility relations. In the brief concluding section I turn to the implications of internalism for our understanding of the content of moral principles, showing how the internalist approach to morality leads to a relational interpretation of its requirements.

1. Rightness and Motivation

Traditional internalists postulate a noncontingent connection of some kind between morality and motivation. But how exactly should the connection they envisage be understood? The most common version of the position, which has been called "moral judgment internalism" (cf. Darwall 1983, p. 54), is cashed out in psychological terms. The idea here is that sincere endorsement of a moral judgment carries with it some tendency to be motivated to comply with the judgment. According to this view, there is a distinctive psychological condition that must be satisfied if an agent is to count as accepting the claim expressed by a moral judgment.[1]

Moral judgment internalism has figured prominently in metaethical discussions during the past century. It has been appealed to by expressivists, for instance, who claim that moral judgments are not the kind of cognitive attitudes that aim to represent the way the world is but involve instead desires or pro-attitudes of some kind, which moral assertions express or give voice to.[2] They argue that moral judgments are necessarily motivating and that we can make sense of this dimension of moral thought only if we understand those judgments to express the kind of noncognitive attitudes that are essentially involved in motivations to act. Indeed, it seems fair to say that moral judgment internalism in some form is the primary consideration alleged to support expressivist approaches—it is the expressivist's Ur-argument, if you will. But the thesis is notoriously problematic. The basic difficulty with it is that it is very hard to see how one could defend moral judgment internalism against possible counterexamples to it in a way that does not simply beg the question.

Traditionally, opponents of moral judgment internalism invoke the figure of the skeptic about morality.[3] This is someone who understands moral

---

[1] Moral judgment internalism, as formulated in the text, raises large interpretative questions. To which moral judgments does it apply? How exactly is the notion of motivation to be understood? I shall bracket such issues in my discussion.

[2] For two recent statements, see Blackburn (1998, ch. 3) and Gibbard (2003, pp. 8–11).

[3] See, for example, Brink (1989, ch. 3); also Svavarsdóttir (1999).

language well enough but who doubts or rejects the significance of moral properties and distinctions in reflecting about how to act. The stance of the moral skeptic seems a coherent one, insofar as we can imagine a person who is competent at moral discourse but who questions its significance for his or her own practical reflection. Indeed, we can imagine this happening in our own case, envisaging a trajectory that takes as its starting point our present commitment to moral ends and arrives at the position of the skeptic. In this scenario, we would retain our actual competence with moral predicates and distinctions but lose any concern to comply with moral requirements, having come to doubt the significance of those requirements for our deliberation about what to do. The prospect of this imaginary trajectory in our thinking about morality will probably seem horrifying from our present point of view, and the skepticism in which it terminates may in fact be substantively mistaken. But it is a perfectly intelligible scenario, and yet moral judgment internalism appears to rule it out on grounds that seem questionably a priori.

We should therefore reject moral judgment internalism. But there is a deeper insight in this position that we should also try to hang on to. What is attractive about internalism, I believe, is the thought that moral considerations at least purport to have normative significance. They present themselves to us as reasons for action, in the basic normative sense of being considerations that count for or against courses of action that are open to us.[4] Thus it is not merely a brute fact about us that we tend to find ourselves drawn to actions that we judge to be morally right or valuable. From the first-person point of view, these moral characteristics strike us as considerations that recommend or speak in favor of the actions to which they apply. Furthermore, the fact that they strike us as normative in this way is connected to our tendency to be motivated in accordance with the moral judgments that we endorse. Here is one way we might develop this insight into an account of the relation between moral properties, moral judgments, and motivation.

Assume, first, that it is a condition of rationality that agents are motivated in accordance with the normative judgments that they sincerely endorse. It is presumably not impossible to fail to be motivated in accordance with such judgments; something like this happens, for instance, in cases of weakness of will and in some forms of self-deception. But when such cases arise, it is natural to say that the agents involved in them are irrational, insofar as they fail to be motivated as they themselves judge that they ought to be. It is thus part of being a rational agent to have dispositions to action (and thought) that are in accordance with the normative reasons one acknowledges to obtain.

Assume, second, that moral considerations do in fact represent genuine reasons for action, having the status of considerations that, for any agent,

---

[4] For this sense, see Scanlon (1998, ch. 1).

count for or against that agent's acting in certain specified ways. If this is the case, then we can say that agents are necessarily motivated to act in accordance with moral requirements to the extent they are deliberating correctly and are otherwise practically rational. The condition of correct deliberation rules out cases in which an agent does not acknowledge the truth of moral judgments or does not acknowledge that such judgments have normative significance for practical reflection. And the rationality condition rules out agents whose motivations fail to align with their own verdicts about what there is reason to do, in the style of weakness of will.

The combination of these two conditions—which I shall henceforth refer to as internalism about motivation—provides a plausible (if rough) characterization of the action-guiding dimension of morality. The requirement combines a claim about the effects of a certain class of judgments, namely normative judgments about what there is reason for one to do, with a substantive thesis about morality, to the effect that it is itself a source of reasons in this normative sense.

The position that results from this combination of claims leaves room for the kind of moral skepticism that is excluded a priori by moral judgment internalism. Indeed, there are two points at which space might open up between an agent's sincere moral judgments and his or her motivations to action. First, a person might accept both the truth of some moral judgment and the normative significance of the judgment thus arrived at without intending to act accordingly. We might believe, for instance, that we are morally obligated to help victims of political persecution in our community, and that our being so obligated speaks strongly in favor of acting accordingly, without really caring about whether we ourselves succeed in providing such assistance when we are in a position to do so. In this scenario, we fail to be motivated in accordance with normative claims that we ourselves accept. Insofar as we accept the normative authority of moral principles for practical deliberation, however, it would not be very plausible to describe us as skeptics about morality. We will rather be acting in ways that are questionable or misguided by our own lights, a condition that involves irrational weakness of will (something along the lines of fecklessness or depression) rather than moral skepticism strictly speaking.

In a different scenario, we might acknowledge the truth of moral judgments without yet accepting that conclusions about what is morally right and wrong have any normative significance at all for us (or perhaps for any agent). Thus we might accept that we are morally obligated to help the locally oppressed without granting that this fact by itself counts in favor of our doing anything to provide such assistance when we can. This in fact seems to describe much better the outlook of a moral skeptic. What skeptics typically doubt or challenge is the normative significance of morality—the idea (for instance) that one ought to help the politically persecuted in one's community just because and insofar as the failure to do so would be wrong.

While allowing for these possibilities, however, the motivation condition, as I have formulated it, still gives expression to the idea that there is a noncontingent connection between morality and motivation. At its heart is the thesis that rightness and other moral considerations represent reasons for people to act in accordance with them. This thesis is a version of the position that is sometimes called "rationalism" in ethics; if it is true, then we can say that those agents who fail to be motivated to act in accordance with their moral judgments are making a substantial mistake of some kind. Either they are failing to acknowledge the normative significance of facts about moral rightness and permissibility, insofar as they deny that people have reason to act only in ways that are morally permissible. Or they grant this normative dimension of morality but irrationally fail to do what they themselves acknowledge that they have reason to do. Conversely, when we form intentions that are in compliance with moral principles, our being motivated in this way is not a mere optional extra, something that just happens to be true of us as a contingent matter of psychological fact. Rather, it is a response that is rendered appropriate by the nature of the moral considerations that we judge to obtain, insofar as those considerations do in fact constitute reasons for acting in accordance with them. They are considerations that merit our compliance with them, and it is in that sense that moral motivation is noncontingently connected to the moral principles it is responsive to.

But what is the connection between rationalism, in the sense at issue here, and moral concepts? Does it follow a priori that if X is the right thing for me to do, then X is something that I have a very strong reason to do? Or is the normative standing of moral considerations a merely contingent fact about them, one that isn't guaranteed by correct application of the concepts involved in moral judgment? The issues here are delicate ones.

On the one hand, it is certainly part of our conventional understanding of morality that it constitutes a domain of reasons for action. Thus we typically cite moral considerations in discussion with other people as factors that are of direct normative significance, counting for or against options that are under active consideration. We raise our children to treat moral considerations in this way, for example. Furthermore, many of us structure our (adult) deliberations on the supposition that moral considerations have normative standing, taking facts about rightness and moral value to have direct significance for our decisions about what to do. These considerations suggest to me that it is one of the familiar platitudes about morality that its central concepts (such as rightness and permissibility) are imbued with normative significance. On the other hand, there has to be room for the skeptical position that coherently questions whether people really do have reason to comply with the standards that define what is morally right and wrong. The skeptical position might be mistaken as a matter of fact, but it isn't merely confused; as I suggested earlier, one can grant that it would be wrong to do X and yet without contradiction deny that this is a reason against acting in that way.

The best way to do justice to these twin pressures, it seems to me, is to take an element of revisionism to be endemic to the skeptical position. Skeptics, insofar as they deny that moral rightness is reason-giving, are denying one of the platitudes that help to fix the meaning of the concept of the morally right. They are thus denying that there is anything in the world that completely answers to this moral concept. It doesn't follow, however, that the position they are adopting is merely confused or incoherent. In saying that people don't have reason to comply with the standards of moral rightness, they can be interpreted as suggesting that the properties in the world that most closely approximate to our concept of the morally right are not properties that have normative significance. Morality cannot, as a result, be everything that it represents itself as being, insofar as one of the platitudes that help to fix the concept turns out to be false as a matter of fact. But this strikes me as a plausible thing to say about the kind of skepticism I have been considering. It is a modestly revisionist position, denying something that strikes us as partly constitutive of the basic moral concepts in the first place, namely the direct significance of the properties they describe for deliberative reflection about what we are to do.

This brings out a second respect in which the connection between morality and motivation is noncontingent on the internalist position I have been sketching. Given the rationalist thesis that moral considerations are reasons for action, the motivation to comply with them is a response that is appropriate to its proper object. But this thesis itself is noncontingently connected to the central moral concepts in such a way that an account of morality that denies the thesis will therefore be at least modestly revisionary.

2. Rightness and Responsibility

Let's now turn to responsibility, considering how an internalist position might look that is modeled on the view sketched in the preceding section.

The first thing to note is that it is not plausible to suppose that attributions of responsibility are built into the act of moral judgment. The judgments that one might expect most closely to involve such attributions are judgments that acknowledge moral shortcomings, including above all judgments to the effect that an agent has acted wrongly or impermissibly. These are the kinds of things that people are typically blamed for, and internalism about responsibility might accordingly be understood to hold that judgments of wrongdoing amount to acts of blame. But this form of "moral judgment internalism" seems implausible, and for reasons that are similar to the reasons that speak against moral judgment internalism about motivation. One can sincerely believe that an agent has acted wrongly without blaming the agent on that account, and this defeats the suggestion that there is an a priori necessary connection between judgments of moral wrongdoing and blame.

Appreciation of this point will be enhanced by brief reflection on the nature of blame. Philosophers have offered a variety of conflicting accounts of moral blame, and there isn't space here to discuss their merits in any detail. So I will cut to the chase and simply assert that on the view I find most attractive, blame should be understood in terms of the reactive emotions of resentment, indignation, and guilt (Wallace 1994). To blame a person for something, on this view, is to think or judge that the person has done something morally impermissible and to be subject on that account to an appropriate emotion from this class that is directed toward the wrongdoer. If the agent has done something to wrong me in particular, for instance, then I will react with blame when I resent the agent for having treated me in this way. Understood in these affective terms, blame is a matter of one's emotional responses to lapses from the standards defined by moral requirements. In particular, it is a way of being exercised by such lapses that shows that one has internalized a concern for moral values. One cares about those values, where this in turn involves a characteristic form of emotional vulnerability to offenses against them. Blame can be understood as a manifestation of one's attachment to morality; it is a reaction that reveals that it matters to one whether people succeed in complying with moral requirements in their interactions with each other (cf. Wallace 2011, sec. 5).

If these brief remarks are on roughly the right lines, however, then it should hardly be surprising that judgments of moral wrongdoing can come apart from either blame or its expression. To judge that a person has acted wrongly is to judge that the person has fallen short by reference to the standards that determine what it is morally permissible to do. But it is an elementary feature of human psychology that we are able to make judgments of this kind even if we do not particularly care about the standards that are at issue in the judgments. We can acknowledge that moral ends have been flouted, for instance, without particularly valuing the forms of relationship that are promoted and made possible by pursuit of those ends. Under these conditions, we will not be prone to blame in the cases in which we acknowledge wrongdoing to have occurred, insofar as we will not have internalized the concern for moral values that is a precondition for emotional reactions of this distinctive kind.

As we saw in the preceding section, however, internalism about motivation is not in any case plausibly understood to involve a necessary psychological connection between moral judgment and the reactions with which it is taken to be noncontingently connected. We do better, I suggested, to think of this connection in normative terms, taking it to rest on the standing of moral considerations as reasons for the motivational responses with which it is noncontingently linked. Let us now turn to the question of how this model might be applied to the case of internalism about responsibility.

There are, I believe, two respects in which we might plausibly understand moral wrongness to be connected normatively to our responsibility reactions. First, the values around which morality is organized might be understood to be values that people in general have good reason to internalize and to care about. These stances involve, as we have seen, forms of characteristic emotional vulnerability, including in particular a tendency to experience the reactive emotions in cases in which people act in ways that flout moral requirements. Even if it is true that we can acknowledge cases of moral wrongdoing while failing to internalize in this way a concern for moral ends, it might still be the case that we in general have reason to adopt this distinctive affective stance, developing the kind of concern for moral ends that would render us susceptible to the reactive sentiments when those ends are offended against. And indeed this seems to be the view that many of us implicitly adopt in our practices of moral education and habituation. We don't think that it is optional for our children to be brought up to care about moral values but seem to view those values as ones that everyone has good reason to internalize. Our interactions with children are accordingly designed in part to inculcate in them an emotional commitment to morality, of the kind that will leave them systematically vulnerable to negative reactions of blame and opprobrium when people wantonly disregard moral requirements in their interactions with others.

Morality in this way seems to differ from many other domains of value. There are plenty of things that we acknowledge to be genuine goods without taking it to be important that all members of the younger generation should be brought up to internalize a specific concern for them. Philosophy, for instance, is an exceptionally worthwhile activity (in my humble opinion). And yet it would hardly be a failing on our part if our children should fail to develop an emotional commitment to this particular activity, coming instead to care about (say) physics or cabinetmaking. Morality seems different in this respect, constituting a domain of value that we all have reason to become emotionally invested in. We might be wrong to think this, of course, but if so it would come as a shock and a surprise, overturning an assumption that is central to our understanding of morality.[5]

So this is one way morality might plausibly be understood to stand in a normative relation to responsibility. A second normative connection that might plausibly be taken to obtain links moral facts about human actions to specific attributions of responsibility for those actions. Thus the fact that A has deliberately done something wrong is at least a defeasible reason for those who have been wronged to resent A for having treated them in this way. It makes sense to react in this way to acts of this kind, and such reactions are therefore rendered appropriate or even called for by the fact that the actions to which they are directed were morally impermissible.

---

[5] This suggests that it is a kind of conceptual truth that morality has this sort of normative significance for our attitudes of caring and concern. I return to the suggestion at the end of the present section.

In saying this, I mean primarily to be alluding to the fact that blame reactions would not be fair or fitting in the complete absence of wrongdoing on the part of the agent at whom they are directed. Deliberate wrongdoing on the agent's part renders blame appropriate, insofar as this reaction is not objectionable in the way it would be if the agent's behavior had been beyond moral reproach.[6] But blame seems called for by wrongdoing in a somewhat stronger sense as well: given the general reasons we have to internalize the kind of concern for moral ends that renders us vulnerable to reactive sentiments in the first place, those emotions are positively appropriate responses to actions that are wantonly impermissible. A failure to experience them when, for instance, someone has wronged us would tend to indicate the absence of the sort of emotional investment in moral values that we generally take to be desirable. The point is not that we have a moral obligation to blame people under circumstances of this kind; I do not believe that it is generally wrong—much less that we generally wrong others—when we fail to respond to deliberate immorality with the reactions constitutive of blame.[7] But such reactions are not merely optional either. We can have positive reasons to blame people, just as we have positive reasons to experience other kinds of emotions (fear, for example, or sadness or even love), even if it is not morally wrong to fail to respond to those reasons in practice.

By the same token, the fact that A has complied with moral requirements in A's interactions with other people provides A with a certain level of normative protection from the emotional reactions that are characteristic of blame. If A's treatment of other people does not involve any moral wrongdoing, then it would ordinarily not be appropriate for them to react to A's actions with the kind of opprobrium and focused hostility that are involved in blame. This is another aspect of the normative connection between an individual's behavior and the responsibility reactions of others.

Of course, the reprehensible moral features of an agent's actions often fail to generate responsibility reactions on the part of other people as a matter of fact. We might, for instance, be strangely indifferent to the fact that A has wronged us, or alternatively feel resentful of A despite the fact that A has not done anything that is genuinely impermissible. But these reactions would often be subject to normative objections of various kinds, for instance, as too mild or as unduly harsh and, well, blaming, objections that imply that there are good reasons for modulating one's reactions to what A has done. This is the sense in which we might take there to be a normative connection between the moral

---

[6] Compare the discussion of "no blameworthiness without fault" in my 1994 (ch. 5).

[7] Thanks to Coleen Macnamara for pressing me to be clearer on this point. There are some situations in which it might seem morally wrong to fail to be exercised about wrongdoing in the way characteristic of blame; we might owe it to the victim of wrongdoing, for instance, to stand up for his claims by blaming the wrongdoer. But these circumstances are somewhat special and do not generalize to all cases.

qualities of actions and the specific reactions that those actions might evoke on the part of people variously affected by them.

Any plausible development of this position will require significant qualification. There may be normative connections between the moral qualities of actions and our responsibility-involving reactions to them, but the connections are capable of being defeated or overridden in particular cases. Thus many cases of wrongdoing are too remote from my own life and experience for it to be plausible to think that I have good reason on balance to become emotionally exercised about them. Particularly if the wrongdoing that is at issue is not egregious and the individuals involved are unknown to me, it might be meddlesome or sanctimonious of me to react to the wrongdoing with indignation. The fact that the victim was wronged would perhaps give us some reason to blame the agent, but the reasons are outweighed on the other side by a variety of considerations that count against reacting in this way.

Another set of cases of this general kind might be those that involve acts of wrongdoing by agents whose powers of moral competence and control are seriously impaired. Even when such agents have wronged me in particular, the fact that they lack the general capacities for moral understanding and control would ground a strong moral objection to my reacting with the standard feelings of blame, so that blame is not a reaction that is really called for or appropriate (on balance) under the circumstances (see Wallace 1994, ch. 6). Here again we might think of facts about wrongdoing as providing reasons for opprobrium that are defeated by the reasons against reactions of this kind, given other relevant facts about the agent of the wrongdoing in the case at hand.

I have so far described two respects in which we might plausibly understand morality and responsibility to be connected to each other normatively. These connections, assuming them to obtain, give a sense to the suggestion that morality and responsibility are related in a way that is not merely accidental or contingent. Holding people responsible isn't a purely optional stance that we might or might not adopt toward them, as we happen to see fit. Rather, it is a response that is inherently answerable to facts about the moral qualities of people's actions, and this in two distinct respects. First, the values around which morality is organized are ones that we all have reason to internalize and to care about, so that we become susceptible to the emotional reactions constitutive of blame on occasions when those values are thwarted or defeated. Second, the moral qualities of individual actions give us defeasible reasons both for blaming their agents and for refraining from blaming them, depending on the qualities that are instantiated in the actions they perform.

There is a third and final point to make as well. In discussing internalism about motivation, I suggested that it might in part be taken to involve a thesis about the concept of morality. The thesis is to the effect that it is part of our understanding of the concept of morality that moral considerations, such as rightness or permissibility, are reasons for action. This thesis might turn out to be false, but if so that result would involve a modest revisionism about morality, the concession that nothing in the world fully matches the contours of our concepts of moral rightness and permissibility. I now want to formulate a similar thesis about the relation between moral concepts and responsibility.

The basic idea is that it might plausibly be taken to be one of our platitudes about morality that moral standards regulate responsibility relations between people. Thus the standards that determine what it is right or permissible to do have it as part of their function to be internalized emotionally, in the way that renders us susceptible to blame reactions when those standards are violated. On this view, it is part of our concept of morality that, for instance, moral wrongness is not only a reason for action (a reason, specifically, to avoid actions that have the property) but also a reason for responsibility reactions (a reason, specifically, for blaming the agent who performs an action with this property). An important consideration in support of this interpretation of the concept of morality is the fact that we tend to identify a society's moral standards by looking to the requirements that are implicit in the reactive sentiments of its members. Our collective moral standards, on this plausible way of seeing things, just are (in part) the standards whose deliberate violation attracts the emotional opprobrium of blame on the part of the members of our community.

In saying this, of course, I don't mean to be saying that we are infallible about what morality requires of us. We might attach opprobrium to the wrong things, blaming people when they engage in eccentric sexual practices with other consenting adults, for instance, and failing to blame them when they turn their backs on the basic human needs of vulnerable members of our community. We could express this possibility by saying that our moral standards are mistaken or misguided in cases of this kind, and this tells us something about the concept of morality: that we think of morality as a set of standards that function to regulate our responsibility relations with each other, giving people reasons for reactive sentiments when they are violated.

Note too that this conceptual point about morality should not be taken to entail that moral standards are in fact reasons for such responsibility reactions. There is room for a skeptical position about responsibility that is analogous to the kind of moral skepticism discussed in the preceding section. This view would hold that the violation of moral standards is not, after all, something that we have good reason to respond to with negative reactive emotions. If I am right, then this skeptical position, just like the corresponding skepticism about moral reasons discussed earlier, would involve some element of revisionism about morality. It would maintain, for instance, that our concepts of moral rightness or permissibility are not fully realized in the world as we find it, precisely insofar as the standards that determine rightness and permissibility do not appropriately regulate our responsibility relations with each other. Our feeling that this outcome would involve a degree of revisionism is a reflection of the basic idea that a normative connection to responsibility relations is built into our concepts of moral rightness and permissibility.

3. Refining the Position

Internalism about responsibility has considerable appeal, but it cannot be accepted in precisely the form in which it has so far been stated. I shall approach the need for refinement by considering a more general issue, having to do with the relation between permissibility, responsibility, and the agent's intent.

At first glance, it seems extremely natural to suppose that the moral permissibility of our actions might at least sometimes depend on the intentions with which they are performed, including in particular the reasons for which we decide to carry them out. Thus it appears to be wrong to fire an employee because the employee has declined your sexual advances, even if it would be permissible to fire the same employee for any of a range of other reasons that might be available in the case. Similarly, refusing to rent an apartment to someone on account of his or her race seems to be wrong, even when one has wide discretion to decide for oneself whom one will enter into a contractual agreement of this kind with. Debates about just war and the ethics of abortion have also frequently invoked principles (such as the doctrine of double effect) that make the permissibility of actions that bring about harm depend in part on the agent's reasons for choosing to perform them.

But these appearances might be questioned. T. M. Scanlon, for instance, has recently mounted an interesting argument for the conclusion that the permissibility of actions almost never depends on the intentions with which agents carry them out (2008, chs. 1–3). His case for this conclusion rests in part on ingenious interpretations of the moral principles that determine permissibility for the problem situations, interpretations that attribute at most derivative importance to the agent's reasons for action. But intent clearly has great moral significance of some kind, and another part of Scanlon's argument is designed to locate its importance in features of moral thought that are distinct from permissibility. Specifically, Scanlon distinguishes between two dimensions of moral assessment, permissibility and meaning, contending that intent matters greatly to the latter even though it is virtually irrelevant to the former. The meaning of our actions is largely a function of the attitudes that are expressed in them, where this in turn depends on our reasons for doing what we do. Scanlon argues that responsibility relations are organized primarily around questions of meaning in this sense rather than questions of permissibility. By acting with contempt or indifference toward someone, we impair our relationship with her, in ways that give her reasons to make the adjustments in her attitudes and behavior that are constitutive of blame, on Scanlon's account of it

(2008, ch. 4). So the intentions with which actions are performed, as part of the meaning of those actions, matter greatly for questions of blame, even if they have virtually no significance for questions about the permissibility of what we have done.

On the surface this position seems to conflict with the internalist view of moral rightness and permissibility that was sketched in the preceding section. Internalism holds that moral properties of this kind have normative significance for our responsibility relations, insofar (for example) as we have reason to blame people when their actions are impermissible. It also holds that it is in the nature of a conceptual truth about morality that the properties it characterizes have this kind of significance, being suited to constitute responsibility relations between people. But if blame is responsive to intent, and intent is in turn largely irrelevant to questions of permissibility, it appears that the internalist position must be mistaken. Moral properties do not, after all, have the direct normative significance for our responsibility relations that it attributes to them.

One might respond to this challenge by questioning Scanlon's account of permissibility. But I do not wish to take that path. I believe Scanlon goes too far in denying the relevance of intent to permissibility, but he is surely right that there are many central cases in which it is not plausible to suppose that moral principles are sensitive to the meaning of the actions they regulate.[8] Nor do I wish to dispute his assumption that questions of meaning are central to blame. Instead I shall argue that the internalist position can be developed in a way that does justice to these two desiderata; indeed, once it is properly understood, internalism about responsibility can help to resolve a puzzle that Scanlon's remarks about permissibility and meaning raise for his larger moral theory.

The puzzle comes into focus when we ask why people should comply with the principles that determine what it is morally right to do. This is the question as to the reason-giving force of moral rightness or permissibility, which is central to the version of internalism about motivation that was presented in section 1. Scanlon himself subscribes to an internalist position of that kind, insofar as he accepts that the impermissibility of an action is a strong reason for just about anyone not to perform it. His own interpretation of this normative aspect of moral properties connects it to a valuable form of relationship between people, which he calls mutual recognition (1998, ch. 4). We relate to people in this way when we are able to justify our behavior to those who might be affected by it, by appeal to principles that it would be unreasonable for

---

[8] For a penetrating discussion of this part of Scanlon's argument, see Kolodny (2011). The account of the moral excuses I offered in my 1994 (ch. 5) assumed that impermissibility always depends on intent. This now seems to me to be mistaken; the remarks that follow are in part an attempt to explain the significance of the agent's quality of will for questions of blame, given the assumption that impermissibility is at least sometimes independent of the agent's attitudes.

anyone to reject as a basis of general agreement. The reason-giving force of moral permissibility thus gets traced to the fact that the principles that define it are conditions for the possibility of valuable relationships of this kind.

Here's the thing about mutual recognition, however. Understood intuitively, this is a way of relating to people that is largely constituted by the attitudes we adopt toward them. To stand in this relationship with others is to acknowledge them as independent sources of claims and to regulate one's behavior accordingly, striving to act in ways that will be justifiable specifically to them. It is thus a matter of the quality of will with which one acts. But if permissibility is independent of matters of intent of this kind, then Scanlon's account of the normative significance of this consideration for action seems to be called into question. Acting permissibly would not appear to be sufficient for mutual recognition, insofar as we can comply with principles of the moral right without having any particular concern for the standing of others as sources of claims against us. Indeed, permissibility does not even appear to be necessary for mutual recognition, insofar as we might fail to do what is objectively right even while sincerely and wholeheartedly endeavoring to act in ways that are justifiable to those affected by what we do. But if permissibility is neither necessary nor sufficient for mutual recognition, and if the value of mutual recognition is in turn the basis of our moral reasons for action, then why should we care about permissibility per se? This is the puzzle to which I alluded earlier.

A first step toward resolving the puzzle is to acknowledge that reasons for action are themselves reasons for intention. Thus if the impermissibility of X-ing is a reason not to do X, then it is itself a reason to intend not to do X, because and insofar as X-ing would be impermissible. Scanlon himself holds something like this view, defending it with the observation that actions involve "judgment-sensitive attitudes" precisely on account of the states of mind of the agent that render their doings intentional performances in the first place (as opposed, for instance, to mere spasms or twitches [1998, pp. 18–22]). We are rational to the extent that we succeed in adjusting our judgment-sensitive attitudes in response to our beliefs about our reasons, and in the case of reasons for action this is a matter of forming intentions to do what we believe there is reason for us to do.

It follows from this that those agents who are responding correctly to the reason-giving force of moral properties such as permissibility and rightness will necessarily act with a certain distinctive quality of will. They will acknowledge that the impermissibility of X-ing (say) is a reason not to X, and they will form the intention not to X for this reason. But this is the very quality of will that plausibly constitutes the necessary and sufficient subjective condition for mutual recognition. We take people to be independent sources of claims, subjects to whom justification is owed, just in case we grant the reason-giving force of permissibility and regulate our intentions in accordance with this consideration. The upshot is this: permissibility might not itself be a condition of mutual recognition, strictly speaking. But if we postulate that it is a consideration with normative significance for human action, then agents will achieve the attitudes constitutive of mutual recognition when (and only when) they respond correctly to this consideration, acknowledging its reason-giving force and adjusting their intentions accordingly. The attitudes important to mutual recognition are thus not attitudes that make actions permissible in the first place (since by hypothesis permissibility often doesn't depend on the agent's intent at all). They are rather the attitudes one forms when one responds appropriately to permissibility as a reason for action.

It is a consequence of this interpretative suggestion, however, that the connection between mutual recognition and the reason-giving force of permissibility becomes somewhat elusive. As I noted earlier, Scanlon appeals to mutual recognition to illuminate the normative significance of moral permissibility; this suggests that our reasons for caring about permissibility are provided by the fact that permissibility makes possible relations of mutual recognition. But this suggestion now seems to be a mistake. Our moral reasons for action, the reasons we directly respond to when we act morally, are constituted by considerations of permissibility and rightness themselves. Mutual recognition is a kind of secondary effect, brought about when we acknowledge the normative significance of those considerations in our deliberations about what to do.[9] It is an important question, which I cannot go into here, how Scanlon's reflections about mutual recognition might shed light on the reason-giving force of permissibility and rightness if relationships of this kind are not the agent's primary reasons for acting morally.[10]

With these remarks in place, let us now return to the question of the normative significance of permissibility and rightness for responsibility. The worry about this, to put it crudely, was that blame is a response to the meaning of an agent's actions (in Scanlon's sense) and that questions of permissibility are distinct from questions of meaning. This seemed to call into question the normative connection between permissibility and blame that internalism about responsibility postulates. But the discussion of mutual recognition points the way to a resolution of this concern. We need to refine our understanding of the normative connection that is at issue, taking it to be mediated via the attitudes of the agents whose actions are up for moral assessment. Thus to say that permissibility and rightness are normative for our responsibility

---

[9] This corresponds to the first-person perspective of the agent who manifests attitudes of mutual recognition. Such an agent cares fundamentally about complying with the objective conditions of moral permissibility, not just achieving the subjective conditions for mutual recognition. Thus if you point out to me that I'm acting in a way that is really objectionable, I won't respond by saying, "That's all right, I'm sincerely trying to do the right thing, and that's all that really matters." Rather, insofar as I'm sincerely trying to do the right thing, I'll be very concerned about whether what I'm doing is morally permissible in fact.

[10] I say something about this issue in my paper "Scanlon's Contractualism" (2006, ch. 12, sec. 3).

reactions is to say that those reactions are properly responsive to agents' attitudes toward the moral properties in question. Those who sincerely strive to comply with the principles that determine permissibility thereby acquire normative protection from blame and opprobrium for what they do. Conversely, attitudes of indifference to these moral considerations, or of blatant contempt for them, provide others with defeasible reasons to react to the agent with blame and opprobrium.

This is, on reflection, nothing less than we should expect, given the idea discussed in section 1 that moral considerations are in the first instance reasons for action (an idea that Scanlon himself accepts). Their having this status means that we ourselves respond correctly to such considerations when we regulate our intentions in accordance with them, striving to do what is right and to act only in ways that are morally permissible. When we internalize a concern for these reasons, one consequence will be that we as agents aim to comply directly with them, in ways that acknowledge their normative standing for our actions. But the responsibility reactions of blame and opprobrium are backward-looking responses, directed toward *agents* on account of the things they have done. In cases in which these emotional responses are at issue, our internalized concern for moral values will lead us to focus on the attitudes of the agents we are responding to and to consider whether those attitudes reflect a due appreciation for the reason-giving force of rightness and permissibility. What we care primarily about, in this distinctive context, is not whether the agents up for assessment really acted in ways that were permissible but whether they had the qualities of will that are constitutive of mutual recognition, responding to moral considerations in just the way we take ourselves to have reason to respond to them in the first-person perspective of deliberation. This is just what I meant in suggesting that the normativity of permissibility for responsibility is mediated via the attitudes of the agents who are up for assessment.

Consideration of the issue of intent and permissibility has thus led us to an improved formulation of internalism about responsibility. Strictly speaking, what is normative for our responsibility reactions is not the permissibility or impermissibility of what people do but the attitudes latent in their actions toward moral considerations of this kind. Morality is suited by its nature to constitute a framework for responsibility relations, insofar as people's attitudes toward it provide the normative basis for such relations.

4. Conclusion: Individualistic and Relational Conceptions of Morality

In this brief concluding section, I want to look at the implications of internalism about responsibility for our understanding of the nature of moral requirements.

Some moral theories are individualistic, focusing on the obligations that people stand under as agents considered in isolation from each other. Perfectionism (in both its Aristotelian and modern variants) is individualistic in this sense, conceiving moral (or better, ethical) standards as means to the realization of an ideal for human agents and as deriving their significance primarily from this function. But many other modern theories seem to be individualistic in the same sense. Utilitarianism, for instance, conceives of moral standards in maximizing terms, telling individuals that it is wrong to act in ways that are suboptimal in their effects on the interests of sentient beings. Whether or not a particular agent is responsive to this standard of wrongness would appear to be completely independent from the question of whether other people have reason to respond to the action with reactions characteristic of blame.

For example, utilitarians often hold that lifestyles of bourgeois consumption are morally objectionable in a world in which there are vast numbers of people living under conditions of extreme need. So long as these conditions persist, individual expenditures on consumer goods will be hard to justify in utilitarian terms, insofar as greater utility would be achieved by donating the funds at issue to an organization such as Oxfam or Doctors without Borders. But it is another matter entirely whether we should blame individuals when they display attitudes of disregard toward this moral consideration. On the utilitarian approach, blame should be treated like any other intervention into the causal order and assessed according to whether it is likely to be optimific in its effects on the welfare of those affected by it. Thus it is sometimes argued that it would be wrong to blame affluent individuals when they fail to organize their personal lives according to the principles of utilitarian consumption. Doing so might just discourage and demoralize them, making it clear how onerous morality would be if they actually took it seriously as a basis for ordering their lives, with the effect that those who are blamed would do even less to contribute to improving the conditions of the billions of people whose lives are characterized by deprivation and disease (see, e.g., Singer 2011, pp. 213–15). For these same reasons, it might even be for the best not to encourage children to internalize the kind of emotional commitment to utilitarian standards that would render them disposed to react to deliberate moral infractions with such sentiments as resentment and indignation.[11] The question of the attitudes of an individual toward moral standards thus seems to be completely independent from the question of whether those same attitudes provide others with a normative basis for reactions of blame.[12]

---

[11] Compare Henry Sidgwick's sympathetic discussion of the possibility of an esoteric morality in his *The Methods of Ethics* ([1874] 1981, bk. 4, ch. 5).

[12] By the same token, a conscientious effort to comply with the utilitarian principle will notoriously not suffice to provide protection from the opprobrium of others. We can easily imagine circumstances in which it might be optimific, and therefore required by utilitarian lights, to react to such a conscientious agent with the reactions characteristic of blame.

On the internalist approach, by contrast, things are otherwise in this respect. This approach takes the attitudes of agents toward moral considerations to have direct normative significance for the responsibility reactions of others. Moral standards must be ones that we have good reason to become emotionally invested in. There must be something about them that gives an agent's attitudes toward them a special normative significance for our responsibility reactions, protecting from opprobrium those who conscientiously strive to comply with them and rendering those who are indifferent to them specially vulnerable to blame and opprobrium. Utilitarian and perfectionistic theories seem deficient when viewed in this light. They take moral requirements to derive from an individual's relation to impersonal value or to an ideal of human attainment. But there is nothing in the nature of such requirements that would seem to explain why our attitudes toward them have the normative significance for responsibility relations that internalism postulates. Why should other people become exercised by the fact that you are indifferent to an ideal of human perfection, or that you do not take sufficiently seriously the claims made on your behavior by impersonal value? Theories of this kind might turn out to be correct at the end of the day. At the very least, however, the internalist approach will entail that they are revisionist in some measure, denying an interpersonal dimension of morality that seems to us to be essential to it.

In response, it might be suggested that there are versions of individualistic theories that do not leave it a contingent matter whether we have reason to respond to deliberate wrongdoing with attitudes of blame and opprobrium. Consider a version of perfectionism that holds that it is a virtue, part of the ideal of a flourishing human life, for agents to internalize the kind of concern for moral values that makes them prone to blaming reactions when people flout those values. On a theory of this kind, morality itself would enjoin us to respond with something like blame to instances of deliberate wrongdoing, and it would therefore seem that there is a nonaccidental connection between such behavior and the responsibility reactions.

A theory of this kind would not really do justice, however, to the internalist position I have been developing in this paper. There are two aspects to the problem. First, on the perfectionist account, what makes actions wrong, in general terms, is that performing them would be incompatible with virtue. This is an individualistic approach, as I said earlier, which holds that the rightness and wrongness of actions is a question of the agent's relation to an ideal of human perfection. But there is nothing in this general way of thinking about morality that explains why an agent's attitudes toward rightness and wrongness should *themselves* provide a normative basis for the responsibility reactions. It is only when we supplement the general account with a specific, substantive theory of virtue that we introduce a reason for people to adopt blaming responses toward episodes of deliberate wrongdoing.

Second, the reason that is introduced by the substantive theory of virtue seems to be a reason of the wrong kind. I should react to deliberate wrong-doing on the part of others, according to the perfectionist theory, because a failure to do so would instantiate a vice on my part. My reason for blaming, in other words, is provided by considerations having to do with my own relation to an ideal of human attainment. According to internalism, by contrast, what provides me with a reason for the responsibility reactions is, in the first instance, the attitudes of the person whom I would blame. It is because that person has displayed indifference or contempt toward moral standards that I have reason to hold the person responsible. This is precisely the normative connection between rightness and responsibility that internalism postulates, and it points toward an essentially interpersonal dimension of morality. Insofar as the per-fectionist theory under consideration remains individualistic, it continues to have a revisionistic character, even if it yields the conclusion that morality gives us a reason of some kind to blame others when they flout moral standards.[13]

What, by contrast, would a nonrevisionist account of moral standards look like? It would be an account of the nature of those standards that makes ap-parent why people's attitudes toward them provide a normative basis for re-sponsibility relations. Most promising in this respect are theories that interpret moral requirements as essentially directional or relational, insofar as they are grounded in the claims or entitlements of other agents. If it is morally imper-missible that I do X, on this approach, this is because someone has a claim against me that I not do X. Actions are permissible, by contrast, when nobody has a claim against me that I not perform them. But if it is in the nature of morality that it is relational in this way, then we can immediately see why peo-ple's attitudes toward moral standards should have direct normative signifi-cance for the responsibility reactions. Indifference to moral requirements will in effect be indifference to the claims of other individuals. And we generally have good reason to care about whether people display this attitude in their interactions with each other.

More specifically, we each have compelling reason to care about whether other people are indifferent to moral standards when their attitudes amount to

---

[13] There are versions of both perfectionism and consequentialism that might come closer to accom-modating the internalist insight. Consider rule consequentialism, in the version that holds that actions are wrong just in case they would be prohibited by general rules that it would be optimific for the members of community to internalize and to follow (where internalization precisely involves a ten-dency to blame people when they exhibit attitudes of indifference toward those general rules). This theory seems to do a better job than the perfectionism considered in the text at capturing the spirit of internalism about responsibility. If it does so, however, that will be because it incorporates into its general account of rightness the relational element I go on to discuss. On this approach, rightness is no longer understood individualistically but is taken to be defined by principles that are suited by their nature to provide a basis for responsibility relations between people. (Whether this is the best way to develop a relational understanding of rightness is another matter, which I cannot go into here.)

indifference toward *our* moral claims. In these cases, indifference to moral requirements is tantamount to disregard of our own moral standing. The paradigmatic response to such an attitude is resentment, which is an emotion that is called for in cases in which other people act with a lack of consideration for our own claims against them, and which is also the most basic form of moral blame. On the relational conception of morality, attitudes of indifference to moral requirements thus have direct normative significance for the responsibility reactions of those whose claims are disregarded. The very thing that makes an action wrong—its failure to honor someone's claims—also itself provides a powerful reason for the holder of the claim to react with resentment. By the same token, agents achieve normative protection from these basic responsibility reactions through the conscientious attempt to comply with moral requirements in their dealings with each other. Attitudes of this kind acknowledge the legitimate claims of those affected by the agent's actions, and this in turn undermines the normative basis for resentment.

Other responsibility reactions are, I believe, parasitic on the relational structure that is latent in resentment, and the normative significance of an agent's attitudes for general questions of responsibility operates through their significance for the individuals whose claims are directly affected by them. Thus indignation and guilt may be understood to be attitudes that are adopted vicariously, on behalf of an individual whose claims have been disregarded by another agent. We feel indignation when we acknowledge that one person has acted with a lack of consideration toward the claims of another, and we are subject to guilt in cases in which we acknowledge that we ourselves have done the same. Internalizing a concern for relational requirements is in the first instance a matter of coming to care that our own claims are recognized by others in their interactions with us. But this concern naturally extends to the claims of other agents as well, disposing us to indignation and guilt in cases in which people act with a lack of consideration for those claims. By adopting attitudes of this kind, we therefore open ourselves to the opprobrium not only of those whose claims we disregard but potentially of the entire moral community as well; conversely, we can protect ourselves from responsibility reactions of this kind through the sincere effort to respect others' claims against us.

Of course, I have done nothing to defend a relational conception of morality in this paper. But that seems to me the kind of moral theory we will be pushed toward if we accept the internalist conception of morality that I have been trying to sketch. And to the extent the internalist approach is found attractive, this will be one important consideration in favor of the relational conception.

13

What Is an Excuse?

Erin I. Kelly

Our intuitive sense that some wrongdoing is excused prompts questions about how to distinguish between the objects of two different judgments: the judgment that an agent's act is wrong and the judgment that the agent is to blame for so acting. What moral issues are settled through these different judgments? And what of moral significance is signaled when they come apart—when an agent acts wrongly but is not to blame? These issues are underexplored but important, for they help to illuminate the moral interest of our evaluation of persons as well as the range of responses we might take toward persons who act in similar ways.

In the first section of this paper, I appeal to intuitions that mark the distinction between a judgment that an agent's act is wrong and the judgment that an agent is to blame for so acting. I try to clarify this distinction and the sense of its importance. In the remaining sections I attempt to rationalize it. I will propose that different normative criteria guide these two different sorts of judgments. Judgments of wrongness express deontological requirements of justification and, in particular, justification to persons who are affected by the action type in question. Deontological moral requirements are often understood to specify forms of behavior that cannot be justified to persons who are negatively affected, even when those negative effects are balanced, overall, by good consequences to other people. I think to say that requirements are deontologically prohibited is also to say that the behavior in question cannot be justified to persons who are affected negatively by it, even when the wrongdoer's actions do not express ill will or when the wrongdoer is not responsible for her ill will.

Excusing conditions, in contrast with deontological requirements of justification, signal considerations of fairness that restrict the appropriateness

For critical comments and helpful discussion of ideas in this paper, I am grateful to Micah Bluming, Justin Coates, Mario De Caro, John Goldberg, Abby Jacques, Lionel McPherson, Jeanne-Marie Musca, Sigrun Svavarsdóttir, Will Tadros, Neal Tognazzini, the Boston University Ethics Group, the Syracuse University Department of Philosophy, and the Department of Philosophy at Università Roma Tre.

of blame as a response to wrongdoing. I propose that these fairness considerations help to determine when compassion appropriately tempers blame.[1] But considerations that render compassion appropriate are not deontic norms: their role is not to specify the conditions under which we are required to feel compassion or to refrain from experiencing it. Neither are they mere permissions.[2] Instead they track the limits of those circumstances under which wrongdoers are worthy of the blaming responses to which we might be drawn. They help us to understand when it is that blame is misdirected.

1

We don't merely evaluate what people do; we evaluate *them* as persons, in view of how they act. We think a person's actions bear on her qualities as a person. Our moral appraisal of persons is signaled by judgments, attitudes, and behavior we direct toward them in view of the moral qualities of their actions. These responses might include what are commonly referred to as the "reactive attitudes" of resentment and moral indignation and the tendency to engage in retributive behavior. These responses are commonly associated with condemning and punishing. But blaming responses might also be understood, more broadly, to include less retributive sentiments, such as disappointment, sadness, or resignation. Although they are not oriented punitively, these attitudes respond to an agent's demonstrated capacity for wrongdoing and take it seriously. They may be accompanied by behavioral responses that are not retributive in nature, such as calling for an explanation or apology, lowering or otherwise changing expectations regarding future interactions, breaking off a relationship, trying to make the wrongdoer feel guilty or make amends, and so on. These responses, as I understand them, need not be thought of as retributive in nature because they need not involve commitment to the idea that the wrongdoer should suffer or otherwise pay a price as a matter of justice. They call for something else—correction of the wrongdoer's fault, for example, or reparative attention by the wrongdoer to the victim. Soliciting guilt feelings may be thought of as a step in remediating the wrongdoer's character. Apology may be called for as a way of recognizing the standing of the victim. Although not retributive, I submit that these responses might qualify as blame when they

---

[1] I rely on compassion as the paradigm reactive attitude associated with mitigating blame. Still we might think of compassion as belonging to a family of emotions and attitudes that includes pity, sympathy, empathy, understanding, sorrow, and the like. Different excusing conditions might draw on this pool of attitudes and emotions in different ways.

[2] Here I follow some recent work by Sigrun Svavarsdóttir (2011).

accompany or express moral criticism of a person. Specifically, blaming responses accompany moral criticism of a person for harboring judgments or attitudes that interfere with the confidence other people should have about her prospects for meeting their reasonable moral expectations. Blame points to a person's moral unreliability and traces it to a standing aspect of his or her character, dispositions, or personhood.

Thus far I have suggested that blame is oriented by perceptions of wrongdoing. But our sense of the appropriateness of blame may also help to solidify our judgment that a person has acted wrongly.[3] Blaming responses may serve to sharpen our attention to what exactly a person has done wrong. Feeling insulted or affronted may prompt one to understand better how one has been mistreated. To be clear, I do not endorse a view that would reduce judgments of wrongdoing to those of blameworthiness (cf. Gibbard 1990). A guiding interest of my approach is in how judgments of wrongdoing and blameworthiness sometimes come apart, as well as in how they interact.

I will group retributive and nonretributive responses together, broadly, as blaming responses. I follow T. M. Scanlon in grouping together as blaming responses all responses that signify the meaning of a wrongdoer's morally criticizable attitudes and judgments for relationships in which she is involved.[4] What I want to call attention to at present, however, is not the variety of responses that might be identified, generally speaking, as blaming behavior. What interests me is the striking difference in blaming responses we might find appropriate to similar transgressions. Some persons seem to be more to blame than others for the wrongs they commit. Similar hurtful words, similar morally criticizable acts of dishonesty, or the same type of criminal behavior coming from different persons might inspire differences in the blaming responses we deem to be appropriate. Irritable remarks that stem from jealousy seem more worthy of blame than irritable remarks provoked by physical pain. The greedy wife who kills her husband seems more to blame than the murderous battered wife.

Some of this variation in blaming responses has to do with the positional nature of blame. Scanlon has described this as a matter of the standing a given person or group has to blame some wrongdoer (2008, pp. 175–79, 206–10). We might feel less entitled to blame the battered wife in part because the abuse she endured is facilitated by morally objectionable aspects of gender-based relationships that we do not consistently challenge or reject, even though we should. We might feel that we, collectively, have let her and others like her down by failing to protect her rights or properly to empower her with opportunities. We may

---

[3] I thank Amelie Rorty for pressing me on this point.

[4] See Scanlon (2008, ch. 4, especially 128–29). Scanlon stresses that questions of meaning differ from questions of permissibility. This fits with my suggestion (following Svavarsdóttir) that there is an interesting domain of moral judgment that is not governed by deontic norms.

thus feel that we lack an appropriate position from which to blame her; sharing in the blame, even remotely, may seem to disqualify us from dishing it out. Engaging in moral criticism under the circumstances seems evasive and morally distasteful.

The positional nature of blame can to some extent be segregated from the basis for making judgments of blameworthiness. Determinations of blameworthiness, while not entirely apositional, are less positional. They may be positional in the sense that it can be inappropriate for some people to engage in judgments of a person's blameworthiness, much less blaming, because, for example, doing so gives the impression of distracting from their own complicity. But other people who lack standing to blame because, for example, they are uninvolved, may perfectly well assess blameworthiness, namely, that the agent has acted in ways that give some persons reasons to blame her.

Despite the relative apositionality of judgments of blameworthiness, these judgments can vary across subjects for the same sort of morally criticizable act. Some persons seem to be more worthy of blame than others are for similar acts.[5] Many people would agree that a person who is desperate for money to treat a sick child is less blameworthy for a theft she commits than someone who does it for fun or to buy video games. Most people would agree that child "soldiers" who murder or maim civilians are less blameworthy than their adult counterparts.

Our judgments of blameworthiness might vary in this way without thereby indicating moral bias or lack of objectivity. A person's difficult circumstances or complicated psychological dynamics have a bearing on our evaluations of her. The circumstances and psychology of an agent may lead us, for good reasons, to find her less blameworthy for her morally criticizable behavior than we would judge someone else to be.[6] In some cases, something interferes with familiar processes of inference from wrong action to blameworthy agency. Some wrongdoing, we think, is wholly or partly excused.

Some analyses of excuses underplay the difference between our moral appraisals of action versus agent. Peter Strawson maintains that excuses undermine the ordinary sense of an agent's having done wrong by demonstrating that there was no faulty judgment, disregard, or ill will on the agent's part (2003, pp. 77–78). This position has been influential and is defended by R. Jay Wallace, among others (1994, p. 135; see also chs. 5, 6). According to Strawson and Wallace, excuses point to a missing link between the act and the agent's intentions and attitudes; her bad acts contrast with her "good will," or, at least, with the absence of bad will. We are all familiar with excuses like these: "She didn't

---

[5] Some of it might have to do with moral pluralism: differences in moral judgments and attitudes compatible with full rationality. But I think it does not come down only to this.

[6] John Martin Fischer and Neal Tognazzini (2011) describe these sorts of cases as occupying a space between morally attributing an act to an agent and holding that agent morally accountable.

mean it"; "He didn't understand what he was doing"; "She was only trying to help." One sort of excuse—for example, "He was pushed"—shows that the agent did not really even act; agency was undermined by circumstantial or intervening conditions.

In fact, by undermining connections between action and will, excusing conditions, so understood, render all excused wrongs only marginally the agent's actions. Being pushed is but an extreme example of an act the agent does not intend, approve of, or identify with, including what the agent is tricked, manipulated, or intimidated into doing. The result is that wrongdoing is only apparent: the excused agent didn't really *do* something wrong; it only seems so until the excuse is unearthed. Excuses of this sort do not raise deeper issues about the difference between moral evaluations of act and agent. Rather, they imply that these evaluations are one and the same. What normally or usually would be wrong is not wrong under excusing conditions.

This approach is challenged by a range of cases in which, it seems to me, we draw a clear distinction between our moral appraisal of an action and our varying attitudes toward the agent. These are cases in which an agent acted wrongly and in so doing demonstrated moral disregard for others. The act is clearly ascribed to the agent, and it is not morally justified or permissible. An excuse establishes that although the agent acted wrongly she should not be blamed or should not fully be blamed.

Examples extend from the ordinary to the extraordinary: the parent under emotional strain who yells at her kid, the child who is mistreated by her parent and in turn bullies another child, the inmate who brutalizes another to avoid appearing weak, the solider in a field of battle who shoots a civilian on orders from a superior, the alcoholic who drives after drinking, the compulsive who tells a lie, the paranoid schizophrenic who commits an act of hateful violence. We might feel that such agents are excused, in whole or in part, from blame for their morally faulty actions. The circumstances or psychological vulnerabilities of these agents fit uncomfortably with the presumptions of our blaming attitudes and judgments. Yet in each of these cases the agent acts intentionally and for reasons we can criticize on moral grounds.

The range of cases I have in mind as morally significant is broader than the class of considerations recognized by the law as excuses from criminal liability. The excuses that are legally recognized as defenses are notoriously narrow. Circumstances providing excuses are mostly limited to duress, coercion, and some mistakes when they show lack of *mens rea*. Psychologically excusing abnormalities are limited to insanity, which is narrowly understood. Insanity as a legal defense is a person's inability, at the time the crime was committed, to distinguish between right and wrong. Insanity, so understood, is an extreme and rare instance of the broader category of mental illness. Most morally disabling forms of mental illness, including significant impairments to moral motivation, compassion for others, and the like, would not be recognized as legal defenses against criminal liability. I will not here analyze or criticize legal criteria for criminal liability. I note, however, that these criteria do not depend on blameworthiness, as I understand it. A person might be guilty of criminal wrongdoing without this establishing her moral blameworthiness. The mental or circumstantial obstacles she faces might excuse her from moral blame, even though her intentional behavior violates criminal laws. Moreover, although less relevant to the matters under discussion, some types of actions prohibited by criminal laws are not morally wrong.

To be clear, then, I am interested in cases of excused wrongdoing that might not all succeed as legal defenses against charges of criminal wrongdoing. Furthermore, I am interested in the idea that a person might be excused only in part, or to some extent, for her wrongdoing. That is, I am interested in the scalar nature of excuses. The aspect of law most connected with the scalar nature of excuses concerns whether punishment should be mitigated. Typically these determinations are made in a separate sentencing phase of a criminal procedure, after the defendant has pled guilty or been found guilty at trial. In the sentencing phase, considerations concerning the defendant's character and circumstances may be introduced as relevant to the question of how much punishment the defendant should receive. Although my main topic is moral accountability, not the norms of criminal procedure, the legal practice that separates the sentencing phase from the finding of criminal guilt lends support to and is supported by my contention that judging the blameworthiness of an agent is and should be guided by a distinct set of norms from those we consult to evaluate the moral quality of a person's action.

In challenging Strawson and Wallace's picture, I am drawing on the intuition that persons might be excused, in whole or in part, from being suitable subjects of blame, despite their violating the requirements of morality and acting wrongly. I will now take up some moral reasons we might have to maintain that an agent who is excused from blame can nevertheless have acted wrongly—the judgment Strawson and Wallace resist.

2

Morality facilitates relationships of respect and consideration between people who may or may not care personally about one another. By offering criteria to guide our thinking, morality helps us to specify our mutual obligations, both personal and impersonal. Often, if not always, these criteria take the form of principles. Public recognition of moral principles helps to ease conflicts between people that are aggravated by the bias of self-and group-interest. Furthermore, the equal standing of persons under the scope of general moral principles promotes a sense of greater commonality and mutual sympathy. In these and other ways, social life is enhanced by common principles of morality, when those principles are justified, principles that are general in scope.

The public and pragmatic dimensions of morality generate some pressure within moral thinking to handle exceptions to general principles by tempering blame rather than complicating action-guiding norms. Expanding principles to include their exceptions and qualifications is cumbersome. It requires either that we narrow our specification of the relevant action types captured by a moral principle in order to reflect relevant contextual factors, or that we enumerate qualifications and exceptions to more general principles so as properly to acknowledge such factors. Either of these strategies can detract from general principles that are intuitively appealing enough to capture our attention when we seek guidance from morality. To avoid this, we abstract, to some extent, in our moral thinking from details that characterize differences in the circumstances to which we apply our principles. Sometimes these details, including the various factors that make it difficult to act morally, have a bearing on what it is reasonable to expect people to do. It may not be reasonable to expect a person to deal forthrightly with someone who has betrayed her in the past, and we might not blame her for withholding or manipulating the truth. Or perhaps more obviously, we would not reasonably expect someone suffering from an attack of paranoia to refrain from making groundless accusations against other people, and we would be unlikely to blame her for her remarks. We might maintain, however, that the manipulation and groundless accusations were morally objectionable. We might believe that persons who were hurt by these actions were done wrong. When we formulate action-guiding norms that prohibit people from doing wrong, we meaningfully abstract from circumstances that mitigate blame.

We also abstract, to some extent, from differences in people's capacities for moral understanding and moral motivation. Morality affirms standards that most people are able to meet, even if some people cannot because they lack the capacity to understand or to care about it. Affirming moral standards makes sense when many and perhaps most people are or might be responsive to them. It is true that some persons are, in fact, not responsive to morality's demands and are very unlikely to change. Furthermore, among those, some persons lack the capacity to respond to morality's demands. But this does not defeat the social purposes served by action-guiding principles that many persons can and do abide by.

These abstractions might seem merely to represent pragmatic compromises to the justifiable content of moral requirements, but pressures to abstract and to generalize in moral thinking about right and wrong have the support of certain important normative considerations. There are moral reasons to treat all rational persons as capable of moral action, even though in fact some are not. Moral capacity, as I understand it, is the capacity to act for moral reasons. As I have indicated, a person's capacity for morality has both cognitive and motivational dimensions. A morally capable person is capable of understanding morality's requirements and so of regulating her behavior. Not only can she recognize that other persons are sentient, concerned about their future, have meaningful relationships, et cetera, but she also has a sensibility that moves her to care about these facts. In asserting that some people lack moral capacity, I am supposing that psychological factors influence our receptivity to moral reasons, in both cognitive and emotional respects. Cognitive and emotional factors influence the reach of moral considerations as reasons for particular persons (see Kelly and McPherson 2010).

Let us set aside the class of persons who are obviously incapacitated, generally speaking, to evaluate reasons for action of any sort: prudential, moral, or instrumental, even merely concerning the means to immediate gratification. Persons who are thus incapacitated are, in an obvious sense, irrational and unfit for practical directives of a reason-giving nature. This leaves us with the category of broadly rational persons. We might owe it to all rational persons to treat them as though they are capable of responding to the demands of morality, even though some people in fact lack the capacity to understand or to be motivated by those demands. It might be arrogant and disrespectful to presume to know who has and who lacks a capacity for morality. It is certainly far from clear which persons have and which lack moral responsiveness, especially since a person might conform to the requirements of morality for reasons of self-interest. Persons who are capable of guiding their actions with moral considerations may reasonably object to being treated as though they are not, since this is bound to limit their relationships with other people. In this sense, moral ought judgments unproblematically presume moral capacity.

Still, we might have grounds to doubt a person's capacity for morality when she fails to demonstrate the understanding or concern morality requires. And we might worry that grounds to doubt a given person's capacity to meet morality's demands should unsettle our confidence about how morally to appraise her actions. While we might feel comfortable directing all rational persons to strive to meet moral requirements, when it comes to judging what a person has done, we might hesitate. It is possible that in some morally relevant domain of action a person just does not care about moral directives—moral reasons have no "authority" for her. Either she cannot cognitively grasp them or they do not resonate motivationally with her. This might represent a limit to her moral capacity.[7]

The worry I am considering is whether it makes sense to judge a person's actions to be morally wrong and to have violated her moral obligations if, in fact, that person could not have acted well. Suppose that she was not, under the circumstances, capable of appreciating the relevant moral reasons or was not, generally speaking, capable of appreciating certain kinds of moral reasons. While the limits of a person's moral capacity are real, I think it does make sense to hold all rational persons up to common standards of moral evaluation. Even

---

[7] For further discussion of points in this paragraph and the next, see my 2012.

if there are persons who do not and could not act as they morally should, there is a clear sense in which any wrongdoer ought to have acted better than she did. The moral ought, as I will understand it, is fixed by what a morally motivated person would do. A reason to fix the standard of moral evaluation in this way is that only this standard properly acknowledges the moral costs, to victims, of wrongdoing. It is morally suspect to claim that, because a particular person could not have treated the victim as she ought to have, that victim has not been wronged.

Moral assessment of behavior must be properly responsive to those persons who are done wrong by the type of behavior in question. Morally we should ask whether behavior that affects them could be justified to them. Action types that reasonably are or could be objectionable to persons affected by them are wrong, whether or not the agents who commit those wrongs were capable of acting well. This standard of justifiable behavior makes sense on the assumption that many people in fact are capable of acting in accordance with morality, even if some are not. Since I have set aside cases of persons who are not even weakly responsive to reasons, what I am affirming is the relevance of moral standards for evaluating the behavior of persons who are at least minimally rational. A morality that is not pointless because it effectively guides many people can be used to evaluate any minimally rational person's acts. In formulating such a morality we have reason to separate evaluations of an agent's blameworthiness from the evaluation of her actions.

The sense I am attempting to give to the distinction between wrongdoing and blameworthiness bears a certain affinity to the deontological structure of some moral dilemmas. I have in mind situations in which the agent must choose between a set of bad options and seems forced to choose the least bad or least objectionable of all the action options available to her. As Thomas Nagel imagines, one might have to twist the arm of an innocent child in order to further morally urgent aims (1986, p. 176). While the act might be, on balance, justified, Nagel's point is that it cannot so clearly be justified to the victim. From the victim's perspective, the agent might only be excused and perhaps not entirely; what the agent has done is not without negative moral remainder. There is an affinity here with the normative structure of excuses, although not an exact parallel. In Nagel's example, the agent wrongs the victim, while not acting wrongly overall. The agent's wrong to the victim is excused by her justifiable purpose. In the cases of excused wrongdoing that interest me, there is no such purpose. The common element in Nagel's scenario and the one I am considering is the insistence on not subsuming costs to the victim in an overall calculation of what it is reasonable to expect of an individual agent. Those costs are instead highlighted in a deontological assessment of the agent's act.

The value of assessing the significance of an agent's wrongful harming of another person, apart from appraising the agent's blameworthiness for so acting, is developed in tort law. Tort law offers a framework that clearly distinguishes between judgments of wrongful harming and blameworthiness. Victims of a tort are entitled to collect damages when they offer adequate evidence that harms they have suffered were wrongfully caused by some other party, regardless of whether that party intended harm, demonstrated ill will in causing the harm, or brought about beneficial consequences, on balance, by so acting. In fact the tortious conduct might have been morally commendable along either of these dimensions: intention and wider consequences. A person who is praiseworthy for a heroic act, such as saving a life, might nevertheless be liable for compensating the owner of property damaged in the course of her act.

Tort law aims to compensate victims for harms wrongfully caused by the defendant. Facts about the defendant's mental state or the further consequences of her act are not germane to the victim-centered, rights-based focus of judgments of tort liability. The notion of fault required to establish the defendant's tort liability is "objective." Typically it involves the judgment that a reasonable person would not have engaged in the type of behavior exemplified by the defendant without recognizing (1) the risk of its causing harm to others and (2) that harm so caused would constitute grounds for appropriate compensation to the victim.[8] Furthermore, the type of behavior is such that people cannot reasonably be expected to obviate the risk to them associated with the conduct in question. A defendant might be found to be at fault for harms that are wrongful, in this sense, despite that fact that she is less reasonable than other persons, that she did her best to take care not to harm others, that she minimized harms overall, or that she was responding justifiably to a morally urgent problem. The relevant standard of fault is a generalized standard: it describes the conduct of a reasonably prudent person in situations of a relevant kind. This standard is used to establish that a victim has been wrongfully harmed and should be compensated even though the tortfeasor's mental state is virtuous and despite the fact that in a particular case, beneficial consequences of the defendant's tortious act might accrue to other persons or even to the victim herself. Legal scholars disagree about whether the rationale for tort law has the moral structure of corrective justice (see Coleman 2001). It is not my task to enter into that dispute here. Still there seems to be an affinity between the moral dynamics that I am discussing and the structure of tort law.

I have argued that, setting aside persons with demonstrated incapacities to appreciate reasons of any sort—hedonistic, prudential, or moral—we should extend the deontological requirements of morality to everyone else. Moral ought judgments extend to persons who discount the importance of moral reasons, provided that such persons are capable of appreciating reasons of any sort—prudential, egotistical, or otherwise.[9] Their rational faculties make them

---

[8] For this formulation I am indebted to George E. Smith.

[9] Matthew Talbert (2008) takes a similar position and from it concludes that it is appropriate to direct blaming responses to all minimally rational wrongdoers. I resist Talbert's conclusion.

candidates for moral obligation and moral assessment, whether or not morality will or could be effective in directing them. Morality effectively moves many people, and that is enough reason to maintain moral standards to assess action. Victims of wrongdoing can meaningfully be said to be morally entitled to the regard that morally motivated persons would give them.

We have good reasons to believe that most persons are capable of acting morally and that all rational persons are subject to morality's demands and assessments. While morality presumes general compliance, it need not presume the possibility of universal compliance. General compliance gives us good reason to maintain, for all rational persons, standards dictated by moral considerations. So we should assume that morality is addressed to rational agents, that is, to agents who respond to reasons, even though not all rational agents are morally capable. Only persons who can understand and be motivated by morality can be said to be morally capable.

3

The general (but not universal) presumption of moral capacity underlying deontological moral requirements suggests a role for excuses: excuses point to the limits of an individual's moral capacity and the relevance of these limits for assessing her blameworthiness. Excuses point to reasons for doubting that a person whose behavior we morally judge to have been wrong was in fact capable of having acted better. While wrongdoing does not depend on the wrongdoer's moral capacity to have acted well, perhaps blameworthiness does. Blameworthiness presupposes moral capacity; excuses point to its absence. Those who are excused could not (or probably could not) have acted for moral reasons.[10] While we might judge their actions, we should not blame them for acting badly. Call this analysis of excuses the Incapacity Thesis.

In fact Strawson and Wallace use a version of the Incapacity Thesis to demarcate a class of cases in which an agent intentionally acts contrary to morality yet is not to blame. They do not, however, understand such cases as cases in which excuses operate. Instead they place these cases in a separate category in which persons are exempted from moral responsibility because they are defective as agents. Wallace writes, "Thus, whereas excuses inhibit responsibility for a particular act by showing that a morally accountable agent has not done anything morally impermissible in the first place, exemptions block responsibility for a particular act by showing that an impermissible act has been

---

[10] This view fits with a familiar notion of desert: namely, that those who could not have done otherwise cannot be said to deserve blame for their wrongdoing. Those who lack excuse for their wrongdoing, by contrast, and hence could have acted well, deserve blame. The operative notion of blame here tends to be retributive in nature.

done by someone who is not, in general, a morally accountable agent" (1994, p. 156). On this line of thinking, an agent is exempted from accountability because that person lacks, in a broader way, what Wallace refers to as "powers of reflective self-control." These are the agent's powers, generally speaking, to understand moral reasons and to regulate her behavior on their basis (p. 157). Agents who are exempted from responsibility have a defective capacity, either permanently or for a limited period of time, to grasp and comply with moral reasons.[11]

Appealing to this model of defective moral agency does not do justice to the full range of cases I have specified. While there are some cases of intentional wrongdoing in which the agent lacked the capacity, more broadly, to recognize and respond to moral reasons, not all cases in which blame is misdirected fit this description. Some cases in which blame is mitigated are cases in which the agent may have demonstrated a healthy capacity to grasp and to abide by moral reasons, generally speaking, and has not lost this general capacity, even under the excusing conditions. Appealing to a highly general account of an agent's capacity for morality is too crude an instrument to account for the scalar nature of excusing conditions and for selective exemptions from an agent's general accountability, such as cases of acting under stress and cases of certain focused psychological pathologies.

The relevant moral capacity could, of course, be construed more narrowly: as the capacity to recognize moral reasons of a certain type or under certain circumstances. Thus it would be more plausible to claim that exempting conditions track an agent's moral incapacities. The trouble with this proposal is that it opens the door too widely to the skeptic, who worries that any instance of wrongdoing might be excused in this sense. Even normal and rational agents might have been caused to act by psychological factors they could not have overcome.[12] People can have moral blind spots, some erratic patterns in their psychological dispositions, and psychological pathologies that do not interfere with most ordinary functioning. This psychological complexity entails that it becomes very difficult to tell whether an agent has or lacks the relevant capacity. We cannot reliably make out the distinction between an unexercised capacity and an incapacity. Blame might never gain a reliable foothold.

Skeptical doubts about whether a person possessed the capacity to distinguish and act from the particular moral reasons she neglected under the circumstances

---

[11] In Wallace's view, such agents are exempted not only from blame for their morally impermissible behavior but also from the moral obligation to act as morality prescribes, since "it does not seem fair to demand that people comply with such obligations unless they have the general ability to grasp those reasons and to regulate their behavior accordingly" (1994, p. 161). In section 2 of this paper, I argued that all minimally rational persons are subject to moral directives and are obligated to act morally. Contra Wallace's suggestion, this would include persons who lack the general capacity to recognize moral reasons and to regulate their behavior accordingly.

[12] As discussed below, I think that this shows the retributivist notion of desert is unstable.

in which she acted wrongly are serious.[13] Taking the skeptic's challenge seriously, I propose that a reasonable assessment of when blameworthiness is mitigated or averted cannot depend on fine discriminations about capacity. This means that Wallace's strategy of using moral incapacity to mark off a separate class of cases in which an agent intentionally does wrong but is not to blame will not work.

I propose instead that excuses function by undermining what normally are reasonable expectations about how a person should be motivated.[14] Excuses do not challenge our notions about how a morally motivated person would act. For this reason they do not challenge our evaluations of right and wrong action. Nor do they entail that the excused agent was incapable of having satisfied morality's demands. The point of excuses is to address obstacles to moral motivation, both cognitive and emotive, and to do this based on a normative standard. The normative standard is a moral one, but the norms that regulate it are different from the norms that guide our appraisal of actions as right or wrong. In evaluating an agent's blameworthiness, we assess how reasonable it is to expect an agent to act morally in the face of obstacles. At the margin we might wonder whether we should retain the assumption of the agent's moral capacity under those circumstances (or more generally)—but this is the outer margin only. Within the scope of many excuses, we do not necessarily relinquish our belief that the agent could have avoided wrongdoing. Instead, we might think that morality itself requires that we relax our expectations that she should have. Circumstances surrounding an agent's disregard for morality sometimes challenge the appropriateness of ordinary moral expectations by unsettling the ordinary presuppositions of our expectations. This is the case if obstacles seem too much reasonably to require the agent to bear without experiencing inner conflict, ambivalence, indifference, or stress that might lead her morally to fail to act well. A blameworthy person is someone we think should have remained committed to moral ends, under her difficult circumstances and despite internal psychological obstacles. We might think that despite her difficult circumstances, the moral demands on her were not unreasonable. Perhaps this is because we all face difficult circumstances at one time or another. Those who are not blameworthy are persons whose commitment to morality is too much to require—obstacles to success are too devastating. Moral expectations would be strangely inhuman.

One way to express this rationale for excuses is to say that it seems unfair that the requirements of morality are so much harder for some people to meet.

---

[13] Wallace himself seems to recognize this (1994, pp. 183–86). He sets these skeptical doubts aside, however, because he claims that what matters is not a person's ability to exercise her reflexive powers of self-control under the circumstances; rather what matters is simply her possession of such powers (see p. 183). I find this position implausible and hard to reconcile with Wallace's acceptance of selective exemptions from an agent's general accountability (see pp. 169, 179).

[14] Gary Watson (2004, p. 72) makes a similar suggestion, although he does not elaborate it.

While our moral judgments of right and wrong reflect our acceptance of moral luck—the recognition that the moral rightness or wrongness of a person's actions depends on a range of factors beyond the agent's control—our judgments of blameworthiness are uncomfortable with it, and legitimately so.[15] A person with the misfortune to be faced with tough moral choices might fail to act well. Our recognition of the difficult circumstances under which she acted in morally criticizable ways bears on our assessment of what her wrongdoing says about her. Obstacles to moral success might challenge our sense that it is fair to blame, not because we lack standing or because we judge that the agent's capacity to choose to act in line with morality has been compromised, but because an agent's confrontation with significant obstacles to moral understanding or moral motivation calls out for our compassion. This is not to say that the moral costs of wrongdoing are not real or important. Our judgment of a person's acts as wrong acknowledges their seriousness. Compassion is, in this way, compatible with moral criticism (see Watson 2004, pp. 244–45).

Judgments that circumstances can mitigate blame despite an agent's wrongdoing express morality's recognition that the stringency of its requirements varies contextually in a way that can be unfair. Judgments of what it is reasonable to expect of a person, under the circumstances, are moral judgments regulated by norms that address unfairness in the distribution of moral demands. This normative appraisal of unfairness can stand in tension with a deontological appraisal of the content of the demand the agent faces. Our compassion for the wrongdoer alleviates this tension, to some extent, by leading us vicariously to share in the burden of unfair moral demands.

4

I have stressed a distinction between two sorts of moral judgments, guided by two sorts of normative standards. The first sort concerns the evaluation of actions. Like the legal criteria of tort liability, judgments of actions as right or wrong are structured by principles that attain a certain generality. I have suggested that such moral principles should meet requirements of justification, especially to the victim, and that they are expressed by our understanding of how a morally motivated person would act. I stressed a parallel with the role of objective criteria in establishing tort liability, criteria that refer to generalized standards of reasonable conduct. Both moral principles for evaluating conduct as wrong and legal criteria for judging conduct as tortious express general standards for regulating and evaluating behavior that are characterized by a victim-centered focus.

---

[15] On the notion of moral luck, see Nagel (1979, ch. 3).

The second sort of moral judgment I have discussed concerns judgments we make about the extent to which we think it is reasonable to expect a particular person to overcome obstacles to moral motivation. These judgments deal more directly with threats to morality in worldly circumstances and in our psychologies. Reasonable expectations about how a particular person should be motivated to act are regulated by considerations of fairness. Our sense that a particular person is unfairly burdened by contingencies the rest of us rarely encounter triggers a judgment that compassion is appropriate and that the circumstances that call for our compassion temper a person's worthiness of blame.

This claim about fairness and compassion goes against the Kantian view that we may always reasonably expect a rational person to overcome the appeal of her inclinations and disinclinations when so acting would conflict with the demands of morality. On this Kantian view, it is always reasonable to blame wrongdoers. This view depends on an uncompromising premise maintaining the autonomy of rational agents from psychological obstacles and, accordingly, asserting the categorical nature of all moral demands. It is the categoricity of morality's demand that rational agents demonstrate "good will" that I challenge here.

The Kantian view is reflected in Strawson's and Wallace's position that those persons who fail to act as the morally motivated person would act and are excused either did not really do something wrong or they are defective as agents, incapable of responding morally to reasons. As we have seen, Strawson and Wallace maintain that when persons are excused from blame despite demonstrating ill will, it is because their capacity for reflexive self-control is diminished or malfunctioning. I am suggesting a different paradigm. Excuses do not necessarily indicate either lack of ill will or an agential incapacity. Rather, they point to obstacles that trigger our compassion. They help us to identify ways in which the requirements of morality can be very difficult to meet—not for everyone, but for some people and under some circumstances. Sometimes wrongdoing is excused, even when accompanied by ill will, not because an agent could not have exercised reflexive self-control but because moral action is so hard under the circumstances, be those circumstances marked by internal or external obstacles. The obstacles the agent faces are significant enough that we should relax our notion of what it is reasonable to expect, even though we may not relinquish our understanding of the actions morality demands.

Let me pause at this juncture to consider an objection.[16] The view I have presented might seem to be too crude. It might be argued that it is not simply the relative difficulty of the moral task that triggers excuses. It is also the genealogy of the obstacles the agent faces. When these obstacles themselves have

---

[16] I am grateful to Emily Robertson for pressing this objection.

resulted from the agent's morally flawed behavior, their presence may fail to incite our compassion or to constitute an excuse. We feel much less sympathy for someone who is struggling with the results of her own bad choices—for example, someone who gambles away her paycheck or who is incarcerated for committing a crime—than we do for someone whose troubles are not of her own making. This explains the ambivalence that many people feel about whether an addict's wrongdoing under the influence of her addiction is excused. While an addict craving a drug might lack a normal capacity to recognize and be motivated by moral reasons, this impairment might have resulted from bad choices she made at a time when she did not lack this capacity.

The account I am developing accommodates and analyzes the intuitions underlying such responses as follows: we assess whether the circumstances creating the obstacles an agent presently faces are circumstances that the agent ought to have avoided and could have avoided without undue burden. We want to know whether the agent had a fair opportunity to have avoided the circumstances or conditions (e.g., poverty, addiction) that now are extremely difficult for her to overcome and may factor into bad choices she now makes. If avoiding the circumstances that now pose serious difficulties for her moral performance would have been too much reasonably to expect of her, then her blameworthiness is called into question. In this way, the analysis I am proposing applies genealogically. If, at the earlier stage, we find that a person did have fair opportunity to have avoided present constraints on her choices, we may find her blameworthy, even though she now faces difficulties that would cause most people to falter. I believe this suffices to accommodate the intuition that people are accountable for problems they have caused themselves to have.

5

I turn now to some further implications. The way I have proposed to understand how excuses function may seem to imply that wrongdoing that is not excused is blameworthy: when a wrongdoer lacks an excuse, she is blameworthy. This would mean that persons with appropriate standing would not be misguided to blame her. Is this right? The answer depends on how we understand blameworthiness. If a person is worthy of blame when she is not motivated in ways that it is reasonable to expect her to be, then lacking excuse would imply blameworthiness. Wrongdoing without excuse would be blameworthy.

This makes sense if we understand blame as, for example, involving an emotionally tinged judgment that such a person has disappointed and may well again disappoint moral expectations and thus is impaired, for morally significant reasons, in her relationships with other people (see Scanlon 2008,

ch. 4). Emotions naturally connected with this judgment include disappointment, regret, frustration, sadness, and longing. The judgment of blameworthiness might be rationally related to recognizing reasons that relevant people
share to change their expectations, intentions, and emotional investment in
relating to the wrongdoer. Those persons themselves would have reason to
make those changes, that is, to engage in blame. Other people might not have
such reasons.

This notion of blame is substantial, but it is not retributive in nature. A retributive notion of blame requires a further premise: that the wrongful agent
could have acted as morality requires. I have claimed that doubting any given
wrongdoer's capacity to have acted well is coherent. This implies that lacking
excuse for wrongdoing would not suffice to substantiate an agent's moral capacity. Someone who we think should have remained committed to moral
ends, under her difficult circumstances and despite internal obstacles, might
in fact have been incapable of doing so. But although I cannot argue this point
fully here, the justification of retributive blame seems to depend on the wrongdoer's moral capacity to have acted well. Her deservingness of blame seems to
depend on having this capacity. That is, it seems to depend on the Kantian
view. If I am right about this, then wrongdoing without excuse would not
imply the appropriateness of retributive responses. There is room for the skeptic's challenge to the appropriateness of retributive blame.

Blame in either sense I have just discussed is a weak rationale for criminal
punishment. Retributive blame lacks adequate justification, or so I have
claimed. Nonretributive blame lacks adequate position-independent creden-
tials: since nonretributive judgments of blameworthiness fail to pick out reasons all persons have to engage in blame, these judgments would seem to be
too narrowly tailored to serve as a rationale for a public institution. Insofar as
criminal punishment has expressive value, it is best understood to express not
an offender's blameworthiness or the blame an offender deserves but rather
social condemnation of the offender's wrongdoing. As Joel Feinberg puts it,
"What justice demands is that the condemnatory aspect of the punishment
suit the crime, that the crime be of a kind that is truly worthy of reprobation"
(1970, p. 118). Social condemnation of criminal acts, scaled according to the
social harmfulness of their types, can and should be distinguished from directing blame toward offenders.

6

I have proposed that excuses represent a threshold of reasonable expectations
formed by reference to norms about the burdens we morally expect persons,
generally speaking, to bear in order to do the right thing. It seems unfair to
expect some persons to bear much greater burdens in order to meet moral

requirements on action. Our judgments about whether an agent is excused, or is excused to some extent, will connect with certain sentiments, and I have stressed a connection with compassion. Whether or not excused wrongdoers lack the capacity to meet morality's demands, we can recognize that the obstacles they face would be deeply unsettling to almost anyone.

This approach to understanding excuses makes sense of scenarios that trigger our compassion and helps to illuminate the value of compassion as an attitude that is available to us as we reckon with people who have made moral mistakes. We come to view a person's mistakes through the lens of a common standard for judging moral commitment. This standard recommends modesty and restrains moral high-handedness by urging us to refrain from holding other people to a higher standard than one that we ourselves could confidently meet. Conversely, for our own moral and psychological health and the vitality of relationships in which we emotionally invest, we might better appreciate that it can be very difficult to live responsibly.

Our sense that compassion is called for might also, strangely enough, help to confirm our sense that an agent has acted wrongly. Our compassion expresses the painful realization that the outcome of the agent's action, and indeed the action itself, were morally troubling. We share in the response that a morally sensitive agent would experience. We do this in part via the recognition that the agent may not have been adequately situated fully to anticipate or to take on this response. We feel it, in effect, on her behalf or, if the agent feels regret, to lessen its sting. Thus, unlike a compassionate response to the phenomenon of "agent-regret," whereby an agent regrets the outcome of an action of hers that was not wrong, compassion in this connection adheres more directly to our assessment of the agent's action as morally wrong.[17] We attempt to soften the connection between the agent and her wrongful act.

The recognition that a wrongdoer faced obstacles that would have led many or most people astray does not entail a normative requirement to feel compassion toward the wrongdoer. A moral requirement would be too strong, and not just because feelings cannot readily be willed. Requiring compassion would seem to neglect the significance of the moral wrong done, especially for those people who have suffered because of it. But although considerations that render compassion appropriate do not require us to feel it, they do enable us to understand how and why someone could be worthy of it. And if we understand that someone is worthy of compassion, we can see that blame would be misdirected. Judgments moderating our sense of an agent's blameworthiness share characteristics with what Sigrun Svavarsdóttir refers to as "value-based criticism of attitudes." Svavarsdóttir writes, "[V]alue-based criticism of attitudes does not take the form that the agent fails to have a required attitude

---

[17] On agent-regret, see Williams (1981, ch. 1).

towards an object or has an impermissible attitude towards an object. Rather, the criticism is that the agent's attitudes are misdirected: his emotional or motivational energies are *wasted* by directing them at things not worth them or by *not* directing them at things worth them" (2011, p. 39).

Blame, as I have described it, characterizes a range of responses to wrongdoing. This range of behavioral responses is not restricted to emotional reactions. It might also include, I have suggested, demands for apologies, explanations, and the like, as well as changes in our expectations and interests in relating to the wrongdoer. For example, a person's wrongdoing may undermine our trust and affect our friendship. I do not mean to deny, however, that blaming responses are often imbued with strong emotion. When this emotion is misdirected, we pay a price. When we become emotionally invested in negative moral assessments of persons whose failures do not set them apart from most people, we lose sight of our common human frailty and an appreciation of the contingencies of our moral successes as well as our failures. By congratulating ourselves we distract ourselves morally. We lose sight of the collective nature of our moral achievements and of the moral obligations we have to protect one another from morally hazardous circumstances. And when we resent wrongdoers who are not blameworthy, we waste opportunities to retain them as members of the moral community.

In sum, while it seems to me that we are not morally required to enter into a wrongdoer's perspective enough to appreciate the difficulty of the obstacles that led her to falter, the possibility of a compassionate recognition of the reasons for a person's moral failures humanizes relationships and opens possibilities for understanding, forgiveness, and an honest reckoning with faults we might share. This is not the subject of moral imperatives, but we might find our relationships to be worthy of these possibilities.

14

The Standing to Blame: A Critique

Macalester Bell

When is it morally appropriate to blame? Philosophers have articulated and defended various accounts of *blameworthiness*; these discussions usually focus on familiar metaphysical questions about what kind of freedom is necessary for moral responsibility and whether this freedom is compatible with the truth of determinism.[1] But there is another condition that is often thought to be relevant to the propriety of blame: according to many, a would-be blamer must have *standing* to blame. Even if the target satisfies the conditions of blameworthiness—however blameworthiness is understood—blame is morally appropriate only when the blamer has standing. I will call this the standard account, and I hope to show that it ought to be rejected.[2]

The Dreamlife of Angels provides a vivid example of how one's standing to blame may be challenged:

> Isa and Marie are two young women who meet in a sewing factory and quickly become good friends. Although Marie is in a romantic relationship with the affable and poor Charly, she longs to escape her hand-to-mouth existence and starts seeing the wealthy and cruel Chriss behind Charly's back. Marie eventually breaks up with Charly and dives headlong into a troubled relationship with Chriss. Chriss is abusive and unfaithful, and Marie responds by becoming increasingly fixated on him. She turns moody and withdraws from Isa. Hurt by what she sees as Marie's selfish

Earlier versions of this paper were presented at Union College and at Fordham University, and I'd like to thank audience members for their thoughtful questions and useful suggestions. I am very grateful to the editors of this volume and to Leo Zaibert for helpful written comments. Finally, I'd like to thank Marilyn A. Friedman for permission to cite unpublished work.

[1] Of course, since P. F. Strawson's "Freedom and Resentment" (1962), many have become convinced that the propriety of blame is not, at bottom, a metaphysical issue at all.

[2] Defenders of the standard account include Cohen (2006), Duff (2010), Friedman (2011), Sabini and Silver (1982), Scanlon (2008), Smith (2007), Wallace (2010), Watson (1987b), and Wertheimer (1998).

abandonment of their friendship, Isa confronts Marie. As Isa sees it, Marie owes it to herself and to their friendship to end her ill-fated romance. Blocking the door in an attempt to keep Marie from heading out to see Chriss, Isa shouts: "Don't humiliate yourself, you're not his dog!" before asking, "This guy's everything? Can't you think of anything else?" Marie responds by pushing Isa against the door and screaming, "Mind your own business!" before storming out of the apartment.

When a person is reproached, there are several ways for her to respond: she might accept that blame is appropriate, express her contrition, and ask for forgiveness; she might deny that blame is appropriate and explain that she had an excuse for her behavior; she might deny that blame is appropriate and explain that her behavior was justified; or she might deny that blame is appropriate because she didn't perform the act in question. In each of these responses the target either accepts or challenges the content of the reproach. But there is another way of responding to moral criticism: one may dispute the blamer's *standing* to blame in the first place. "Who are you to judge?" and "Who do you think you are?" are very common responses to unwelcome reproach. In telling Isa to mind her own business, Marie attempts to deflect Isa's criticism by dismissing her standing to blame.

Defenders of the standard account have articulated several conditions that a person must meet to have standing to blame:

1. Y's wrongdoing is X's business. That is, X has an identifiable stake in Y's wrongdoing. Let's call this the Business Condition.
2. X and Y are contemporaries and inhabit the same moral community. Let's call this the Contemporary Condition.
3. X has not engaged in similar wrongdoing in the past. Let's call this the Nonhypocritical Condition.
4. X is not responsible for or complicit in Y's wrongdoing. Let's call this the Noncomplicit Condition.

One or more of these conditions must be satisfied in order for someone to have standing to blame. If one lacks standing to blame, then one's reproach necessarily lacks moral propriety and may be dismissed without consideration of its content.[3] Very often those who defend the standard account do so with the aim of limiting or eliminating blame: the standing conditions will rarely be satisfied, and because of this, few persons, if any, will have standing to blame. I aim to show that responding to unwelcome blame by claiming that the critic lacks

---

[3] Some, e.g., Cohen (2006), hold that blame is *impossible* if the would-be blamer lacks standing, while others argue that blame that fails to meet the standing conditions *lacks moral propriety*. I characterize the standard account as I do in order to be charitable: the claim that blame is impossible if the would-be blamer lacks standing is even less defensible than the view that such blame is always morally inappropriate. However, I do think that some forms of hypocrisy make it the case that subjects' apparent expressions of blame are mere pretenses. I will say more about this in section 3.

standing is usually, as the informal fallacies of ad hominem and tu quoque suggest, utterly beside the point.

I will begin by sketching an account of the nature and value of blame. I will then turn to the arguments that have been offered in defense of the standing conditions and show why they ought to be rejected. Despite my criticisms, I do acknowledge that there is a kernel of truth in the standard account: blame is *positional*; that is, the moral propriety of blame sometimes depends on the relationship between the blamer and the target. However, the standard account, as it is typically presented, fails to adequately capture the positionality of blame. While defenders of the standard account suggest that the ethics of blame is exhausted by considerations of fittingness and standing, the moral dimensions of blame are better appreciated by focusing on our responsibilities within this domain. As critics, targets, and third parties, we have special responsibilities, and I will close by briefly describing these responsibilities of reproach.

1. Blame

What is involved in blaming someone? At a minimum, for X to blame Y for some action *a*, X must believe that Y performed *a*, X must believe that *a* is wrong, and X must express this belief in some form of communication.[4] In addition X must believe that Y is blameworthy for *a* (however blameworthiness is understood); X does not believe that any excusing or exempting conditions obtain. However, there is more to blame than the belief that the target has culpably done wrong. Isa doesn't just *believe* that Marie is degrading herself and neglecting their friendship; she is *angry* with her for it. To blame is to be liable to a range of negative emotions: if X blames Y for *a*, then X judges Y to be blameworthy for *a*, and X is liable to hostile emotions such as resentment, indignation, or contempt toward Y. If X blames herself for *a*, she judges herself to be blameworthy for *a* and is liable to self-directed negative emotions such as guilt and shame. Let's call this the Hostile Attitude Account of blame.[5] According to this account, the activity of blaming is partially constituted by a liability to a range of negative emotions.[6]

---

[4] We may also coherently blame persons for their character traits and attitudes, but to simplify what is already a complex topic, I shall focus on blaming persons for their actions.

[5] Some (but not all) of the negative emotions that partially constitute blame on the Hostile Attitude Account are tokens of what Strawson called the "reactive attitudes." Reactive attitudes are forms of *moral address* (see Watson 1987b; Darwall 2006); that is, they address a complaint to their target and call for some response.

[6] According to the Hostile Attitude Account, a person blames only if she *experiences* hostile attitudes. Simply judging that such attitudes would be warranted is not sufficient for one's stance to count as blame. If X believes that Y culpably did wrong, judges that indignation would be warranted, but feels no hostile attitudes toward Y, then we should say that X judges Y to be blameworthy but does not blame.

Two qualifications: First, as I'm using the term, blame is synonymous with "reproach," "condemnation," and "moral criticism." Admittedly these terms differ somewhat in regard to their force. We can account for these differences in terms of the strength of the negative attitudes expressed; for example, condemnation is partially constituted by a more hostile set of negative emotions than moral criticism. Second, I've been using "blame" to refer to the activity of *expressing* some attitude toward an offender. One may also blame someone in one's heart, as it were, without open communication. Some defenders of the standard account believe that there are standing conditions even for privately held blame (see, e.g., Smith 2007; Wallace 2010), but I am particularly interested in the ethics of expressed blame, and I will use the term "blame" to refer to its expression.

Not everyone thinks that blame is partially constituted by negative emotions. For example, T. M. Scanlon (2008) has defended a relational account of blame according to which blame involves judging the target to manifest a relationship-impairing attitude and taking one's relationship to be modified in light of this impairment. And George Sher (2006) has argued that blame is constituted by a belief that someone has acted badly and a desire that the target had not so acted. Neither Sher nor Scanlon thinks that a liability to hostile attitudes is an essential component of blame.

I cannot offer a complete defense of the Hostile Attitude Account here, but I do think we have reasons to prefer it to its rivals. There is surely more to blame than the belief-desire combination identified by Sher. One could harbor this attitude and simply feel sorry for the wrongdoer or sad that he did wrong. But to blame is to stand against wrongdoing; simply feeling sad about a person's wrongdoing is not to blame him for it. Scanlon's relational account also has difficulty accounting for blame's characteristic force.[7] One could believe that the target manifests a relationship-impairing attitude, take one's relationship with the target to be modified in light of this impairment, and respond with sad resignation. Again, being prone to melancholic resignation is not to stand against wrongdoing. The Hostile Attitude Account best captures the important sense in which blame involves *resisting* wrongdoing. While I think we have good reason to prefer the Hostile Attitude Account to its rivals, we do not need to settle this issue here. In what follows, I will use "blame" and its synonyms to refer to expressions of a judgment of blameworthiness and some hostile attitude. Even defenders of alternative accounts of blame should admit that we sometimes "blame" in this way.

I will focus on whether morally appropriate blame must meet the standing conditions outlined earlier, and in taking up this question I will assume that the target of blame really is blameworthy. That is, I will assume that the negative

---

[7] For a similar criticism of Scanlon's account, see Wallace (2011).

emotions that partially constitute blame are *fitting*; that is, they correctly present their targets. Those who defend the standard account claim that even in cases where blame is fitting, it will utterly lack moral propriety if it fails to satisfy blame's standing conditions.[8] In order to assess the standard account, we need a clear understanding of the aims and value of blame. Let's turn now to these issues.

2. The Aims and Value of Blame

Blame has five distinct aims and corresponding modes of value. First, blame marks the damage done to our relationships through wrongdoing (Scanlon 2008). Not only does blame signal relational damage, but it also prepares persons to repair this damage by focusing the subject's attention on the wrong done and motivating her to demand that the target change his ways. Second, it is difficult to see how, in the complete absence of blame, wrongdoers could know that they have done wrong. Reproach is valuable, in part, because it educates its target about the norms violated through wrongdoing (Calhoun 1989, p. 405). Third, being blamed often has motivational value for the target (p. 405). Since being criticized is psychologically painful, the possibility of being on the receiving end of moral criticism may motivate some offenders to do what they can to avoid future blame.

When we blame, we point to reasons why the target should not have acted as he did, and we attempt to put the target into a position to appreciate these reasons.[9] If a moral agent comes to a full appreciation of his past wrongdoing, he will take steps to change how the wrong done in the past has affected the present. Normally this will involve making some sort of reparation (e.g., an apology) to the victims of his past wrongdoing. Of course, it may not always be possible for the blamer to put the wrongdoer in a position to appreciate his past wrongdoing. The target of blame may be dead, far away, or so morally

---

[8] Some may insist that the four standing conditions outlined in the introduction are part of blame's *fittingness conditions*. But this is not how defenders of the standard account present these conditions. Instead they argue that even if blame is fitting and accurately presents its target, there are *further* conditions—the standing conditions—that blame must meet in order to be morally appropriate. Moreover, we have independent reasons to reject this claim. Consider resentment-tinged blame: resentment presents its target as having done wrong. Insisting that the content of resentment includes the judgments that the wrongdoing is the blamer's business, that the target is a contemporary, that the wrong in question is not something that the blamer has done or would do, and that the blamer is in no way responsible for the wrongdoing is indefensible. Claiming that the content of blame includes even one of these judgments would require defense. I am grateful to Jada Strabbing for pressing me to say more on this point. For a discussion of the distinction between fittingness and other modes of attitude assessment, see D'Arms and Jacobson (2000).

[9] For more on the distinction between pointing to a reason to ϕ and putting a person in a position to appreciate her reason to ϕ, see Bell (forthcoming).

corrupt that he cannot be brought to appreciate the damage wrought by his wrongdoing. Some see blame that is not or cannot be given uptake by the target as failed or incomplete,[10] but I think this is a mistake. Blame does not simply address the target; it also addresses other members of the moral community. This brings us to blame's fourth aim and mode of value: blame educates and motivates others in the moral community. Upon witnessing a stern rebuke, onlookers may be reminded of their reasons not to perform similar acts, and blame for another may motivate them to avoid being targets of moral criticism in the future.

Fifth, blame is valuable as a way of standing up for one's values. Condemning wrongdoing is a central way for persons to express their moral commitments and avoid condonation. The moral value of Isa's criticism of Marie is not determined solely by whether it aided or benefited Marie. Isa might not have been able to live with herself if she hadn't confronted Marie. To stand in silence as someone does something one thinks is wrong is to fail to show proper care for oneself and one's values and can constitute condonation of the wrong done. To condone a wrong means to overlook it, let it pass, or otherwise fail to take it seriously qua wrongdoing. The condoner is not ignorant about right and wrong; instead she is aware of the wrongdoing and in some limited sense disapproves of it but nevertheless does not treat it as seriously as she should. One cannot avoid condonation simply by retaining the *belief* that a wrong was done. In fact, someone who believes that a person did something wrong but is disposed to look the other way or treat the person as if he had not done wrong is precisely the sort we would criticize as condoning the wrong (see Hughes 1995, p. 114). Whether silence constitutes condonation is partially determined by how others in one's community see one's connection to the offender. Your silence may constitute condonation if you are associated with the wrongdoing or wrongdoer, and this association can take many forms. For example, your silence may constitute condonation if the wrong was done by someone close to you, or done to someone close to you, or if the wrong was brought to your attention, or if you have condemned similar wrongs in the past, and so on. To a large degree, whether your silence will constitute condonation is a matter of social conditions that are beyond your control. We do, however, have ways of avoiding condonation; the clearest way is by expressing our condemnation of the offense, and part of the value of blame is that it gives us a way to avoid condonation.

Some will object that the forward-looking aims of blame are, in fact, blame's only true aims. For example, Garrath Williams insists that the aim of blame "is to improve the culprit's conduct by addressing her sense of what is morally

---

[10] See, e.g., Frye (1983, p. 89). While Frye makes this point about anger in particular, she would likely draw a similar conclusion about blame more generally.

acceptable" (2003, p. 431, emphasis deleted). Unfortunately, Williams does not say much in defense of his preferred characterization of blame. Perhaps one could reconstruct an argument for his position by arguing that blame is partially constituted by resentment, and resentment aims only to change the target's future behavior. But we have reason to reject this position. Resentment clearly has both forward-looking and backward-looking aims; it calls for responses from the target and bystanders, but it is also a way of standing against past wrongdoing.

Others may insist that blame is fundamentally backward-looking; any consequences of blame are simply side effects of what is essentially a backward-looking stance (Sher 2006). I acknowledge that blame is backward-looking and can be valuable only if it fits its target, but I see no reason to deny that blame *also* has forward-looking aims. This is not to say that every effect of blame should be characterized as one of its aims; blame may have side effects that are not directly related to its aims. But there is no reason to deny that blame's educational and motivational aspects are part of its aims. Surely a token of blame is more successful and valuable qua blame if it educates, motivates, and helps the blamer avoid condonation. These features are not simply happy side effects of blame but constitutive parts of its aims and value.

A complete understanding of the value of blame must take into account its multiple aims: in part, blame expresses the subject's backward-looking attitudes about the wrong done, but it also seeks to motivate and educate. If we acknowledge blame's multiple aims and modes of value, we should conclude that many of the arguments given in support of the standard account ought to be rejected, or so I shall argue.

3. The Standing to Blame

Defenders of the standard account have articulated several standing conditions. If a person fails to satisfy one or more of these conditions, then she lacks standing to blame.[11] Let's consider each condition in turn.

3.1. BUSINESS CONDITION

First, one may question whether it is the would-be blamer's *business* to blame; this is how Marie attempts to deflect Isa's criticism. According to the most prominent version of this line of thought, standing to blame is analogous to the doctrine of standing in law (Sabini and Silver 1982). Standing is the term used to signify that one has the right to initiate a lawsuit, and in the United

---

[11] For a discussion of several ways standing can be questioned, see Duff (2010).

States only those who have been directly injured have a right to sue for damages.[12] Similarly, defenders of the Business Condition insist that one must have been directly injured by the target's actions in order to have standing to blame.

Appealing to legal standing in order to justify the Business Condition is problematic for at least two reasons. First, those who make this sort of argument ignore the fact that the doctrine of legal standing is contested. For example, Catherine Mackinnon has suggested that the standing doctrine oppresses women: since many of the injuries that women experience are collective injuries, no one woman is able to show that she is differentially injured by unjust practices. Given the nature of their injuries, many will fail the "injury in fact test" that the doctrine of standing requires (1991, pp. 238–39). Since the doctrine of legal standing is open to this and other criticisms, we ought to be suspicious of those arguments that appeal directly to legal standing in an attempt to explicate and defend the Business Condition. Second, even if we put these worries to one side, there are practical reasons why we might want to adopt a strict doctrine of standing in the law but not in our moral lives. Given the limited resources of our courts, we may decide that it makes sense to restrict the number of persons who can sue for damages. But our moral lives are not limited in this way. Thus it is not clear why an appeal to legal standing should ground or even illuminate the standing to blame.

Others may attempt to defend the Business Condition by arguing that when we blame without standing we evince a moral fault. Angela Smith argues that a general reticence to interfere in the affairs of others helps maintain the smooth functioning of society. In order to diminish friction in our social lives, we need a well-developed sense of what is and is not "our business." Smith asks us to imagine attending a party where we encounter a man who constantly interrupts and belittles his wife's contributions to the conversation. She argues that blaming the husband would be morally inappropriate unless one is a close associate of the couple (2007, p. 478). For her, the Business Condition is justified because we ought to respect persons' privacy: "The rights of privacy are such that it is generally not our business to reproach others for their minor moral faults unless we stand in a special relation to them and/or have a relevant stake in the matter" (p. 478, n. 18). Smith does not elaborate on what is involved in having a "relevant stake" in the wrongdoing of others, but she clearly thinks that few would have such a stake in the case she describes.

Despite Smith's claims, it is not at all clear that blaming in the absence of a special relationship or relevant stake in the wrongdoing would violate the target's privacy. Smith's own example does not help her case: the husband in this

---

[12] The U.S. Supreme Court has ruled that those who have standing must meet the following three conditions: (1) The person "must have suffered an 'injury in fact'—an invasion of a legally protected interest"; (2) this injury must be causally connected to the complaint; (3) it must be "likely" that this injury will be redressed by a favorable decision (*Lujan v. Defenders of Wildlife* 1992).

case seems to evince inappropriately hostile attitudes toward his wife (and perhaps toward women in general), and this is hardly a "minor moral fault."[13] If the man publicly expresses his derogatory attitudes in this way, one surely wouldn't violate his *privacy* by challenging these attitudes. Similar considerations would apply to other cases of wrongdoing. Concerns about privacy actually seem to tell *against* the Business Condition. According to the standard account, one must establish that one has standing to blame; the default presumption is that one lacks the standing that morally appropriate blame requires. But in order to establish that one has standing, a would-be blamer would likely need to disclose aspects of her private life that have nothing to do with the offense. While a person need not reveal anything about herself in order for it to be *true* that she has standing to blame, a target will have reason to take the content of some criticism seriously only if he *believes* that the criticizer has standing. In order to make a convincing case that she has standing to blame, a critic would need to explain how she is connected to the wrongdoer, and satisfying this condition may require her to divulge aspects of her private life that she would prefer not to disclose. In this way, the standard account has the potential to lead to greater violations of privacy than standingless blame. Finally, even if a token of blame did violate a target's privacy, it doesn't follow that the critic would necessarily lack the standing to blame. Blamers may evince all sorts of moral faults in their critical interventions, but these faults need not undermine the moral appropriateness of reproach in every instance. I will say more about this below.

3.2. CONTEMPORARY CONDITION

The Contemporary Condition states that the blamer must inhabit the same moral community as the person blamed. Very roughly, two persons can be said to inhabit the same moral community if they see the same considerations as reason-giving and employ the same moral concepts. If the target is dead or inhabits a moral community far removed from the critic's community, it would be impossible for the target to give criticism uptake. According to those who defend the Contemporary Condition, to blame someone who is unable to give blame uptake would be to make a mistake or to engage in a hopeless fantasy (see Williams 1995b, p. 73). A necessary condition of morally appropriate criticism is that the blamer is a moral contemporary of the target.

The Contemporary Condition brings out the important responsibility critics have to attempt to understand the motives of their targets and blame in

---

[13] We do sometimes have good reasons for responding to persons with contempt, but there is no reason to suppose that the husband's contempt for his wife in Smith's example is justified. As Smith presents it, this is supposed to be a case where blame for the husband is fitting, but only some people have the standing to actually blame him for his morally inappropriate attitudes.

such a way that targets can reasonably be expected to give the blame uptake (if uptake is possible). This sort of blame will be more difficult to secure across moral distance. However, the difficulty, or even impossibility, of securing the target's uptake does not always render blame morally inappropriate. If the aims of blame were exclusively forward-looking, then blame across historical or moral difference could be dismissed as pointless fantasy. But as I have argued, blame's aims are both forward-looking and backward-looking. Even in cases where the target cannot give blame uptake, blame may still have a point as a way of motivating and educating others in the moral community or defending the blamer's values. Thus we should reject the Contemporary Condition.

Some may worry that I'm here conflating the issue of whether blame has a *point* with whether it is *morally appropriate*: blame may have a point even when its target cannot give it uptake, but just because a token of blame has a point, it doesn't follow that it is morally appropriate.[14] While some may wish to distinguish between blame's point and its moral propriety, this is not relevant to my argument against the standard account. Those who defend the Contemporary Condition assume that if blame cannot be given uptake by its target, then it is pointless, and if blame is pointless, then it is morally inappropriate. It is the first claim that I reject. If blame is a fitting response to some wrong done, it is not necessarily rendered pointless by the target's inability to give it uptake, and because of this, it is not necessarily rendered morally inappropriate.[15] Moreover, I am not here conflating blame's point with its moral propriety. A token of blame is morally appropriate when it is fitting and achieves at least one of its multiple aims. However, as I will argue in the final section of this essay, we would do better to think about the ethics of blame in terms of our critical responsibilities rather than simply in terms of whether blame meets the bar of moral appropriateness.

3.3. NONHYPOCRISY CONDITION

According to the Nonhypocrisy Condition, one forfeits one's standing to blame if one manifests the same flaw that one attempts to criticize in another. Such a stance evinces hypocrisy, and hypocrisy always undermines standing.

Some defenders of the Nonhypocrisy Condition claim that blame is a speech act, and for it to come off, certain conditions must be met. Specifically, one must have the authority or standing to condemn (Cohen 2006). Just as an

---

[14] I am grateful to the editors for pushing me to say more on this issue.

[15] I am here assuming, as do defenders of the standard account, that blame fits its target. If blame is unfitting, then it cannot be morally appropriate even if it has motivational and educational value for others. Fittingness is a necessary, though not sufficient, condition for blame's moral appropriateness. Those who defend the standard account insist that even when blame is fitting, it is always morally inappropriate if one lacks the standing to blame, and it is this claim that I think we ought to reject.

actor in robes lacks the authority to marry two persons when he utters the words "I pronounce you husband and wife" or a spectator making the "T" sign with his hands lacks the authority to call fouls, hypocritical criticizers lack the standing to blame. Suppose we grant that blame is a speech act and has illocutionary force only when its felicity conditions are met. It is clear that determining who has authority to blame is a very different activity from determining who has authority to officiate weddings or call technical fouls. In the latter cases, we may look to our practices and conventions to determine who has the authority to perform the relevant speech acts. But determining who has authority to condemn is a fundamentally normative matter and not something that we can simply read off of our practices. If one is going to claim that hypocrites lack standing, then substantive arguments for this claim must be given; the general appeal to speech act theory cannot, by itself, support the Nonhypocrisy Condition.

What arguments might one give in support of the claim that hypocrisy always undermines a person's standing to blame? One could argue that hypocritical blamers don't really understand the moral badness of what they condemn. If one does not or cannot acknowledge one's own flaws, then one is not in a position to apprehend the same flaws in another. A version of this view is reflected in a famous passage from the Gospels: "Thou hypocrite, first cast out the beam out of thine own eye; and then shalt thou see clearly to cast out the mote out of thy brother's eye" (Matthew 7:5). According to this line of thought, a person's past immorality compromises his present moral vision, and a failure to understand one's own moral faults is an impediment to seeing these faults in another.

We ought to reject this way of justifying the Nonhypocrisy Condition. While past wrongdoing may compromise a person's moral vision, it may also improve it. Wrongdoers often have knowledge of the costs of wrongdoing that others lack. Suppose, for example, that Isa had, in the past, impaired one of her friendships by chasing after a no-good man. Under these circumstances, Isa's firsthand experience of the pleasures of obsessive love and the damage wrought by this kind of relationship might provide Marie with additional reasons for taking the content of Isa's criticism seriously. Past wrongdoing may give the wrongdoer a deeper appreciation of the damage wrought by wrongdoing. If hypocrisy undermines a blamer's standing to blame, it cannot be because past wrongdoing always compromises one's moral vision.

According to a more promising line of argument, hypocritical criticizers lack standing because they don't really respect their targets as moral equals or value the norms violated (Wallace 2010; Friedman 2011). There is, some note, a deep tension in hypocritical blame: the would-be blamer stands against what he criticizes out of a purported allegiance to morality, yet at the same time, his past actions show that his declaration of allegiance is insincere. The hypocrite says one thing with his mouth and another with his actions. Moreover, this stance reveals that the hypocrite takes the interests of those he blames to be less important than his own: the hypocrite seeks to protect himself from moral criticism but is willing to reproach others. This attitude may be thought to constitute a denial of equal moral standing.

R. Jay Wallace offers a version of this defense of the Nonhypocrisy Condition. Wallace argues that there is a kind of hypocrisy, which he calls "hypocritical moral address," that is distinctly objectionable and undermines the hypocrite's standing to blame. According to Wallace, blame gives rise to a commitment to examine one's own attitudes and past behaviors, but hypocritical blamers fail to live up to this commitment: "[T]he moral objection to hypocritical blame can accordingly be understood to be that hypocrites have failed to live up to the commitment that they have undertaken through the attitudes that constitute their blame" (2010, pp. 326–27). In failing to critically scrutinize their own attitudes and past behavior as they adopt hostile attitudes toward others, hypocrites treat others' interests as less important than their own; that is, they fail to abide by the principle of equality that grounds the commitment to self-scrutiny. To be committed in this way, one must be willing to "admit publicly to one's own moral failings," and hypocrites are unwilling to do this (p. 329, n. 37).

I think we have reason to reject Wallace's defense of the Nonhypocrisy Condition. Despite what he suggests, blame does not carry with it a commitment to self-scrutiny. Wallace seeks to defend this claim on the basis of an observation he makes about the hostile attitudes that partially constitute blame: sometimes subjects of resentment and indignation may learn things about themselves and their values through the experience of blaming another. For example, if I blame you for lying to me, this may lead me to reflect on my own mendacious past, realize I've done wrong, and commit to doing better in the future. Under these circumstances, a subject's past wrongdoing no longer renders her a hypocrite (in Wallace's sense of the term), and her attitude ceases to be morally objectionable (Wallace 2010, p. 326). From this observation about the value of some tokens of blame, Wallace concludes that blame is partially constituted by a commitment to self-scrutiny that is, in turn, grounded by the principle of equality. But it is not at all clear how these claims follow from his observation that blame may give the blamer a deeper appreciation of her own past wrongdoing. Consider a related case: grief for another's loss may give a subject insight into her own values and motivate her to express these values though her actions; for example, a person who grieves for the misfortunes of children in faraway places may reflect on the children in need in her local community and her past indifference to their plight, and this reflection may motivate her to volunteer at a local youth center. In this way, grief for the calamities of others can be a means to learning about one's own values and can spark moral self-improvement. But we shouldn't conclude from this observation that grief always carries with it a commitment to self-scrutiny. Instead, the lesson we should draw is that grief may sometimes have educational and motivational value for the griever. So too the hostile attitudes that constitute blame may sometimes be valuable for the subject. But this observation about blame's value does not establish that blame always carries with it a commitment to self-scrutiny that the hypocrite fails to satisfy. To make this further claim is to offer a moralized (and therefore distorted) analysis of the hostile attitudes that partially constitute blame.

Hypocrisy is a moral fault, and Wallace is right to stress that people often evince hypocrisy in their critical interventions. In fact, people may, and frequently do, evince a wide variety of moral faults through their blame: they can show meanness, pettiness, stinginess, arrogance, and so on. But while people may manifest hypocrisy and other faults in their critical interventions, there is no reason to conclude that these faults always undermine a person's standing to blame. As we have seen, blame has multiple aims and modes of value. The educational or motivational value of blame is not undermined by the blamer's hypocrisy; we can learn from the morally corrupt just as we can learn from the morally pure.

A defender of the Nonhypocritical Condition may push back and insist that there is something particularly problematic about the fault evinced by the hypocritical critic, especially if we accept the Hostile Attitude Account of blame. The hypocritical blamer does not actually value what she claims to value: she claims to care about violations of moral norms, but her own behavior reveals that she doesn't treat these violations as important; she expresses affective attitudes that she doesn't genuinely or fully experience.

In response we should distinguish between three different kinds of hypocrisy. Some hypocrites do care about the norms they blame others for violating, but they are weak-willed and don't, due to their weakness, act in accordance with their values. This sort of hypocrite feels remorse and shame in response to her moral failings and strives to improve herself. We may contrast weak-willed hypocrites with clear-eyed hypocrites. Clear-eyed hypocrites only *pretend* to care about the norms in question and feign the negative affective attitudes at the heart of blame. Molière's Tartuffe would be a good example of this kind of hypocrite. Clear-eyed hypocrites don't really harbor hostile attitudes toward those they "blame," nor do they believe that the target's action is wrong; they merely pretend to have these attitudes. So, on the Hostile Attitude Account, clear-eyed hypocrites don't really blame when they utter what sound like condemnations. However, I don't think that we should conclude that clear-eyed hypocrites lack the *standing* to blame. First, respect for privacy gives us good reason to reject the Nonhypocritical Condition even when this is restricted to clear-eyed hypocrites. We can't know whether someone is engaging in clear-eyed hypocritical criticism without performing a detailed investigation of the critic's evaluative history. But respect for privacy militates against the moral propriety of this kind of investigation. We should not have to publicly sort through all of our dirty—and clean—laundry in order for the content of our criticism to be taken seriously. Second, those who defend the Nonhypocritical Condition seem to conflate *failing* to blame and *lacking standing* to blame. Consider a similar case: suppose that a person expresses gratitude for some assistance but doesn't actually feel grateful at all; instead, the person inwardly seethes with resentment at being put in the position of a supplicant. There is much we could say about the moral faults evinced by such a person, and we would be right to describe him as *feigning* gratitude rather than *expressing* gratitude. But one thing we clearly shouldn't say is that this person lacks the *standing* for gratitude. So too clear-eyed hypocrites may feign blame and evince all sorts of faults though their attitudes, but it would be a mistake to describe them as lacking the standing to blame. Since we often cannot ascertain whether someone is a clear-eyed hypocrite without violating his privacy, we have reason to take the content of feigned blame seriously.

In addition to weak-willed and clear-eyed hypocrites there is a third type of hypocrite: the exception-seeking hypocrite. This kind of hypocrite really does care about moral standards and genuinely harbors hard feelings for those who do wrong. Nevertheless, he engages in the same kind of behavior that he criticizes and sees his own behavior as morally justified. So, for example, he may denounce cheaters and sincerely believe that cheating is wrong, but when he cheats he sees his actions as simply taking what is his due. As with other forms of hypocrisy, there is a tension between the values he endorses through his blame and the values expressed through his actions. But unlike the clear-eyed hypocrite, he takes himself to value what he claims to value though blame, and unlike the weak-willed hypocrite, he doesn't realize that his own actions are wrong. He genuinely blames others while seeing himself as blameless. Again, such a person evinces a fault, but this fault does not undermine his standing to blame. This kind of hypocrite is self-deceived: he doesn't realize that in taking what he thinks he deserves he is in fact cheating. Of course, we may find this sort of self-deception blameworthy; the person in this example *should* realize that what he is doing is cheating, and if he is going to blame others for cheating, consistency demands that he also blame himself. We may even say that such a person fails to treat those he blames as his moral equals. But just because a person is self-deceived, inconsistent, and inegalitarian, it doesn't follow that he lacks the standing to blame.

3.4. NONCOMPLICITY CONDITION

According to the fourth condition, one's standing to blame is compromised if one is complicit in the wrongdoing that is the focus of one's blame. In this case, blame isn't dismissed because the blamer has, in the past, performed the type of action that he criticizes; instead, the person's blame is dismissed because the blamer is partly responsible for the wrong that is the focus of his criticism.

My response to this condition mirrors my previous arguments against the first three standing conditions, and for this reason I shall be brief. Those who blame others for the very wrongs that they are partially responsible for evince a serious fault: we should avoid complicity in immoral practices, and when we discover we've been complicit, we should take responsibility for our misconduct and attempt to right our wrongs. A person who is complicit in wrongdoing and makes no attempt to address her complicity is morally flawed and merits blame. Such a person would better spend her time addressing and attempting to right her own past wrongs rather than blaming others for acts that she is partially responsible for. Nevertheless, complicity does not undermine one's standing to blame.

As in the case of hypocritical blame, targets can learn from and be motivated by blame that comes from a person with faults, just as they can learn from and be motivated by blame from moral saints. In fact, observing complicitous condemnation can lead targets and bystanders to a better appreciation of the wrong in question. The jarring hypocrisy of this stance can help to provide insight into the seriousness of the wrong done. Of course, being the target of complicit blame does not always lead to this kind of understanding, but insofar as it can reasonably be expected to have these kinds of effects, this sort of blame may be morally valuable.

3.5. THE POSITIONALITY OF BLAME

I have argued that we have reasons to reject the arguments given in support of the four standing conditions outlined in the introduction. However, I do admit that there is a kernel of truth at the core of the standard account: blame is, in two important respects, *positional*. Whether a person is in a position to blame depends, in certain cases, on the relationship between the subject and the target of blame.[16] Sometimes we are not all equally well positioned to criticize an offender because we are not all equally well positioned to hold the offender to certain standards. For example, two old friends from art school may hold one another to standards of artistic integrity, even though it may be inappropriate for others to hold them to these standards. What makes it appropriate for the friends to hold one another to these standards is that their relationship is partially constituted by norms concerning artistic excellence.[17] The relationships between children and parents, friends, colleagues, and compatriots are all partially constituted by norms that structure the relationships and give rise to certain expectations. We can describe these as "relationship-dependent norms." Relationship-dependent norms are those norms that proscribe what we owe to one another *as relations*, which is distinct from what we owe to one

---

[16] For a discussion of the positionality of moral and legal responsibility, see Kutz (2007).
[17] A similar example is used to make a different point in Bell (2011).

another *as persons*.[18] Only those who are party to the relationship are in a position to hold persons to these relationship-dependent norms. If a casual acquaintance were to blame one of the artists for lacking artistic integrity, the artist could reasonably reply that the criticizer is not in a position to blame him for this fault even if he has in fact compromised his artistic integrity. In cases of relationship-dependent norms, the moral appropriateness of blame depends on the relationship between the subject and the target of blame. But there are other norms that we are *all* in a position to hold one another to. Many of the norms violated in cases of wrongdoing do not have the kind of positionality characteristic of relationship-dependent norms. Or to put the point in another way, we are all well positioned to hold people responsible for serious wrongdoing and injustice. The standard view fails to properly account for the positionality of blame. For the standard account does not distinguish between relationship-dependent norms and other norms.

There is a further sense in which blame is positional: whether someone is in a position to blame will depend on the emotional tone of her blame. For example, only immediate victims are in a position to blame resentfully because resentment presents its target as having wronged the subject. Indignation, on the other hand, lacks this feature; nonvictims are in a position to blame indignantly even when they are not positioned to blame resentfully. Only those subjects who stand in the right relations to their targets may fittingly respond with certain hard feelings (such as contempt and resentment), and because of this, only those who stand in these relations may blame in particular ways.

Some might worry that in acknowledging what I've described as the kernel of truth in the standard account I've actually ended up completely capitulating to its defenders. My claim that blame is positional may be interpreted as simply another way of saying that blame admits of standing. But in arguing that blame is positional, I am not surreptitiously endorsing the standard account. First, to argue that blame is positional is to make a claim about blame's fittingness conditions: in some cases, the fittingness of blame depends on the relationship between the subject and the target. The standard account characterizes standing as something distinct from fittingness. According to the standard account, one may lack the standing to blame even when one's blame is fitting, and this claim I reject. Second, according to the standard account, if one lacks standing to blame, then one's blame may be dismissed completely without taking into account its content or affective tone. But if we accept that blame is positional in the ways that I've described, it may be the case that a person's resentment-tinged blame is unfitting, but his indignation-tinged blame would be fitting. Accepting the positionality of blame allows us to recognize and appreciate

---

[18] There is now a large literature on what grounds special obligations. Since my arguments here do not depend on a specific understanding of our special responsibilities and obligations, I will not take up this issue here.

important distinctions between different kinds of blame and their moral relevance; this is not something that we can easily do on the standard account. Finally, it is worth stressing again that most moral norms are not relationship-dependent. We are all in a position to hold one another to norms of respect and beneficence, for example. Thus the relationship-dependence of some norms does not give us reasons to dismiss criticism directed toward, say, an abusive man we encounter at a dinner party; we are all well positioned to hold one another to norms of respect for persons.

4. Responsibilities of Reproach

Defenders of the standard account seem to worry that if we give up the idea that blame has strict standing conditions, our moral lives will be overrun with blame. Blame's standing conditions are thought to provide a bulwark against moralism and excessive condemnation.

I don't think that the threat of moralism gives us reason to accept the standard account. In fact, the standard account seems to encourage the very moralism that its defenders decry. If the only people with the standing to blame are those with pristine moral records, this suggests that blame is a kind of privilege that is given as a reward to the morally pure. This strikes me as a highly moralistic, and disturbing, characterization of blame. Instead, blame is better understood as a tool that we may all use to learn from one another and express our moral values, no matter how blemished our moral records may be. Moreover, nothing in my arguments entails that we have overriding reasons to spend the majority of our time reproaching people. It is impossible to provide a concise formula for when we do or don't have overriding reasons to blame because our reasons to blame depend on contextual factors. These reasons become stronger in direct relation to the value of blame, and the value of a particular token of blame depends on the extent to which the token realizes blame's multiple aims. Whether blame would be valuable in a particular situation may depend on factors such as one's position vis-à-vis the target. A person associated with a wrongdoer by birth or convention may have reasons to blame (so as to avoid condonation) that others lack. However, the blame of the scold or indiscriminate blamer is unlikely to be valuable. When a person is constantly blaming others, her blame will tend to be quickly dismissed, and because of this it will lack educational and motivational value. While excessive blame may help blamers avoid condonation, a person could avoid condonation without devoting all her energies to blaming others.

Rather that characterizing the ethics of reproach solely in terms of blame's fittingness and the critic's standing, we should pay more attention to our special responsibilities within the domain of criticism. Targets, blamers, and bystanders all have distinct responsibilities regarding reproach. As targets, we can respond excellently or poorly to blame we receive. Targets of blame should resist the temptation to try to undermine criticism by bringing up the moral record of the criticizer. While it can be hard to hear, we often have reason to give uptake to criticism voiced by the morally flawed. This does not mean that we must accept the criticism as accurate, but we should consider the content of the blame and take its claims seriously.

Blamers have additional responsibilities. First, and most obviously, we should criticize only when we have good reason to believe that the target really has done wrong or evinces an objectionable character trait (Friedman 2011). Very often there will be epistemic barriers to blaming those who are not close to us. We don't know, for example, whether the seemingly able-bodied stranger we see parking in a spot reserved for the disabled is a swindler or someone whose disability is not easily observed. Here, unlike in Smith's example of the belittling husband, concerns about privacy and respect do give us reason not to pry. In addition, blamers should not aim to break down their targets. While the expression of some opprobrium is necessary in order to stand up for our values and avoid condonation, criticism need not be especially acerbic in order to achieve this end. Moreover, brutal criticism does not aid the offender, and it is unlikely that this sort of criticism will lead to moral change. Finally, it is less morally appropriate to criticize someone who is trying to change his ways and who has already reproached himself for his past offense.[19] Since blame is valuable in part as a form of aid to the target, if the target is already reproaching himself for his past wrongdoing, criticism from others no longer has value as a form of aid. Blame may still have value for the criticizer under these conditions, but it is less likely that one's silence can reasonably be taken as condonation of the wrong. Once the offender has repudiated his wrongdoing, one can associate (or be associated) with him without as great a risk that one's association will constitute condonation.

Bystanders also have distinct responsibilities regarding reproach. We should pay attention to the critical activities of those around us even when we do not have a clear stake in the criticism. Of course, this does not mean that we should interfere in affairs that have nothing to do with us, but we ought to take the content of publicly articulated criticism seriously. We may end up rejecting the criticism as misplaced, but in giving the criticism uptake we may learn new things about wrongdoing. In cases where the target of blame will not or cannot give the criticism uptake, bystanders may have additional roles to play. If we determine that reproach is warranted, then we may have reason to reach out to blamers in order to reassure them that a wrong was indeed done. This is particularly important in cases where groups of persons have warranted grievances against those who are unable, or unwilling, to give their blame

---

[19] For a defense of this point on different grounds, see Adams (1985).

uptake. Under such circumstances, third parties may have reason to address the blame through institutional mechanisms such as memorials or reparations.

Many of us are tempted to deflect unwelcome criticism by insisting that those who blame us lack the standing to criticize. I have argued that this common response, while understandable, is misguided. Those who defend the standard account characterize blame as something persons should be protected from; some go so far as to say that a fundamental aim of morality is to shield us from blame (Wallace 2010). These philosophers see standing as having an important role to play in protecting persons from blame. I reject this characterization of the relationship between blame and morality. If anything is protecting or shielding in this domain it is blame: blame helps to shield and protect us from the moral damage wrought by wrongdoing. Rather than attempting to limit blame by appealing to the objectionable notion of standing, we should take seriously our special responsibilities as critics, targets, and bystanders.

{ 15 }

Standing in Judgment

Gary Watson

Yet the obvious fact is that we all live in neighborhoods which are at
different distances from the Kingdom of Ends, and it seems merciless
to give this obvious fact no weight.

—CHRISTINE KORSGAARD, *CREATING THE KINGDOM OF ENDS*

1

The radio station at my former university occasionally broadcast messages
urging listeners who are experiencing suicidal or otherwise destructive impulses to discuss their problems in the "nonjudgmental" setting of the university's counseling center. What was advertised, I take it, was a place
where members of the university community might disclose and discuss
disturbing thoughts and inclinations without fear of recrimination or
rejection. This nonjudgmental response contrasts, apparently, with the reception that such disclosures would be apt to receive in dormitories or
even at home.

The explicit discourse of nonjudgmentalism is most familiar in this sort of
clinical context. Presumably a nonjudgmental posture, however that is to be
understood, is recommended for effective counseling and therapy. Jon Schreiber, a director of a health and wellness center in Berkeley, has a suggestion
about how we should understand this posture: "When you are nonjudgmental,

This paper derives from a lecture delivered at Cumberland Lodge, Windsor, England, sponsored by the
Philosophy Department of Birkbeck College, University of London, and subsequently delivered as the
Austin-Hempel Lecture at Dalhousie University. Many thanks to my hosts and audiences on those
occasions, especially to Gregory Scherkoske. Since then I've received helpful comments from more
people than I can remember; those I can remember include Svetlana Beggs, William Bracken, Stephen
Gardiner, Peter Graham, Richard Kraut, Coleen Macnamara, Miriam McCormick, Michael Rosenthal,
Angela Smith, Bill Talbot, and Ken Westphal. I am especially grateful for the philosophical advice of
Marcia Baron, Victoria McGeer, and the editors of this volume.

you totally *accept the other person exactly as they are.*[1] But the promotion of nonjudgmentalism is not confined to such settings, and even the therapeutic literature often emphasizes nonstrategic reasons that apply to human relations quite generally. For example, one of the most widely read texts of the recovery movement makes the following plea: "Try never to judge. . . . Each mind is so different, actuated by such different motives, controlled by such different circumstances, influenced by such different sufferings, you cannot know all the influences that have gone to make up a personality."[2] In his emphasis on nonjudgmentalism as a crucial part of twelve-step programs, Bill Wilson adduces a further consideration: "Finally, we begin to see that all people, including ourselves, are to some extent emotionally ill as well as frequently wrong, and then we approach true tolerance and see what real love for our fellows actually means."[3] The implication of both claims is that nonjudgmentalism is not just a virtue in the work of clinical practitioners but, on a clear view of the human condition, something required by more general ideals and virtues.

There is something right about this, I think, but also something alarming. What would "never judging" or "accepting people exactly as they are" or regarding oneself and others "as to some extent emotionally ill as well as frequently wrong" come to, and why would these stances be at all desirable? If 'never to judge' means suspending our critical intelligence or not holding one another morally answerable, then nonjudgmentalism writ large amounts to nihilism, complacency, or a loss of moral nerve.[4] The possession and exercise of critical judgment is clearly central not only to healthy ethical relations but also to moral personhood. Seen in this way, *non*judgmentalism looks like the vice.[5]

Yet it is a mistake simply to dismiss the everyday discourse of judgmentalism as moral rubbish: as evasion, or as an attempt to pathologize human affairs. It points to important values and ideals that warrant our attention, articulation, and assessment. The term itself is unbeautiful and no doubt too clumsy to collect the subtle distinctions that are wanted here. But it can lead us fruitfully into the insufficiently explored territory of second-order virtues and vices, that is, virtues and vices pertaining to how we respond to the moral shortcomings of ourselves and others. My aim in this paper is to delineate an important subset of these.

---

[1] As reported in Martin Miller, "If I'm OK and You're OK, Are There Any Bad Guys?," Los Angeles Times, January 27, 2002 (my italics). This is—totally—what you'd expect a director of a wellness center in Berkeley to say.

[2] Anonymous (1975), as quoted in Care (1996, p. 178). I have been much influenced by Care's sensitive and groundbreaking work on related subjects; see also his 2000. (Thanks to Geoffrey Sayre-McCord for alerting me to the relevance of Care's work.)

[3] From Alcoholics Anonymous (1953, p. 92), as quoted in Care (2000, p. 174, n. 14). Wilson was a cofounder of Alcoholics Anonymous.

[4] It amounts to nihilism if it means we lack the authority to make moral claims and demands on one another. I expand on this below.

[5] Walter Kaufmann counters the churchy discourse of nonjudgmentalism by inverting Matthew 7:1: "Judge, that you may *be* judged" (1963, p. 305, my emphasis).

To anticipate, I shall initially distinguish two (overlapping) types of vice or fault (and corresponding virtues) that plausibly belong under the heading of being judgmental (or nonjudgmental). One type concerns a tendency to find the worst in people, a kind of fault-finding that amounts to *interpretive ungenerosity*. The second type concerns ways of responding to the perceived faults of others, in particular the readiness to dismiss others or to foreclose or restrict important human relations with them on the basis of those perceptions of fault. Those who are judgmental in this way are, as I shall say, *too unaccepting* of the faults of others. The two types of vice, then, are (1) failures of interpretive generosity (roughly, too readily attributing fault in the first place) and (2) being too unaccepting of others' faults.[6] Ultimately, I'll suggest, being too unaccepting is crucial to being judgmental in both forms.

2

To focus the discussion, consider some examples.

THE PACIFIST FATHER

A man with strong antimilitarist convictions is deeply troubled by his daughter's decision to join the military and to participate in what the father regards as a particularly unjust war. This clash might estrange them from one another for a time, even permanently. Instead, perhaps soon, the father might come to accept this decision on the part of his daughter. What this involves, roughly, is successfully resolving not to allow what he takes to be his daughter's morally problematic decision to damage their relationship.[7] If the father refuses or fails to overcome this estrangement, the daughter might naturally complain, "You are too judgmental on this issue. You won't brook any disagreement from anyone about this. If they support the war, you write them off."

THE FUNDAMENTALIST MOTHER

A friend of mine told me the following story. He had (anxiously) phoned his parents to report his recent separation from his spouse and their decision to end their fifteen-year marriage. After an awkward moment of silence, his mother coldly replied, "You know how your father and I feel about divorce. It

---

[6] As we'll see, my understanding of nonacceptance *passim* relies heavily on something very close to T. M. Scanlon's idea of impaired relationships, especially in his 2008.

[7] They might agree to discuss certain writings that defend the other's position, remaining open to the possibility that there is some merit there. Perhaps they will come to see this as hopeless, though, and the openness as phony. They may instead just reach an understanding that on this matter they will be at odds, and that it is a subject best avoided.

is forbidden by the Church. What you are proposing to do is very wrong." The mother's first response is to take the moral measure of her son's conduct instead of (also) offering some comfort and concern, of engaging with the plight of her son and daughter-in-law in some less dismissive way ("Are you sure there are not alternatives? Have you given enough thought to the matter?").[8] As a result, the son remained alienated from his parents for years.

THE CONDESCENDING MOTHER-IN-LAW

Here's an example from Iris Murdoch's *Sovereignty of the Good*: "A mother, whom I shall call M, feels hostility to her daughter in law, whom I shall call D. M finds D quite a good-hearted girl, but while not exactly common yet certainly unpolished and lacking in dignity and refinement. D is inclined to be pert and familiar, insufficiently ceremonious, brusque, sometimes positively rude, always tiresomely juvenile. M does not like D's accent or the way D dresses. M feels that her son has married beneath him" (1971, p. 17).

THE PREJUDICED SALESMAN

A salesman in a computer store is repelled by the appearance of a heavily tattooed and body-pierced customer, whose comportment strikes him as tasteless and even offensive. After ignoring her for a time, he reluctantly attends to the transaction, but coldly and with evident disdain.

3

In attempting to evoke the reader's sense of these cases as exemplary of a kind of judgmentalist vice, I have relied tacitly on assumptions about the contexts. Making some of these explicit will underscore some important preliminary points.

First, our sense of the responses in these cases as judgmental depends on a conception of what is appropriate to and significant about the relations in question. It matters in *the fundamentalist mother* that the son is calling on her as his mother, not, say, as a representative of the Catholic League. We expect something different from parents. It is no surprise that the examples of judgmentalism that come most vividly to mind involve domestic relationships. It is here that 'judgment' matters most to the possibility and the quality of those relations. Still, this should not cloud our view. As we see from the examples with which I opened

---

[8] This looks also to be an example of *moralizing*, since the mother's first concern is to frame the issue in moral terms when that shouldn't have been what was most salient. However, a judgmental reaction in this context could also be ethical in some nonmoral sense. Imagine the women's response was based on grounds of social class rather than religion. "Divorce is just not done in our sort of family. That's not the way we do things." This variation on the case brings it in some ways closer to the third example below.

the essay, and from *the prejudiced salesman*, the virtues and vices under consideration are by no means confined to intimate relations. Although they are especially problematic in relation to her son's new wife, M's condescension would be objectionable even as reactions to a colleague or to a stranger on a train.

Second, obviously, our understanding of these attitudes as vices depends not only on the relationship in question but on the relative significance of the putative faults to which they are reactions. It would be quite another matter if the parents were responding to their children's decisions to join a murderous terrorist cell. Our attribution of the vice can be contestable in both of these dimensions.

Third, reactions can be more or less judgmental. Many responses short of writing someone off can count as judgmental. *The antimilitarist father* can be too judgmental without breaking off normal relations altogether. We often harbor estranging sentiments without expressing them even nonverbally (as might be the case in two of our examples). The persistence of the father's feelings of disapproval mark a degree of estrangement, but his keeping them to himself may reflect a strong affirmation of the importance of the relationship. Sometimes concealment rather than elimination is the best one can do.

A final preliminary point: Being judgmental often involves *blaming* too readily, but on some accounts the last two examples, at least, raise a question about this. The attitudes of M and the salesman express primarily *contempt* and *disdain*, and on some prominent views of blaming those will not in themselves be blaming attitudes. On a very standard view, blame is understood to involve holding certain "reactive attitudes" such as resentment, indignation, and (in the self-regarding case) guilt, attitudes that are directed toward individuals in virtue of their offensive attitudes *toward others*. It is implausible to suppose (at least we need not suppose) that M's judgmental stance presumes such a view of D, though that might be part of the salesman's view of the customer.

Suffice it to say that blaming and "judging" in the sense under consideration here are at the very least significantly overlapping categories. It seems to me true and important that D's putative vulgarity is something M *holds against* her (a telling phrase). But it may be that "holding against" is a broader category than blaming (moral or nonmoral). That question is important for the larger themes of this book, but for my purposes we can set it aside.

4

In my preliminary remarks, I distinguished, as candidates for judgmentalism, two sorts of failure, of what I called interpretive generosity and of being too unaccepting of the faults of others.[9] Before discussing these in turn, note that

---

[9] There are important self-reflexive forms of these faults, which I touch on very briefly below.

only some of my examples (clearly *the condescending mother-in-law* and per-haps less clearly *the prejudiced salesman*) fall under the first type. In our opening example of the counseling center, what is broadcast is the promise to provide visitors with a welcoming reception, no matter how disturbed or dis-turbing their thoughts. Whatever one thinks of the merits of the parents' posi-tions on military participation or divorce, the salient issue raised in these cases is not the content of their views but how they respond to others on the basis of those judgments.

This suggests an apparent infelicity in the preliminary categories. It is nat-ural to think that judgmentalism must involve faults of *judgment*, and only failures of interpretive generosity explicitly do that. However, on further re-flection, we should locate the primary vice of judgmentalism in the faulty ways in which one's judgment conditions one's relations with others. Or so I shall propose. Nevertheless, failures of interpretative generosity are worth exam-ining for the supporting role they play in this primary vice. Before developing these points, I want to consider and reject an alternative way of construing the vice of judgmentalism.

NONJUDGMENTALISM AS "NEUTRALITY"

To begin with, we should reject the tempting thought that nonjudgmentalism is to be understood in terms of a kind of neutrality or suspension of judgment in the narrow sense of 'assessment,' although that understanding is suggested by some of the rhetoric in this area. 'Try never to judge' is naturally taken in this way, and a stance of neutrality looks at first sight to be just what is wanted for being nonjudgmental. But even in clinical contexts, that injunction cannot plausibly be construed in this way. In many cases, the fact that someone has or is inclined to act wrongly or badly is very much part of the framework of the interaction. For the purpose of the interaction may well be to help the indi-vidual to avoid committing, or to come to terms with the fact that he has com-mitted, a great wrong. Suppose his struggle is with his sexual inclinations regarding children or with his having abandoned his family. Advising the in-terlocutor to have no opinions about the moral quality of the inclinations or the deed in question would be wildly misguided. The man's struggle is with inclinations to wrongdoing or with guilt and shame for what he's done or felt. That's the problem with which he needs help. Moral neutrality would avoid the issue and disable the interlocutors from understanding and addressing the central problem. Similarly the authors of *Twenty-four Hours a Day* are not challenging or calling for a suspension of our assessments of the comparative merits of a life devoted to alcohol. It is part of the assumed background that those in treatment have damaged themselves and likely mistreated others.

To be sure, there are many cases in which the problem is to help people see that what they have done or tried to do is *not* appropriately to be regarded as shameful or wrong. In that case, we would work toward the rejection of the premise on which they approach the interaction. But importantly this is not a neutral or nonmoral stance in which one suspends judgment but a challenge to a negative judgment held by the subject.

Since nonjudgmentalism is called for even here, the equation of nonjudgmentalism with "suspending moral evaluation" cannot be right. Instead the injunctions to neutrality and to "suspend judgment" should be understood in a different sense of 'judgment.' What is required, it seems, is to refrain from "*passing* judgment." To follow the legal metaphor somewhat, the idea is that it is out of order for me to hold trial, to stand as judge and jury. That's not my business, at least in this context. So construed, "Try never to judge" may still be a questionable generalization, but it is not to be dismissed as inconsistent with robust moral assessment.

NONJUDGMENTALISM AND SKEPTICISM

Before saying more about how this "verdictive" sense of 'judgment' is related to judgmentalism as nonacceptance, I want to mention, just to set aside, the common idea that nonjudgmentalism involves *skepticism*. Indeed one or another of two types of skepticism comes up in this context. One sort is ethical: that judging others is problematic because there are no valid interpersonal ethical standards. The second type of skepticism concerns responsibility: we should not judge because people are just products of their environment and in particular of pathologies for which they cannot be faulted.

These are, of course, familiar positions, and no doubt some who caution against judging others do so on one or both of these grounds.[10] Ethical skepticism cannot be the right basis of our target notion, however, since nonjudgmentalism as we are conceiving it *is* an ethical position. It cannot simply reject the validity of interpersonal ethical norms. (Obviously it is committed to not being judgmental about judgmentalism itself, but there is no incoherence in that.) There are admittedly intimations of skepticism about responsibility in some of the passages I've quoted, but they seem to me inessential to the issue.

"To understand is to forgive" is a slogan that is often intoned in this context. And it seems right to think of being forgiving as part of not being judgmental.

---

[10] Compare Albert Einstein: "I do not at all believe in human freedom in the philosophical sense. Everybody acts not only under external compulsion but also in accordance with inner necessity. Schopenhauer's saying, 'A man can do what he wants, but not want what he wants,' has been a very real inspiration to me since my youth; it has been a continual consolation in the face of life's hardships, my own and others', and an unfailing well-spring of tolerance. This realization mercifully mitigates the easily paralyzing sense of responsibility and prevents us from taking ourselves and other people all too seriously; it is conducive to a view of life which, in particular, gives humor its due" (1982, pp. 8–9). Einstein's talk of "not taking ourselves or others too seriously" invites the worry about seriousness mentioned in the beginning of the essay.

Being nonjudgmental is being "understanding," and understanding in this sense is something we often ask of one another and are often grateful to receive. But it is a familiar point that the slogan cannot coherently express the second type of skepticism, since forgiveness presupposes an attribution of responsibility and fault. The understanding that underlies the readiness to forgive is not that there is no responsibility but that all of us are liable to go wrong in important ways, a realization that tempers one's judgment in a sense that it is our aim to unpack. At any rate, nothing in the case for nonjudgmentalism as I construe it denies that we are answerable to one another on the basis of interpersonally valid norms.

5

Let me return at last to my preliminary classification of types of judgmentalism. The conception of judgmentalism as a failure of interpretive generosity is suggested by two related themes in the passages I quoted earlier. First, the passage from *Twenty-four Hours a Day* ("you cannot know all the influences that have gone to make up a personality") alleges something of general ethical significance in our epistemic position, namely, that we are obscure to one another in rather deep ways. Second, Wilson here pleads for "tolerance" on the basis of what he takes to be our common lot: we are all "frequently wrong" and "to some extent emotionally ill." This is a claim, apparently, about the circumstance of alcoholic and nonalcoholic alike, the recognition of which is said to be integral to "true tolerance" and "real love."[11]

The question "Who are you to judge?" can express two distinct challenges, one regarding the character of the judge, the other having to do with the judge's competence to declare an authoritative table of values and to condemn those who depart from it. Both are questions of standing or qualification. The first thought is that our being "frequently wrong" ourselves morally disqualifies us from judging others.[12] The second thought concerns our ethical epistemic position: "What makes you think you know better than others how to live?" (This question expresses ethical humility, not the kind of ethical skepticism considered earlier.) On this second construal, the fault is a kind of arrogance or dogmatism or self-satisfaction regarding one's own values. Something of this sort is at stake in the charge of ethnocentrism—that someone is ready to condemn or dismiss other ways of life without real appreciation of what they involve.

---

[11] I consider the connection with tolerance below. Denis de Rougemont connects the Christian ideal of the love of one's neighbor (*agape*) with "an *acceptance* of him or her in the whole concrete reality of his or her affliction and hope" (1983, p. 71, my emphasis).

[12] The first question of standing is insightfully explored, for example, in Dworkin (1999), Scanlon (2008), and Wallace (2010).

This second worry has some obvious similarity to the fault of interpretive ungenerosity with which we are concerned here, but it does not get to the heart of what Wilson et al. have in mind. Once again, they do not question unfavorable assessments of alcoholic lives. More important, it is possible to be too satisfied with one's own values—uncurious and fatuously parochial—without a readiness to condemn, put down, or exclude those who differ on some point.

The nonjudgmental ideal invoked in these remarks suggests something in addition to epistemic humility; it also calls for us to be mindful of the general fragility of human agency, of how imperfectly actual human beings tend to satisfy the standards of clarity and control we presume in our mutual dealings.[13] Even the most fortunate of us struggle with our own demons, and the failure to keep this vividly in mind leads to a tendency to be overly severe with others. The recognition of these limits of our knowledge and agency recommends both a kind of interpretive generosity and an *acceptance* of others (faults and all) that is characteristically lacking in judgmental people.[14]

6

The lessons of interpretive generosity are commonplace. Your neighbor is (by all appearances) rude to you, or worse, but your resentment is tempered or dissipated when you come to realize what great stress he has been under. (He's been in chronic pain, say, or has just lost a job or a loved one.)[15] A poignant historical instance of this is Beethoven's famous lament in his "Heiligenstadt Testament": "Oh you men who say that I am malevolent, stubborn or misanthropic, how greatly do you wrong me; *you do not know the secret causes of my*

---

[13] A main theme of Care's later work (cited above) is the importance for human relations, including relations with oneself, of the knowledge that we are virtually all (in one way or another) "damaged agents." I am also beholden to Care for the emphasis on "generosity" in connection with judgmentalism: "A serious respect for the responsibilities that members of the moral community have to and for each other should be tempered with a certain generosity toward individuals, given the degree to which the perspective on the human condition that suggests that there are fixed elements of character seems plausible" (Care 1996, p. 29). Such generosity might be interpretive, but it seems to me that acceptance is itself a kind of generosity to the person accepted.

[14] Of course, someone can display the vice of judgmentalism without being a judgmental person tout court. It is not uncommon for one's judgmentalism to be occasional or quite selective. A person might be judgmental only on selected issues, just as a father might be a paradigm of the overly stern judge with his sons but a model of understanding and generosity with his colleagues.

[15] Arlie Hochschild reports "how one air stewardess handles angry passengers without getting angry herself: 'I pretend something traumatic happened in their lives. Once I had an irate [sic] that was complaining about me, cursing at me, threatening to get my name and report me to the company. I later found out that his son has just died. Now when I meet an irate [sic] I think of that man'" (1983, as quoted in Elster 1999, p. 261). This passage illustrates the adoption of a nonjudgmental stance for strategic (in this case self-protective) reasons. But the technique can also serve the broadly ethical ideals that concern me here.

seeming." What appeared to family and acquaintances as arrogance or indifference on Beethoven's part was often due (so he says) to his deafness or to his excruciating embarrassment about this impairment.

The passage quoted earlier from Murdoch's *The Sovereignty of the Good* provides an excellent illustration of both the failure of interpretative generosity and its overcoming. After her "first thoughts about D," M begins to change her view: "D is discovered to be not vulgar but refreshingly simple, not undignified but spontaneous, not noisy but gay, not tiresomely juvenile but delightfully youthful, and so on" (1971, p. 18). One can see this transition of the mother-in-law either as coming to a truer view of D or as coming to a more favorable understanding that is equally consistent with the evidence. In either case, the initial take is a reading of D that is in part distorted by M's own needs and fears. It is in this way unjust and in a manner unloving (which is, of course, Murdoch's main theme here).

As Murdoch presents the case, M's fault looks like a vice of misjudgment in a basic sense; it leads to a distorted reading of the daughter-in-law. Note that M's interpretation could be a distortion even if it were accurate as far as it went; its partiality highlights the worst. What's crucial here, it seems to me, is that her take on her daughter-in-law is not just off in this way, but serves as a prelude to and pretext for a dismissal or rejection of D as a suitable mate for her son. The ungenerous interpretation is in effect the mother's brief for nonacceptance, for a stance of rejection if not hostility, or at least for maintaining the distance of superiority.

These examples reveal (at least) two different points at which we can fail in interpretative generosity: first, in our initial characterization of others' conduct and, second, in what we make of that characterization. One may be too quick, in the first place, to read someone's behavior as rude rather than shy, harsh rather than honest. But even where the former attributions are accurate enough, the interpretively generous person will be more hesitant to epitomize the others in these terms. Fault-finders are those who are inordinately preoccupied with the putative misdeeds of others. They are fault-finders because they are fault-trackers.[16] And that is ethically problematic not just because fault-finders might get it wrong but because it is a setup for an overall *verdict*.

In contrast, nonjudgmental people will be reluctant to engage in the business of coming to such verdicts, having a lively sense that there is likely to be a lot more to the story. Even if it is right to construe Beethoven's behavior as rude or aloof (rather than merely uncommunicative), it might well be too severe to expect someone suffering that sort of disability to behave perfectly correctly. Even if our inconsiderate neighbor has not lost his job or a loved one, for all we know he is subject to equally extenuating stresses and strains. We should, then, not be so quick to dismiss him as merely a jerk (or worse).

---

[16] Often this preoccupation reveals something about the agent's attitude to herself. One suspects that judging others is self-protecting because it is self-inflating. However, some people do seem to be equally hard on themselves.

Compare the judgmental and nonjudgmental variations of the story of *the pacifist father*. Both stories involve the conviction that the daughter's decision to join the military is morally objectionable. In that sense of the term, the judgmental and nonjudgmental responses are based on the same 'judgment,' and the fault in question lies not in the judgment but in the response. But in a different sense, the judgmental father's response is itself a kind of judging. In this stronger sense of 'judgment,' judging is a complex attitude comprising judging in the weaker sense of assessing and dismissing the other on the basis of that assessment.

When the authors of *Twenty-four Hours a Day* implore the reader, "Try never to judge," then, I understand them to be cautioning primarily against judging of this verdictive type. Again, what is in question is not whether someone has wasted his life and harmed others by addiction to drink but how we regard the individual in view of this assessment. We are urged to refrain (or at least to try, for it's a demanding task) from dismissing others simply as losers, as weak, as irredeemably defective in ways that differentiate them significantly from you and me. Interpretive generosity is adopting an interpretation of others according to which they are not to be dismissed in these kinds of ways.

7

Thus nonjudgmentalism is not a matter of faulty judgment in the narrow sense but of how one responds to others on the basis of those judgments. What makes interpretative ungenerosity itself judgmental, I have proposed, is precisely its connection to being unaccepting, to judging in this stronger sense. This last point becomes clearer when we consider cases in which this connection is absent.

We speak of some people as being too critical (hypercritical), and sometimes this amounts to a charge of judgmentalism. But not always. I might read your manuscript uncharitably just because it is critical of my cherished views or because I am jealous of your talent. Being too critical need not be self-serving, though. Imagine that as a critic of poetry I have standards that virtually no one, including myself, could meet; only a handful of geniuses are worth taking seriously, according to me. This severe standard may prevent me from seeing the value in these works and giving their authors the credit they deserve. But it need not involve nonacceptance in the sense I have been trying to identify. I could unfairly think my son to be a rotten poet without in any way thinking less of him as a son or a person.[17] If I did think this, then I would manifest at

---

[17] My son might be angered or hurt by my severe assessment of his talents. Perhaps my opinion is important to his self-assessment, and in particular it may be important to his sense of our relationship that I appreciate his work. Hence my lack of appreciation may well damage our relationship. For this reason, a blunt statement of my opinion may be insensitive, but neither that fault nor the ensuing damage to our relationship has anything to do with nonacceptance on my part.

least two faults: in my assessment of his work and in my inappropriately conditioning my relation with him on such assessments. We may well use the term 'judgmental' to describe the former interpretive fault by itself, but without its connection with nonacceptance it is importantly different.

Similarly, familiar usage might classify *being opinionated* as a kind of judgmentalism. The former term denotes a readiness to form and express one's views in an uncompromising way and to be dismissive of rival opinions. Like being hypercritical, being opinionated might display, among other things, an objectionable closed-mindedness and lack of humility. Nevertheless, unless these faults of judgment dispose one to dismiss not just other opinions but the authors of those opinions, they do not seem to me to involve the fault under consideration here.

Consider as well the relative who is constantly monitoring your life, hinting that you are drinking too much, or exercising too little, or letting the kids watch too much television. However inappropriate, this sort of hypercritical attention may well not be judgmental; it may manifest a kind of anxious love without disposing him to anything like an alienation of affection or regard. In this sense he may not for a moment hold these things against you.

This seems to be the best explanation of why Murdoch's example of interpretative ungenerosity is so conspicuously a case of judgmentalism. Recall M's initial thoughts about her daughter-in-law: "D is inclined to be pert and familiar, insufficiently ceremonious, brusque, sometimes positively rude, always tiresomely juvenile. M does not like D's accent or the way D dresses. M feels that her son has married beneath him." If it is important for the sake of good family life that M be (and not just to appear to be) on good terms with D, then M must either change her perspective of D or somehow manage to accept her into the family despite that assessment. It is difficult, if not impossible, to maintain unimpaired personal relationships of a familiar sort with someone one thinks of as "vulgar" or "tiresomely juvenile." In contrast to the example of the father who judges his son's poetry too harshly, these epithets are themselves complaints and accusations, displaying distance and dismissal. That's why M seems not just hypercritical but judgmental.[18]

8

To take stock, I have proposed that interpretative ungenerosity is judgmental only when it is implicated in some way with nonacceptance, where that consists in imposing inappropriate conditions on being in (fully) good terms with

---

[18] Perhaps seeing M as "not vulgar but refreshingly simple, not undignified but spontaneous, not noisy but gay, not tiresomely juvenile but delightfully youthful" is at least as warranted as the pejorative view. In any case, the nonpejorative alternative might not be within M's grasp, at least in the short term. In that case, for the sake of the relationship, she might try to change her focus, if not her assessment. Without reaching the position of rejecting the original thoughts as simply wrong, M might manage to stop *thinking* these thoughts,

others. The distinction here is between making objectionable demands on one's relationships and making objectionable assessments of whether someone meets those demands. Both involve inappropriately holding certain things against another, but the fault is located in different places.

Is the fault of nonacceptance sufficient as well as necessary for being judgmental? I am inclined to think not. Consider a father who fails to (fully) accept his children just because they are homely, or of average intelligence, or the wrong gender. These are faults of nonacceptance, to be sure, but it seems to me less natural to speak of judgmentalism here than in *the pacifist father* and *the fundamentalist mother*. In the cases we have taken to be exemplary of this vice, there is some (at least loosely) ethical negative assessment of the other's conduct or attitudes and a questionable demand that the other change or else.

Contrast the case just mentioned with parents whose affection or regard for their daughter was negatively affected by her choice of a career as a realtor over a promising future as an academic. This seems a candidate for judgmentalism because, like the earlier cases, the lack of acceptance is based on some kind of *charge* against the daughter. In contrast, the father isn't *charging* his child with being a girl or being dull or homely (though that's a possible case, I suppose). He simply cares less about his child on this account.

But I am not confident that this is the right conclusion or the right basis for the conclusion. In some plain sense the father holds it against his children that they are not smarter (and so on); he writes them off. Perhaps both conclusions conform equally with common usage, such as it is. It may be fruitless to try to regiment the discourse of 'judgmentalism' to this extent, since it is not clear that anything is at stake. In any event, the conclusion that the father's nonacceptance on these grounds is not judgmental clearly does not imply that his response is any less objectionable. On the contrary, it is in some ways more so since it responds to the children as desirable or undesirable things rather than as persons. So I'll leave open the question of whether being too unaccepting is a sufficient condition of being judgmental. What concerns me in the remainder of the paper is primarily the nature and normativity of acceptance.

9

Here a pair of images from Raimond Gaita is helpful. Judgmentalism, he suggests, is "an ever-present readiness to point the finger at others and to turn one's back on them" (2000, p. 96).[19] These images are distinct; finger-pointing

---

attending instead to what after all are D's "better" qualities. If a friend were now to say to her, "Isn't D rather boorish?," M may reply, "Perhaps, but she has so many good qualities, doesn't she?," thereby granting the unfavorable assessment intellectually, as it were, but refusing to frame her daughter-in-law in these terms.

[19] Gaita also calls this 'moralism.' (Thanks to Svetlana Beggs for calling my attention to Gaita's discussion.) Note that here Gaita is using the term to refer to a general trait. Since I am assuming

is engaged, whereas turning one's back signals disengagement. However, it seems right to conjoin these images because the responses they represent are importantly linked. Finger-pointing is the accusation, as it were, and turning one's back is the conviction (or sentence). In a legal context, the first is a prelude to something like punishment. And punishment paradigmatically takes the form of excluding the accused from our lives in one way or another. We turn our backs when we reject the defense or the apology or the pleas for understanding or mitigation, and we turn our backs once the cell door slams shut.

Turning one's back on someone is a vivid trope for judgmental nonacceptance, but obviously nonacceptance is typically more nuanced and less dramatic than that. To continue to mix anatomical metaphors, one's back may not be turned, but one's shoulder may be colder, one's arms less open. Acceptance and its difficulties are nicely portrayed by the following exchange in George Eliot's novel *Middlemarch* between Fred Vincy and his father. The young man has just decided to pursue a living in business rather than to enter the clergy, as required by his parents' designs. Invoking yet another anatomical image, the elder Vincy initially responds to the announcement in this way: "Very well; I have no more to say. I wash my hands of you. I only hope, when you have a son of your own he will make a better return for the pains you spend on him." The father not only criticizes Fred's decision but takes it to have profoundly impaired their relationship. "Fred lingered; there was still something to be said. . . . 'I hope you will shake hands with me, Father, and forgive me the vexation I have caused you.' Mr. Vincy from his chair threw a quick glance upward at his son, who had advanced near to him, and then gave his hand, saying hurriedly, 'Yes, yes, let us say no more'" (1994, pp. 568–69). On this basis, Fred expressly concludes that his father had "accepted his [Fred's] decision and forgiven him" (p. 569). In accepting his son's hand, Mr. Vincy thereby signifies that he is taking Fred (and his unwelcome decision) back into his life. In doing so, the father retracts his initial expression of rejection.

In general, acceptance *establishes* or *settles* something. In this case, it is now taken as part of their common understanding, and their life together, that Fred will be a businessman rather than a member of the clergy. When one accepts something, one takes certain things as settled, as not being issues. Idiomatically put, one "moves on" or "lets go." This eliminates (or attempts to eliminate) certain kinds of distances and discord. What is signaled by a handshake here might have been conveyed by the utterance "I accept your decision." Signaling that you do or don't accept someone as your student or your husband can have the consequence that these relationships, with their constitutive commitments, are or are not, by that very fact, established.

---

throughout that, like all virtue and vice terms, we can speak of particular actions as in some sense displaying a vice or virtue without attributing the general trait to the agent, I ignore this part of his characterization.

However, in the contexts that interest us here, no utterance or other signal, however sincere, will suffice. For part of what is established by acceptance is a set of "attitudes" that cannot obtain just in virtue of such performances or decisions. Acceptance means that the problematic trait or fact has been incorporated into their mutual life without significantly interfering with full filial relationships. Later on Fred might lament that his father has not, after all, accepted his vocation, and this would not imply that Mr. Vincy's original declaration had been insincere. As we've seen, acceptance often requires struggle, can take a good bit of time, and genuine attempts at acceptance can fail. Mr. Vincy might find that he can't accept Fred's decision after all, that he is merely resigned or that he remains partially unsettled, encountering residues of resistance. In some cases, the best answer to the question "Has someone accepted another's decision?" is simply "Sort of."

As we've also seen, acceptance is in question only in the context of an actual or potential relationship. To update the example from *Middlemarch*, academic parents might not accept the decision of their gifted daughter to depart from her promising professional track to pursue a career as a realtor. But it makes no sense to speak of strangers accepting this decision or not. There is simply no standing or occasion for them to do so. You are not in a position to accept or reject the alcoholic excesses or dim-wittedness or personal slovenliness or sexual impotence of someone unless you are in a position to assume or discontinue a relationship to which these features are thought to be relevant.[20]

It may seem that this view of judgmentalism as nonacceptance cannot without strain be applied to relations among strangers, for whom no (further) interaction is in the offing.[21] The interaction between the customer and the prejudiced salesman was no doubt impaired by his attitudes, but this seems incidental to the case. We would think him equally judgmental if he felt this way while viewing the customer from afar, as she was being helped by his colleague. In what meaningful sense has he inappropriately failed to accept her into a relationship? It does seem to me appropriate to speak of the salesman as not accepting the customer as one to whom various courtesies and regard are owed, even though there is no likelihood, or perhaps even possibility, that he will ever have any actual dealings with her. His attitudes do actually impair his "relationship" with her, I want to say, even though that consists in this case in the truth of certain counterfactuals about their interactions.

Both interpretive generosity and accepting others' faults are practical stances. To determine that someone's behavior was not, or may not have been, disrespectful, despite appearances, may be to adopt a take on the person that differs from belief; it may be a determination to proceed, practically and epistemically, on this premise.[22] Likewise, accepting someone's fault is an (effective)

---

[20] Philippa Foot wants to say something similar about approval; see her 1978 (ch. 14).

[21] I am grateful to Miriam McCormick for pressing this objection.

[22] For the distinction between belief and acceptance, see Bratman (1999, ch. 2).

determination to set some feature F aside as a significant factor in your relationship with that person going forward. To call these practical stances, however, is not to say that one has it in one's volitional power to take them or not.

These are various examples of accepting someone's being F as a member of certain relationships. Once again, sometimes the relationship in question is the relationship with oneself. The core idea is the same in the reflexive case as in the interpersonal case, but the phenomenon and its norms are considerably complicated by self/other asymmetries. (For one thing, accepting what one regards as another's wayward ways may be required by respect for his independence. This cannot be a reason for accepting one's own shortcomings.) One wants an accommodation with one's faults that enables one to go on without alienation or self-deception. As in other-regarding acceptance, this is sometime possible and generally desirable, but there is no reason to think that it is always so.[23]

10

Early on we asked: How can accepting people for "what they are" be a virtue if what they are is something rather disagreeable or even vicious, by one's lights? The worry was that acceptance of serious shortcomings would show a failure of moral seriousness[24] or lack of integrity.[25] Can a general virtue of nonjudgmentalism as acceptance (as distinct from a strategic attitude confined to clinical settings or designed to mitigate the strains of interpersonal involvement) be affirmed in the face of these worries about seriousness and integrity? Unsurprisingly, this challenge echoes traditional debates about the liberal virtue of political tolerance, since that is also a matter of acceptance.

This link between nonjudgmentalism, acceptance, and tolerance is suggested in some of the passages we have already considered, as well as by the literature on political toleration. What is difficult about the virtue of toleration, as T. M. Scanlon says, is that it "requires us to accept people and permit their practices even when we strongly disagree with them" (2003a, p. 187). This means, in the political context, "accepting them as equals" (p. 190). John

---

[23] I explore the self-regarding case more fully in "Acceptance and Self-Acceptance" (unpublished).

[24] Speaking of the advice "Forget it and go on," Care remarks, "[O]ne sometimes suspects that those who can follow it, that is, those who can easily jettison problematic chunks of the past, are not fully serious people" (2000, p. 41).

[25] Arthur Kuflik addresses what is in effect this worry about tolerance in terms of 'compromise': "How is it possible for persons to be compromising to each other without compromising their own moral integrity in the bargain?" (1979, p. 38). The worry about integrity explains why 'compromise' and 'compromising' often have a pejorative sense. But so does 'uncompromising.' See also Williams (1996).

Horton writes that "the tolerant person is not too judgmental toward others. In becoming less judgmental, a person becomes more tolerant" (1996, p. 38).[26]

The general form of the reply to this challenge is implicit in what has been said already: higher-order considerations concerning how to respond to ethical differences often require that we reach accommodation with one another. These considerations pertain primarily to the importance of maintaining good terms with one another. The answer to the worries about integrity and seriousness in political contexts invokes the same idea, namely, the ethical reasons we have to accommodate differences in order to preserve (and constitute) important relationships.

I follow Scanlon in identifying these relationships in political and general moral contexts as those of mutual respect or recognition. The ideal underlying the practice of political tolerance, Scanlon suggests, is the avoidance of "a form of alienation from one's fellow citizens" (2003a, p. 194).[27] Respect calls for willingness to accept differences. And this requires a resistance to the readiness to dismiss or disregard others as citizens of equal standing. What this amounts to clearly differs from what is at issue in personal relations. Observance of and respect for the forms and substance of civility and common political standing may be all that is required for nonalienated relations among citizens. In a family in good order, the virtue of being accepting of differences requires more than what we mean by tolerance.

The pacifist father is not intolerant toward his fellow citizens when he protests and campaigns strenuously against the militarist policies they support. Nor is he being judgmental if he excludes his rabidly hawkish neighbor from the invitation list for his dinner parties. In contrast, he cannot be said to have accepted his daughter's military vocation just by including her in family gatherings and keeping up appearances of paternal affection. What is required is not just civility and nonoppression but love.

In real life, civility and respect might be the best we can achieve even among family. In national and international relations, we are extraordinarily lucky to accomplish even that much. The difficulty here is posed (hyperbolically) by Rousseau's contention that "it is impossible to live in peace with people one believes to be damned; to love them would be to hate the God who punishes them; it is an absolute duty either to redeem or to torture them" (1968, pp. 186–87).[28]

---

[26] Recall the passage quoted earlier from Alcoholics Anonymous, *Twelve Steps and Twelve Traditions*. When "we begin to see that all people, including ourselves, are to some extent emotionally ill as well as frequently wrong, . . . we approach true tolerance and see what real love for our fellows actually means" (1953, p. 92).

[27] See also Allan Gibbard, who (following John Rawls) contrasts a mere Rawlsean modus vivendi with a regime of tolerance that "allows [us] to live in a kind of mutual respect" (1990, p. 243).

[28] Thanks to Martha Nussbaum for calling my attention to this passage.

11

Acceptance requires more than putting up with others as a modus vivendi; it consists in accommodating (rather than eliminating) conflicts for the sake of the nonstrategic value of being on good terms with them. That's why it raises issues of seriousness and integrity. To be a genuine virtue, acceptance as accommodation must leave room for the parties to acknowledge and express their disagreements in ways that are consistent with a commitment not to let those differences impair the relationships in question.

Hence nothing I've said is meant to suggest that acceptance of another's decisions or attitudes entails remaining silent about one's moral positions. In personal relations in particular, a plausible ideal is what might be called *engaged* acceptance.[29] This ideal would call for honest engagement with the other's standpoint, which might mean both challenging its defensibility and maintaining an openness to the possibility of coming closer to agreement. But as we know, these transactions are delicate. Some disagreements are so sharp and fundamental that further discussion is fruitless and even disrespectful. There is a difference between engaging and taking on the project of changing the other. A mother who badgers her gay daughter by continually pinning advertisements for "homosexual therapy" on her pillow shows how far she falls short of acceptance.

Very often what is wanted (and required) for good terms in a relationship is not just acceptance but affirmation. We may well be unable to have good personal relations with those who see our religion or sexual orientation as a misfortune or worse, and hence as something that has to be accommodated. Rousseau's remark points to a tension, if not absurdity, in talk of "hating the sin but not the sinner," especially in cases in which the "sin" is central to someone's conception of what's important to her. The recipients of this sort of "tolerance" are bound to find it offensive. On certain matters and in certain relationships, we may rightly be unwilling to accept anything less than affirmation.

12

There is reason to think that, to attain autonomy and self-respect as individuals, we need nonjudgmental acceptance from at least some people who matter to us. The British psychologist Elizabeth Newson argues that

> a successfully integrated personality structure requires that a sense of personal worth be dovetailed with a sense of the needs of others; and that the major sources of these understandings are, in the first case, the

---

[29] I am indebted to Victoria McGeer for this phrase and for the idea it conveys.

special partiality which parents have for their children, and in the second case, the fairness and evenhandedness which the child may hope to expect from other adults, and which will indeed be fully backed up by his parents. (1978, pp. 23–24)

Newson's thesis is that this "partiality" gives the child a sense of himself as someone of "value and substance" that cannot be obtained just by being treated fairly, as one person among others, by the culture at large. It requires the parents, or someone in a long-term caretaking role, to give him a sense of himself as someone with "individual power," as "someone to be reckoned with" (p. 22), with a "mind of his own."[30] This partiality requires an acceptance (within limits) of the child's peculiar propensities in a way that could not be expected generally outside the family. (Parents "often strike a kind of unstated bargain with the child that he may bend the rules at home in exchange for complying with them elsewhere" [p. 20].) Newson conjectures that it is important to this sense of "personal worth" that the child knows that the parents defer to his idiosyncrasies by not always requiring him to live up to all of the cultural standards which they share—that he knows that, despite those standards, they accept him as someone who sucks his thumb and draws on the walls with crayons—for the time being, at least.[31] These accommodations might be merely indulgent if they obstructed the goal of enabling the child eventually to deal effectively with the demands of the larger society. On the other hand, without these accommodations we are less likely to achieve a sense of "personal worth." This acceptance affirms that these relationships—and hence the individuals—have an importance that is not merely contingent on harmonizing with others' values.

Newson's thesis sheds light on the value of nonjudgmental acceptance quite generally. Such acceptance honors others' individuality, respects them as beings with minds of their own. One can value *them* without valuing what they value by according them room to pursue their particular ends and express their distinctive tastes.[32] The importance of sharing values with others is undeniable, but there is a way in which affirming and loving others can be manifested all the more by accepting them, faults and all. For that reflects a less

---

[30] Part of what is at stake here was memorably put by one of the parents in Newson's study: "If he's going to grow up with his 'yes' being 'yes' and his 'no' being 'no,' he's going to have to have a mind of his own when he's young, isn't he?" (1978, pp. 10–11).

[31] "Perhaps it is even important that parents also enhance this sense of power in the child by occasionally demurring: that the child should know that they want him to give up the dummy, or that they don't like children fighting in the home, but nevertheless accept it in their own despite" (Newson 1978, p. 23).

[32] Of course, accepting someone's distinctive tastes or standards, in this sense, might be accepting her as someone whose tastes and standards are not all that distinctive, as someone whose values and outlook are pretty ordinary. That's "who she is." And that might be all she asks or even needs to be accepted as.

conditional form of love or regard than what is required for relations among more like-minded souls. It is in this kind of context that we are most likely to speak of accepting people for who they are, not because we are assuming some essentialist view of the individual but because the acceptance is not made conditional on demands to change.

To be sure, it is not obvious a priori that taking a nonaccepting stance will be worse for the well-being of the parties involved.[33] This could mean worse for their relationship or worse all told for each party individually. It might be best for you, and required by our friendship or my parental responsibilities, for me to refuse to accept certain behavior by you, even at the risk of impairing or ending the friendship. Acceptance is only contingently in the service of love. Nevertheless, Newson's studies suggest a general human connection here.

13

I hope to have shown that, despite its excesses, common discourse about judgmentalism identifies a range of important ethical faults. I also hope to have clarified to some extent their variety and nature. In general, nonjudgmentalism guards against a tendency to allow appraisals (even when sound) to underwrite a stance of estrangement or hostility or superiority toward others—a stance, as I've called it, of nonacceptance. Someone who is too ready to break off or significantly qualify interpersonal relationships because of the perceived faults of others exhibits this fault. Someone who is too unaccepting fails to respond to the reasons there are to maintain good (or at least decent) relations in the face of deep differences and disagreements. These higher-order reasons explain why acceptance does not necessarily compromise our integrity as individuals of principle.

I've emphasized that acceptance and its norms are relative to a relationship, that acceptance is multidimensional, and that there is such a thing as being too accepting. It is clear to me (contrary to Schreiber) that very often we should *not* accept the other person exactly as he is. It all depends on how he is, exactly, and on the relationship in question. Getting this right seems to me one of our most familiar and difficult ethical struggles.

---

[33] As Richard Kraut has emphasized to me.

{ REFERENCES }

Abramson, Lyn, Martin Seligman, and John Teasdale. 1978. "Learned Helplessness in Humans: Critique and Reformulation." *Journal of Abnormal Psychology* 87: 49–74.

Adams, Robert. 1985. "Involuntary Sins." *Philosophical Review* 94: 3–31.

Ahmed, Eliza, Nathan Harris, John Braithwaite, and Valerie Braithwaite. 2001. *Shame Management through Reintegration*. Cambridge: Cambridge University Press.

Alcoholics Anonymous. 1953. *Twelve Steps and Twelve Traditions*. New York: Alcoholics Anonymous World Services.

Alicke, Mark D. 2000. "Culpable Control and the Psychology of Blame." *Psychology Bulletin* 126: 556–74.

Alicke, Mark D., Teresa L. Davis, and Mark V. Pezzo. 1994. "A Posteriori Adjustment of A Priori Decision Criteria." *Social Cognition* 8: 286–305.

Alicke, Mark D., David Rose, and Dori Bloom. 2011. "Causation, Norm Violation and Culpable Control." *Journal of Philosophy* 108: 670–96.

Altham, J. E. J. 1973. "Reproach." *Proceedings of the Aristotelian Society* 74: 263–72.

Anderson, Elizabeth. 1993. *Value in Ethics and Economics*. Cambridge, Mass.: Harvard University Press.

Anonymous. 1975. *Twenty-four Hours a Day*. Revised edition. Center City, Minn.: Hazelden.

Armstrong, D. M. 1980. *The Nature of Mind and Other Essays*. Ithaca, N.Y.: Cornell University Press.

Arpaly, Nomy. 2003. *Unprincipled Virtue: An Inquiry into Moral Agency*. Oxford: Oxford University Press.

Arpaly, Nomy. 2006. *Merit, Meaning, and Human Bondage: An Essay on Free Will*. Princeton, N.J.: Princeton University Press.

Austin, J. L. 1962. *How to Do Things with Words*, 2nd edition. Ed. J. O. Urmson and M. Sbisá. Cambridge, Mass.: Harvard University Press.

Ayer, A. J. 1954. "Freedom and Necessity," In *Philosophical Essays*. New York: St. Martin's Press.

Beardsley, Elizabeth Lane. 1957. "Moral Worth and Moral Credit." *Philosophical Review* 66: 304–28.

Beardsley, Elizabeth Lane. 1960. "Determinism and Moral Perspectives." *Philosophy and Phenomenological Research* 21: 1–20.

Beardsley, Elizabeth Lane. 1969. "A Plea for Deserts." *American Philosophical Quarterly* 6: 33–42.

Beardsley, Elizabeth Lane. 1970. "Moral Disapproval and Moral Indignation." *Philosophy and Phenomenological Research* 31: 161–76.

Beardsley, Elizabeth Lane. 1979. "Blaming." *Philosophia* 8: 573–83.

Bedau, Hugo Adam, and Erin Kelly. 2010. "Punishment." In *The Stanford Encyclopedia of Philosophy*, Spring edition. Ed. Edward N. Zalta. http://plato.stanford.edu/archives/spr2010/entries/punishment/.

Bell, Macalester. 2011. "Globalist Attitudes and the Fittingness Objection." *Philosophical Quarterly* 61: 449–72.

Bell, Macalester. Forthcoming. "Forgiveness, Inspiration and the Powers of Reparation." *American Philosophical Quarterly*.

Bennett, Christopher. 2002. "The Varieties of Retributive Experience." *Philosophical Quarterly* 52: 145–63.

Bennett, Christopher. 2003. "Personal and Redemptive Forgiveness." *European Journal of Philosophy* 11: 127–44.

Bennett, Christopher. 2008. *The Apology Ritual: A Philosophical Theory of Punishment.* Cambridge: Cambridge University Press.

Bennett, Jonathan. 1980. "Accountability." In *Philosophical Subjects: Essays Presented to P. F. Strawson.* Ed. Zak van Straaten. Oxford: Clarendon Press.

Blackburn, Simon. 1998. *Ruling Passions.* Oxford: Clarendon Press.

Bok, Hilary. 1998. *Freedom and Responsibility.* Princeton, N.J.: Princeton University Press.

Boxill, Bernard 1976. "Self-Respect and Protest." *Philosophy and Public Affairs* 6: 58–69.

Boyd, Robert, and Peter J. Richerson. 2005. *The Origin and Evolution of Cultures.* New York: Oxford University Press.

Braithwaite, John. 2002. *Restorative Justice and Responsive Regulation.* Oxford: Oxford University Press.

Brandt, Richard. 1958. "Blameworthiness and Obligation." In *Essays in Moral Philosophy.* Ed. A. I. Melden. Seattle: University of Washington Press.

Bratman, Michael. 1999. "Practical Reasoning and Acceptance in a Context." In *Faces of Intention.* Cambridge: Cambridge University Press.

Bratman, Michael. 2007. *Structures of Agency: Essays.* New York: Oxford University Press.

Brink, David. 1989. *Moral Realism and the Foundations of Ethics.* Cambridge: Cambridge University Press.

Calhoun, Cheshire. 1989. "Responsibility and Reproach." *Ethics* 99: 389–406.

Care, Norman. 1996. *Living with One's Past.* Lanham, Md.: Rowman & Littlefield.

Care, Norman. 2000. *Decent People.* Lanham, Md.: Rowman & Littlefield.

Carlsmith, Kevin M., Timothy D. Wilson, and Daniel T. Gilbert. 2008. "The Paradoxical Consequences of Revenge." *Journal of Personality and Social Psychology* 95: 1316–24.

Ciocchetti, Christopher. 2003. "Wrongdoing and Relationships." *Social Theory and Practice* 29: 65–86.

Clarke, Randolph. 2009. "Dispositions, Abilities to Act, and Free Will: The New Dispositionalism." *Mind* 118: 323–51.

Coates, D. Justin, and Neal A. Tognazzini. 2012. "The Nature and Ethics of Blame." *Philosophy Compass* 7: 197–207.

Cohen, G. A. 2006. "Casting the First Stone: Who Can, and Who Can't, Condemn the Terrorists?" *Royal Institute of Philosophy Supplement* 58: 113–36.

Cohen, Stephen. 1977. "Distinctions among Blame Concepts." *Philosophy and Phenomenological Research* 38: 149–66.

Coleman, Jules. 2001. "Torts and Tort Theory: Preliminary Reflections." In *Philosophy and the Law of Torts.* Ed. Gerald J. Postema. Cambridge: Cambridge University Press.

Copp, David. 2008. "'Ought' Implies 'Can' and the Derivation of the Principle of Alternate Possibilities." *Analysis* 68: 67–75.

D'Arms, Justin, and Daniel Jacobson. 2000. "The Moralistic Fallacy: On the 'Appropriateness' of Emotions." *Philosophy and Phenomenological Research* 61: 65–90.

Darwall, Stephen. 1983. *Impartial Reason*. Ithaca, N.Y.: Cornell University Press.

Darwall, Stephen. 2006. *The Second-Person Standpoint: Morality, Respect, and Accountability*. Cambridge, Mass.: Harvard University Press.

Darwall, Stephen. 2007. "Moral Obligation and Accountability." *Oxford Studies in Metaethics* 2: 111–32.

Darwall, Stephen. 2010a. "But It Would Be Wrong." In *Moral Obligation*. Ed. E. F. Paul, F. D. Miller Jr., and J. Paul. Cambridge: Cambridge University Press.

Darwall, Stephen. 2010b. "Moral Obligation: Form and Substance." *Proceedings of the Aristotelian Society* 110: 24–46.

Darwall, Stephen. 2010c. "Precis: The Second-Person Standpoint." *Philosophy and Phenomenological Research* 81: 216–28.

Darwall, Stephen. 2011. "Justice and Retaliation." *Philosophical Papers* 39: 315–41.

de Rougemont, Denis. 1983. *Love in the Western World*. Princeton, N.J.: Princeton University Press.

de Sousa, Ronald. 1987. *The Rationality of Emotion*. Cambridge, Mass.: MIT Press.

de Sousa, Ronald. 2004. "Emotions: What I Know, What I'd Like to Think I Know, and What I'd Like to Think." In *Thinking about Feeling: Contemporary Philosophers on Emotions*. Ed. R. C. Solomon. Oxford: Oxford University Press.

Deigh, John. 1995. "Empathy and Universalizability." *Ethics* 105: 743–63.

Deigh, John. 2012. "Reactive Attitudes Revisited." In *Morality and the Emotions*. Ed. Carla Bagnoli. Oxford: Oxford University Press.

DeLancey, Craig. 2001. *Passionate Engines: What Emotions Reveal about Mind and Artificial Intelligence*. Oxford: Oxford University Press.

Dillon, Robin. 1992. "Respect and Care: Toward Moral Integration." *Canadian Journal of Philosophy* 22: 105–32.

Dilman, Ilham. 1979. *Morality and the Inner Life: A Study in Plato's Gorgias*. Basingstoke, U.K.: Macmillan.

Dostoevsky, Fyodor. (1880) 1990. *The Brothers Karamazov*. Trans. Richard Pevear and Larissa Volokhonsky. New York: Farrar, Straus, and Giroux.

Double, Richard. 1991. *The Non-Reality of Free Will*. New York: Oxford University Press.

Driver, Julia. 1992. "The Suberogatory." *Australasian Journal of Philosophy* 70: 286–95.

Duff, R. A. 1986. *Trials and Punishments*. Cambridge: Cambridge University Press.

Duff, R. A. 2001. *Punishment, Communication and Community*. Oxford: Oxford University Press.

Duff, R. A. 2008. "Legal Punishment." In *The Stanford Encyclopedia of Philosophy*. Ed. Edward N. Zalta. http://plato.stanford.edu/entries/legal-punishment/.

Duff, R. A. 2009. "Legal and Moral Responsibility." *Philosophy Compass* 4: 978–86.

Duff, R. A. 2010. "Blame, Moral Standing and the Legitimacy of the Criminal Trial." *Ratio* 23: 123–40.

Dworkin, Gerald. 1999. "Morally Speaking." In *Reasoning Practically*. Ed. Edna Margalit. Oxford: Oxford University Press.

Ebels-Duggan, Kyla. 2010. "Dealing with the Past: Responsibility, History, and Salience." Unpublished manuscript.

Einstein, Albert. 1982. *Ideas and Opinions*. New York: Crown.

Ekman, Paul. 1972. *Emotions in the Human Face*. New York: Pergamon Press.

Ekman, Paul. 1992. "An Argument for Basic Emotions." In *Basic Emotions*. Ed. N. Stein and K. Oatley. Hillsdale, N.J.: Lawrence Erlbaum.

Eliot, George. 1994. *Middlemarch*. London: Penguin Books.

Elster, Jon. 1983. *Sour Grapes*. Cambridge: Cambridge University Press.

Elster, Jon. 1999. *Addiction: Entries and Exits*. New York: Russell Sage Foundation.

Fara, Michael. 2008. "Masked Abilities and Compatibilism." *Mind* 117: 843–65.

Fehr, Ernst, and Urs Fischbacher. 2004a. "Social Norms and Human Cooperation." *Trends in Cognitive Sciences* 8: 185–90.

Fehr, Ernst, and Urs Fischbacher. 2004b. "Third-party Punishment and Social Norms." *Evolution and Human Behavior* 25: 63–87.

Fehr, Ernst, and Simon Gachter. 2002. "Altruistic Punishment in Humans." *Nature* 415: 137–40.

Feinberg, Joel. 1970. *Doing and Deserving*. Princeton, N.J.: Princeton University Press.

Feinberg, Joel. 1986. *Harm to Others*. New York: Oxford University Press.

Fingarette, Herbert. 1957. "Blame: Its Motive and Meaning in Everyday Life." *Psychoanalytic Review* 44: 193–211.

Fischer, John Martin, and Mark Ravizza. 1998. *Responsibility and Control: A Theory of Moral Responsibility*. Cambridge: Cambridge University Press.

Fischer, John Martin, and Neal A. Tognazzini. 2011. "The Physiognomy of Responsibility." *Philosophy and Phenomenological Research* 82: 381–417.

Fitzgerald, F. Scott. 1995. *The Great Gatsby*. New York: Scribner.

Foot, Philippa. 1978. "Approval and Disapproval." In *Virtues and Vices*. Berkeley: University of California Press.

Frank, Robert H. 1988. *Passions within Reason: The Strategic Role of Emotions*. New York: Norton.

Frankfurt, Harry. 1969. "Alternate Possibilities and Moral Responsibility." *Journal of Philosophy* 66: 829–39.

Frankfurt, Harry. 1971. "Freedom of the Will and the Concept of a Person." *Journal of Philosophy* 68: 5–20.

French, Peter A. 1976. "Senses of 'Blame.'" *Southern Journal of Philosophy* 14: 443–52.

Friedman, Marilyn. 2011. "How to Blame People Responsibly." Unpublished manuscript.

Frye, Marilyn. 1983. "A Note on Anger." In *Politics of Reality*. Trumansburg, N.Y.: Crossing Press.

Gaita, Raimond. 1991. *Good and Evil: An Absolute Conception*. Basingstoke, U.K.: Macmillan.

Gaita, Raimond. 2000. *A Common Humanity*. 2nd edition. New York: Routledge.

Gardner, John. 2007. *Offences and Defences*. Oxford: Oxford University Press.

Gibbard, Allan. 1990. *Wise Choices, Apt Feelings: A Theory of Normative Judgment*. Cambridge, Mass.: Harvard University Press.

Gibbard, Allan. 2003. *Thinking How to Live*. Cambridge, Mass.: Harvard University Press.

Ginet, Carl. 1990. *On Action*. Cambridge: Cambridge University Press.

Glover, Jonathan. 1970. *Responsibility*. London: Routledge and Kegan Paul.

Goldie, Peter. 2000. *The Emotions: A Philosophical Exploration*. Oxford: Oxford University Press.

Greenspan, Patricia. 1981. "Emotions as Evaluations." *Pacific Philosophical Quarterly* 62: 158–69.

Griffiths, Paul E. 1997. *What Emotions Really Are*. Chicago: University of Chicago Press.

Haji, Ishtiyaque. 1998. *Moral Appraisability: Puzzles, Proposals, and Perplexities*. New York: Oxford University Press.

Hampton, Jean. 1988a. "Forgiveness, Resentment, and Hatred." In Jean Hampton and Jeffrie G. Murphy, *Forgiveness and Mercy*. Cambridge: Cambridge University Press.

Hampton, Jean. 1988b. "The Retributive Idea." In Jean Hampton and Jeffrie G. Murphy, *Forgiveness and Mercy*. Cambridge: Cambridge University Press.

Hampton, Jean, and Jeffrie G. Murphy. 1988. *Forgiveness and Mercy*. Cambridge: Cambridge University Press.

Harman, Gilbert. 1977. *The Nature of Morality*. Princeton, N.J.: Princeton University Press.

Hart, H. L. A. 1968. *Punishment and Responsibility*. Oxford: Clarendon Press.

Held, Virginia, ed. 1995. *Justice and Care: Essential Readings in Feminist Ethics*. Boulder, Colo.: Westview Press.

Helm, Bennett. 1994. "The Significance of Emotions." *American Philosophical Quarterly* 31: 319–31.

Henrich, Joseph, and Natalie Henrich. 2007. *Why Humans Cooperate: A Cultural and Evolutionary Perspective*. New York: Oxford University Press.

Hertzberg, Lars. 1975. "Blame and Causality." *Mind* 84: 500–515.

Hieronymi, Pamela. 2001. "Articulating an Uncompromising Forgiveness." *Philosophy and Phenomenological Research* 62: 529–55.

Hieronymi, Pamela. 2004. "The Force and Fairness of Blame." *Philosophical Perspectives* 18: 115–48.

Hieronymi, Pamela. 2007. "Rational Capacity as a Condition on Blame." *Philosophical Books* 48: 109–23.

Hieronymi, Pamela. 2008. "Review: Sher's Defense of Blame." *Philosophical Studies* 137: 19–30.

Hobart, R. E. 1934. "Free Will as Involving Determinism and Inconceivable without It." *Mind* 43: 1–27.

Hobbs, James. 2012. "'Ought' Claims and Blame in a Deterministic World." PhD dissertation, Cornell University.

Hochschild, Arlie. 1983. *The Managed Heart*. Berkeley: University of California Press.

Honderich, Ted. 1988. *A Theory of Determinism*. Oxford: Oxford University Press.

Horton, John. 1996. "Toleration as a Virtue." In *Toleration*. Ed. D. Heyd. Princeton, N.J.: Princeton University Press.

Houston, Barbara. 1992. "In Praise of Blame." *Hypatia: A Journal of Feminist Philosophy* 7: 128–47.

Hughes, Paul M. 1995. "Moral Anger, Forgiving and Condoning." *Journal of Social Philosophy* 25: 103–18.

Humberstone, I. L. 1971. "Two Sorts of 'Ought's." *Analysis* 32: 8–11.

Hume, David. (1739) 1978. *A Treatise of Human Nature*. Oxford: Oxford University Press.

Hume, David. (1748) 1977. *An Enquiry Concerning Human Understanding*. Ed. Eric Steinberg. Indianapolis: Hackett.

Hurley, Elisa A., and Coleen Macnamara. 2010. "Beyond Belief: Toward a Theory of the Reactive Attitudes." *Philosophical Papers* 39: 373–99.

Husak, Douglas. 2010. "Review of Alan Brudner's Punishment and Freedom: A Liberal Theory of Penal Justice." *Ethics* 120: 841–46.

Jackson, Frank, and Philip Pettit. 1995. "Moral Functionalism and Moral Motivation." *Philosophical Quarterly* 45: 20–40.

Johnstone, Garry, ed. 2003. *Restorative Justice: Ideas, Values, Debates*. Cullompton, U.K.: Willam.

Johnstone, Garry, and Daniel W. Van Ness, eds. 2007. *Handbook of Restorative Justice*. Portland, Oreg.: Willan.

Kaufmann, Walter. 1963. *The Faith of a Heretic*. New York: Anchor Doubleday.

Kelly, Daniel. 2011. *Yuck!: The Nature and Moral Significance of Disgust*. Cambridge, Mass.: MIT Press.

Kelly, Erin I. 2012. "Moral Capacity." Unpublished manuscript.

Kelly, Erin I., and Lionel K. McPherson. 2010. "The Naturalist Gap in Ethics." In *Naturalism and Normativity*. Ed. Mario De Caro and David Macarthur. New York: Columbia University Press.

Kenner, Lionel. 1967. "On Blaming." *Mind* 76: 238–49.

Knobe, Joshua. 2003. "Intentional Action in Folk Psychology: An Experimental Investigation." *Philosophical Psychology* 16: 309–24.

Knobe, Joshua, and Ben Fraser. 2008. "Causal Judgment and Moral Judgment: Two Experiments." In *Moral Psychology, Vol. 2: The Cognitive Science of Morality: Intuition and Diversity*. Ed. W. Sinnott-Armstrong. Cambridge, Mass.: MIT Press.

Kolodny, Niko. 2003. "Love as Valuing a Relationship." *Philosophical Review* 112: 135–89.

Kolodny, Niko. 2011. "Scanlon's Investigation: The Relevance of Intent to Permissibility." *Analytic Philosophy* 52: 100–123.

Korsgaard, Christine. 1996. *Creating the Kingdom of Ends*. New York: Cambridge University Press.

Kuflik, Arthur. 1979. "Morality and Compromise." In *Compromise in Ethics, Law, and Politics*. Ed. James Roland Pennock and John W. Chapman. New York: NYU Press.

Kukla, Rebecca, and Mark Lance. 2009. *"Yo!" and "Lo!": The Pragmatic Topography of the Space of Reasons*. Cambridge, Mass.: Harvard University Press.

Kutz, Christopher. 2007. *Complicity: Ethics and Law for a Collective Age*. New York: Cambridge University Press.

Lacey, Nicola. 2008. *The Prisoner's Dilemma*. Cambridge: Cambridge University Press.

Lazarus, Richard. 1991. *Emotion and Adaptation*. Oxford: Oxford University Press.

Lenman, James. 2006. "Compatibilism and Contractualism: The Possibility of Moral Responsibility." *Ethics* 117: 7–31.

Lewis, David. 1980. "Mad Pain and Martian Pain." In *Readings in Philosophy of Psychology*. Ed. N. Block. Cambridge, Mass.: Harvard University Press.

Lewis, Michael, and Douglas Ramsey. 2005. "Infant Emotional and Cortisol Responses to Goal Blockage." *Child Development* 76: 518–30.

Little, Margaret. Forthcoming. "The Deontic Fallacy." In *Thinking about Reasons: Essays in Honour of Jonathan Dancy*. Ed. D. Bakhurst, B. Hooker, and M. Little. Oxford: Oxford University Press.

MacKinnon, Catherine A. 1991. *Toward a Feminist Theory of the State*. Cambridge, Mass.: Harvard University Press.

Macnamara, Coleen. 2011. "Holding Others Responsible." *Philosophical Studies* 152: 81–102.

Macnamara, Coleen. Forthcoming. "'Screw You!' & 'Thank You.'" *Philosophical Studies*.

Manne, Kate. 2011. *Not by Reasons Alone*. PhD dissertation, MIT.

Marcus, Ruth Barcan. 1966. "Iterated Deontic Modalities." *Mind* 75: 580–82.

Mason, Michelle. 2003. "Contempt as a Moral Attitude." *Ethics* 113: 234–72.

Mason, Michelle. 2011. "Blame: Taking It Seriously." *Philosophy and Phenomenological Research* 83: 473–81.

McGeer, Victoria. 2011. "Co-Reactive Attitudes and the Making of Moral Community." In *Emotions, Imagination and Moral Reasoning*. Ed. R. Langdon and C. MacKenzie. London: Psychology Press.

McKenna, Michael. 1998. "The Limits of Evil and the Role of Moral Address: A Defense of Strawsonian Compatibilism." *Journal of Ethics* 2: 123–42.

McKenna, Michael. 2012. *Conversation and Responsibility*. New York: Oxford University Press.

McKenna, Michael, and Paul Russell, eds. 2008. *Free Will and Reactive Attitudes*. Burlington, Vt.: Ashgate.

McKenna, Michael, and Aron Vadakin. 2008. "Review of George Sher, *In Praise of Blame*." *Ethics* 118: 751–56.

McLaughlin, Eugene, Ross Fergusson, Gordon Hughes, and Louise Westmarland, eds. 2003. *Restorative Justice: Critical Issues*. London: Sage.

Mele, Alfred, and Steven Sverdlik. 1996. "Intention, Intentional Action, and Moral Responsibility." *Philosophical Studies* 82: 265–87.

Menkel-Meadow, Carrie. 2007. "Restorative Justice: What Is It and Does It Work?" *Annual Review of Law and Social Science* 3: 161–87.

Moore, Michael. 1997. *Placing Blame*. Oxford: Oxford University Press.

Morris, Herbert. 1981. "A Paternalistic Theory of Punishment." *American Philosophical Quarterly* 18: 263–71.

Morse, Stephen J. 2008. "Psychopathy and Criminal Responsibility." *Neuroethics* 1: 205–12.

Murdoch, Iris. 1971. *Sovereignty of the Good*. New York: Schocken Books.

Murphy, Jeffrie G. 1988. "Forgiveness and Resentment." In Jean Hampton and Jeffrie G. Murphy, *Forgiveness and Mercy*. Cambridge: Cambridge University Press.

Nadelhoffer, Thomas. 2004a. "The Butler Problem Revisited." *Analysis* 64: 277–88.

Nadelhoffer, Thomas. 2004b. "Praise, Side Effects, and Intentional Action." *Journal of Theoretical and Philosophical Psychology* 24: 196–213.

Nadelhoffer, Thomas. 2006. "Bad Acts, Blameworthy Agents, and Intentional Actions: Some Problems for Jury Impartiality." *Philosophical Explorations* 9: 203–20.

Nagel, Thomas. 1979. *Mortal Questions*. Cambridge: Cambridge University Press.

Nagel, Thomas. 1986. *The View from Nowhere*. New York: Oxford University Press.

Nelkin, Dana. 2011a. *Making Sense of Moral Responsibility*. Oxford: Oxford University Press.

Nelkin, Dana. 2011b. "Review of Thomas Scanlon, *Moral Dimensions*." *Philosophical Review* 120: 603–7.

Newson, Elizabeth. 1978. "Unreasonable Care: The Establishment of Selfhood." In *Human Values: Lectures of the Royal Institute of Philosophy*. Ed. G. Vesey. Atlantic Highlands, N.J.: Humanities Press.

Nichols, Shaun. 2002. "Norms with Feeling: Towards a Psychological Account of Moral Judgement." *Cognition* 84: 221–36.

Nichols, Shaun. 2007. "After Compatibilism: A Naturalistic Defense of the Reactive Attitudes." *Philosophical Perspectives* 21: 405–28.

Nichols, Shaun, and Ron Mallon. 2006. "Moral Dilemmas and Moral Rules." *Cognition* 100: 530–42.

Noddings, Nell. 1984. *Caring: A Feminine Approach to Ethics and Moral Education*. Berkeley: University of California Press.

Norcross, Alastair. 2006. "Reasons without Demands: Rethinking Rightness." In *Blackwell Contemporary Debates in Moral Theory*. Ed. J. Dreier. Oxford: Blackwell.

Nussbaum, Martha. 2001. *Upheavals of Thought*. Cambridge: Cambridge University Press.

Pereboom, Derk. 1995. "Determinism al Dente." *Noûs* 29: 21–45.

Pereboom, Derk. 2001. *Living without Free Will.* Cambridge: Cambridge University Press.

Pereboom, Derk. 2007. "Hard Incompatibilism" and "Response to Fischer, Kane, and Vargas." In J. Fischer, R. Kane, D. Pereboom, and M. Vargas, *Four Views on Free Will.* Oxford: Blackwell.

Pereboom, Derk. 2009. "Free Will, Love and Anger." *Ideas y Valores* 141: 5–25.

Pereboom, Derk. Forthcoming. "Frankfurt Examples, Derivative Responsibility, and the Timing Objection." *Philosophical Issues.*

Pettit, Philip. 2001. "The Capacity to Have Done Otherwise: An Agent-centred View." In *Relating to Responsibility: Essays for Tony Honoré on His Eightieth Birthday.* Ed. P. Cane and J. Gardner. Oxford: Hart.

Priestley, Joseph. 1788. "A Free Discussion of the Doctrines of Materialism and Philosophical Necessity." In a Correspondence between Dr. Price and Dr. Priestley, part III, pp. 147–52. Reprinted in Joseph Priestley, *Priestley's Writings on Philosophy, Science, and Politics.* Ed. John Passmore. New York: Collier.

Prinz, Jesse J. 2004. *Gut Reactions: A Perpetual Theory Of Emotion.* New York: Oxford University Press.

Radzik, Linda. 2004. "Making Amends." *American Philosophical Quarterly* 41: 141–54.

Radzik, Linda. 2009. *Making Amends.* Oxford: Oxford University Press.

Rappaport, Roy A. 1999. *Ritual and Religion in the Making of Humanity.* Cambridge: Cambridge University Press.

Rawls, John. 1971. *A Theory of Justice.* Cambridge, Mass.: Harvard University Press.

Raz, Joseph. 1999. *Practical Reasons and Norms.* Oxford: Oxford University Press.

Raz, Joseph. 2001. *Value, Respect, and Attachment.* Cambridge: Cambridge University Press.

Reis-Dennis, Samuel. 2010. "Blame." Undergraduate honors thesis, Cornell University.

Roberts, Robert C. 1988. "What an Emotion Is: A Sketch." *Philosophical Review* 47: 183–209.

Roberts, Robert C. 2003. *Emotions: An Essay in Aid of Moral Psychology.* New York: Cambridge University Press.

Robinson, Gwen, and Joanna Shapland. 2008. "Reducing Recidivism." *British Journal of Criminology* 48: 337–58.

Rosch, Eleanor. 1972. "Universals in Color Naming and Memory." *Journal of Experimental Psychology* 93: 10–20.

Rosch, Eleanor. 1973. "Natural Categories." *Cognitive Psychology* 4: 328–50.

Rosen, Gideon. 2006. "The Alethic Conception of Blameworthiness." Unpublished manuscript.

Rousseau, Jean-Jacques. 1968. *The Social Contract.* Ed. Maurice Cranston. London: Penguin.

Russell, Paul. 2000. "Compatibilist-Fatalism." In *Moral Responsibility and Ontology.* Ed. T. van den Beld. Dordrecht: Kluwer.

Russell, Paul. Forthcoming. "Responsibility, Naturalism, and the 'Morality System.'" In *Oxford Studies in Agency and Responsibility.* Ed. David Shoemaker. Oxford: Oxford University Press.

Sabini, John, and Maury Silver. 1982. *Moralities of Everyday Life.* Oxford: Oxford University Press.

Scanlon, T. M. 1988. "The Significance of Choice." *Tanner Lectures on Human Values* 8: 149–216.

Scanlon, T. M. 1998. *What We Owe to Each Other.* Cambridge, Mass.: Harvard University Press.

Scanlon, T. M. 2003a. "The Difficulty of Tolerance." In *The Difficulty of Tolerance*. Cambridge: Cambridge University Press.

Scanlon, T. M. 2003b. "Punishment and the Rule of Law." In *The Difficulty of Tolerance*. Cambridge: Cambridge University Press.

Scanlon, T. M. 2008. *Moral Dimensions: Permissibility, Meaning, Blame*. Cambridge, Mass.: Harvard University Press.

Schlick, Moritz. 1939. "When Is a Man Responsible?" In *Problems of Ethics*. Ed. D. Rynin. New York: Prentice-Hall.

Schroeder, Mark. 2011. "Ought, Agents, and Actions." *Philosophical Review* 120: 1–41.

Scott, Walter. (1815) 1995. *Rob Roy*. New York: Penguin Books.

Searle, John R., and Daniel Vanderveken. 1985. *Foundations of Illocutionary Logic*. Cambridge: Cambridge University Press.

Seidman, Jeffrey. 2009. "Valuing and Caring." *Theoria* 75: 272–303.

Seneca. 1995. "On Anger." In *Seneca: Moral and Political Essays*. Ed. John M. Cooper and J. F. Procopé. New York: Cambridge University Press.

Shapland, Joanna, Gwen Robinson, and Angela Sorsby. 2011. *Restorative Justice in Practice*. London: Routledge.

Sher, George. 2006. *In Praise of Blame*. Oxford: Oxford University Press.

Sherman, Lawrence, and Heather Strang. 2007. *Restorative Justice: The Evidence*. London: Smith Institute.

Sherman, Lawrence W., Heather Strang, and Daniel J. Woods. 2000. "Recidivism Patterns in the Canberra Reintegrative Shaming Experiment (RISE)." Report. Australian National University, Canberra.

Sherman, Nancy. 1997. *Making a Necessity of Virtue*. Cambridge: Cambridge University Press.

Shoemaker, David. 2007. "Moral Address, Moral Responsibility, and the Boundaries of the Moral Community." *Ethics* 118: 70–108.

Shoemaker, David. 2011. "Attributability, Answerability, and Accountability: Toward a Wider Theory of Moral Responsibility." *Ethics* 121: 602–32.

Shoemaker, David. Forthcoming. "On Criminal and Moral Responsibility." *Oxford Studies in Normative Ethics*. New York: Oxford University Press.

Sidgwick, Henry. (1874) 1981. *The Methods of Ethics*. London: Macmillan.

Singer, Peter. 2011. *Practical Ethics*. 3rd edition. New York: Cambridge University Press.

Skorupski, John. 1999. "The Definition of Morality." In *Ethical Explorations*. Oxford: Oxford University Press.

Smart, J. J. C. 1961. "Free-Will, Praise, and Blame." *Mind* 70: 291–306.

Smilansky, Saul. 2000. *Free Will and Illusion*. Oxford: Oxford University Press.

Smith, Adam. 1759. *The Theory of Moral Sentiments*. London: A. Millar.

Smith, Angela M. 2005. "Responsibility for Attitudes: Activity and Passivity in Mental Life." *Ethics* 115: 236–71.

Smith, Angela M. 2007. "On Being Responsible and Holding Responsible." *Journal of Ethics* 2: 465–84.

Smith, Angela M. 2008a. "Character, Blameworthiness, and Blame: Comments on George Sher's *In Praise of Blame*." *Philosophical Studies* 137: 31–39.

Smith, Angela M. 2008b. "Control, Responsibility, and Moral Assessment." *Philosophical Studies* 138: 367–92.

Smith, Michael. 2003. "Rational Capacities, or: How to Distinguish Recklessness, Weakness, and Compulsion." In *Weakness of Will and Practical Irrationality*. Ed. Sarah Stroud and Christine Tippolet. Oxford: Oxford University Press.

Smith, Nick. 2008. *I Was Wrong: The Meanings of Apologies*. Cambridge: Cambridge University Press.

Solomon, Robert. 1973. "Emotions and Choice." *Review of Metaphysics* 27: 20–41.

Solomon, Robert. 2004. "Emotions, Thoughts and Feelings: Emotions as Engagements with the World." In *Thinking about Feeling: Contemporary Philosophers on Emotions*. Ed. Robert C. Solomon. Oxford: Oxford University Press.

Spinoza, Baruch. (1677) 1985. "Ethics." In *The Collected Works of Spinoza*. Vol. 1. Ed. and trans. E. Curley. Princeton, N.J.: Princeton University Press.

Squires, J. E. R. 1968. "Blame." *Philosophical Quarterly* 18: 54–60.

Sripada, Chandra. 2005. "Punishment and the Strategic Structure of Moral Systems." *Biology and Philosophy* 20: 767–89.

Sripada, Chandra, and Stephen Stich. 2007. "A Framework for the Psychology of Norms." In *The Innate Mind: Culture and Cognition*. Ed. P. Carruthers, S. Laurence, and S. Stich. Oxford: Oxford University Press.

Stern, Lawrence. 1974. "Freedom, Blame, and Moral Community." *Journal of Philosophy* 71: 72–84.

Stocker, Michael. 1983. "Psychic Feelings: Their Importance and Irreducibility." *Australasian Journal of Philosophy* 61: 5–26.

Stocker, Michael. 1987. "Emotional Thoughts." *American Philosophical Quarterly* 24: 59–69.

Stocker, Michael, with Elizabeth Hegeman. 1996. *Valuing Emotions*. Cambridge: Cambridge University Press.

Strang, H. 2002. *Repair or Revenge: Victims and Restorative Justice*. Oxford: Clarendon Press.

Strawson, Galen. 1986. *Freedom and Belief*. Oxford: Clarendon Press.

Strawson, Galen. 1994. "The Impossibility of Moral Responsibility." *Philosophical Studies*. 75: 5–24.

Strawson, P. F. 1962. "Freedom and Resentment." *Proceedings of the British Academy* 48: 1–25.

Suikkanen, Jussi. 2011. "Intentions, Blame, and Contractualism." *Jurisprudence* 2: 561–73.

Svavarsdóttir, Sigrun. 1999. "Moral Cognitivism and Motivation." *Philosophical Review* 108: 161–219.

Svavarsdóttir, Sigrun. 2011. "Value as a Norm for Attitudes." Unpublished manuscript.

Tadros, Victor. 2005. *Criminal Responsibility*. Oxford: Oxford University Press.

Tadros, Victor. 2009. "Poverty and Criminal Responsibility." *Journal of Value Inquiry* 43: 391–413.

Tadros, Victor. 2011. "Criminalization and Regulation." In *The Boundaries of the Criminal Law*. Ed. R. A. Duff, Lindsay Farmer, S. E. Marshall, Massimo Renzo, and Victor Tadros. New York: Oxford University Press.

Talbert, Matthew. 2008. "Blame and Responsiveness to Moral Reasons: Are Psychopaths Blameworthy?" *Pacific Philosophical Quarterly* 89: 516–35.

Talbert, Matthew. 2012. "Moral Competence, Moral Blame, and Protest." *Journal of Ethics* 16: 89–109.

Taylor, Charles. 1985. "Self-Interpreting Animals." In *Human Agency and Language: Philosophical Papers I*. Cambridge: Cambridge University Press.

Tognazzini, Neal A. 2012. "Blame as a Volitional Activity." Unpublished manuscript.

van Inwagen, Peter. 1983. *An Essay on Free Will*. Oxford: Oxford University Press.

Van Ness, D. W., and K. H. Strong. 2010. *Restoring Justice: An Introduction to Restorative Justice*. New Providence, N.J.: Matthew Bender.

Vihvelin, Kadri. 2004. "Free Will Demystified: A Dispositional Account." *Philosophical Topics* 32: 427–50.

Von Hirsch, Andrew. 1986. *Past or Future Crimes: Deservedness and Dangerousness in the Sentencing of Criminals*. New Brunswick, N.J.: Rutgers University Press.

Walker, Margaret Urban. 2006. *Moral Repair: Reconstructing Moral Relations after Wrongdoing*. Cambridge: Cambridge University Press.

Wallace, R. Jay. 1994. *Responsibility and the Moral Sentiments*. Cambridge, Mass.: Harvard University Press.

Wallace, R. Jay. 2006. *Normativity and the Will: Selected Papers on Moral Psychology and Practical Reason*. Oxford: Clarendon Press.

Wallace, R. Jay. 2007. "Reasons, Relations, and Commands: Reflections on Darwall." *Ethics* 118: 24–36.

Wallace, R. Jay. 2010. "Hypocrisy, Moral Address, and the Equal Standing of Persons." *Philosophy & Public Affairs* 38: 307–41.

Wallace, R. Jay. 2011. "Dispassionate Opprobrium: On Blame and the Reactive Sentiments." In *Reasons and Recognition: Essays on the Philosophy of T. M. Scanlon*. Ed. R. Jay Wallace, Rahul Kumar, and Samuel Freeman. New York: Oxford University Press.

Wallace, R. Jay, Rahul Kumar, and Samuel Freeman, eds. 2011. *Reasons and Recognition: Essays on the Philosophy of T. M. Scanlon*. New York: Oxford University Press.

Watson, Gary. 1975. "Free Agency." *Journal of Philosophy* 72: 205–20.

Watson, Gary. 1987a. "Free Action and Free Will." *Mind* 96: 145–72.

Watson, Gary. 1987b. "Responsibility and the Limits of Evil: Variations on a Strawsonian Theme." In *Responsibility, Character, and the Emotions: Essays in Moral Psychology*. Ed. Ferdinand Schoeman. Cambridge: Cambridge University Press.

Watson, Gary. 1996. "Two Faces of Responsibility." *Philosophical Topics* 24: 227–48.

Watson, Gary. 2001. "Contractualism and the Boundaries of Morality." *Social Theory and Practice* 28: 221–41.

Watson, Gary, ed. 2003. *Free Will*. 2nd ed. Oxford: Oxford University Press.

Watson, Gary. 2004. *Agency and Answerability*. Oxford: Clarendon Press.

Watson, Gary. 2011. "The Trouble with Psychopaths." In *Reasons and Recognition: Essays on the Philosophy of T. M. Scanlon*. Ed. R. Jay Wallace, Rahul Kumar, and Samuel Freeman. New York: Oxford University Press.

Wertheimer, Roger 1998. "Constraining Condemning." *Ethics* 108: 489–501.

Williams, Bernard. 1981. "Persons, Character, and Morality." In *Moral Luck: Philosophical Papers 1973–1980*. Cambridge: Cambridge University Press.

Williams, Bernard. 1995a. "Internal Reasons and the Obscurity of Blame." In *Making Sense of Humanity and Other Philosophical Papers*. Cambridge: Cambridge University Press.

Williams, Bernard. 1995b. "Nietzsche's Minimalist Moral Psychology." In *Making Sense of Humanity and Other Philosophical Papers*. Cambridge: Cambridge University Press.

Williams, Bernard. 1996. "Toleration: An Impossible Virtue?" In *Tolerance: An Elusive Virtue*. Ed. David Heyd. Princeton, N.J.: Princeton University Press.

Williams, Garrath. 2003. "Blame and Responsibility." *Ethical Theory and Moral Practice* 6: 427–45.

Winch, Peter. 1972. "Ethical Reward and Punishment." In *Ethics and Action*. London: Routledge.

Wolf, Susan. 1990. *Freedom within Reason*. New York: Oxford University Press.

Wolf, Susan. 2011. "Blame, Italian Style." In *Reasons and Recognition: Essays on the Philosophy of T. M. Scanlon*. Ed. R. Jay Wallace, Rahul Kumar, and Samuel Freeman. New York: Oxford University Press.

Wollheim, Richard. 1968. *Art and Its Objects*. Harmondsworth, U.K.: Penguin.

Zehr, Howard. 2002. *Little Book of Restorative Justice*. Intercourse, Penn.: Good Books.

Zimmerman, Michael J. 1988. *An Essay on Moral Responsibility*. Totowa, N.J.: Rowman and Littlefield.

{ INDEX }

24912914R10200

Printed in Poland
by Amazon Fulfillment
Poland Sp. z o.o., Wrocław